Humana Festival '98
The Complete Plays

Humana Inc. is one of the nation's largest
managed health care companies
with more than 6 million members in its health care plans.

The Humana Foundation was established in 1981
to support the educational, social, medical and cultural development
of communities in ways that reflect
Humana's commitment to social responsibility
and an improved quality of life.

Humana Festival '98
The Complete Plays

Edited by Michael Bigelow Dixon
and Amy Wegener

Contemporary Playwrights Series

SK
A Smith and Kraus Book

A Smith and Kraus Book
Published by Smith and Kraus, Inc.
PO Box 127, Lyme, NH   03768

Manufactured in the United States of America

Cover and Text Design by Julia Hill
Text Conversion and Layout by Joel A. Smith
Cover artwork © Rafal Olbinski

First Edition: September 1998
10 9 8 7 6 5 4 3 2 1

Library of Congress Cataloguing-in-Publication Data
Contemporary Playwrights Series
ISSN 1067-9510

Contents

Acknowledgements

The editors wish to thank the following persons for their invaluable assistance in compiling this volume:

Josh Abrams
Sarah Achbach
Meghan Davis
Emily Gnadinger
Adrien-Alice Hansel
Rene Humphrey
Hilary Redmon
Megan Shultz
Joel A. Smith
Val Smith
Alexander Speer

Rande Brown
Jason Fogelson
Lorraine Kisly
George Lane
Sterling Lord
Carl Mulert
Howard Rosenstone
Katharine Shields
Helen Tworkov

Foreword

The Humana Festival has been leaving tracks for twenty-two years now, but somehow it has never seemed more American. As I watched them playing in repertory over a three-day period, I realized that beyond a shadow of a doubt not a single one of these plays could have been written in another culture. This fact didn't seem thematic, it seemed character-based. These were Americans in trouble, and even the trouble was deeply American. American love stories, American poetic sensibilities, American guilt, American geographies of land and spirit, American yearnings for (and fears of) success. I hadn't felt as defined in time and space since the last time I went through passport control.

Sometimes American writers take critical heat for not being political enough. I have an English acquaintance who calls the plays he sees here "squabbles at the dinner table," but it's a bum rap. Americans see that every issue refines down to relationships and those relationships refine down to family or family soon-to-be. American writing for the stage usually buries its metaphors in the specific and its politics in the home. That doesn't mean it isn't political. The politics of mother and daughter, or lovers, or father and son are, one step abstracted, the politics of the nation. You'll certainly see that in this collection. This time around they are rife with politics yet-to-come in a new millennium, and they get at that by centering around the children, whose experience of the culture now will define the issues of the twenty-first century. Politics by implication. These characters don't have the "big picture" as they lead their American lives. The audience or the reader has to discover that fruit on the tree. Personally, I'd call that treating the audience with respect. American writers, they have their own way of doing things, and these are absolutely and to-the-core American writers.

Jon Jory
Producing Director
Actors Theatre of Louisville

Editors' Note

The Humana Festival of New American Plays—it means many things to many people. For playwrights, it's a grand opportunity to refine and realize their visions on stage for an international audience. For critics, it's an annual checkup on the dramatic temperature of our time. Louisville audiences consider it a chance to witness something new, and maybe catch a rising star—that next award-winning play. For theatre producers across America and abroad, it's part of an ongoing search for something that just might work back home. Development scouts from other media come in search of emerging talent and fresh material. Leaders of the Humana Foundation say the Festival expresses their belief that America's arts are a precious natural resource. And everyone at Actors Theatre of Louisville uses the occasion to celebrate new American contributions to the age-old art of playwriting.

What's crucial about these many viewpoints isn't simply that they co-exist—what else would you expect in the relativist atmosphere of a postmodern universe? No, what's crucial is that the Humana Festival creates a space for all of them. The Festival's "user-friendliness" allows its impact to far exceed any one perspective, event, or set of interpretations, and here's how that works. First of all, 30,000 people see the plays, and their experiences generate an ongoing dialogue about the work. For those who can't be in the audience, there are dozens of critics conveying the event in print, or at least their versions of it. Next come the plays in future productions: at theatres everywhere, in movie houses (a film of *Resident Alien* is in the works), and on the radio (*Acorn* has already been aired by National Public Radio). Finally, there's this book, which presents the plays, though significantly revised, in the form in which they first arrived at Actors Theatre of Louisville.

So how do you like to experience your plays—as stage performances, through discussions and reviews, via film and radio adaptations, or by reading the published texts? The very fact of this menu demonstrates the amazing ripple effect of the Humana Festival—from one playwright to so many minds via so many media. This book is part of that cultural phenomenon—and so are you. Enjoy.

Michael Bigelow Dixon & Amy Wegener

Humana Festival '98
The Complete Plays

Ti Jean Blues

adapted from the works of Jack Kerouac

by JoAnne Akalaitis

BIOGRAPHY

JoAnne Akalaitis was Co-Artistic Director and Co-Founder of the New York City-based Mabou Mines. She worked with this company for 20 years as an actor, writer, director and designer on such productions as *Dressed Like an Egg* (writer, director, designer and performer), *Dead End Kids* (director and writer of feature film adaptation) and Beckett's *Cascando* (director and designer). Her other directing credits include: *Iphigenia* at the Court Theatre in Chicago, *Endgame* and *The Balcony* at American Repertory Theatre, *The Screens* at The Guthrie Theater, '*Tis Pity She's a Whore* at The Goodman Theatre, *Green Card* (which she also wrote) at Mark Taper Forum, *Dance of Death* at Arena Stage, *In the Summer House* at Lincoln Center, *The Visit* at New York City Opera, *Cymbeline* and *Henry IV, Parts 1 and 2* at New York Shakespeare Festival, where she was the former Artistic Director. Currently Co-Chair of the Directing Program at Juilliard's Drama Division, Ms. Akalaitis is the recipient of five Obie Awards for direction and production, the Drama Desk Award, the NEA Award for Sustained Artistic Achievement, a Guggenheim Fellowship, Rockefeller and NEA grants for playwriting and opera, and the National Theatre Residency Grant at the Court Theatre. Several of her plays have been published by Broadway Play Publishing. She has also published articles in *American Theatre* magazine, *Performing Arts Journal* and *The New York Times*.

HUMANA FESTIVAL PRODUCTION

*Ti Jean Blue*s was first performed at the Humana Festival of New American Plays in March 1998. It was directed by JoAnne Akalaitis with the following cast:

ACTOR 1	Jesse Sinclair Lenat
ACTOR 2	Christopher Michael Bauer
ACTOR 3	Spencer S. Barros
ACTOR 4	Lisa Louise Langford
ACTOR 5	Gretchen Lee Krich

and the following production staff:

Scenic Designer	Paul Owen
Costume Designer	Jeanette deJong
Lighting Designer	Greg Sullivan
Sound Designer	Martin R. Desjardins
Properties Designer	Ron Riall
Stage Manager	Christine Lomaka

Assistant Stage Manager. . . . . Kathy Preher
Dramaturgs . . . . Amy Wegener & Meghan Davis
Movement Coordinators . . . . Michelle H. Strier
                                        Arthur Allen Doederlein
American Sign Language Coach . . . . Mark Sawyer-Dailey
Casting . . . . Laura Richin Casting

MUSIC

Prisoner of Love (aka Melodies for Saxophone) composed by Philip Glass. Music was used by special arrangement with Dunvagen Music Publishers, Inc.

Jesse Sinclair Lenat, Christopher Michael Bauer, Spencer S. Barros,
Lisa Louise Langford and Gretchen Lee Krich
in *Ti Jean Blues,* adapted from the works of Jack Kerouac by JoAnne Akalaitis

22nd Annual Humana Festival of New American Plays
Actors Theatre of Louisville, 1998
photo by Richard Trigg

Ti Jean Blues

ACTOR 4 & ACTOR 5: Transcendental, transcendental, we shall dance a mad cadenza.

ACTOR 1: I was never really interested in writing. Jack was—Jack wasn't just *interested* in writing. I mean, whatever else Jack was doing, he had to write. It's like you gotta breathe, or shit, or eat. He was always writing. And no matter how much of his life was having a job—or riding around in a car, or traveling or this or that—he always found some time to scrawl in the little books. He really had a memory like few men that you meet. Like he used to say—"That's why they call me Memory Babe," which is what they used to call him in Lowell, Mass. He had a *fantastic* memory.

ACTOR 2: One gray afternoon in Centralville when I was probably 1, 2 or 3 years old, I saw a cluttered dark French Canadian shoe repair shop all lost in gray bleak wings infolded on the shelf. It was the day I learned to say door in English...door, door, *porte, porte*—this shoe repair shop is lost in the rain of my first memories and's connected to the Great Bathrobe Vision.

I'm sitting in my mother's arms in a brown aura of gloom sent up by her bathrobe—the bathrobe of the family, I saw it for 15 or 20 years—that people were sick in—old Christmas morning bathrobe, but the brown of the color of life, the color of the brain, the gray brown brain, and the first color I noticed from the crib so dumb. I'm in my mother's arms her robe sends auras of warm brown (the brown of my family)—so now when I bundle my chin in a warm scarf in the wet gale—I think on that comfort in the brown bathrobe—or as when a kitchen door is opened allowing fresh ices of air to interfere with the fragrant heat of cooking...say a vanilla pudding...

ACTOR 5: I am the pudding

ACTOR 4: winter is the gray mist.

ACTOR 2: A shudder of joy ran through me—when I read of Proust's teacup—

ACTOR 5: all those saucers in a crumb—

ACTOR 4: all of History by thumb—

ACTOR 2: all of a city in a tasty crumb—I got all my boyhood in vanilla winter waves around the kitchen stove. It's exactly like cold milk on hot bread pudding.

The brown that I saw in the bathrobe dream, and the gray in the shoeshop day, are connected with the browns and grays of Pawtucketville—
ACTOR 4 & ACTOR 5: the black of Doctor Sax came later.
ACTOR 1: Be in love with your life every detail of it

(Music: Charlie Parker. Chair business, getting someone's attention at a party mudra, throwing dolls. Music stops.)

ACTOR 3: Everything goes away from me girls visions, anything, just in the same way and forever and I accept lostness forever

(Music: Philip Glass.)

ACTOR 2: Lowell (Mass.) High School
ACTOR 5: Horace Mann School for Boys
ACTOR 4: Columbia College (1940-42)
ACTOR 1: Got an A from Mark Van Doren in Shakespeare at Columbia
ACTOR 2: Flunked chemistry at Columbia
ACTOR 3: Played football on varsities
ACTOR 4: Also track, baseball, chess teams
ACTOR 5: SUMMARY OF PRINCIPAL OCCUPATIONS
ALL: AND/OR
ACTOR 4: JOBS
ALL: Everything:
ACTOR 1 & ACTOR 2 & ACTOR 3: Let's elucidate:
ACTOR 5: scullion on ships
ACTOR 3: gas station attendant
ACTOR 4: deckhand on ships
ACTOR 1: newspaper sportswriter
ACTOR 2: railroad brakeman
ACTOR 4: script synopsizer
ACTOR 5: soda jerk
ACTOR 3: railroad yardclerk
ACTOR 4: railroad baggagehandler

ACTOR 1: cottonpicker

ACTOR 2: furniture mover

ACTOR 5: sheet metal apprentice

ACTOR 4: forest fire lookout

ACTOR 3: construction laborer

ALL: INTERESTS

ACTOR 1: HOBBIES I invented my own baseball game, on cards, extremely complicated, playing a whole 154-game season among eight clubs, with all the works, batting averages, E.R.A. averages, etc.

ACTOR 2: SPORTS Played all of them except tennis and lacrosse and skull

ALL: SPECIAL Girls

(Girl mudra. Music stops.)

ACTOR 5: The whole thing forms one enormous comedy, seen through the eyes of poor Ti Jean (me), otherwise known as Jack Duluoz, the world of raging action and folly and also of gentle sweetness seen through the keyhole of his eye.

ACTOR 1: PLEASE GIVE A BRIEF RESUME OF YOUR LIFE

(Music: Philip Glass.)

ACTOR 4: Had beautiful childhood, roamed fields and riverbanks day and night, wrote little novels in my room, first novel written at age 11, also kept extensive diaries.

ACTOR 5: Had good early education from Jesuit brothers at St. Joseph's Parochial School in Lowell; as child traveled to Montreal, Quebec, with family. Took long walks under old trees of New England at night with my mother and aunt.

(Music stops.)

ACTOR 2: Bye and bye you'll rise to the sun and propel your mean bones hard and sure to huge labors, and great steaming dinners, and spit your pits out, aching cocklove nights in cobweb moons, the mist of tired dust at evening—

ACTOR 3: the corn

ACTOR 4: the silk

ACTOR 1: the moon

ACTOR 5: the rail—

ACTOR 2: that is known as Maturity—but you'll never be as happy as you are now in your quiltish, innocent book-devouring boyhood immortal night.

(Shift. Music.)

ACTOR 3: Decided to become a writer at age 17 under influence of Sebastian Sampas, local young poet who later died on Anzio beach head

ACTOR 2: To Sebastian Sampas

> April 15, 1941
> New York City

Sebastian—

I read Wolfe at 4 A.M. this morning—I saw Walt Disney's "Fantasia" the other night. Wasn't it magnificent, especially Bach's Staccato [sic] & Fugue. George came over the weekend, and we possessed the bodies of a few women; had little discussion on Union Square with a few Reds; roamed Greenwich Village; and sat by the Hudson on Sunday, ending the afternoon by gazing rapturously at some original Greek sculpture. George also burped loudly in the face of a genuine burper.

ALL: Write soon.

ACTOR 2: Jean

(Shift.)

ACTOR 1: read the life of Jack London at 18 decided to also be an adventurer, a lonesome traveler; Influenced by my older brother Gerard Kerouac who died at age 9 in 1926 when I was 4, was great painter and drawer in childhood

ACTOR 2: I saw my brother in a satin coffin, he was nine, he lay with the stillness and the face of my former wife in her sleep, accomplished, regretted—

ACTOR 1: I thought I was a phantom,
me, myself,

Suffering. One night I saw
    my older brother Gerard
Standing over my crib with wild
    hair, as if he had just
    pee-visited the pail
    in the hall of snores
    and headed back for his room
    was investigatin the Grail.

ACTOR 4: when you die
ACTOR 2: you muffle
ACTOR 3: in your sigh
ACTOR 1: the thorny hard
ACTOR 5: regret of rocks
    of life-belief.
ACTOR 2: I knew, I hoped, to go be saved.

ACTOR 4: But I saw my father die,
ACTOR 3: I saw my brother die,
ACTOR 1: I saw my mother die
ACTOR 2: my mother my mother my mother
    inside me—

ACTOR 5: Saw the pear trees die,
    the grapes, pearls, penny trees—
Saw little girl with black dress
And spots of rose on each cheek,
    die.

(Music. Shift.)

ACTOR 3: My father was completely honest man full of gaiety; soured in last years over Roosevelt and World War II and died of cancer.

ACTOR 2: Ha ha ha ha! What a town when you come to think of it—*Lowell*— Well it's where my little woman hung her curtains. *God*, I'm just tryna please. If I cant please You, and the world, and Ti Jean too, then I cant please the lion and the angel and the lamb all at the same time neither.

Thank you God, and get those Democrats outa there before this country goes to hell!

ACTOR 3: Mother still living, I live with her a kind of monastic life that has enabled me to write as much as I did. My mother's name Gabrielle, learned all about natural story-telling from her.

(Music stops.)

ACTOR 4: Jack always tried to please his mother. It seemed to eat away at him. He went off with the Beat Generation, but he always worried about his mother.

ACTOR 1: I keep falling in love
    with my mother,
I dont want to hurt her
—Of all people to hurt.
Every time I see her
    she's grown older
But her uniform always
    amazes me
For its Dutch simplicity
And the Doll she is,
The doll-like way
    she stands
Bowlegged in my dreams,
Waiting to serve me.

    And I am only an Apache
    Smoking Hashi
    In old Cabashy
    By the Lamp

(Shift.)

ACTOR 3: Read and studied alone all my life

ACTOR 1: Set a record at Columbia College cutting classes in order to write a daily play and read, say, Louis Ferdinand Céline, instead of "classics."

(Music stops.)

ACTOR 3: Had own Mind

ACTOR 2: Am known as a "Madman bum and angel" with "naked endless head" of "prose."

ACTOR 5: Always considered writing my duty on earth.

ACTOR 4: Am actually not "beat" but strange solitary crazy mystic.

ALL: Final plans:

ACTOR 2: hermitage in the woods, quiet writing of old age, mellow hopes of Paradise

ALL: (which comes to everybody anyway)

(Shift.)

ACTOR 2: TO ALLEN GINSBERG

> [December 28, 1952
> New York City]

> Allen—
> I've been digging your mad little pad and I took the terrible liberty of borrowing The Complete Oeuvres Genet, upon my word I won't lose it and'll return it very soon— The mystery not only of the French language but Genet's dawn—I didn't tell you about the thieves and fairies of Mexico and the one they call Negress—*Negra*—Also, yr. radio is superb, Lester Young in the afternoon on WHOM or Vivaldi on WNYC—Too much drinking & excitement for me—LIFE IS A LARK NOW.

ACTOR 1, ACTOR 4, ACTOR 5, ACTOR 3: Ti Jean

ACTOR 4: Be crazy dumbsaint of the mind

(Music: Monk.)

ACTOR 1: Dostoevski

ACTOR 5: Spengler

ACTOR 2: 52nd Street

ACTOR 3: West End Bar

ACTOR 4: Coleman Hawkins

ACTOR 1: Shostakovich

ACTOR 5: Stravinsky

ACTOR 4: Schönberg

ACTOR 3: Stendhal

ACTOR 1: *Blood of the Poet*

ACTOR 3: Kafka

ACTOR 2: Genet

ACTOR 4: Céline

ACTOR 1: Blake

ACTOR 5: Rimbaud

ACTOR 3: Yeats

ACTOR 2: *Finnegan's Wake*

ACTOR 4: Shakespeare

ACTOR 2: Proust

ACTOR 3: Thoreau

ACTOR 1: Times Square

ACTOR 4: Denver

ACTOR 1: New Orleans

ACTOR 3: Seattle

ACTOR 2: Desolation Peak

ACTOR 5: The Diamond Sutra

ACTOR 4: O God in the Heavens, what a fumbling, hand-hanging, goof world it is, that people actually think they can gain anything from either this, or that, or thissa, or thatta, and in so doing, corrupt their sacred graves in the name of sacred-grave corruption.

(Shift.)

ACTOR 3: Berkeley

ACTOR 1: Tangiers

ACTOR 2: Sheridan Square

ACTOR 4: Lower East Side

ACTOR 1: San Francisco

ACTOR 3: Market Street

ACTOR 2: North Beach

ACTOR 5: Chinatown

ACTOR 2: There O I always came and walked and negotiated whole Friscos in one afternoon from the overlooking hills of the high Fillmore where

Orient-bound vessels you can see on drowsy Sunday mornings of poolhall
goof.

ACTOR 3: Over Harrison and down to the Embarcadero

ACTOR 3 & ACTOR 1: and around Telegraph Hill

ACTOR 3, ACTOR 1 & ACTOR 5: and up the back of Russian Hill

ACTOR 3, ACTOR 1, ACTOR 5 & ACTOR 4: and down to the play streets of
Chinatown

ALL: and down Kearney back across Market to Third and my wild-night neon
twinkle fate there, ah,

ACTOR 2: the immense girders of Oakland Bay still haunting me and all that
eternity too much to swallow and not knowing who I am at all but like a
big plump longhaired baby.

ACTOR 5: And there's my room, small, gray in the Sunday morning, now all
the franticness of the street and night before is done with, bums sleep—

ALL: my mind whirls with life.

ACTOR 3: Mexico City

ACTOR 1: Mexico City Bop
    I got the huck bop
    I got the floogle mock
    I got the thiri chiribim
        bitchy bitchy bitchy
        batch batch
    Chippely bop
        Noise like that
        Like fallin off porches
        Of Tenement Petersburg
        Russia Chicago

ALL: O Yay.

ACTOR 1: Like, when you see,
        the trumpet kind, horn
        shiny in his hand, raise
        it in smoke among heads
        he bespeaks, elucidates,
        explains and drops out,
        end of chorus, staring
        at the final wall

where in Africa
the old men petered
out on their own account
using their own Immemorial
Salvation Mind
SLIPPITY BOP

ACTOR 2: Wolfe
ACTOR 1: Melville
ACTOR 4: Greyhound bus

(Music stops.)

ACTOR 3: Hector's Cafeteria

(Music. Shoulder shake dance.)

ACTOR 1: I went to Hector's, the glorious cafeteria of Cody's first New York vision when he arrived in late 1946 all excited with his first wife; A glittering counter—decorative walls—sections of the ceiling high mirrors—brownwood panels with coat hooks and sections of rose-tint walls—But ah the counter! as brilliant as B-way outside!

ACTOR 2: great rows of diced
ACTOR 2 & ACTOR 3: mint jellos
ACTOR 2: in glasses
ACTOR 3: diced strawberry
ACTOR 1 & ACTOR 2 & ACTOR 3: jellos
ACTOR 4 & ACTOR 5: gleaming red
ACTOR 1 & ACTOR 2 & ACTOR 3: jellos
ACTOR 2: mixed with
ACTOR 2 & ACTOR 4 & ACTOR 5: peaches and cherries
ACTOR 4: cherry
ACTOR 1 & ACTOR 2 & ACTOR 3: jellos
ACTOR 4: top't with whipcream
ACTOR 1: vanilla custards top't with
ACTOR 4 & ACTOR 5: cream
ACTOR 5: great

ACTOR 4 & ACTOR 5: strawberry
ACTOR 4 & ACTOR 5 & ACTOR 3: shortcakes already
ACTOR 4 & ACTOR 5, ACTOR 3 & ACTOR 1: sliced in
ALL: twelve sections
ACTOR 1 & ACTOR 2 & ACTOR 3: Huge salads
ACTOR 1: cottage cheese
ACTOR 5: pineapple
ACTOR 4: plums
ACTOR 3: egg salad
ACTOR 2: prunes
ALL: everything
ACTOR 4: vast baked apples
ACTOR 3: tumbling dishes of grapes
ACTOR 5: immense pans of cheesecake
ACTOR 2: of raspberry cream
ACTOR 1 & ACTOR 2 & ACTOR 3: cake
ACTOR 1: of flaky rich Napoleons
ACTOR 3: of simple Boston
ACTOR 1 & ACTOR 2 & ACTOR 3: cake, armies
ACTOR 1: of éclairs
ACTOR 2: of enormously dark chocolate (gleaming scatological brown)
ACTOR 1: of deepdish strudel
ALL: of time and the river
ACTOR 3: of freshly baked powdered
ACTOR 3 & ACTOR 2: cookies
ACTOR 1: of glazed strawberry-banana desserts
ACTOR 5: wild glazed orange
ACTOR 5 & ACTOR 1 & ACTOR 2 & ACTOR 3: cakes
ACTOR 4: pyramiding glazed desserts made of
ACTOR 4 & ACTOR 5: raspberries
ACTOR 3: whipcream
ACTOR 1: lady fingers
ACTOR 1 & ACTOR 2 & ACTOR 3: sticking up
ACTOR 2: vast sections reserved for the splendors of
ACTOR 2 & ACTOR 4 & ACTOR 5: coffee cakes and Danish crullers
ACTOR 3: All interspersed with white bottles of rich mad milk
ACTOR 2: Then the bread bun mountain—
ACTOR 2 & ACTOR 1: Then the serious business,

ACTOR 1 & ACTOR 2 & ACTOR 3: the wild steaming fragrant hot-plate counter

ACTOR 1: Roast lamb,

ACTOR 1 & ACTOR 3: roast loin of pork,

ACTOR 1 & ACTOR 2 & ACTOR 3: roast sirloin of beef, baked breast of lamb, stuffed pepper, boiled chicken

ACTOR 1: stuff'd spring chicken,

ACTOR 1 & ACTOR 4 & ACTOR 5: things to make the poor penniless mouth water

ACTOR 1 & ACTOR 2 & ACTOR 3: big sections of Meat fresh from the ovens, and a great

ACTOR 4 & ACTOR 5: knife

ACTOR 2: sitting alongside

ACTOR 4: The coffee counter the urns the cream jet

ACTOR 3: the steam

ACTOR 2: But most of all it's that shining glazed sweet counter

ACTOR 5: showering like heaven

ACTOR 1 & ACTOR 2 & ACTOR 3: an all-out promise of joy

ALL: in the great city of kicks.

ACTOR 1: But I haven't even mentioned the best of all

ACTOR 5: the cold cuts and sandwiches and salad counter—

ACTOR 4 & ACTOR 5: with pans of mountainous spreads that have cream cheese coverings sprinkled with chives and other bright spices, the pink lovely looking lox—

ALL: cold ham—Swiss cheese—the whole counter gleaming with icy joy,

ACTOR 1: salty and nourishing—

ALL: cold fish, herrings, onions

ACTOR 2: great loaves of rye bread sliced

ACTOR 1: so on

ACTOR 4 & ACTOR 5: egg salads big enough for a giant decorated and sprigged on a pan—in great sensuous shapes

(Music stops.)

ACTOR 1: (Poor Cody in front of this in his scuffled-up beat Denver shoes, his literary "imitation" suit he had wanted to wear to be acceptable in New York cafeterias which he thought would be brown and plain like Denver cafeterias, with ordinary food)—

ACTOR 4: Dizzy Gillespie

ACTOR 3: Dickinson
ACTOR 1: Lester Young
ACTOR 5: Billie Holiday
ACTOR 1: Lautréamont
ACTOR 2: Huxley
ACTOR 4: Wells
ACTOR 3: Aeschylus
ACTOR 5: Goethe
ACTOR 1: The Cotton Club
ACTOR 2: Tolstoy
ACTOR 3: Baudelaire
ACTOR 4: Birdland
ACTOR 1: Basie
ACTOR 5: Brooklyn Bridge
ACTOR 2: Charlie Parker

(Shift. Music starts.)

ACTOR 1: Charley Parker, forgive me—
    Forgive me for not answering your eyes—
    For not having made an indication
    Of that which you can devise—
    Charley Parker pray for me—
    Pray for me and everybody
    In the Nirvanas of your brain
    Where you hide, indulgent and huge,
    No longer Charley Parker
    But the secret unsayable name
    That carries with it merit
    Not to be measured from here
    To up, down, east, or west—
    —Charley Parker, lay the bane,
        off me, and every body

(Shift.)

ACTOR 3: BUDDHA
ACTOR 5: Balzac

ACTOR 4: Byron
ACTOR 2: Hemingway
ACTOR 1: Whitman

(Shift.)

ALL: I saw my father die
    I saw my brother die
    I saw my mother die
    Every one of us born to die

(Music: Philip Glass.)

ACTOR 5: Write what you want bottomless from bottom of the mind
ACTOR 1: Blow as deep as you want to blow
ACTOR 2: We blop
ACTOR 1: and plop in the waters
ACTOR 4: of slaughter
ACTOR 3: and white meat
ALL: and die
    one by one.

(Music: Artie Shaw, "Begin the Beguine.")

ACTOR 3: It was at the dance. The Rex Ballroom; with coat attendants in a drafty hall,
ACTOR 4: fresh snow spilled on the boards;
ACTOR 1: the rosy girls and handsome boys running in,
ACTOR 2: the boys clacking heels, the girls in high heels, short dresses of the Thirties showing sexy legs.
ACTOR 3: A jitterbug kid, Whitey St. Claire, introduced me to Maggie.
ACTOR 1: I tried and tried to work that chick!
ACTOR 5: I suppose you're wondering what an Irish girl can be doing at a New Year's Eve dance unescorted. You're a football player Whitey said.
ACTOR 3: Whitey?
ACTOR 5: Whitey that introduced us, dummy. Do you get hurt often? my brother Roy gets hurt all the time that's why I hate football. I suppose

you like it. You've got a bunch of friends. They look like a nice bunch of fellas—

ACTOR 2: She was nervous,

ACTOR 4: curious,

ACTOR 1: gossipy,

ACTOR 2, ACTOR 4 & ACTOR 1: womany.

(Shift.)

ACTOR 5: Got a girl?

ACTOR 3: In high school—Pauline Cole is my girl, I meet her under the clock every afternoon after third bell—

ACTOR 5: And you tell me right away you got a girl! You're French Canadian aintcha? I bet all the girls go for you, I bet you're gonna be a big success.

ACTOR 3: Oh—not exactly—

ACTOR 5: But you're only sixteen years old, you're younger than me, I'm seventeen—That makes me old enough ha ha.

ACTOR 2: I put my hard arm around her soft waist and took her dancing awkward dumb steps under the balloons and crinkly pop funhats of New Year's Eve America—

ACTOR 1: Boy and girl, arms around each other, Maggie and Jack, in the sad ball floor of life, already crestfallen, corners of the mouth giving up—love is bitter, death is sweet.

ACTOR 4: Maggie loves you. She's madder about you than I can ever remember her being about anybody else.

ACTOR 3: Huh?

ACTOR 4: Maggie loves you, but dont try her patience—tell her you want to marry her or sumptin.

ACTOR 2: In the variety of the tone of her words, moods, hugs, kisses, brushes of the lips, and this night the upside-down kiss over the back of the chair with her dark eyes heavy hanging and her blushing cheeks full of sweet blood and sudden tenderness, the startling sudden sweet fall of all her hair over my face and the soft downward brush of her lips, in the mouth of life when life is young.

ACTOR 3: I held her captured upside down, and savored the kiss which first had surprised me like blind man's bluff, as she descended to me from the upper dark where I'd thought only cold could be and with all her heavy lips and breast in my neck and on my head and sudden fragrance of some

5 & 10 cheap perfumes the little hungry scent of perspiration warm in her flesh like preciousness.

(Shift.)

ACTOR 1: I think we were both frightened later when we'd hold a kiss for 35 minutes until the muscles of our lips would get cramps.

ACTOR 2: Sometimes our teeth'd grind, our mouths burn from interchanged spittle, our lips blister, bleed, chap—We were scared.

ACTOR 3: I ate her lips and she ate mine.

ACTOR 1: Ah I loved my Maggie, I wanted to eat her, bring her home, hide her in the heart of my life the rest of my days.

ACTOR 4: Well how's your love affair with Maggie Cassidy coming along?

ACTOR 3: my sister'd ask, grinning from behind a sandwich,

ACTOR 4: or did she give you the air because of Moe Cole!

ACTOR 3: You mean Pauline? Why Pauline?

ACTOR 4: You dont know how jealous women get—that's all they think about—You'll see—

ACTOR 3: I dont see anything.

ACTOR 1: *Tiens*

ACTOR 3: my mother's saying

ACTOR 1: here's some bacon with toast I made a big batch this morning. Never mind the tennis courts, it's gonna be awright if you just stick to your guns there like a real French Canadian boy—listen, Ti Jean, you'll never be sorry if you follow a clean life.

ACTOR 2: Hey Zagg, what do you call that hold? Zeet? Hey Zagg?

ACTOR 3: Mouse? Remember the winter it was so cold they had frostbites in the Principal's office with doctors?—

ACTOR 1: And the time we had that snowball war on Wannalancitt—

ACTOR 3: I used to walk home every noon me and Eddy Desmond—he was the laziest guy in the world, he didn't want to go to school in the afternoon.

ACTOR 1: Ah the old days! All I ask is a chance in this ga-dam world to earn a decent living and support my mother and see that all her needs are answered—

ACTOR 3: Where's Scotty workin now?

ACTOR 2: Didnt you hear?—out in Chelmsford, they're building a big war airplane base, Scotty and all the old WPA bums—he's making a million dollars a week—I love Scotcho—Dont catch *him* going to no high school and no business school courses—

ACTOR 1: You're quiet, Zagg—that damn Maggie Cassidy's got you boy, s'got you boy!

ACTOR 2: Dont let no broad get you, Zagg—love aint worth it—what's love, *nothin.*

ACTOR 3: No, love is *great* Mouse—something to think about—

ACTOR 2: Zagg You Babe! Screw her! Zeet? Have a good one for me!

ACTOR 1: Zagg, screw her then leave her take it from an old seadog,—women are no good, forever 'tis written in the stars—Ah! Kick em in the pants, put em in their place—There's enough misery in this world, laugh, cry, sing, tomorrow is nothing—Life my dear Zagg is immerelensum! Dont let her get you down, Zagguth.

ACTOR 3: I wont, Mouso.

ACTOR 5: Hmm. Isnt he dreamy?

ACTOR 4: I don't know. He looks sleepy all the time.

ACTOR 5: That's the way I like—

ACTOR 4: Oh get away—how do you know how you like?

ACTOR 5: Wouldn't you like to know? Ask—

ACTOR 4: Ask *who*?

ACTOR 5: I'm—Oh, there's the bell.

ACTOR 5: Sometimes you get me. Sometimes I cant stand how I love you.

ACTOR 3: Hah?

ACTOR 5: Jacky! I love you Jacky. Why do you make me so mad! Oh you make me so mad! Oh I love you so! Oh I wanta kiss you! Oh you damn fool I want you to take me. I'm yours dont you know?—all, all yours—you're a fool Jacky—Oh poor Jacky—Oh kiss me—*hard*—

ACTOR 5: I wish you were older.

ACTOR 3: Why?

ACTOR 5: You'd know more what to do with me—

ACTOR 3: If—

ACTOR 5: No! You dont know how. I love you too much. What's the use? Oh hell!—I love you so! But I hate you! Oh go home!! Kiss me! Lie on top of me, crush me—I know you're too young, I'm robbing the high school cradle.

ACTOR 3: Ah—

ACTOR 5: You have no trade—You have a career ahead of you—

ACTOR 3: No no—

ACTOR 5:—be a brakeman on the railroad, we'll live in a little house by the tracks, play the 920 Club, have babies—I'll paint my kitchen chairs red—I'll paint the walls of our bedroom deep dark green or sumpin—I'll kiss you to wake up in the morning—

ACTOR 3: Oh Maggie that's what I want!

ACTOR 5: No! Oh Jack it's too late.

ACTOR 3: I dont wanta go.

ACTOR 5: You gotta go.

ACTOR 3: Ah okay.

ACTOR 5: I dont want you to go—Jacky—I love you I love I love you—You better go home, dear—You gotta go to school tomorrer—You'll never get up.

ACTOR 3: Okay Maggie.

ACTOR 5: Say you love me when you wake up in the morning, to yourself—

ACTOR 3: Maggie that house by the railroad tracks, the red chairs…I…I…cant—dont want to do anything else with anybody else—ever—I'll tell—I'll—We'll—Ah Maggie.

ACTOR 2: She'd cradle my broken head in her all-healing lap that beat like a heart; my eyes hot would feel the soothe fingertips of cool, the joy, the stroke and barely-touch, the brooding river in her unfathomable springtime thoughts—The dark flowing enriched silty heart—Irish as peat, dark as Kilkenny night, red-lipped as red-rubied morn on the Irish Sea bringing tears to my eyes to be an Irishman too and lost and sunk inside her forever—her brother, husband, lover, raper, owner, friend, father, son, grabber, kisser, keener, swain, sneaker-upper, sleeper-with, feeler, railroad brakeman in red house of red babycribs and the joyous wash Saturday morning in the glad ragged yard—

ACTOR 5: "Jack—Jack, marry me some day."

ACTOR 3: "Yes, yes, always—nobody else."

ACTOR 5: "You sure there's nobody else?"

ACTOR 3: "Well who could be?"

(Shift.)

ACTOR 5: There was something deep between Jack and me, something nobody else understood or knew about. After that book Maggie Cassidy came out I had a lot of trouble. People calling me and the neighbors talking. It was awful. Jack was so sweet. He was a sweet, good kid, and the people of Lowell didn't understand him. They never did. Nobody ever reads here. They wouldn't even put up a plaque for him.

ACTOR 1: Ah life, God—we wont find them any more the Nova Scotias of flowers! No more saved afternoons! The shadows, the ancestors, they've all walked in the dust of 1900 seeking the new toys of the twentieth century just as Céline says—but it's still love has found us out, and in the stalls was nothing, eyes of drunken wolves was all.

ACTOR 2: Ask the guys at the war

(Music.)

ACTOR 3: I have the persistent feeling that I'm gonna die soon, only the feeling, no real I think wish or "premonition," I feel like I've done wrong, to myself the most wrong, I'm throwing away something that I can't even find in the incredible clutter of my being but it's going out with the refuse en masse, buried in the middle of it. I get so sick thinking of the years I wasted.

(Music stops.)

ACTOR 1: Jack was just—ah, you know, he couldn't be led, and he was recalcitrant, and he was a pig, and he was this that and the other but he was everything in a man that Edie ever thought could exist. Edie Parker was the best woman Jack ever got involved with, bar none. Jack didn't really have problems with *women,* women had problems with Jack. He didn't really want to be cornered into a situation where you're building something. If someone said, "Let's get married and move to the suburbs," he'd, like, disappear. Anything that tended to trap Kerouac, whether it was a woman, or a job, or a jail sentence—it was something he didn't want to get involved with.

ACTOR 2: Edie at that time was kind of a cute-looking chick. She had blonde hair, green eyes, and she wore her hair kind of fluffy.

ACTOR 3: Accept loss forever

(Music: Billie Holiday, "Too Marvelous for Words.")

ACTOR 4: Following the abortion of our child, Jack Kerouac and I decided to get our own apartment. We would drop out of school and work, so that Jack could continue his writing. We found the right place at 420 West 119th Street, apartment #28, in the New Year of 1942, just after the attack on Pearl Harbor. The war was upon us. We felt as if we had very little time. We had to be alone, our love was choking us; we needed each other, desperately.

(Music changes.)

ACTOR 2: But it was a year of low, evil decadence. Not only the drugs, the morphine, the marijuana, the horrible Benzedrine we used to take in those days by breaking open Benzedrine inhalers and removing the soaked paper and rolling it into poisonous little balls that made you sweat and suffer (lost thirty pounds in three days the first time I tried it an over dose) but the characters we got to know—

I ran with horror from home to "them" and then from "them" to home but both equally dark and inhospitable places of guilt, sin, sorrow, lamentation, despair. It wasnt so much the darkness of the night that bothered me but the horrible lights men had invented to illuminate their darkness with.

ACTOR 1: That feeling when you wake up with the delirium tremens with the *fear* of eerie death dripping from your ears,

ACTOR 3: the feeling of being a bentback mudman monster groaning underground in hot steaming mud pulling a long hot burden nowhere,

ACTOR 1: the feeling of standing ankledeep in hot boiled pork blood,

ALL: ugh,

ACTOR 4: of being up to your waist in a giant pan of greasy brown dishwater

ACTOR 5: The face of yourself you see in the mirror with its expression of unbearable anguish

ALL: so hagged and awful with sorrow

ACTOR 2: you cant even cry for a thing

ACTOR 1: so ugly,

ACTOR 3: so lost.

(Music.)

ACTOR 2: TO STELLA SAMPAS

Dec. 10, 1952
Mexico City, Mexico

Dear Stella,

Your beautiful letter reached me in California as I was preparing to travel to Mexico, so the delay—I've not been ignoring your letters but they've been finding me in out-of-the-way-places, and I didn't know what to say—during a recent long, dark depression with thoughts of suicide sometimes. Thank you for sympathizing with my "literary obscurity"—it's a bitch—I have to work on my feet for a living, on railroads, and my feet have been bad for 5 years—I've been in several hospitals, stopped smoking—

My dearest hope is to come back to Lowell, with my mother, and make a home—eventually get married again— to some girl that loves me, not hates me—hate is madness—But nothing can prevent me from returning to Lowell, and walk all I please those hallowed streets of life— Good luck, excuse this sentimental letter, love to whole family.

Jack K.

ALL: (Write)

ACTOR 4: He went off with the Beat Generation but he always worried about his mother.

ACTOR 5: You're a genius all the time.

ACTOR 2: I've decided to hitch-hike with my seventy dollars and hit all the bars in the snow of the great land between here and Frisco—if I freeze to death it won't be from lack of beer and *food* (!) I'm to meet ship and renew old strange acquaintance with L.A., the actual ORIGIN of the B-movie and center of the California Night. In front of Holland Tunnel I wait. I will—no ride—spend dollars for bus ticket.

ACTOR 1 & ACTOR 2 & ACTOR 3: This trip in depth, then, beginning, New York

ACTOR 3: pull out fast—at New Brunswick wild Air Force gang in Levis get on with satchels of whiskey, wine and jewelry for wives in Colorado Springs

ACTOR 2: the leader is big handsome Ben from San Antone, his buddy is crazy snap-knife Doug with blond hair

ACTOR 5: Ben says he was knifed in Amarillo, an X in his back, got a buddy to hold the gang at bay with a shotgun and *stomped* all four one by one, stomped one's tongue out accidently

ACTOR 4: They call their cocks "hammers," cunts a "gash" and do the up-your-ass fingersign slapping finger down into palm

ALL: wham

ACTOR 5: Bus went through pretty

ALL: Princeton

ACTOR 5: made me homesick for oldfashioned Eastern Xmas Dammit

ACTOR 1: then into

ALL: Pennsylvania

ACTOR 3: in

ALL: Harrisburg

ACTOR 2: I jogged in eighteenth-century streets

ACTOR 3: Turnpike in snow to

ALL: Pittsburgh

ACTOR 1: I on dexies feel relaxed,

ACTOR 3: eat my first two ham sandwiches outdoors while Negro cleans out bus and others eat ham and eggs inside

ACTOR 2: At

ALL: Deerfield

ACTOR 4: I walk up and down highway in intense sunny cold of old Ohio

ACTOR 5: Then

ALL: Cleveland

ACTOR 4: and bought a pint of whiskey cheap

ACTOR 5: Cream of Kentucky

ACTOR 3: from Cleveland to Toledo I

ACTOR 1: walked,

ACTOR 2: ran,

ACTOR 3: froze,

ACTOR 1: Then across to Indiana and the lights of Xmas trees of supper evening coming on in little towns like LaGrange and Angola

ACTOR 5: (remember Fred MacMurray and Barbara Stanwyck going home to Indiana at Xmas?)

ACTOR 3: then into

ALL: Chicago

ACTOR 2: and the fantastic big red neon of ITS night

ACTOR 1: around midnight

ACTOR 3: the great glitter in the cold lakeshore night

ACTOR 1: (Dreiser should have seen, but he *did!*)

ACTOR 3: I saw no bop, hurried

ACTOR 2: saw North Clark trucks with girlieshow flaps

ACTOR 5: Across Illinois to Davenport,

ACTOR 4: where I woke up just before dawn,

ACTOR 2: dug the Mississippi again,

ACTOR 3: the ninth time,

ACTOR 5: thing to do is

ALL: GO ON

ACTOR 4: over frost fields to Muscatine, Keota (the Golden Buckle of the Corn Belt), I walked in freezing morn while others ate joyous breakfasts

ACTOR 1: at

ALL: Council Bluffs

ACTOR 1: everything was gray and Western and inevitable,

ALL: bam, in Omaha it's snowing

ACTOR 5: a blizzard

ACTOR 2: dirty old scabrous shithouse character watches me shit, another sells me comb for dime, I eat sandwiches

ACTOR 4: (now down to bread and boiled eggs)

ACTOR 2: in Omaha doorway facing Missouri River Street down by warehouses in huge blizzard, I look real handsome passing plate glasses, like new cowboy, old scabrous finds me, wants sandwich or dime, I say "Get money from the rich!" recalling Dostoevsky

ACTOR 3: in toilet read, take dexy

ALL: storm is thick

ACTOR 5: three beers, which start me and send me buzzing, also dexy,

ACTOR 4: so from North Platte to Cheyenne I am

ALL: DRUNK

ACTOR 1: and finish all the whiskey, talking to everybody, seat jumping, running out with old man to piss at Chappell, busdriver says

ACTOR 2: "I know there's a bottle on this bus—if anybody needs a rest stop speak up."

ACTOR 3: and I say

ACTOR 1: "This gentleman needs to go to the restroom"

ACTOR 4: bravado at height

ACTOR 1: Till at Cheyenne I was stone cold out when they woke us up to change buses

ACTOR 2: next stop wonderful drowsy winter afternoon Mormon town I believe Wasatch

ACTOR 1: (dunno)

ALL: Wendover, Wells, Elko, Winnemucca, Lovelock

ACTOR 3: Finally I get to dig that crazy Reno high on Dexy at 6:30 am booming with roulette and house girls, and tic-kid with money so handsome and tragic at faro table, three fags watching, and soldier asking for girl at bar and Jewish New York handsome gambler with girls, and those *cunts* it's a sin that town

ACTOR 5: then the new fag driver with ONE glove

ACTOR 1: up the mountain and home in Truckee, just like Lowell,—over Donner Pass, and down to fogs of California

ALL: Colfax, Auburn, Roseville

ACTOR 2: and over to Frisco

ACTOR 3: waited in saloon at Mission and Sixth till Cody showed up with ONE precious stick that rode us high-crazy-yelling-wild clear into the Little Harlem Satnite where they told us Buddy'd slashed his woman and for want of money I gave away my MexCity wallet to gal who, Five Guys Named Moe in the crazy drizzling Negress morning I screwed forty-eight hours later—

ALL: Oh mad!

ACTOR 2: Now down in L.A. to meet ship

ALL: L.A. Xmas

ACTOR 2: the Great American Saturday afternoon

ACTOR 2 & ACTOR 1: but in L.A. and at Xmas shopping peak

ACTOR 2: just like Lowell is South Broadway

ACTOR 1: but in a warm strange sun.

ACTOR 1 & ACTOR 3: L.A. Playland

ACTOR 2: but there's something inexpressibly sad right now

ACTOR 3: in this beat old Playland

ACTOR 1: at the coffee counter

ACTOR 2: Bing's "White Christmas"

ACTOR 1 & ACTOR 2 & ACTOR 3: on juke

ACTOR 2: some sadness that draws my mind apart and makes me want to moan—

(Music: Charlie Parker. Dance.)

ACTOR 1: Josephine wants to come back via Lushy-Mushky Bust Colo., of course Josephine wants to cuk 7 Fuck (what mistakes dear me cuk 7 Fuck would be SOME FUCK) and I was saying she wants to fuck and fuck (fuck and fuck I meant to write but didn't capitalize the 7) she wanted to fuck and fuck or that is fuck and fuck and has or rather and has been doing so, Oh for goodness sakes, here is the sentence, Josephine wants to fuck and fuck and has been doing so with Irwin and me regular as pie and spent 4 days with me giving skull and getting skull, Mac and girl and me and everything and everybody but kitchen sink, weekend climaxed by my bringing colored guitarist and pianist and colored gal and all three women took off tops while we blew two hours me on bop-chords.

ACTOR 2: But there's an awful paranoiac element sometimes in orgasm that suddenly releases not sweet genteel sympathy but some token venom that splits up in the body—I feel a great ghastly hatred of myself and everything, the empty feeling far from being the usual relief is now as tho I've been robbed of my spinal power right down the middle on purpose by a great witching force—I feel evil forces gathering down all around me, from her. The moment I see her again "She's doing something else"—I leer and I dont feel sorry at all—"My God she should get to a nunnery!"

(Music.)

ACTOR 4: O his father was dead
ACTOR 1: and O his mother was dead
ACTOR 3: and O his sister was dead
ACTOR 2: and O his whereabout
ALL: was dead was dead.

ACTOR 1: In Pueblo, Colorado, in the middle of the winter Cody sat in a lunch-cart at three o'clock in the morning in the middle of the
ACTOR 1 & ACTOR 4 & ACTOR 5: poor unhappy thing
ACTOR 1: it is to be wanted by the police in America or at least in the night
ACTOR 2: (slapping dime down on counter like killing a fly with hand)
ALL: America,
ACTOR 3: the word,
ACTOR 5: the

ACTOR 5 & ACTOR 4: sound

ACTOR 5: is the

ACTOR 5 & ACTOR 4: sound

ACTOR 5: of my unhappiness,

ACTOR 3: the pronunciation of my

ACTOR 1 & ACTOR 2 & ACTOR 3: beat

ACTOR 3: and

ACTOR 1 & ACTOR 2 & ACTOR 3: stupid

ACTOR 3: grief

ACTOR 1 & ACTOR 2 & ACTOR 3: America

ACTOR 2: is being wanted by the police,

ACTOR 4: pursued across Kentucky and Ohio,

ACTOR 3: sleeping with the

ACTOR 3, ACTOR 4 & ACTOR 2: stockyard rats

ACTOR 3: and howling tin shingles of gloomy hideaway silos,

ACTOR 1: is the picture of an axe in *True Detective Magazine*,

ALL: America is where you're not even allowed to cry for yourself. America

ACTOR 1: (TEENAGE DOPE SEX CAR RING!!)

ACTOR 2: is also the red neon and the

ACTOR 2 & ACTOR 4 & ACTOR 5: thighs

ACTOR 2: in the cheap motel—

ACTOR 5: It's where at night the staggering drunks began to appear like cock-roaches

ACTOR 5 & ACTOR 1 & ACTOR 2 & ACTOR 3: when the bars close—

ACTOR 3: It is where

ACTOR 3 & ACTOR 5: people

ACTOR 3, ACTOR 5 & ACTOR 1: people

ACTOR 3, ACTOR 5, ACTOR 1 & ACTOR 2: people are

ACTOR 4 & ACTOR 5: weeping and chewing their lips in bars as well as lone beds and

ACTOR 1 & ACTOR 2 & ACTOR 3: masturbating

ACTOR 1: in a million ways in every hiding hole you can find in the dark—

ACTOR 2: It has evil roads behind gas tanks where

ACTOR 1 & ACTOR 2 & ACTOR 3: murderous dogs

ACTOR 2: snarl from behind wire fences and cruisers suddenly leap out like get-away cars but from a crime more secret, more baneful than words can tell—

ACTOR 1: It is where Cody Pomeray learned that people aren't good,

ACTOR 2: they want to be bad—

ACTOR 5: where he learned they want to cringe and beat,

ACTOR 4: and

ACTOR 4 & ACTOR 1 & ACTOR 2 & ACTOR 3: snarl

ACTOR 4: is the name of their lovemaking—

ACTOR 1: America took dark paints and made

ACTOR 1 & ACTOR 4 & ACTOR 5: hollows around a young boy's eyes,

ACTOR 1: and made his cheeks sink in.

ACTOR 2: Ah and nobody cares but the heart in the middle of US that will reappear

ACTOR 4: when the salesmen all die.

ALL: America's a lonely crockashit.

ACTOR 1: It's where the miserable fat corner newsstand midget sleeps in the lunchcart with a face that looks as if it had been repeatedly beaten on the sidewalk—

ACTOR 4: Where ferret-faced hipsters who may be part-time ushers are also lushworkers and half queer

ACTOR 5: Where people

ACTOR 5 & ACTOR 1: wait

ACTOR 5, ACTOR 1 & ACTOR 2: wait

ACTOR 1 & ACTOR 2: poor married couples

ACTOR 5: sleep on each other's shoulders on

ACTOR 1 & ACTOR 2: worn brown benches

ACTOR 5: while the

ACTOR 5, ACTOR 1 & ACTOR 2: nameless

ACTOR 5: blowers and air conditioners and

ACTOR 5, ACTOR 1 & ACTOR 2: motors

ACTOR 5: of America

ACTOR 5 & ACTOR 1 & ACTOR 2 & ACTOR 3: rumble

ACTOR 5: in the dead night—

ACTOR 3: where Negroes,

ACTOR 4: so drunk,

ACTOR 1: so raw,

ACTOR 2: so tired,

ACTOR 3: lean black cheeks on the hard arms of benches and sleep with pendant brown hands and pouting lips the same as they were in some moonlit Alabama shack when they were little like Pic or some Jamaica, New York nigger cottage with pickaninny ricket fence and sheepdogs

ACTOR 1: and Satnite busy-cars street of lights and around-the-corner glitter and suggestion of good times in tall well-dressed

ACTOR 1 & ACTOR 5: black

ACTOR 1, ACTOR 5 & ACTOR 4: men

ACTOR 1, ACTOR 5, ACTOR 4 & ACTOR 2: walking

ALL: gravely thither

ACTOR 4: where the young worker in brown corduroys, old Army shoes, gas station cap and two-toned "gang" jacket of a decade ago dozes head down at the trolley stop with his right hand palm-up as if to receive from the night—

ACTOR 1: "I'm alone, I'm sick, I'm dying, see my hand uptipped, learn the secret of my heart, give me your hand, take me to the safe place. I've had enough, I give up, I quit, I want to go home, take me home O brother in the night, take me home, lock me in safe—My mother, my father, my sister, my wife and you my brother and you my friend—but no hope, no hope, no hope, I wake up and I'd give a million dollars to be in my bed, O Lord save me."

ACTOR 2: I hear the click of a newcomer's heels,

ACTOR 2, ACTOR 5, ACTOR 3, & ACTOR 4: the litany of voices

(Music. Chair dance.)

ACTOR 2: TO NEAL CASSADY

> [April] '53
> [San Luis Obispo, Calif.]
> Hello to Carolyn

Dear Neal—

Things are slow in SLO but I imagine no faster in San Jose. I am now ready to return to the feverish intensities of the big city. I am racking my brain trying to figure my next move in life. One of them will be a month in the forest in the mountains. (JOHN THE BAPTIST) After that, Mexico, and this time a cunt will live with me.

Loss & tedium of life are driving me slowly inside insane—I've tried every angle of my mind to figure what to do. I've been getting sillydrunk again lately and disgusting myself. I want to live a quiet life but I am so weak for booze.

God I don't set store in anymore—Jesus Christ was a liar.
I don't even believe in Melville or Wolfe any more—&
even Proust & Joyce I wonder why they bothered.

In closing, I want you to remember the night we met in
Watsonville and you said "We don't talk any more" with
tears in your eyes…Forgive me, O Neal, for everything that
I done wrong. Holy Angels bless you.

ALL: Jack

ACTOR 5: Believe in the holy contour of life

ACTOR 2: O what stories, what things been happenin on this end of the
groanin old about-to-sink pink American land. O it's too much, where to
start, my ears are ringing, I'm going mad. San Francisco, 1955.

ACTOR 1: Out we jumped in the warm mad night hearing a wild tenorman's
bawling horn across the way going "EE-YAH! EE-YAH!"

ALL: "Go, go, go!"

ACTOR 3: "Blow, man, blow!"

ACTOR 1: A bunch of colored men in Saturday night suits were whooping it
up.

ACTOR 2: Crazy floppy women wandered around in their bathrobes,

ACTOR 5: bottles clanked in alleys

ACTOR 1: In back of the joint beyond the splattered toilets, scores of men and
women stood against the wall drinking wine-spodi-odi and spitting at the
stars…wine, whiskey and beer.

ACTOR 3: The behatted tenorman was blowing, a rising and falling riff that
went from "EE-yah!" to a crazier "EE-de-lee-yah!"

ACTOR 4: Uproars of music and the tenorman

ALL: *had it*

ACTOR 4: and everybody knew he had it. They were all urging that tenorman
to hold it and keep it with cries and wild eyes; he was raising himself from
a crouch and going down again with his horn, looping it up in a clear cry
above the furor.

ACTOR 2: A six-foot skinny Negro woman was rolling her bones at the man's
hornbell, and he just jabbed it at her, "Ee! ee! ee!" He had a foghorn tone.

ALL: Everybody was rocking and roaring.

ACTOR 3: Groups of colored studs stumbled in from the street. "Stay with it
man!"

ACTOR 2: "Whoo!"

ACTOR 3: said Cody. He was rubbing his chest, his belly, his T-shirt was out, the sweat splashed from his face.

ALL: Boom, kick.

ACTOR 3: Chinese chords, they shuddered the piano in every timber, chink and wire,

ALL: *boing!*

ACTOR 5: and finally the tenorman decided to blow his top and crouched down and held a note in high C for a long time as everything else crashed along skittely-boom.

ACTOR 4: It was just a usual Saturday night goodtime, nothing else; the bebop winos were wailing away, the workingman tenors, the cats who worked and got their horns out of hock and blew and had their women troubles, saying things, a lot to say, talkative horns, you could almost hear the words and better than that the harmony.

ACTOR 1: Summer and Frisco blowing mad.

ALL: all of it insane, sad, sweeter than the love of mothers yet harsher than the murder of fathers

(Shift.)

ACTOR 2: Cody was in a trance. The tenorman's eyes were fixed straight on him; he had found a madman who not only understood but cared, and they began dueling for this; everything came out of the horn, no more phrases, just cries, cries,

ALL: "Baugh"

ACTOR 2: and down to

ALL: "Beep!"

ACTOR 2: and up to

ALL: "EEEEE!"

ACTOR 2: and he tried everything, up, down, sideways, upside down

ACTOR 1 & ACTOR 2 & ACTOR 3: dog fashion

ACTOR 2: horizontal, thirty degrees, forty degrees and finally he fell back in somebody's arms and gave up and everybody pushed around and yelled

ALL: "Yes, yes, he done blowed that one!"

ACTOR 5: Cody wiped himself with his handkerchief.

ACTOR 3: Up steps Freddy on the bandstand and asks for a slow beat and looks sadly out the open door over people's heads and begins singing "Close

Your Eyes." Freddy's wearing a tattered suede jacket, a purple shirt with white buttons, cracked shoes and zoot pants without press; he didn't care. He looked like a pimp in Mecca, where there are no pimps; a barren woman's child, which is a dream; he looked like he was beat to his socks; he was down, and bent, and he played us some blues with his vocals and in arpeggios of applause staggered off the platform ruefully, broodingly, nonsatisfied, artistic, arrogant. He sat in the corner with a bunch of boys and paid no attention to them. They gave him beers. He looked down and wept. He was the greatest.

ACTOR 1: Cody and I went over to talk to him. We invited him out to the car. In the car he suddenly yelled

ACTOR 2: "Yes! ain't nothing I like better than good kicks! Where do we go?"

ACTOR 3: "Later! later!"

ACTOR 1: said Freddy

ACTOR 3: "I'll get my boy to drive us down to Jamson's Nook, I got to sing. Man I *live* to sing. Been singing 'Close Your Eyes' for a month—I don't want to sing nothing else. What are you two boys up to?"

ACTOR 1: We told him we were going to New York tomorrow.

ACTOR 3: "Lord, I ain't never been there and they tell me it's a real jumping town but I ain't got no cause complaining where I am. I'm married you know."

ACTOR 2: "Oh yes? And where is the little darling tonight and I bet she's got a lot of nice friends...man..."

ACTOR 3: "What do you mean? I tole you I was married to her, didn't I?"

ACTOR 2: "Oh yes, Oh yes."

ACTOR 1: blushed Cody.

ACTOR 2: "I was just asking. Maybe she's got a couple of friends downtown, or somethin', you know man, a ball, I'm only looking for a ball, a gang ball, man."

ACTOR 3: "Balls. What's the good of balls, life's too sad to be ballin all the time, Jim.

ACTOR 3 & ACTOR 4 & ACTOR 5: Shee-it.

ACTOR 3: I ain't got no money and I don't care tonight."

ACTOR 4: Freddy's boy showed up at this moment; he was a little taut Negro with a great big Cadillac. We all jumped in. He hunched over the wheel and blew the car clear across San Francisco without stopping once, seventy miles per hour; he was fulfilling his mission with a fixed smile, his destiny. Right through traffic and nobody even noticed he was so good. Cody was in ecstasies.

ACTOR 2: "Dig *this* guy, man—dig the way he sits right in that seat with the feel of the car under his both haunches, a little bit forward, to the left, against the gut of the car and just balls that jack and can talk all night while doing it, O man the things, the things, and Freddy's his boy, and tells him about life, O man the things…the things I could—I wish—let's not stop, man, we've got to keep going now!"

ACTOR 4: And Freddy's boy wound around a corner and bowled us right in front of Jamson's Nook and was parked.

ALL: "Yes!"

ACTOR 5: Whoo, Frisco nights, the end of the continent and the end of the road and the end of all dull doubt.

ACTOR 1: Cody and I raced on to the East Coast. At one point we drove a 1947 Cadillac limousine across the state of Nebraska at 110 miles an hour.

ACTOR 2: "Oh man"

ACTOR 1: said Cody to me as we stood in front of a bar on North Clark Street in the hot summer night,

ACTOR 2: "dig these old Chinamen that cut by Chicago. What a weird town—whee! And that woman in that window up there, just looking down with her big breast hanging from her old nightgown. Just big wide eyes waiting. Wow! Sal we gotta go and never stop going till we get there."

ACTOR 1: "Where we going man?"

ACTOR 2: "We gotta go, we gotta GO."

ACTOR 4: One night I saw Lester, in a reverie on the stand, make such faces in his thoughts—the sneer, the twitch, that Billie Holliday has too, that compassion for the dead; those poor little musicians in Chicago, their love of Lester, early heroisms in a room, records of Lester, early Count, suits hanging in the closet, tanned evenings in the rosy ballroom, you can hear Lester blow and he is the greatness of America in a single Negro musician—he is just like the river, the river starts in near Butte, Montana, in frozen snow caps and meanders on down entire territorial areas of dun bleak land with hawthorn crackling in the sleet, picks up rivers at Bismarck, Omaha, and St. Louis just north, another at Kay-ro, another in Arkansas, Tennessee, comes deluging on New Orleans with muddy news from the land and a roar of subterranean excitement that is like the vibration of the entire land sucked of its gut in mad midnight, fevered, hot, the big mudhole rank clawpole old frogular pawed-soul titanic Mississippi—

ACTOR 5: Lester, so, holding, his horn high in Doctor Pepper chickenshacks, backstreet. Basie Yaysee wearing greasy smeared corduroy bigpants, scuffle-up shoes all slopey Mother Hubbard, soft, pudding, and key ring, early handkerchiefs, hands up, arms up, in wood-brown whiskeyhouse with ammoniac urine from broken gut bottles around fecal pukey bowl and a gal sprawled in it legs spread in brown cotton stockings, bleeding at belted mouth, moaning "yes" as Lester, horn placed, has started blowing, "blow for me mother blow for me,"

ACTOR 1: Miles is still on his daddy's checkered knee, Louis' only got twenty years behind him, and Lester blows all Kansas City to ecstasy and now Americans from coast to coast go mad,

ALL: and everybody's picking up.

ACTOR 3: There is no end to the night. At great roar of Chicago dawn we all staggered out and shuddered in the raggedness. It would start all over tomorrow night.

ALL: We find it, we lose, we wrestle for it, we find it again, we laugh, we moan. Go moan for man. It's the pathos of people that gets us down.

ACTOR 1: "Everybody is laughing at me."

ACTOR 4: "Why?"

ACTOR 1: "Because I want to be a writer."

ACTOR 4: "I'm not laughing."

ACTOR 1: "You're not?"

ACTOR 4: "No. I think it's wonderful."

ACTOR 1: "Well, I'll be a writer. I'll write a lot of books."

ACTOR 4: "More power to you. It's possible. Writers are people like us. But, let me warn you. You're in for a lot of disappointments."

ACTOR 1: "I don't mind."

ACTOR 4: "Then congratulations. Writers can be very important. They can influence countless people."

ACTOR 2: Like Proust be an old teahead of time

(Music: Philip Glass.)

ACTOR 4 & ACTOR 5: And at night the river flows,

ACTOR 2: it bears pale stars on the holy water,

ACTOR 3: some sink like veils,

ACTOR 4: some show like fish,

ACTOR 4 & ACTOR 5: the great moon

ACTOR 2: now high like a blazing milk

ACTOR 1: Now a door slams.

ACTOR 5: The kids have rushed out for the last play,

ACTOR 4: the mothers are planning and slamming in kitchens,

ACTOR 3: you can hear it out in

ALL: swish

ACTOR 3: leaf orchards,

ACTOR 1: on popcorn swings,

ACTOR 2: in the million-foliaged sweet wafted night of sighs,

ACTOR 3: songs,

ACTOR 4: shushes

ACTOR 5: A thousand things up and down the street,

ACTOR 1: deep,

ACTOR 4: lovely,

ACTOR 3: dangerous,

ACTOR 5: aureating,

ACTOR 2: breathing

ACTOR 4: throbbing

ALL: like stars;

ACTOR 1: a whistle,

ACTOR 3: a faint yell;

ACTOR 2: the flow of Lowell over rooftops beyond;

ACTOR 4: the bark on the river,

ACTOR 3: the wild goose of the night

ACTOR 1: yakking,

ACTOR 5: ducking

ALL: in the sand and sparkle;

ACTOR 2: the ululating lap and purl and lovely mystery on the shore,

ACTOR 5: dark,

ACTOR 4: always dark

ACTOR 2: the river's cunning unseen lips murmuring kisses,

ACTOR 1: eating night,

ACTOR 3: stealing sand,

ACTOR 4 & ACTOR 5: sneaky.

ACTOR 1: Write for the world to read and see your exact pictures

ACTOR 5: I was smelling flowers in the yard, and when I stood up I took a deep breath and the blood all rushed to my brain and I woke up dead on my back in the grass. I had apparently fainted, or died, for about sixty seconds. My neighbor saw me but he thought I had just suddenly thrown myself on the grass to enjoy the sun. During that timeless moment of unconsciousness I saw the golden eternity.

ALL: I saw heaven.

ACTOR 4: In it nothing had ever happened, the events of a million years ago were just as phantom and ungraspable as the events of now or of a million years from now, or the events of the next ten minutes.

ACTOR 4 & ACTOR 5: It was perfect,

ACTOR 4 & ACTOR 5 & ACTOR 2: the golden solitude,

ACTOR 4 & ACTOR 5, ACTOR 2 & ACTOR 1: the golden emptiness

ALL: Something-Or-Other

ACTOR 3: something surely humble.

ACTOR 2: There was a rapturous ring of silence abiding perfectly.

ACTOR 5: There was no question of being alive or not being alive

ACTOR 1: of likes and dislikes

ACTOR 4: or near or far

ACTOR 3: no question of giving or gratitude

ACTOR 2: no question of mercy or judgment, or of suffering or its opposite or anything.

ACTOR 5: I call it the golden eternity but you can call it anything you want.

ACTOR 1: As I regained consciousness I felt so sorry I had a body and a mind suddenly realizing I didnt even have a body and a mind and nothing had ever happened and everything is alright forever and forever and forever.

ALL: O thank you thank you thank you.

ACTOR 5: This is the first teaching from the golden eternity.

ACTOR 2: The second teaching from the golden eternity is that there never was a first teaching from the golden eternity. So be sure.

ACTOR 4: What was your last contact with Kerouac?

ACTOR 3: After *The Subterraneans* I didn't see Jack any more. The rumor around the Village was that he was embarrassed about what Hollywood had done to the thing. At the end I'd get reports about what Kerouac had said about the Vietnam War. I felt it came from home—mom, his wife. And when Jack died I was in Harlem.

ACTOR 1: Jack's funeral was very solemn. I went with Peter & Gregory & John in John's car, saw Jack in coffin in Archambault funeral home on Pawtuckville St. Lowell...pallbore through high mass at St. Jean-Baptiste cemetery—Jack in coffin looked large-headed, grim-lipped, tiny bald spot top of skull begun but hair still black & soft, cold skin make up chill to finger touch on his brow, fingers wrinkled, hairy hands protruding from sports-jacket holding rosary, flower masses around coffin & shaped wrinkle-furrow familiar at his brow, eyes closed, mid-aged heavy looked like his father had become from earlier dream decades—shock first seeing him there in theatric-lit coffin room as if a Buddha in *Parinirvana* pose, come here left his message of illusion—wink & left the body behind.

END OF PLAY

Acorn
by David Graziano

BIOGRAPHY

David Graziano is a recent graduate of New York University's Tisch School of the Arts where he earned a B.F.A. in Dramatic Writing. Mr. Graziano lives in New York City where he balances the thrill of writing with the rigors of a day job. He is currently working on both a full-length play and a feature-length screenplay. The premiere of *Acorn* in the Humana Festival at Actors Theatre of Louisville marks his first professional production.

HUMANA FESTIVAL PRODUCTION

Acorn premiered in the Apprentice/Intern Showcase at Actors Theatre of Louisville in December 1997. In March 1998 that production was presented in the Humana Festival of New American Plays, directed by Sandra Grand with the following cast:

Bags . . . . Matthew Damico
Catherine. . . . . Catherine Papafotis
and the following production staff:
Scenic Designer . . . . Paul Owen
Costume Designer. . . . . Kevin R. McLeod
Lighting Designer. . . . . Greg Sullivan
Sound Designer . . . . Mark Huang
Properties Designer. . . . . Mark Walston
Stage Manager. . . . . Charles M. Turner III
Dramaturgs . . . . Michael Bigelow Dixon, Sarah Achbach

CHARACTERS
BAGS

CATHERINE

TIME AND PLACE
The play takes place in Brooklyn. The present.

Catherine Papafotis and Matt Damico
in *Acorn* by David Graziano

22nd Annual Humana Festival of New American Plays
Actors Theatre of Louisville, 1998
photo by Richard Trigg

Acorn

Darkness. Lights come up on a male and a female. The male is Vincent "Bags," he is a 26-year-old unemployed union carpenter. The female is Catherine Dinoffrio, she is an 18-year-old just out of high school who takes care of her invalid father. There is a clothesline with a pulley extending from Bags to Catherine.

CATHERINE: Vincent Baggarusso?…"Bags"?

BAGS: Catherine Dinoffrio? *(Savoring her name.)* Catherine Dinoffrio…

CATHERINE: He disgusts me…

BAGS: It was weird…I mean I'm on this union job…you know…carpentry…a product launch for this new kinda beeper…see I even got one…anyway, at a certain point in the show they wanted these doves to fly out over the crowd…I told them I could build a box that could be flipped over at the right time…you know to let the birds loose…

CATHERINE: I felt trapped…here I am…just out of high school…wanting to go away to college like the rest of the neighborhood and…my father got sick…*(Whispering.)* colon cancer…what was I to do?…Leave him to some Haitian nurse…uh-uh…we're family…

BAGS: I loved jobs like this…I mean cake…pure cake…so I made sure that box was built…you know…good…*(Laughing.)* well I wound up makin' the box so good that it was almost airtight…by the time they flipped the box over all but two of the doves had died…

CATHERINE: I felt bad though…restless…like all boxed in…I felt guilty…like I was waitin' for my father to…die…

BAGS: So the doves fall out and…wham…land on top of some people from Indianapolis…you think they'd stop the show?…uh-uh…anyway I got fired…an' that's how I wound up at my uncle's place…and…ohhh… Catherine…

CATHERINE: Sunday I do the rugs…vacuum and shampoo…Wednesday I make sure my father gets to see the doctor…and every day I do laundry… I got two little brothers and I'll be damned if they look like slobs… wha, my mother?…she cut out as soon as pop was diagnosed…'cause when he was healthy he used to beat—*(Catches herself.)*

BAGS: Well my uncle don't allow no smokin' in his house…good thing too… cause I had to go out into the patio…well one day I was in that patio thinkin' about how I'm almost 26 an' I'm outta work…an' then I look up an' see these little underwears…like from a girl…er, a woman rather…

CATHERINE: I noticed Bags looking at me the second day he moved in…I knew his uncle next door a long time…

BAGS: You ever notice on girl's…I mean, women's underwear…how they got those little ribbons…in the shape of a bow?…shit…that's cute…the guy that invented that?…he's some kinda genius…you know, my mind started goin' an'…before I knew it…

CATHERINE: Before I knew it…he was staring at me every day as I put the laundry out…ten o'clock came and he'd be out there smokin' his cigarette…

BAGS: Don't get the wrong idea…I ain't a freak…I mean I never dress in girls underwear or nothing…

CATHERINE: Something wasn't right about him…he seemed, I don't know… effeminate?

BAGS: My grandfather always said…when a Baggarusso falls in love…he falls! I stared at those underwears so long sometimes…that the sun would hurt my eyes…at least twenty feet high they were…from her window to the telephone pole…well one time I looked down 'cause of the sun an' there were these acorns all over the cement…so I threw some…as a joke…at the window first…and then…

CATHERINE: I was taking in the laundry and all these acorns were in the clothes…my panties especially…in clean clothes!? Uh-uh…I re-washed everything…who knows where those acorns were…

BAGS: It just seemed to fit…I mean…acorns…panties…besides I couldn't touch 'em…they were up too high…I figured for a joke…I could touch somethin' that would touch her underwear…which in turn would touch her…if that's the closest I could come to her, I would be happy…ey, I'm not a freak…just for fun…you know…

CATHERINE: Doing that extra load that day…made me sooo mad! You know what I did?…I took all those acorns and laid them out on his uncle's welcome mat in the shape of what I thought Bags was…an ass…

BAGS: When she gave the acorns back…I knew it was a symbol…she arranged them in the shape of a heart…

CATHERINE: I figured he would get the hint...but after the ass-shaped acorns...he started leaving notes...pinning them...in the night...to my underwear!...on the line!...

BAGS: I stayed up all night writing the note...and I got a ladder from the garage...I rolled the note up real tight and thin and slipped it in the little pink bow on the front of the underwear...

CATHERINE: I had to end this...before my brothers or my father found out...I mean, what if the neighbors saw!?

BAGS: This...now this...was the beginning...to somethin' really special...

CATHERINE: So...I started wearing guy's underwear...I went right out after he put the second note in my panties...and bought some briefs...nice colored ones...couldn't find pink though...

BAGS: On the third night I was puttin' another note...that made three now... and I had to lean off of the ladder a little bit...big ladder...old...rickety...you know sort of into her yard...'cause there was a fence between us...

CATHERINE: You'd be surprised how much more comfortable guy's underwear is than girl's...no wedgies...no nothin'...*(Laughing.)* And that little flap...

BAGS: Well I rolled it up real tight and slipped it in...this note was a little longer so it was harder to get it in the bow on her underwears...and... "bam!"...I lost my balance! The...the ladder kicked out from beneath me and *(Makes hitting sound.)* my leg was broke...I knew it right off the bat...I heard the crack an' everything...

CATHERINE: I got two little brothers and I didn't know that's what it was for! *(Laughing.)* Of course I have no use for it...but it's sooo cute...you don't think I'm a freak, right?

BAGS: Would you know I climbed back over the fence...and put the ladder away and everything...so no one would find out...all with a broken leg!...and I knew my grandfather was laughin'...'cause I could hear him say..."When a Baggarusso falls in love...he falls..." *(Laughing.)*

CATHERINE: Well it worked...the guys' underwear...I wore some every day... I'm even wearing some right now...*(Shows the band.)* He actually stopped writing notes...

BAGS: Needless to say...I couldn't leave her notes anymore...at least not for awhile...man that thing took forever to heal...and itchy!?

CATHERINE: It was nice...but it was a strange sort of silence...and I went back to taking care of my father...

BAGS: I convinced my uncle to switch rooms with me…'cause I told him that his room was closer to the bathroom…well my uncle's room has this great view…of her washline…at least I could see what she wore that day, right? You know…open my window an' maybe smell her detergent… anything…

CATHERINE: I started thinking about what he thought about…

BAGS: I dunno…I mean there were no panties…so I waited…I started thinkin'…maybe she didn't wear any that day…you know…the kinky type…

CATHERINE: His letters *were* kind of romantic…I mean…for a guy who writes with a Brooklyn accent…

BAGS: Well after a week I got pissed…what!? She didn't wear panties for a whole week!? What else? I mean what's she got under her bed? Whips? Hot candle wax? Black mambos?

CATHERINE: I'd like to marry a guy who's romantic…like the "boy next door" type…

BAGS: Uh-uh, I'm sorry…this isn't the type of girl a guy wants to marry…and that guy's underwear out there…it's too big for her brothers…an' her father wears boxers…I know…I been watchin'…

CATHERINE: I cooked and cleaned and vacuumed and flipped channels and shaved my father, but the laundry…I realized laundry for what it was… it's not just another household chore…it's a form of communication…

BAGS: I broke my leg for this…forget it…I stopped waiting…I don't care if all the clothes-lines in all the neighborhoods in the world were full of panties…floral printed, frilly panties…with bows…French cut an' all…who cares!

CATHERINE: Being cooped up in that house like a pigeon…who needs it…I began to miss the notes…more and more and more…

BAGS: I didn't care about women…forgettaboutem! Not real ones at least…I got my uncle to get me couple of old *Cosmos* from the dental office where he works…

CATHERINE: I felt stifled…suffocated…

BAGS: I read up on what women *really* liked for weeks. I took twenty-three romance quizzes…memorized all of the supermodels' names and learned a little more than I needed to know about toxic shock syndrome.

CATHERINE: I was lonely…

BAGS: There's no denyin' it…I was horny…

CATHERINE: I couldn't take it…being so isolated…I just needed a friend…

so…just for kicks…one day…I put one pair of panties up on the clothes-line…nothing sexy…just pink…with a little ribbon shaped like a bow…

BAGS: Oh my god!

CATHERINE: I waited…I decided to leave those panties up there all night long…

BAGS: Oh my god!

CATHERINE: I woke up the next morning…and nothing…Can guys really be that fickle…I mean one minute they're putting notes in your panties and then nothing…just because a girl plays hard to get…

BAGS: I couldn't do nothin'! I tried gettin' the phone number from my uncle… "The father is on his deathbed and you're gonna be messin' with his daughter?" I told him it was alright…I told him about the reappear-ance of the panties an' everything…I told him how it was a symbol…I even told him the real way that I broke my leg…he looked at me like I had a hole in my head…

CATHERINE: So…I saw…he wanted to play hard to get with me now…uh-uh…Catherine Dinoffrio is no man's violin…she won't be played…

BAGS: Oh my god!!

CATHERINE: Yep! Every color…size…shape imaginable…they all went up…I even took a trip to Victoria's Secret and bought some new French cuts, a thong and several silk slips…I read somewhere that silk slips drive men nuts…*Cosmo* I think…I left the panties up overnight…

BAGS: That night I learned how to go down the stairs on my ass…I got out in that patio…looked at all those panties blowing in the moonlight…wit' all those bows…and had my first cigarette in what seemed like months…I picked a single acorn from the ground…I threw it just right…real gentle against the glass…and she came to her window…that night…at her win-dow…Catherine spoke the first words she would ever speak to me…it was the first time I would ever hear her voice…she said…

CATHERINE: You're a freak!…

BAGS: And it's true. Maybe I am.

CATHERINE: We went on our first date two nights after that…and three months from then my father passed away…

BAGS: Yeah…an' four days after that…my uncle threw me out…but now me an' Catherine share our own clothesline…

CATHERINE: Just you me…an' my brothers…

BAGS: Now that's romance…that's romance…(*They kiss. Blackout.*)

END OF PLAY

Dinner With Friends
by Donald Margulies

For Lynn

BIOGRAPHY

Donald Margulies has written many plays including *Collected Stories* (South Coast Repertory [SCR], Manhattan Theatre Club [MTC], Los Angeles Drama Critics Circle Award, Drama-Logue Award, nominated for Drama Desk and Dramatists Guild/Hull-Warriner Awards), *Broken Sleep: Three Plays* (Williamstown Theatre Festival), *The Model Apartment* (Primary Stages, Obie Award, Drama-Logue Award, nominated for Drama Desk and Dramatists Guild/Hull-Warriner Awards), *July 7, 1994* (Actors Theatre of Louisville Humana Festival 1995), *Sight Unseen* (SCR, MTC, Obie Award, Dramatists Guild/Hull-Warriner Award, Drama Desk Award nominee, a Burns Mantle Best Play), *The Loman Family Picnic* (MTC, Drama Desk nominee, a Burns Mantle Best Play), *Pitching to the Star* (included in *Best American Short Plays 1992-93*), and *Found a Peanut* (Joseph Papp/NYSF). *What's Wrong With This Picture?* was produced off-Broadway at MTC and Jewish Repertory Theatre and on Broadway at the Brooks Atkinson Theatre. His adaptation of Sholom Asch's Yiddish classic, *God of Vengeance*, will have its world premiere at A Contemporary Theatre in Seattle in 1999. Mr. Margulies has won grants from CAPS, the New York Foundation for the Arts, the National Endowment for the Arts, and the John Simon Guggenheim Memorial Foundation. He has twice been a finalist for the Pulitzer Prize. A collection of his work, *Sight Unseen and Other Plays*, has been published by Theatre Communications Group. An alumnus of New Dramatists, he is a member of the council of the Dramatists Guild and sits on the board of directors of Dramatists Play Service, Inc. Born in Brooklyn, New York in 1954, he currently lives with his wife, Lynn Street, a physician, and their son, Miles, in New Haven, Connecticut, where he teaches playwriting at the Yale School of Drama.

HUMANA FESTIVAL PRODUCTION

Dinner With Friends was commissioned by Actors Theatre of Louisville and premiered at the Humana Festival of New American Plays in March 1998. It was directed by Michael Bloom with the following cast:

Gabe. . . . . Adam Grupper
Karen . . . . .Linda Purl
Beth . . . . Devora Millman
Tom. . . . . David Byron

and the following production staff:

Scenic Designer . . . . Paul Owen
Costume Designer. . . . . Jeanette de Jong

Lighting Designer . . . . Greg Sullivan
Sound Designer . . . . Michael Rasbury
Properties Designer . . . . Ron Riall
Fight Director . . . . Steve Rankin
Stage Manager. . . . . Becki Owczarski
Assistant Stage Manager . . . . Kristine A. Schipper
Dramaturg . . . . Val Smith
Assistant Dramaturg . . . . Megan Shultz

Casting . . . . Laura Richin Casting

CHARACTERS

KAREN and GABE
and
TOM and BETH
two couples in their forties.

TIME AND PLACE

ACT ONE

SCENE ONE: Karen and Gabe's kitchen in Connecticut. Evening. Winter.
SCENE TWO: Tom and Beth's bedroom. Later that night.
SCENE THREE: Karen and Gabe's living room. Later still.

ACT TWO

SCENE ONE: A house on Martha's Vineyard. Summer. Twelve and a half years earlier.
SCENE TWO: Karen and Gabe's patio. Six months after the events in Act One. Spring. Also, a bar/restaurant in New York. The same day.
SCENE THREE: Karen and Gabe's bedroom. That night.

AUTHOR'S NOTE

The draft of *Dinner With Friends* which follows is essentially the version that was presented in the Humana Festival of New American Plays. It is still a work-in-progress. D.M.

Adam Grupper and David Byron
in *Dinner With Friends* by Donald Margulies

22nd Annual Humana Festival of New American Plays
Actors Theatre of Louisville, 1998
photo by Richard Trigg

Dinner with Friends

ACT ONE
SCENE ONE

Gabe and Karen's kitchen/dining/living room. A wintry night in suburban New England. The present. Gabe and Karen are entertaining their good friend Beth at an informal dinner, which is now moving on to the dessert course. Dishes are being cleared, coffee is being prepared. Four children, now offstage, had been seated at the table with them. Beth is distracted but not impolite.

GABE: Oh, and this *market* she took us to!

KAREN: She took us shopping.

BETH: Uh huh.

GABE: This indoor market: Fish, produce, you name it!

KAREN: Gorgeous stuff. Really.

GABE: Live chickens, live geese...

KAREN: So aromatic. So...colorful. And the faces!

GABE: I got some great shots; I hope they're good, we'll see...

KAREN: *(Over "we'll see...")* The *authority* with which she handled every onion, every red pepper she picked up!

BETH: Huh.

GABE: Yeah, she'd palpate an eggplant just so, and close her eyes and inhale...
(Gabe demonstrates. Beth smiles.)

KAREN: This is someone who's been cooking for over seventy years. Can you imagine? Seventy?!

BETH: *(Over "Seventy?!")* Wow.

GABE: Her relationship to food was so primal, so sexy, really. Gave us a great angle for our piece.

BETH: Huh!

KAREN: *(Over "Huh!")* Well, I don't know about *sexy*…She's this old crone. I can't imagine she was ever a thing of beauty…

GABE: No, but did you see the way she handled the zucchini? Man!

KAREN: *(To Beth.)* Regular or decaf?

BETH: Uh…*(Looks at the clock.)* Better make it decaf.

GABE: Anyway, what a great day.

BETH: Sounds it.

KAREN: The *traffic* to her place was absolutely horrific.

BETH: Oh, really?

GABE: Harrowing. Truly.

    (Beth has gathered a few plates and started for the kitchen; Gabe takes them from her.)

BETH: Let me do something.

GABE: *(Sotto.)* No, no, sit.

    (Beth does, reluctantly.)

KAREN: The rules of the road over there…

GABE: There *are* no rules of the road.

KAREN: It's chaos; it *is*.

GABE: Like the bumper cars in Coney Island.

KAREN: Every driver has his own agenda.

GABE: Yeah, suicide.

    (Beth smiles, but still seems faraway.)

And they don't care *who* they take with them.

KAREN: You have this *sea* of speeding cars, no lines on the road…

BETH: Oh, God…

KAREN: *(Continuous.)* …madmen-and-women honking, shouting curses at one another, hands flying off steering wheels, switching lanes left and right…

BETH: Oh, God!

GABE: No one bothers to signal over there.

KAREN: But you just go with the flow…

GABE: Kinda like life.

KAREN: …and it's really not so bad.

GABE: Oh, no, just white-knuckle time.

KAREN: What are *you* complaining about? *I* did the driving. And I was damn good.

GABE: I know; you *were*. *(To Beth.)* It's true; she's amazing: She drives like a New York cabbie; she *does*. I was too culture-shocked. I thought, Great, our first vacation without the boys and I get us killed. Our bodies'd have to be shipped home through the State Department…

BETH: Uch! Gabe!

GABE: *(Continuous.)* …you and Tom would become the boys' guardians, and raise them on processed foods…*(She swipes at him affectionately for his affectionate dig.)* I'm telling you it was a nightmare.

KAREN: Is that really what was going through your head?

GABE: Absolutely.

KAREN: You are one morbid dude, my darling.

GABE: Yes, and I'm all yours.

(She kisses him.)

BETH: So did you ever get to Milan?

GABE: *(Confused by her question.)* What?

KAREN: This *is* Milan, Beth.

GABE: Emilia lives outside of Milan.

KAREN: Remember?

BETH: *(Over "…Milan.")* Oh, of course, I'm sorry, I thought this was *Florence* you were talking about.

GABE: *(Over "you were talking about.")* No no, we haven't gotten to Florence yet.

KAREN: Is this really boring?

BETH: No no, not at all.

KAREN: It is, we'll shut up.

BETH: No no, go on. I want to hear about it. I *do.*

GABE: Okay, anyway…

KAREN: Why don't we just get to lunch.

GABE: Okay, so we get there in one piece…

BETH: Yeah…?

KAREN: Thanks to my fabulous driving…

GABE: I am *drenched* with sweat from the hellish journey, I stumble out of the car, feeling a bit queasy…

KAREN: And she's preparing this *lunch*…!

GABE: This *feast!*

BETH: Wow.

KAREN: The simplest, freshest…

GABE: Uh! The pomodoro! Tell her about the pomodoro!

KAREN: Right. She had this lovely sunny little pantry…

BETH: Yeah…?

GABE: *Filled* with jars and jars…

KAREN: Jars and jars of her own plum tomatoes picked from her own garden that were the most incredible, succulent...

GABE: You wouldn't believe how *red* these tomatoes were...

BETH: Hm...

GABE: ...and *sweet!*

KAREN: They were so *soft*, Beth...

GABE: Buttery, almost.

KAREN: They *were*. She just crushed them with her bare hands.

BETH: Huh!

GABE: *Pul*verized them...

KAREN: You should've seen...

GABE: *(Continuous.)* ...in her gnarled little hands. It was a riot, this little old lady...

KAREN: It was funny, it really was.

BETH: *(Smiling.)* Uh huh.

GABE: I mean, she's really *tiny*, like 4-10 or something.

KAREN: No...Not quite.

GABE: She's got to be, honey; come on, she's definitely under five feet.

KAREN: No, she's not, not *under*...

GABE: *(Over "...under...")* Think about it, she was like up to *here* on me.

KAREN: Yeah? Maybe.

GABE: She was. Think about it.

KAREN: Maybe you're right.

GABE: And she went on and on—she's a real talker.

BETH: *(Smiling.)* Uh huh.

KAREN: *(Fondly.)* Oh, yes.

GABE: Heavily accented broken English, in that cigarette-destroyed voice of hers. She was like something out of a Fellini movie; *Satyricon* or something.

KAREN: *Any*way.

GABE: Anyway, the pomodoro.

KAREN: The pomodoro was amazing.

GABE: And simple.

KAREN: Amazingly simple. Sautéed garlic...

BETH: Yeah...?

GABE: A *lot* of garlic. Phew!

KAREN: *(Over "Phew!")* A little onion. Finely diced.

GABE: That's right. That was interesting: very little onion.

KAREN: Are you gonna let me tell this, or what?

GABE: Sorry.

KAREN: She crushes the garlic with her *thumb,* by the way. This arthritic, calcified thumb. It was hilarious.

GABE: *(Over "...hilarious.") Mashes* it into the marble counter, *flings* it into the olive oil.

KAREN: Then the tomatoes.

GABE: Five, six pounds of them.

BETH: Huh!

KAREN: Breaks up whatever isn't crushed with the wooden spoon.

GABE: Right. Very deliberately, while stirring, flames shooting, scalding sauce sputtering everywhere.

KAREN: No no, she used a screen.

GABE: You sure?

KAREN: Positive. Then she adds a fistful of parsley...

GABE: Remember: not a measuring spoon in sight.

KAREN: Fresh oregano.

GABE: *And* dried.

KAREN: Fresh basil.

GABE: Whole clumps. She just *tears* at it; *rips* at it with her bare hands. You following this?

BETH: Uh huh.

KAREN: Handful of sugar, handful of salt. Lots of fresh ground pepper.

BOY'S VOICE: *(From downstairs.)* DAD!

KAREN: Throws in some chianti.

GABE: Which she'd been discreetly tucking away the whole time.

BOY'S VOICE: DAD!!!

GABE: *(Calls.)* YES?

KAREN: *(To Beth; over the above.)* It was really a wonderful visit.
    (Beth nods and smiles.)

CHILDREN'S VOICES: *(Over "...a wonderful visit.")* PUT ON A TAPE! WE WANT TO WATCH A TAPE! PLEASE?!

GABE: *(Shouts back)* DANNY CAN DO IT!

BOY'S VOICE: NO, DAD! I CAN'T! *YOU* DO IT!

GABE: *(Over "You do it!")* Yes, you can; Danny, you do it all the time. All you do is put it in and press play...

BOY'S VOICE: I *CAN'T* DO IT! I WANT YOU TO DO IT!

KAREN: *(Over "I want you to do it!" To Gabe.)* Will you just go do it?

GABE: He can do it, he knows how to do it.

BOY'S VOICE: *(Over "...he knows how to do it.")* DAD! WE WANT TO WATCH *THE ARISTOCATS!* IT ISN'T WORKING! *(Etc.)*

GABE: *(Shouts.)* MAKE SURE THE TV IS ON CHANNEL THREE!

BOY'S VOICE: WHAT?

GABE: CHANNEL THREE!

KAREN: Please, Gabe. I hate when you shout back and forth like that. Just go down there and talk to them.

GABE: *(Calls.)* All right, I'LL BE RIGHT DOWN! *(Starts to go.)* Don't talk about Florence without me.

(He goes. Pause. Karen smiles uncomfortably, sensing something is wrong.)

KAREN: So...*(A beat.)* Is everything...? Was dinner...?

BETH: No, no, dinner was great. The lamb and risotto, everything was fabulous.

KAREN: I overcooked the risotto; it was a bit gummy.

BETH: Not at all. It was perfect.

KAREN: We've been running off at the mouth all night; I'm sorry.

BETH: No, no, you're excited. I'm jealous; it sounds like a great trip.

KAREN: It was. It was really good for us. We were so trepidatious about leaving the boys...

BETH: I'm sure.

KAREN: Ten days is a long time.

BETH: It *is.*

KAREN: We missed them terribly. We talked about them all the time, of course...

BETH: Of course.

KAREN: But they were fine. Next time you and Tom'll have to come with us.

BETH: Uh huh.

KAREN: We'd have a blast, don't you think?

BETH: Oh, yeah.

KAREN: Just the four of us?! You would *love* Italy.

BETH: I know; I can't believe I've never been there.

KAREN: Dump the kids with Tom's sister or something. They'd be fine. Believe me, with Danny and Isaac, we came home and it was like, "Oh, hello. You again?"

(They smile. Silence.)

Too bad about Tommy.

BETH: What do you mean?

KAREN: Having to fly to Washington on a night like this.

BETH: Oh, yeah.

KAREN: *His* loss. Oh, well, more food for us.

> *(They smile. A beat.)*
>
> Are you okay?

BETH: Oh, yeah, fine; I'm just a little…I think I may have a migraine coming on.

KAREN: Oh! *(That explains Beth's behavior.)* Well, lay off the wine.

BETH: I am; I have been.

KAREN: You want some Motrin?

BETH: Yeah, that would be great, thanks.

> *(Karen gets pills from a cabinet.)*

KAREN: You know, you really should see a doctor about this.

BETH: I know.

KAREN: You've been getting migraines an awful lot lately.

BETH: Seems that way.

KAREN: I almost forgot: We got you guys something.

BETH: Oh, really? How nice.

> *(Karen gives Beth a wrapped bundle.)*
>
> Thank you. That was so sweet.

KAREN: That's for you and Tom. Just a little something. For the house. *You* know.

BETH: Thanks. Should I open it now?

KAREN: Whatever you like.

> *(Beth unwraps the bundle: placemats and napkins. They somehow make her sad but she tries not to let it show.)*

BETH: Oh, Karen. Thank you so much. What are they?

KAREN: Placemats and napkins.

BETH: They're beautiful.

KAREN: They're from Siena. We spent a day there. Can you use them?

BETH: Oh, God, yes, me?

> *(Gabe returns holding four bowls, which had been the kids' ice cream dessert.)*

GABE: You should see: I wish I had some film.

KAREN: That's right, we ran out of film.

GABE: *(Continuous.)* All four kids, lying on the floor, lined up in a row, heads in hands like this, like four little Raphael cherubs, watching *The Aristocats* for the ninety-seventh time.

> *(Beth suddenly breaks down and sobs.)*

KAREN: Oh, my God…Beth?

GABE: *(Over "Beth?")* What is it?, what's the matter? *(Softly, to Karen.)* Did I miss something here?

(She shrugs, Not that I know of.)

KAREN: Beth, what is it?

BETH: Oh, Karen…Tom's leaving me.

KAREN: What?

BETH: He's leaving me.

GABE: What are you talking about?

BETH: He doesn't love me anymore.

KAREN: What?!

GABE: That can't be…

BETH: He's leaving. He left me. He's gone. *(She breaks down again.)*

GABE: What happened?

BETH: He says he's in love with someone else.

KAREN: Oh, God, you're kidding.

GABE: Who?

KAREN: *(Admonishing.)* Gabe!

GABE: What, I want to know if it's someone we know!

KAREN: What difference does it make?

BETH: It's okay. I don't know, some stewardess.

GABE: A *steward*ess? Tom's in love with a *steward*ess?

BETH: "Nancy" her name is. She lives in Washington.

KAREN: When did he have time to fall in love with a stewardess?

BETH: It wouldn't've taken very long. He's been traveling so much…

KAREN: This is so tacky. He says he's in love with her?

(Beth nods.)

How long has this been going on?

BETH: I don't know, a few months at least, apparently.

KAREN: *(Over "…apparently.")* A few *months*? When did you find out?

BETH: Just the other day; while you were away.

GABE: *(Softly.)* Jeez…

KAREN: What happened?

BETH: He confessed. We had an argument. About the dog. He hates the dog. If the dog chews on the rug, naturally it's my fault, so…*(Takes a breath.)* He told me he was miserable, that he's always been miserable, he's been miserable for so long he doesn't remember what it was like to be happy, I don't know, something like that.

KAREN: *Tom* said that?

BETH: *(Nods, then.)* He said this isn't the life he had in mind for himself, that if he were to stay married to me, it would kill him, he would die young.

GABE: Jesus.

BETH: *(To Gabe.)* Did you know about this?, did he tell you anything?

GABE: *(Over "...anything?")* No. This is...I didn't have a *clue*...

KAREN: We all just went out to eat together. Right before we left.

BETH: I know.

KAREN: That Indian place in Branford. We loved their chicken tikka masala.

BETH: I know; that's right.

KAREN: You seemed fine; both of you did. We had a wonderful time. He didn't seem "miserable" at all.

BETH: I know.

KAREN: I can't believe it. You mean, we were sitting there, kidding around, as always, and he was not only miserable but in love with someone else?
(Beth nods.)
Oh, sweetie, I'm so sorry, this can't be happening...I just...
(To Gabe, off his silence.)
Feel free; jump in any time.

GABE: *(Defensively.)* What.

KAREN: *(Mocking.)* "What."

GABE: I'm listening.

KAREN: *(To Beth.)* So, what's happening? Are you getting therapy? Some counseling?

BETH: *(Shakes her head, then.)* He doesn't want to.

GABE: Doesn't want to?

KAREN: So, what does that *mean?*

BETH: It means it's over. There's nothing more to be done. It's over.

KAREN: Come on! That's *it?* Twelve years, two kids, and he doesn't *want* to?

BETH: He says he feels he's tried for years to work it out, and he's had it, he's spent, and he can't give it anymore.

KAREN: *How? How* did he try?
(Beth shrugs.)

GABE: I can't believe this; it just doesn't sound like him. It's like his body's been snatched and he's been replaced by a pod.

BETH: I know. You should have seen him. The rage! I didn't recognize him. I've never seen that kind of rage in him before!

GABE: Tom is the sweetest guy in the world!

KAREN: Watch out for those sweet guys.

BETH: I'm telling you, this side of him…It was volcanic. He *hates* me.

KAREN: *(Soothing.)* No…

BETH: He does. He says I've ruined his life.

KAREN: Well, this sounds like something else is going on.

BETH: Doesn't it?

KAREN: Some kind of life-crisis thing. God, I wish you'd come with us to Italy.

BETH: I think he's really in trouble. I tried telling him that; that he needs help, but that only made him angrier.

KAREN: Oh, this is classic. You've got to get him some help.

BETH: Good luck. You know Tom, he's suspicious of every kind of therapy you can think of. I'm just worried he's headed for some kind of breakdown.

GABE: Well, what does he want? A trial separation or something?

BETH: No, no, he wants a divorce.

GABE: I can't believe this.

KAREN: Oh, that's ridiculous. A divorce?, just like that?

BETH: That's what he *says*…

KAREN: We'll *talk* to him. *Gabe* will.

GABE: Sure, I'll…

BETH: *(Over "Sure, I'll…")* No, Karen, he wants out. Period. No therapy, no trial *anything*. I told him, Whatever it would take. I would do anything. He doesn't want to hear it. He doesn't want to "prolong the misery."

KAREN: Oh, God, what about the kids? Have you told them?

(Beth shakes her head sadly.)

No? When are you going to?

BETH: I don't know. I don't know what to say. He goes out of town so much, I feel like there's no need to break it to them right away, you know? I figure we can buy some time. They know something's up, there's been tears and testiness. They know mommy and daddy are trying to work out a problem, that's as much as we've told them.

GABE: I don't believe this. I can't believe we're having this conversation.

BETH: If you could've only heard the hateful things he said.

KAREN: Where is this coming from?! I don't understand it! Tom?! Do you think it's drugs?

GABE: Karen…

KAREN: I mean, how do you account for this, this personality change?

BETH: Karen, I've been racking my brain, playing back every little tiff, every long-distance phone conversation of the last several months, and I just…*(She trails off, shakes her head.)*

KAREN: He's crazy about you, Beth! I know it! I've seen it! You can't fake something like that.

BETH: *(Over "…something like that.")* Karen. The things he said to me…This is not a man who's crazy about me, believe me. He's in love with this person. He *is*. He says she's everything I'm not.

KAREN: What is that supposed to mean?

BETH: He says she's completely devoted to him. She hangs on his every word. She's "there" for him.

KAREN: Oh, God, such bullshit.

BETH: Really. The stuff pouring out of his mouth…It's like bad greeting cards. He says I gave him seventy-five per cent, she gives him a hundred-and-twenty.

KAREN: He said that? A hundred-and-twenty percent?
(Beth nods.)
He's into percentages? What's that extra twenty-percent supposed to be?
(Beth and Gabe both look at her.)

GABE: Karen.

KAREN: Oh. *(To Beth.)* What, you didn't go for that extra twenty-percent?

BETH: Apparently not like she does.

KAREN: Did you *know* he was miserable?

BETH: No. That's what he accuses me of: He says I ignored all the signs, that I'm so self-involved…I mean, he never came to me and said, "Honey, I'm miserable" or anything like that. He was moody. Yes. Distracted. I thought it was work, or jet lag…I'd find him staring off into space and ask him what he was thinking and he'd always say, "Nothing."
(Karen looks at Gabe.)

GABE: What.
(Karen shakes her head.)

BETH: I don't know, he's definitely been going *through* something, that much I know. Acting-out stuff.

KAREN: Like what?

BETH: Oh, I don't know that I want to go into it.

KAREN: That's okay.

BETH: Inappropriate stuff. *You* know: sexual stuff. *(A breath.)* We went out to the movies, some *cop* thing he wanted to see, nothing sexy, and Tom like puts my hand in his crotch to *you* know, and I look at him like, What are you crazy?, and he's mortally offended!

KAREN: Was this before or after the girlfriend?

BETH: I think it must have been after he started seeing her.

KAREN: *(Over "...he started seeing her.")* Uh huh, uh huh.

BETH: Some kind of sexual-daring test and I flunked it.

KAREN: One more nail in the old coffin.

BETH: You got it.

GABE: See that? One lousy hand job, you could've saved your marriage.

KAREN: Gabe.

GABE: Sorry.

BETH: I'm sorry to lay this on you guys...

GABE: *(Dismissively.)* Hey...

KAREN: *(Over "Hey...")* Don't be silly...

BETH: This is the last thing you were expecting tonight, huh?

KAREN: Oh, God, yes.

GABE: I still can't believe it.

CHILDREN'S VOICES: *(Off, variously.)* DAD!! FIX THE TAPE! FIX IT! *(Etc.)*

KAREN: *(Shouts downstairs.)* WE HEAR YOU! STOP SHOUTING!

BOY'S VOICE: DAD! IT'S DOING THAT THING AGAIN!

GABE: *(Shouts.)* YOU CAN FIX IT, DANNY!

BOY'S VOICE: I DON'T KNOW HOW!

GABE: I SHOWED YOU! REMEMBER?!

KAREN: *(Shouts, over "Remember?!")* DADDY SHOWED YOU, DANIEL!

GABE: *(Shouts, over "...Daniel!")* THE PLUS AND THE MINUS! PRESS THEM BOTH AT THE SAME TIME!

KAREN: Gabe. *Must* you?

GABE: I'll go down...

KAREN: No no, I will.

CHILDREN'S VOICES: *(Off.)* FIX IT! IT'S STILL DOING IT!

KAREN: *(Shouts.)* ALL RIGHT, ALL RIGHT, I'M COMING!

CHILDREN'S VOICES: *(Off.)* PLEASE!

KAREN: I'M *COMING! STOP SHOUTING!*

> *(She goes downstairs. Gabe and Beth are alone. Awkward silence. He offers her wine. Beth shakes her head, Gabe refills his own glass. Pause.)*

GABE: All the vacations we spent on the Vineyard...Remember the summer you and Karen were both pregnant? *(Beth nods.)* You guys *met* there; we had such great *times* there.

(They ruminate bittersweetly in silence. Gabe sighs, shakes his head incredulously, sips his wine. Children's cheers come from downstairs.)

CHILDREN'S VOICES: *(Off.)* YAYY!!!

GABE: How can he walk away? I don't understand it. How can he just...?

BETH: *(Gets up, distracted.)* I should get the kids; we should get going. *(She picks up one boy's sneaker by its laces, looks around for the other.)* Do you see another one of these?

(Gabe takes her hand in a loving, friendly way.)

GABE: Beth...*(She stops, looks at him. Pause.)* I'm so sorry.

BETH: You thought Tom never should've married me.

GABE: What?

BETH: It's okay, Gabe; I know; Tom told me.

GABE: I never said that.

BETH: It's okay. I just wonder if you were right.

(Karen returns, notes a certain tension.)

KAREN: Why don't we have dessert?

BETH: Oh, I don't know, it's late; I really should get them home.

KAREN: Don't. They're riveted.

BETH: You're right, what am I running home to? *(She sits.)* A few minutes.

KAREN: *(To Gabe.)* You want to do the honors?

GABE: Sure.

(He brings a cake to the table, expertly slices it, while Karen refills coffee, etc.)

BETH: Oh, that looks so good, what is it?

GABE: Limone-mandorle-polenta.

BETH: Mandorle?

GABE: Almond.

BETH: Mm.

KAREN: Instead of white flour, you use polenta.

BETH: Ooo, what a good idea.

GABE: And *six* eggs.

KAREN: It's very eggy.

GABE: And a *ton* of butter.

BETH: *(Tastes it.)* Mm, it's delicious.

KAREN: *(Samples it; approvingly.)* Hm.

GABE: I think it's great.

KAREN: Yeah? You don't think I could've beaten the eggs a little bit longer? Don't you think it could've been a little fluffier?

GABE: No. I think it's good.

BETH: It's wonderful.

KAREN: *(To Gabe.)* Too much vanilla?

GABE: *(Considers this.)* Uh…Possibly.

KAREN: Hm.

(Silence while they eat.)

BETH: *(Sighs.)* I feel so much better now that I told you. All night long, sitting here, I thought I was going to explode. You're my closest friends, you know.

KAREN: Of course we are.

GABE: Of course.

BETH: My closest friends in the world.

(They continue eating dessert in silence.)

Mm, this is so good.

(Karen and Gabe are pensive. End of scene.)

SCENE TWO

Later that night. Beth and Tom's cluttered, messy bedroom in lamp light. Piles of books, magazines and clothes are about. Beth, seeming somewhat vulnerable and bereft in her own home, begins to disrobe, draping her clothes over a NordicTrac and, wearing a tee-shirt and panties, gets into bed. She picks up the napkins and placemats Karen gave her, shakes her head ironically and tosses them aside. Somewhere in the house, a dog barks.

BETH: *(Shouts.)* Sarge! Quiet! *(The barking persists.)* Sergeant, dammit, be quiet!

(The bedroom door opens, startling her; she gasps. Tom, in from the cold, dressed in winter gear, tracking snow in on his boots, stands there. Light from the hallway spills in.)

BETH: Tom! Jesus…

TOM: *(Overlap; whispers.)* Hi. Sorry. I didn't mean to…

BETH: *(Overlap; normal volume.)* Couldn't you at least knock?

TOM: Shhh. I'm sorry.

BETH: You can't just come and go as you please anymore, you know…

TOM: Beth…

BETH: *(Continuous.)* …like some kind of phantom, it's not fair, Tom; if you're gonna go, go.

TOM: I just wanted to…

BETH: *(Continuous.)* Otherwise, I'm gonna have to change the locks.

TOM: Come on, you don't want to do *that*…

BETH: I *am,* that's what I'm gonna have to do.

TOM: *(Over "…have to do.")* Beth…Look, I didn't come here to fight. Okay? I saw the light on; I just wanted to say hi.

BETH: Hi?! Why aren't you in D.C.?

TOM: My flight was cancelled; they closed the airport.

BETH: They *closed* it? Why, the snow's not that bad.

TOM: No, but it *is* getting worse. See?, it's really starting to come down.

BETH: *(Glances out.)* Oh, shit, it is.

TOM: They're saying up to ten inches. National and Dulles are both closed, they've already got like a foot and a half, so I would've been stranded for God knows how long.

BETH: Why didn't you get a room at the airport?

TOM: There *were* no rooms at the airport; you mean a motel?

BETH: Yeah.

TOM: There were no *rooms,* nothing, everything was booked.

BETH: Everything?

TOM: There was not a room to be had, Beth. I swear. You should've seen what was going on there. Everybody shouting and pushing…People can be real animals at times like this. I just didn't have it in me to stay there and sleep on the floor.

BETH: Why didn't you call your friend, the stewardess?

TOM: *(Wearily.)* Travel agent.

BETH: Whatever.

TOM: I did.

BETH: And? Couldn't *she* help you? With all her many connections?

TOM: Not really; no. Besides, I was forty-five minutes from home; I just wanted to come home. You know? All I could think about…was coming home. *(He shrugs. They share eye contact for a moment.)* Don't worry, I'm sleeping in the den.

BETH: Who's worried?

TOM: *(Backing off.)* Well, look, I just wanted to say hi.

BETH: You're melting.

TOM: Huh?

BETH: Your boots. You're making a puddle.

TOM: Oh... *(He sits on the bed to remove his boots.)* I looked in on the kids; they both look pretty wrecked.

BETH: Oh, yeah, they partied hearty. Sam fell asleep in the car. I made a successful transfer, though; he didn't budge.

TOM: He's snoring his head off in there.

BETH: He's getting a cold.

TOM: *(Sympathetically.)* Oh no...

BETH: His nose was running all night. I gave him some Tylenol before we left Karen and Gabe's.

TOM: Liquid or chewable?

BETH: Liquid.

TOM: Wow. And he let you? He usually puts up such a fight. Remember how he'd make himself gag?

BETH: *(Discomfitted by the familiarity of their conversation, she changes the subject.)* Yeah, well, look, I'd really like to be alone right now if you don't mind...

TOM: *(Over "...if you don't mind...")* Yeah, sure...

BETH: Your bedding's in the dryer.

TOM: Oh. Thanks.

BETH: I threw everything in the wash. Your sheets and stuff, they're dry but they're still in the dryer. I wasn't expecting you back.

TOM: I know. Thank you. I'll...

BETH: You might want to grab the extra comforter while you're at it; sounds like it might get awfully cold in there tonight.

TOM: Good idea, thanks. *(Takes blanket from a chest. Sees the placemats.)* What's this?

BETH: Oh. For us. From Italy. A little house gift. Very homey, no? Karen and Gabe, God bless 'em, they know what a disaster I am in the kitchen so they're always giving me things like trivets and cookbooks. I can never tell if they're being remedial or just plain hostile.

TOM: Uh huh.

BETH: *(Continuous.)* In any case, I always find their gifts slightly condescending.

TOM: How was dinner?

BETH: Fabulous. *You* know. When is dinner there *not* fabulous?

TOM: I know. What'd they make this time?

BETH: Oh, *you* know. These incredible recipes they picked up in Italy. Pumpkin risotto, grilled lamb...

TOM: Mm. That *does* sound good. You didn't bring any home by any chance?

BETH: No; I did not.

TOM: The kids eat that, too?

BETH: Of course not, what do you think?, they would never eat anything that good. No, Gabe cooked up some macaroni and cheese for them. From scratch. That was almost as good as the risotto. Then they had Ben and Jerry's for dessert.

TOM: *(Nods; a beat.)* So how are they?

BETH: They're fine. You know. As always. They went on and on about Italy. Thank God their slides weren't back yet.

TOM: *(Smiles, then.)* So what did you tell them?

BETH: About what?

TOM: Why I wasn't there.

BETH: What do you mean? I said you had to go to D.C.

TOM: And they accepted that?

BETH: Why shouldn't they accept that? You're always going *some*where…

TOM: Yeah, but they didn't suspect anything?

BETH: No.

TOM: What did they say?

BETH: What do you mean, what did they say? What did they say about what?

TOM: About my not being there.

BETH: They said they were sorry.

TOM: Sorry about what?

BETH: About your not being there! Jesus! Are you gonna cross-*examine* me now? Look, I'm tired, I'm going to sleep…
(Puffs up her pillow, turns away.)

TOM: I just want to get an idea of what you all talked about, that's all.

BETH: I told you. Italy and stuff. They talked about this famous old Italian cook they're doing a piece on.

TOM: And?

BETH: I don't know, Tom, we talked about a lot of things; what do we ever talk about?

TOM: I don't know, what *do* we talk about?

BETH: Movies, kids, money, the news, I don't know, what we saw, what we read, catching up on this and that. Karen's mom has cataracts; she has to have surgery.

TOM: Is that it?

BETH: I don't know, I don't remember every single goddamn thing.

TOM: You were there like five or six hours.

BETH: Oh, please…

TOM: Right? Like from five to ten, ten-thirty?

BETH: So?

TOM: That's a lot of hours to fill with talk. You mean to tell me the whole evening went by without a word about us?

BETH: Oh, God…You are so paranoid, you know that?

TOM: Oh, really, am I?

BETH: *(Gets under the covers, turns away.)* Look, I'm really not in the mood for this…

TOM: *(Grabs her arm, pulls her to him.)* You told them, didn't you.

BETH: What?!

TOM: You did! You told them!

BETH: Let go of me.

TOM: I knew I shouldn't've trusted you…

BETH: You spoke to them? Already?

TOM: *(His suspicions confirmed, he squeezes her arm.)* No, I didn't speak to them…

BETH: Ow!

TOM: *(Continuous.)* I didn't *have* to speak to them. I knew it! I knew you'd tell them!

BETH: *(Over "…tell them!")* Tom, you're hurting my arm!

TOM: *(Releases her brusquely.)* You promised me you weren't gonna say anything, didn't you promise me?! Not until we both could be there!

BETH: *(Over "..could be there!")* And what did you promise *me?!* Huh? What did you promise *me?!*

TOM: *(Over "…promise me!")* I can't believe you did this! I can't be*lieve* it!

BETH: *(Over "I can't believe it!")* Shhh! You want to wake up the whole house?!

TOM: *(Continuous.)* We were gonna get a sitter and tell them together, face to face, just the four of us, remember?! That's all I asked: Wait for me to get back, we'll tell them together.

BETH: If it was really so important to you, you should've just come tonight, instead of running off to be with your girlfriend!

TOM: Shit, where were the kids?

BETH: What?

TOM: Where were the kids when you told them?

BETH: I don't know…

TOM: You don't *know?!* Were they *sitting* there?!

BETH: No, of course not. They were downstairs, I guess, watching a tape.

TOM: What were they watching?

BETH: What?!

TOM: What tape were they watching?

BETH: Christ, I don't know, Tom...

TOM: You don't know what tape your own children were watching?!

BETH: Oh, for God's sake...I don't know, it was some Disney thing. *The Aristocats.*

TOM: *(Pacing, agitated.)* So, the kids are downstairs watching *The Aristocats* and you're where?

BETH: Oh, Tom, this is ridiculous.

TOM: No no, I want to get the whole picture; I want to see just how this sort of thing could happen. The kids are downstairs and you're in the living room? Huh?

BETH: *(Reluctantly.)* At the table.

TOM: Middle of dinner?

BETH: Right before dessert.

TOM: What was it?

BETH: What?

TOM: The dessert.

BETH: Some kind of lemon-almond cake, made with polenta.

TOM: Was it great?

BETH: Of course.

TOM: So you're sitting there...

BETH: I don't believe this.

TOM: Tell me.

BETH: We were sitting there, chatting, and I lost it. I just...lost it.

TOM: Oh, for Christ's sake...

BETH: *You* try carrying that around with you, keeping it to yourself. I'm only human, Tom. I mean, I'm sitting there with our closest friends, eating their food, drinking their wine, making believe that everything is just dandy...

TOM: Shit.

BETH: And I couldn't contain myself. I tried, I really did.

TOM: Shit shit shit.

BETH: So what? So what if they know? So they know! They were bound to find out!

TOM: That's not the point! *You've* got the advantage now!

BETH: What?! No, I don't.

TOM: Of course you do! You got to them first!

BETH: Tom...

TOM: *(Continuous.)* They heard your side of the story first! Of *course* they're gonna side with you, it's only natural!

BETH: Oh, come on, nobody's taking sides.

TOM: Of course they are!

BETH: They'll make up their own minds!

TOM: Don't be naive! You know how it is! I'm not gonna let you get away with this, Beth.

BETH: What?!

TOM: *(Continuous.)* Gabe and Karen mean too much to me. *We* may be splitting up but I'll be damned if you make me lose them, too!

BETH: Tom, you're overreacting.

TOM: Don't tell me I'm overreacting! You've prejudiced my case! You've turned them against me!

BETH: I have not, Tommy. I was very even-handed.

TOM: Ha! How can you say that?

BETH: I was; I told the truth. They were very sympathetic.

TOM: Of course they were sympathetic. You won them over.

BETH: I did not; stop saying that.

TOM: You *intended* to tell them.

BETH: That is not true! I tried, I really did. I couldn't help it, I broke down!

TOM: Oh, Christ...You *cried?* You actually *cried?*

BETH: Yes. What did you expect? Of course I cried. Everything just spilled out!

TOM: Everything?

BETH: *(A beat.)* Yes.

TOM: Tell me. What did you spill? I want to hear what you spilled.

BETH: Look, this is sick. I'm exhausted. Aren't you exhausted, Tom?

TOM: *(Over "Aren't you exhausted, Tom?")* I want to know what was said. Do you mind? I'm entitled to know.

BETH: You *know* all this, Tom, we've been through this a dozen times.

TOM: *(Over "...a dozen times.")* If you're going to be speaking for the both of us, the least you could do...You owe me that much.

BETH: *(A beat.)* I told them what happened. *You* know.

TOM: Everything? You told them the whole story?

(She nods; a beat.)

And what did they say?

BETH: They were shocked. They were sad.

TOM: They were?

BETH: What do you think? They're our best friends. Of course, they were shocked, they were terribly upset.

TOM: Yeah?

BETH: They didn't see it coming at all, it was a total shock.

TOM: They were sad for *you*, though, right? Because *I'm* such a bastard.

BETH: No, Tom, they were sad for everybody. They were sad for the kids.

TOM: Did you tell them what you did to me, how you killed my self-confidence?

BETH: Oh, Christ, Tom…

TOM: *(Continuous.)* Did you? Did you tell them how you refused to hear me? How I tried to get you to listen to me—for years—but you wouldn't? Did you tell them that?

BETH: *(Over "Did you tell them that?")* No more of this. Please?

TOM: I cried out for help, so many times…

BETH: When? When?

TOM: Never mind, you never paid attention, why should I expect you to remember?

BETH: How did you cry out, Tom, by fucking stewardesses?

TOM: Goddammit, Beth, she's not a stewardess!

BETH: Were your cries detectable by human ears, Tom, or could just the dogs in the neighborhood hear them?

TOM: That's right, go ahead, cut me down, castrate me all over again. That's what you do best.

BETH: *(Over "That's what you do best.")* Oh, please. You know, I hear you say this stuff, Tom…I can't believe that someone I could have been *married* to, for twelve *years!*, that I could have had *children* with!, would be capable of spouting such banal bullshit! It's embarrassing, it really is!

TOM: *(Over "…it really is!")* Even now! Even now you're doing it! Even now you refuse to hear me!

BETH: I "hear" you, I "hear" you! Christ! Tell me your *girlfriend* feeds you this crap, Tommy, I can't believe you came up with it on your own!

TOM: Don't patronize me; I don't need *Nancy* to tell me what I'm feeling…

BETH: *(Over "I don't need Nancy to…")* Oh, yeah?, oh, yeah?, well, what about all the years you patronized *me?!*

TOM: *Patronized you?* I patronized *you?*

BETH: *(Over "…patronized you?!")* Yes! Admit it, Tom, you never took me seriously as an artist! Never!

TOM: *(Over "Never!")* What?! Oh, for God's sake…

BETH: You didn't! You never really supported me, never!

TOM: Oh, come on, I supported you plenty…

BETH: *(Continuous.)* You humored me all along!

TOM: Christ, I supported you for our entire marriage, how can you say I wasn't supportive?! You got a great deal! You needed more time to yourself?, help with the kids?, I got you a nanny…

BETH: *Me* a nanny?

TOM: *(Continuous.)* You needed your own space?, I built you one over the garage! God only knows what the hell you *do* up there all day.

BETH: Fuck you!

TOM: *(Continuous.)* You insist on calling yourself an artist, but where the hell is the art?! You haven't *shown* me anything in years!

BETH: That's 'cause you always made me feel *apologetic* about my work!

TOM: *(Continuing his tirade.)* Hell, you wanted a NordicTrac, I got you a goddamn NordicTrac! As you can see, it's being put to great use! Look at it: It's like a metaphor for our marriage!

BETH: All I ever wanted from you was *respect,* you know that, Tom?—genuine, loving respect—for me, for my art…

TOM: Ah, your art, your art.

BETH: What's the use? Get out of here. Go. Get out.

TOM: *(Over "Go… ")* You held this marriage *hostage* to your goddamn art!

BETH: Out!

TOM: Do you know what it's like having to support something you don't believe in? Do you, Beth? Do you? It's exhausting.

BETH: *(Turning away.)* I don't want to talk anymore…

TOM: The lying, lying to you, lying to myself…

BETH: Go away! Get out!

TOM: *(Over "Get out!")* I couldn't do it anymore. Year after year. The delusion. It was draining me. What was I supposed to tell you, that I thought your "art" sucked?

BETH: What?!

TOM: *(Continuous.)* Huh? Is that what I was supposed to say? That it was just an excuse not to get a fucking job just like everybody else…

BETH: Bastard…

TOM: *(Continuous.)* …and really *do* something with your life?! *(Beth groans in anger and frustration.)* I couldn't do that; how could I do that? It was like extortion. I had to go along with it.

BETH: How dare you! How *dare* you!

(*She strikes him. He grabs her wrists.*)

TOM: You wanna fight? Huh? You wanna fight?

(*He gets into the bed, straddles her.*)

BETH: (*Overlap.*) Let go of me! Let *go* of me!

TOM: Hit me! Hit me! Go ahead and hit me!

BETH: Prick!

TOM: Bitch!

(*She spits in his face. They wrestle, roll around on the bed, inflaming their conflicted passions.*)

TOM: Ballbreaker!

BETH: Liar!

TOM: Dilettante!

BETH: You fuck. I hate you! I hate you so much!

TOM: I could kill you. Right now, I could fucking kill you.

BETH: Try it. I dare you.

(*He suddenly kisses her hard on the mouth. They sob and seethe and wrestle with one another in a desperate, primal dance. Equally aroused, she undoes his pants and he penetrates her; her cry is both ecstatic and sorrowful. End of scene.*)

SCENE THREE

Gabe and Karen's house. Around the same time. Gabe and Karen are on the sofa, finishing off a bottle of wine. Their banter is edgy but always affectionate.

KAREN: Beth and Tom.

GABE: I know.

KAREN: Of all the couples we know...

GABE: I know.

KAREN: Incredible. I never would have guessed. Would you?

GABE: No.

KAREN: Oh, God, Gabe, we introduced them.

GABE: God, you're right.

(*They sit in silence, each lost in thought. They shake their heads, sip their wine.*)

KAREN: *(Re: the wine.)* What do you think of the Shiraz?

GABE: Acidic.

KAREN: Uh huh, I think so, too. *(A beat.)* What he's done to her…She looks like a wraith, doesn't she?

GABE: She does look pretty thin.

KAREN: Oh, I think she looks terrible. Can you imagine what that would be like? You spend your entire adult life with someone, confident that you know and love them and that they know and love you, and it turns out that that person, the one person you completely entrusted your fate to, is an impostor?! Can you *imagine?*

GABE: Now, wait a minute, we don't know the whole story.

KAREN: What is there to know? He was duplicitous; he cheated on her.

GABE: *(Over "…on her.")* Yeah, yeah, but that's not the whole story; that's all we know. It's not as simple as that, Karen, you know that. It never is.

KAREN: That snake.

GABE: Honey. You're talking about someone who up until like two hours ago you thought was salt-of-the-earth!

KAREN: I know; I was wrong. I can't believe I could've been so wrong about a person. Have I ever been so wrong about someone? God, what does this say about my judgment?

GABE: Karen, come on, he's the same person you've known and loved for years.

KAREN: No, he's not; he couldn't be. I'm beginning to think he was *never* that person.

GABE: Honey…

KAREN: Maybe he never existed at all.

GABE: Come on…

KAREN: Maybe he was a figment of our collective imagination. He's very seductive, your friend. He had us convinced he was true blue. He really did. What a sympatico guy: decent, loving, hard-working, a good father…

GABE: He *is* all those things. So he made a transgression…

KAREN: A transgression?!

GABE: *(Continuous.)* It's still the same old Tom…

KAREN: Gabe!, this is more than a mere transgression. How could I ever look him in the eye again? I can't. After what he's done to Beth and the kids…?

GABE: So, what do we do, abandon him? He's my oldest friend!

KAREN: *(Over "He's my oldest friend!")* I don't expect you to do anything. Do whatever you want. I'm saying, *I* can't look at him anymore.

GABE: Maybe he's really in trouble. Maybe he is. What kind of friends would we be if we went ahead and punished him? I've got a feeling Beth is doing a pretty damn good job punishing him herself.

KAREN: She *is* the injured party...

GABE: So, what does that mean, she's the injured party, so we can only stay friends with *her?*

KAREN: I'm telling you I can't *be* friends with him anymore; you can be friends with whomever you like; as far as I'm concerned, someone who conducts his life like this is not to be trusted.

GABE: You are so strict.

KAREN: I am not "strict"—I resent that, that's one of those words...

GABE: Okay; I'm sorry.

KAREN: *(Continuous.)* I'm principled. You can't fault me for being principled...

GABE: But doesn't forgiveness enter into it for you, or are you too principled for that?

KAREN: Some things are not forgivable; this is not forgivable.

GABE: Boy...

KAREN: *(Continuous.)* That's too easy. I'm sorry: Actions have consequences.

GABE: Remind me not to get on your bad side.

KAREN: You do something like this, I'm telling you right now, you are outta here.

GABE: Really?

KAREN: You better believe it. None of that sleeping-in-the-den shit.

GABE: It's for the kids' sake; that's what she said; I can understand that.

KAREN: If he's gonna decimate his family, he doesn't deserve to sleep under the same roof, I'm sorry.

GABE: But it's for the kids!

KAREN: That's a privilege; he's *lost* that privilege.

GABE: Wow. You are really tough.

KAREN: Don't be facetious! There has got to be a price for doing what he did; this neither/nor situation just won't do. I don't know how she can tolerate that. I would just throw him the hell out.

GABE: So, if in a moment of weakness, I sleep with a check-out girl or something, and am foolish enough to confess to you and beg for your forgiveness, you'd tell me, what, to go fuck myself?

KAREN: That's right.

GABE: You mean we couldn't still be friends?

KAREN: No way. Are you kidding?

GABE: We couldn't be friends? *(She shakes her head.)* Not at all? You mean we wouldn't even be civil with one another? *(She shakes her head as if to say, What are you crazy?)* At least now I know where you stand.

KAREN: As if you had any doubt.

(Long pause. They find themselves snuggling closer.)

GABE: The thing is, you never know what couples are like when they're alone; you never do. You know *that:* There's no way of knowing. It's all very mysterious.

(He rests his head on her lap. Pause.)

KAREN: There goes the Vineyard.

GABE: Oh, God, you're right. How would we work that?

KAREN: We couldn't. What, we'd have Beth come with the kids for two weeks, then she would go and Tom would take over? That's ridiculous.

GABE: It sounds awful.

KAREN: What a mess.

GABE: It's like a death, isn't it?

(She nods. Pause.)

KAREN: Why were you so quiet tonight?

GABE: What? What do you mean?

KAREN: When Beth was telling us. You were so silent.

GABE: I wasn't silent. I was shocked, I was stunned.

KAREN: You let me do most of the talking.

GABE: That's not unusual. *(She swats at him.)* Hey! No, I mean it, you *do* do most of the talking.

KAREN: I do not.

GABE: Yes you do. I'm not complaining, or criticizing you, it's a fact. You generally have more to say on any given subject than I do. That's why we work well together: you talk, I write, you edit me.

KAREN: You're evading.

GABE: No, I'm not. Evading what?

(Sits him up again.)

KAREN: I think what Beth was telling us…I think it was very hard for you.

GABE: Of course it was hard. No one wants to hear about his closest friends going through something like this.

KAREN: *(Over "…like this.")* No, no, that's not what I mean. Don't get defensive.

It's just, I think, all this…*marital* talk…It's too close to home. I think it made you very uncomfortable.

GABE: Made *me* uncomfortable?

KAREN: Yes.

GABE: Well, like I said, it's not the most pleasant of topics.

KAREN: Don't play dumb with me, Gabe.

GABE: What?!

KAREN: You're playing dumb.

GABE: No, I'm not, I don't know what you're talking about.

KAREN: You do that, you know, whenever I want you to talk to me about something like this, something important…

GABE: *(Angered, he moves away.)* Oh, great, you trying to pick a fight with me, or what?

KAREN: *(Over "…or what?"; wearily.)* No, Gabe…

GABE: What do you want me to say?, that this whole thing scares the shit out of me? Well, it does. Okay?

(Pause. She nods.)

KAREN: Yes. Good. It does me, too.

(They look at one another. Pause. Headlights are seen through the living room windows; we hear a car pull into the snowy driveway.)

GABE: Who the hell is that? *(Peers out.)* Oh, shit, you're not gonna believe this, I think it's Tom.

KAREN: You're kidding.

GABE: It *is* Tom.

KAREN: He's supposed to be in Washington.

GABE: Well, he's not, he's pulling into our driveway.

KAREN: *(Starting to go.)* I don't want to see him, I'm going to bed.

GABE: Karen! Come on, you can't do that.

KAREN: Why not? I really don't want to see him, Gabe, I really don't.

GABE: *(Over "I really don't.")* You have to. Come on.

KAREN: No I don't; tell him I went to bed. He's not here to see *me*, anyway, he's here to see you; he's *your* friend.

GABE: That's not true. You *love* Tom.

KAREN: No, I *thought* I did.

GABE: You owe it to him to be here. Come on.

KAREN: I don't owe him anything.

(Off, the motor stops running, the headlights shut off. We hear footsteps trudging through the snow.)

GABE: Karen. Please? *(The doorbell rings.)* Don't leave me alone with him.

KAREN: *(Good humoredly.)* Ohhh! *(Meaning, Now I understand.)*

(Karen relents. Gabe opens the door to admit Tom. Snow blows in.)

GABE: Tom. Hi.

TOM: Hi. I know this is crazy; it's really late and everything.

GABE: That's okay, come in.

(Tom enters, tracking in snow.)

TOM: I just had to see you guys.

(Gabe nods, meaningfully. Tom hugs Gabe fiercely.)

GABE: *(Softly.)* I know, I know...

TOM: Here's *another* fine mess I've gotten myself into...

GABE: I'll say...

(Tom then presents himself for a hug to Karen, whose body language tells us she's not interested.)

TOM: It's okay, Karen, you can hug me, I'm not contagious. *(A beat. She coolly drops her guard and lets him hug her.)* Thanks.

KAREN: I thought Beth said you were in Washington.

TOM: Yeah, I never got there. The weather.

(Karen nods.)

GABE: Hell of a night to be out on the road.

TOM: Yeah, I was slipping and sliding...I wasn't gonna just drop in on you like this; I was gonna call you on the way over but I forgot to recharge the phone. Sorry, Karen.

KAREN: Don't apologize to *me*...

(An awkward moment.)

GABE: *(To Tom.)* So. Have you had dinner?

TOM: Actually, no. Just a crappy sandwich at the airport.

GABE: Let me fix you a plate.

(Karen shoots him a look.)

TOM: Oh, no, you don't have to do that...

GABE: It's no problem. Really.

TOM: It's so late...

KAREN: Tom's right, it really *is* late...God, look at the time...

GABE: *(To Tom.)* Don't worry about it. I think a light supper would be just fine.

(Gabe goes to prepare a plate of leftovers.)

TOM: Thanks. *(A beat; calls.)* Hey, you wouldn't happen to have any of that lemon-almond-polenta cake left, would you?

GABE: As a matter if fact we do.

TOM: Oh, great.

KAREN: She told you about that?

TOM: Yeah, she said it was wonderful.

KAREN: You talk about *cake?*

TOM: Yeah. Why not? We *talk...*

(*Pause.*)

KAREN: Well, you two can bond. I'm going to bed.

TOM: Karen, wait. (*She stops.*) Look, I know this is awkward...

KAREN: Not at all.

TOM: It's a lot to digest all at once, I know. You're mad at me, I can tell.

KAREN: No, I'm not.

GABE: Karen...

TOM: This is just what I wanted to avoid: You've already made up your mind.

GABE: No we haven't...

KAREN: It's very late and I'm tired.

TOM: I wanted us to tell you together. I knew this would happen. And so did she. It was really vindictive of her, it really was.

KAREN: Tom. Really. I don't feel like getting into this with you right now. You drop in, unannounced...

GABE: Karen...

TOM: I said I was sorry about that; my car phone was dead...

KAREN: Yeah, well, I'm going to bed. (*Turns to go.*)

GABE: (*Surprised by her behavior.*) Honey!

TOM: I didn't want a night to go by without seeing you guys. I didn't want to lose any more ground.

KAREN: Good night.

TOM: Hey. Aren't you even willing to hear me out? (*She stops.*) I came here...I mean, really, Karen, don't you think you owe it to me? Owe it to our friendship? You guys mean too much to me to just...

GABE: (*Over "You guys...," gently.*) He's right.

KAREN: Okay, you made your point, Tom; you drove all the way over here in a snowstorm to lobby for our support. That's very politic of you.

TOM: I'm not lobbying for anything. I just think you've got to hear me out. You can't just go by what Beth says.

KAREN: It's pretty unambiguous, isn't it, Tom?

TOM: No. It's not. I'm not the villain here. (*She laughs scoffingly.*) If you insist on seeing me as the villain...I could tell you things about Beth...

KAREN: Boy, there's just no end to how low you'll stoop, is there?

GABE: *(Over "…is there?")* Karen…

TOM: *(Continuous.)* Things that might give you a little perspective on all this…Did Beth tell you how she wouldn't touch me anymore?

KAREN: I don't want to hear it.

TOM: *(Continuous.)* Huh? She tell you how she stopped touching me?

KAREN: *(Covering her ears.)* I don't want to hear it!

TOM: But, hey, if you just want to be pissed at me, fine…

KAREN: It's so squalid: A stewardess?!

GABE: Karen…

TOM: *(Overlap.)* What?! Is that what she told you?!

KAREN: *(Continuous.)* I mean, really, couldn't you do better than that?

TOM: *(Continuous.)* She was a stewardess?! Nancy's not a stewardess, she's a travel agent, okay?

KAREN: *(Over "…okay?")* Big deal. I don't care *what* she is, Tom. The point is you fucked her.

GABE: *(Winces.)* Gosh, Karen…

TOM: *(To Karen.)* What are you so angry about? *(To Gabe.)* Jesus, she acts as if I…
    (Gabe shrugs.)

KAREN: Any man who would do that to his wife, to his family…

TOM: Do you think I'd do something like break up my family lightly? Do you, Karen? Is that what you think of me?

KAREN: I don't know *what* I think of you, Tom. I honestly don't.

GABE: Karen…

KAREN: All I know is, she'd better be worth it.

GABE: *(To Karen.)* Look, maybe you'd *better* go to bed.

KAREN: Maybe I should. *(A beat.)* Good night, boys.
    (She goes upstairs. Tom rubs his face with his hands. He groans.)

GABE: Boy, if this is any indication of what it would be like if I ever…

TOM: Man! I knew this wasn't gonna be easy. But I didn't think she'd make it impossible.

GABE: Give it some time. This is all very new for us, you know. *(Tom nods. Gabe presents the plate.)* I could throw it in the microwave if you like.

TOM: *(Over "…if you like.")* No no, this is fine, it looks magnificent.

GABE: Wine?

TOM: Please. *(Gabe pours him a glass.)* Thanks. I want you to know, I really appreciate this. *(Gabe nods.)* I've been feeling so uprooted these days…

GABE: That's understandable.

TOM: Sleeping in the den, living out of a suitcase…*(He tastes the lamb.)* Mmm!

GABE: Good?

TOM: Uh! How'd you do it?

GABE: Very simple. You marinate it overnight.

TOM: Yeah…?

GABE: Lemon juice, olive oil, garlic, rosemary…Then you throw it on the grill, sear it…

TOM: Oh, it's fantastic.

GABE: Thanks.

TOM: Mmm, this is so good.

(Gabe watches Tom eat for a moment.)

GABE: Beth thinks you're having a breakdown.

TOM: Of *course* Beth thinks I'm having a breakdown. If *you* were Beth, wouldn't *you* prefer to think that instead of having to deal with the fact that I can't stand living with her anymore? I haven't gone crazy, Gabe, I've gone sane. I feel better now than I have in a long, long time. I was miserable.

GABE: Really, Tom, I had no idea.

TOM: *(Shrugs.)* Why should you have known? I didn't know it myself.

GABE: What is it, Tom? Is it just sex?

TOM: *Just* sex? No. It's not just sex. Well, of course that's part of it. You know? Ironically? Lately? The sex has been great.

GABE: What do you mean?

TOM: I mean…

GABE: You mean you and Beth…?

TOM: Uh huh.

GABE: You and Beth are still having sex?

TOM: Yeah. Why is that so hard to believe?

GABE: I don't know, it seems to me that given the circumstances…Given the level of hatred and animosity…I don't necessarily see how combat is conducive to great sex.

TOM: You don't? *(Gabe shakes his head.)* Oh, God, it's been so intense! If the sex had been this good when we still had a marriage…

GABE: I must be really out of it. I thought really good sex was the product of trust and love and mutual respect.

TOM: You don't really believe that. *(Gabe shrugs.)* Don't underestimate rage; rage can be an amazing aphrodisiac.

GABE: Huh.

TOM: *(Tastes the cake.)* Mmm! It's really polenta!

GABE: Yeah, there's no white flour in it, just polenta.

TOM: Uh, is that good!

GABE: So you're still making love, huh?

TOM: I wouldn't exactly call it making love. *(A beat.)* She really wouldn't touch me much anymore.

GABE: What do you mean?

TOM: I mean, she wouldn't touch me. The way someone who loved you might casually slip a hand through your arm or onto your shoulder, around your neck or something. *(A beat.)* I did an experiment. I decided I wasn't going to touch her and see how long it would take before she touched me. I'm not talking about sex now; I'm talking about skin-to-skin contact. A simple good night kiss, holding hands. She wouldn't touch me, Gabe. At all. I gave it a week. I couldn't stand it. I broke down and cried.

GABE: Gee...

TOM: I don't know about you, Gabe, but I'm at the point in my life where I want to enjoy myself. I don't want to go through life hoping I'm gonna get lucky with my own wife. You know? You go to bed and you think you're gonna have sex and then you say something, some kind of offhanded remark of no consequence whatsoever, and it pisses her off and the mood is gone and it's lights out and that's it. I must've masturbated more than any married man in history.

GABE: I doubt that. Besides, who ever said marriage meant sex 24 hours on demand?

TOM: I'm not asking for it 24 hours a day, all I'm asking for is a little affection. *(Gabe nods. Pause.)*

GABE: Have there been other women, Tom?

TOM: *(Offended.)* No!

GABE: Sorry.

TOM: What kind of man do you think I am?

GABE: I don't know.

TOM: No, Gabe, there were no other women. There *were* opportunities, though. Oh, yeah. I mean, when you're out of town as much as I am...You're lonely, you're far from home, it doesn't seem like you're living in real time. I began thinking, I'm saving myself, for what? For this hypercritical woman waiting for me back home? For this "marriage"? This "home life"? This wife who made me feel that everything I did wasn't enough or wasn't right or whatever? Who would look at me with withering disappointment. All the time. This accusatory, How could you be so thoughtless look. No matter what I did, it was never enough. Everything I did infuriated her.

GABE: It wasn't always like that, was it? It had to have been good *sometime*...

(Tom shrugs. Pause.)

TOM: I'd be out of town on business and strike up a conversation with a female colleague, or maybe a couple of divorcees with big hair in a hotel bar who'd claw each other's eyes out over you, and suddenly I'd feel competent again, and make them laugh, and feel, Hm, I might still be clever and attractive after all; they'd laugh and look pretty and I'd start to feel good about myself again. It would get late and there'd be that electricity in the air, that kind of buzz I hadn't felt since college days, remember?, when you'd feel that a single move, any move at all, and there'd be sex. But, always the faithful husband, I'd excuse myself and go back to my hotel room and call Beth out of guilt, or hope, and get some shit about something I neglected to do or did badly. Well, by the time I met Nancy —she made me feel good from the first time I talked to her on the phone—I hadn't even laid eyes on her yet—she booked all my travel.

GABE: Uh huh.

TOM: She had this laugh and this great flirty sense of humor, and she said, "I've been talking to you for weeks, I want to meet you already!" And I began to think, Why the hell not? On one hand, there's this woman who makes me feel worthwhile and there's this *other* woman, my wife, who makes me feel like shit. Who would you choose?

(Pause.)

GABE: If only you'd confided in me...

TOM: Gabe...

GABE: If only you'd told me what was going on in your head...

TOM: What, then you'd've tried to "reason" with me?

GABE: Yes.

TOM: Maybe I didn't *want* to be reasonable. I've been reasonable my whole life...

GABE: I could've helped you avoid this mess.

TOM: See, you see it as a mess and I see it as the best thing that could've happened to me!

(Pause.)

GABE: So what happens now, Tommy?

TOM: What do you *mean* what happens now?

GABE: I mean, what are you gonna do? Are you gonna go to someone?

TOM: *Go* to someone?

GABE: A counselor or a therapist or something?

TOM: What would be the point?

GABE: The *point?* Tom, we're talking about your *family.*

TOM: But the marriage is over. What have I been telling you? It's over.

GABE: *(Over "It's over.")* How do you know it's over?

TOM: Because I know. Because as far as I'm concerned it *is* over, it's been over for me for a long time.

GABE: Yeah, that's how you feel now, in the heat of the moment. But don't you want to be absolutely sure you're making the right decision?

TOM: I am making the right decision. Are you questioning my decision?

GABE: Well...

TOM: Are you?

GABE: No. I mean, if I were you...

TOM: You're not me.

GABE: *(Backing off.)* Okay. *(A beat.)* All I'm saying is, Tommy, if I were you, I would want to be certain that there was absolutely no hope whatsoever.

TOM: *(Annoyed; over "...whatsoever.")* Shit...

GABE: I mean, how can you walk away, Tom? How can you throw up your hands and walk away? I don't get it.

TOM: *(Wearily.)* Christ, Gabe...

GABE: Twelve years, Tom. Don't you think you owe it to the kids?

TOM: For Christ's sake...

GABE: *(Continuous.)* What if this is a transient thing or a, a mid-life crisis-thing or something, don't you want to know that? Don't you want to know if this is something that'll pass before you do something irrevocable?

TOM: Look, this is not what I wanted from you, okay?

GABE: I'm merely telling you what I think.

TOM: Yeah, well, I don't want to know what you think.

GABE: Excuse me?

TOM: If you were really my friend...

GABE: Of course I'm your friend, asshole. What do you *mean* if I were really your friend?

TOM: *(Over "...your friend?")* If you were really my friend, you would just listen.

GABE: Just listen?

TOM: Yes.

GABE: Is that what you want? I'm not supposed to say a word?

TOM: That's right. I don't *want* your advice; I don't *want* to know what you think, I just want you to hear me. Is that asking too much?

GABE: Jesus, Tom, you drop this *bomb* on us…We're going to have opinions.

TOM: Yeah, well, I don't want to hear them. All right? My head is spinning with shoulds and shouldn'ts. I've been *through* all this stuff, over and over. It may be news to you but I've been living with this for a long time. I know what I'm doing. I just need you to hear me out.

GABE: All right. Talk. Go ahead.

TOM: *(Softly.)* Never mind.

GABE: Talk. I'm all ears. My lips are sealed. *(Throws away the key.)*

TOM: *(Pause; with difficulty.)* I…I hope you never know…the…*loneliness* I've known. I hope you never do. *(Tom puts down his napkin, gets up.)* Well…*(Tom puts on his jacket, starts to go.)*

GABE: Hey. Tommy. Don't go. I'll let you talk. I will. I'll keep my mouth shut.

TOM: Thanks for dinner.

GABE: Tom.

(Tom waves and goes. We see Tom's headlights and hear him pull away through the snow. Gabe turns off a lamp. He sits, deep in thought, in near darkness for a moment. The stairway light comes on.)

KAREN: *(Off, from the top landing.)* Gabe?

GABE: Yeah?

(Karen, dressed for bed, stands at the top of the stairs.)

KAREN: So? How was that?

GABE: Okay.

KAREN: Come to bed and tell me.

GABE: In a minute.

(She goes up the stairs. He lingers, slowly goes around turning off lamps. He looks around the dimly lit room which suddenly feels cold and strange to him. Silence.)

KAREN: *(Off.)* Honey?

GABE: *(Calls.)* Coming!

(He turns off the last lamp and walks upstairs. Out of sight, at the landing, he switches off the stairway light.)

(End of Act One.)

ACT TWO
SCENE ONE

In the black, we hear the "All Things Considered" theme. Lights up: A house on a hill on Martha's Vineyard. Twelve and a half years earlier. Much of this utilitarian 1960s-vintage house (which was built by Gabe's family) is made of glass, so the view overlooking the ocean is pretty spectacular. The large, main room is used for sitting, dining, and cooking. (A working kitchen is required; a meal will actually be prepared during the scene.) An exterior deck which wraps around the house is visible through the huge windows. It is around six on a summer evening; daylight fades to dusk during the course of the scene (west is stage left). Karen listens to the radio while preparing a marinade of soy sauce, balsamic vinegar, lime, ginger, and garlic. (She later makes bruschetta by dicing tomatoes, onion, and garlic, sautéeing it and serving it on toasted baguette; Gabe will wash greens in a spinner and make a salad.) Soon Gabe is seen on the deck before entering with bags of groceries, flowers, liquor.

GABE: Hi-i-i.

KAREN: Hi-i-i. Where'd you go?

GABE: I stopped at Morning Glory. I thought we could use some flowers.

KAREN: Nice.

(They kiss. He trims the flowers and arranges them in a bottle.)

GABE: Tom here yet?

KAREN: No, no sign of him.

GABE: Where's your friend?

KAREN: She's still not back from her walk.

GABE: Ah, yes, communing with the skunk population, teaching them tai-chi
or something. *(Karen smiles at him with mock-disapproval.)* Did you get a
load of the relaxation tapes she listens to? She listens to them constantly.

KAREN: Gabe...

GABE: *(Continuous.)* All that shimmery, tinkly new-age shit.

KAREN: So what? It helps her relax. It's not like she's subjecting *you* to it...

GABE: Yes she is; I can hear the treble through her headphones. I don't know
how she can listen to that stuff: It would just send me running to the
bathroom all the time. *(A beat.)* What's she so tense about, anyway? Was
she like this at work?

KAREN: No...Well, she *is* a little high-strung...

GABE: High-strung: Great. Hey, *I* know: Let's introduce her to Tom! Tom'll straighten her out, give her peace of mind.

KAREN: She's fun. I *do* think Tom could be good for her, he's essentially a good guy. He just needs to find the right woman.

GABE: Uh huh. And Beth is the right woman.

KAREN: I don't know; maybe. What's wrong with Beth?

GABE: Have you seen her sketchbook? Whoa.

KAREN: There's no harm in *introducing* them…They're grown-ups, they can do whatever they want, that's out of our hands.

GABE: You sure?

KAREN: Yes. What's the worst that could happen?

(Pause. He unpacks liquor: four whites, four reds, dark rum, gin, tonic, and two six-packs of beer.)

GABE: *(Sarcastically.)* You think we've got enough to drink?

KAREN: We're gonna need every last drop.

(Gabe smiles. A beat. He snuggles behind her at the counter and kisses her neck. She continues mincing garlic.)

KAREN: What are you doing?

GABE: *(Kissing her nape.)* Nothing.

KAREN: Gabe. No, really, what are you doing?

GABE: Can't I kiss my wife?

KAREN: Go ahead, kiss your wife, but why is it you always get amorous whenever people are about to arrive any minute?

GABE: No I don't.

KAREN: Yes you do, Gabe. What is that about?

GABE: Forget it. *(He gets out the salad spinner, rinses romaine, etc. She looks at him then resumes mincing.)*

KAREN: Now you're sulking.

GABE: I'm not sulking.

KAREN: Come on, honey, I'm mincing garlic and you're feeling amorous; tell me: what am I supposed to do about this?

GABE: You could try putting down the knife. *(Pause. She acquiesces, puts down the knife, leans against the counter. He kisses her.)* That wasn't so bad now, was it? *(She puts her arms around him. An intimate game ensues, which they play utterly straight, i.e., no baby talk.)* Uh oh.

KAREN: What.

GABE: *(Looks at his watch.)* You know what time it is?

KAREN: What.

GABE: It's time for me to scare you.

KAREN: *(Playing along.)* Oh, no, please don't.

GABE: I do; it's time.

KAREN: No, Gabe, please?

GABE: Sorry. A man's got to do what a man's got to do.

KAREN: Please, please don't.

GABE: Sorry, Sweetie. It can happen any time now.

KAREN: *(Pleading.)* No…

GABE: Any second.

KAREN: Gabe, please…

GABE: Sorry, kid. That's just the way it is. *(A beat. He shouts, "Boo!" She jumps.)* Works every time.
   (She kisses him. Their kisses become more fervent.)

KAREN: There's no time…Do we have time? We can't…We shouldn't…

GABE: Why not?
   (Their kissing progresses. Through the glass, we see Tom, wearing a knapsack, arrive after a long bike ride. He parks his bike on the deck and enters. He sees Gabe and Karen kissing and caressing. He backs away as if to go but decides to lurk and watch. Karen catches his eye and abruptly stops.)

GABE: What. *(She indicates with her eyes, he turns.)* Oh. Tom. Hi.

TOM: Carry on, don't mind me, it was just getting good.

KAREN: How long have you been standing there?

TOM: Ten, fifteen minutes.

KAREN: Jerk.
   (She kisses Tom's cheek.)

TOM: Nice to see you, too.
   (The men embrace.)

GABE: Welcome. How was the ferry?

TOM: Good. Beautiful. Boy, the ride from Vineyard Haven gets longer every year.

GABE: No, you just get older every year.

KAREN: We could've picked you up.

TOM: No, I wanted to ride.

GABE: Beer? Wine?

TOM: Yes!

GABE: Which?

TOM: Beer.

KAREN: How were things in the city?

TOM: Sticky.

GABE: Beck's, Bass, Heineken.

TOM: Uh, I don't care.

GABE: How about Bass?

TOM: Fine. *(Gabe hands him a bottle.)* Thanks. So, you guys look pretty good; you look like you're on vacation or something.

GABE: Funny how that happens.

TOM: So where's this woman you're setting me up with?

KAREN: It's not a set-up. *(To Gabe.)* Did you tell him it was a set-up? *(Gabe shrugs.)* Don't call it a set-up. That sounds so cheap and scheming. We just thought you two might like each other, that's all.

TOM: That's okay with me. I have no problem with cheap and scheming.

GABE: It's not like it's a blind date. You already met her.

KAREN: At our wedding.

TOM: Yeah, so you said; I don't remember.

GABE: Remember, right at the end?, the woman dancing all by herself on the dance floor doing that weird Kabuki shit?

KAREN: Gabe!

GABE: What.

TOM: *(Simultaneously; to Gabe.)* You're kidding. *(Gabe shakes his head.)* Her?

KAREN: Now, wait a minute, that really isn't fair. It was a wedding! She had a little buzz on, she was feeling expansive.

TOM: So *that's* the woman in question. I didn't actually meet her, but I did observe her, yes.

GABE: Yeah, I think Beth *has* been under observation.

KAREN: You know, this is not funny. Beth is really...she's really a uniquely gifted person.

TOM: Uh huh. That much seemed clear. *(Gabe cracks up.)*

KAREN: *(To Gabe.)* Why are you doing this?

GABE: I'm only joking. Beth is great. You're gonna love her. And this is not a set-up.

(Tom laughs, Karen shakes her head.)

TOM: So, is she here yet?

GABE: *(Nods.)* She drove up with us Thursday night.

KAREN: She must've gone to the beach to paint or something.

TOM: She paints?

KAREN: Yeah and she's very good, too.

GABE: *(Equivocally.)* Well...

KAREN: *I* like her stuff!

TOM: What does she do?

GABE: She does this, I don't know what you'd call it: these Expressionistic, neo-psychotic...

KAREN: *(Angered.)* Gabe!

GABE: What?

KAREN: *Why are you doing this?!*

GABE: What does it matter what I think? Tom can decide for himself if he thinks she's any good.

TOM: Yeah.

KAREN: *(Over "if he thinks she's...")* You're being incredibly negative and I wish you would cut it out!

GABE: He asked me what I thought! What difference does it make? Jesus...
(Silence. They continue to cook.)

TOM: *(Facetiously.)* Gee, it's really generous of you guys to be setting your friends up. I guess you just want us to be as happy as *you* are, huh? That's really sweet.

KAREN: *(Smiling.)* Screw you.
(Beth comes in from a long hike looking sunburned and pretty, wearing a shoulder bag bursting with art supplies and headphones around her neck. She shyly avoids making eye contact with Tom, who sits smiling pleasantly.)

BETH: *(Entering.)* Hello?

KAREN: Hi!

GABE: Hi-i-i.

BETH: I'm not late, am I?

GABE: Not at all.

BETH: I totally lost track of time.

KAREN: Where did you go?

BETH: Oh, it was glorious. The light! On the ocean! I walked all the way down to the beach...Where you took me yesterday?

KAREN: Lucy Vincent Beach?

BETH: Yes!

KAREN: Wow, that's some walk.

BETH: Uh! I love this place!

GABE: I know.

BETH: I am in love.

TOM: This your first time on the Vineyard?

BETH: *(Ignores him; to Karen.)* I walked all along the beach, past those spectacular clay cliffs?

KAREN: Uh huh.

BETH: The *light!*

GABE: I know.

BETH: I'm telling you, the cliffs *glow!*

KAREN: They *do,* don't they.

BETH: They're this brilliant terra cotta.

KAREN: Uh huh.

BETH: And these people, these beautiful men and women, were cavorting in the clay…

GABE: Oh, yeah.

BETH: *(Continuous.)* …and the *light* on their bodies…

TOM: Were they naked?

BETH: *(A beat, looking at him for the first time.)* Excuse me?

TOM: I was just wondering if they were naked.

BETH: Some of them.

GABE: I'm sorry; Beth, this is Tom. Tom…

TOM: Hi. *(He extends his hand; they shake hands.)*

BETH: I remember you. *(To Karen.)* I do remember him.

KAREN: I knew you would.

TOM: Wait wait: I don't think we ever…

BETH: At the wedding. I talked a lot to the woman you were with. She was a public defender.

TOM: Not anymore. I mean, she's still a public defender, I'm just not with her anymore.

BETH: Oh, that's too bad.

TOM: Not necessarily.

BETH: She seemed great.

TOM: *(Equivocally.)* Uh…

BETH: As I recall, *I* talked to her a lot more than you did. Maybe if you paid more attention to her…

GABE: Moving right along…

KAREN: Would you like something to drink?

BETH: I would love something to drink.

GABE: Beer, wine, red, white…? Rum and tonic?

BETH: Oo, yeah, a rum and tonic; a rum and tonic sounds great.

GABE: You got it. *(Gabe prepares one.)*

TOM: So, is this your first trip to the Vineyard?

BETH: Yeah it is. *(Mostly to Karen.)* And now I see what makes people so fanatical about this place: The terrain!

KAREN: Uh huh.

GABE: That's right.

BETH: *(Continuous.)* It's this incredible mix of beach and woods and hills and farmland.

GABE: I know.

BETH: Rock and sand and trees.

KAREN: Uh huh.

BETH: It's like Scotland or something.

KAREN: Uh huh.

TOM: You've been to Scotland?

BETH: No.

TOM: Me, neither. I've been coming here…Gabe, *how* long have I been coming here?

GABE: The first time was the summer between freshman and sophomore year, so that's, what, twelve years.

BETH: Wow, you guys have known each other forever, right?

TOM: Uh huh. Yeah.

GABE: *(Simultaneously.)* First day of freshman orientation.

TOM: Was it the first day?

GABE: The first *hour.* We met on line at breakfast. We amused each other with gross comments about the food.

TOM: That's right! I'd forgotten that.

KAREN: Even then he cracked wise about food.

GABE: Only now I get paid for it.

BETH: All these years. That is really remarkable.

GABE: Or really neurotic, depending on how you look at it.

TOM: *(Taking mock-offense.)* Hey!

GABE: No, it is, it's great. Tommy and I had this co-dependent thing going: I'd have these paralyzing crushes and he'd hit on these women before I could ever bring myself to make the first move.

TOM: What? That's a lie.

GABE: I'm exaggerating only slightly.

TOM: That is not true.

GABE: Tommy. Bubbie. Think about it.

TOM: All right: Cathy What'shername, I admit.

GABE: Yeah, and what about the *other* Kathy. There was Kathy with a K and Cathy with a C.

TOM: Right! The Two Kathys. I forgot about that.

GABE: Two Kathys, two broken hearts.

KAREN: Poor thing.

GABE: And Emily, remember Emily? And Mindy Glazer?

TOM: Okay, okay. See now: *Karen* I could go for, but she wouldn't have me.

GABE: *(Mock alarm.)* Ohhhh...

TOM: He can't give you what I can give you, Karen. I *know;* remember I *lived* with him for four years; I've seen him naked.

KAREN: I have no complaints.

TOM: Touché.

GABE: *(To Karen.)* Thank you. *(He gives her a kiss.)*

BETH: *(To Tom.)* So I guess I'm supposed to say I've heard so much about you.

TOM: Have you?

BETH: Enough. *What* do you do?

TOM: Oh, I'm just another jaded lawyer, burnt-out at thirty-one but hanging in there for want of anything better to do.

BETH: Uh huh.

TOM: And you?

KAREN: Beth's an artist.

BETH: Karen...

KAREN: A damn good artist.

BETH: No...

TOM: Neat.

BETH: "Neat"?

TOM: *You* know...So: *How* do you know Karen?

BETH and KAREN: Doubleday.

TOM: Oh, right.

BETH: In-house promo: She wrote the copy, I designed it.

KAREN: What a team.

TOM: You still there?

BETH: No, I got out.

KAREN: She left me. *(To Beth.)* It's just not the same without you.

BETH: You'll survive.

KAREN: It's not.

BETH: *(To Tom.)* I'm free-lancing now. Now I'm at Warner.

TOM: Uh huh.

BETH: Mass-market paperbacks. Direct-mail to booksellers, that sort of thing.

TOM: *(Seemingly with interest.)* Uh *huh*.

BETH: You "Uh huh" as if you think what I do is interesting; it's not. If I'm still doing this five years from now, do me a favor, shoot me.

TOM: *(Making eye contact; seductively.)* Okay; if you insist.

(His gaze unnerves Beth.)

KAREN: Beth is really a terrific artist.

BETH: I wish you would stop saying that.

TOM: What kind of stuff do you do? Expressionistic, neo-psychotic...?

BETH: Excuse me?

(Gabe glares at Tom in disbelief.)

TOM: I mean...What style? Whatayacallit, realistic...?

BETH: I hate labels.

TOM: Oh, okay.

BETH: Do you know art?

TOM: Not really.

BETH: Then why ask for labels? Why not just take it at face value?

TOM: *(Pointing to her notebook.)* Can I see?

BETH: *(Outraged.)* No!

TOM: Oh. Okay.

BETH: Why should I let you see it?

TOM: I don't know, I just...

BETH: I mean, forgive me: Who are you to me, anyway?

(Gabe clears his throat, for effect.)

TOM: You're right, I'm nobody.

BETH: Sharing one's art...That comes with trust. It's a gift. I never show my art on the first date.

TOM: Oh, is this a date? *(Looking to his hosts.)* I thought this *wasn't* a date.

BETH: Excuse me. *(Goes to Karen for refuge.)* So, what can I do? Give me something to do.

GABE: Here. Make a dressing. *(Gives her a jar, ingredients.)*

BETH: How do you want me to do it?

GABE: Four parts oil to one part vinegar. A little Dijon...

TOM: *(Approaches Beth.)* So I actually remember you from their wedding, too.

BETH: What do you remember?

TOM: You dancing. Right toward the end. When you were by yourself.

BETH: *(Embarrassed.)* Oh, God, I can't believe you saw me.

TOM: Sure I saw you; I was watching you. You looked beautiful. I mean, your dancing. It was quite a sight.

(Karen and Gabe exchange looks. Beth, distracted by Tom's attention, has lost count in her measurements; she pours it down the drain and mixes it again.)

BETH: That was a fun wedding.

KAREN: Was it? I don't even remember. Is that my wine?

BETH: *(Over "Is that my wine?")* Oh, come on, you know it was. You guys really know how to throw a wedding.

TOM: *(To Beth.)* They know all this stuff; they're perfect.

(Beth smiles, nods.)

KAREN: *(Over "You guys really know...")* I really don't; I have very little recollection of it, I was in an altered state most of the time.

GABE: Honey, you were a wreck. *(To the others.)* She made me gather everyone together for the ceremony ten minutes early; she was in a panic.

KAREN: It's true; I was.

BETH: I *remember.*

GABE: *(Continuous.)* She said to me, "If we're gonna do it, let's do it; I want to do it *now.*"

KAREN: It's true.

GABE: *(Continuous.)* So, what did I do, dutiful husband that I am? I rushed around to everyone and said, "Quick, get over there, Karen wants to do it *now!*" I had to *push* people away from the hors d'ouevres; my future depended on it.

KAREN: I don't think I got to try a single hors d'ouevre.

GABE: You didn't miss anything.

BETH: So does it *feel* different? Being married?

KAREN: Um...*(To Gabe)* What do *you* think?

GABE: I think it does. It feels...*calmer* than before. *(To Karen)* Don't you think? *(She nods.)* Even when we were just living together. The social pressure that comes with being single is gone. You can actually relax a little.

TOM: Really?

KAREN: Uh huh. What was nebulous and noncommittal is now right out-there, in sharp focus: We're married. We're a married couple.

BETH: It's like, Okay, now you can get on with your life.

KAREN: Exactly.

(Serves bruschetta. Ad lib responses.)

BETH: That sounds wonderful. When you're single—*and* of a certain age, you spend so much energy...

TOM: I know. I wouldn't mind getting married, having kids, the whole bit. This single stuff is getting awfully tired. I mean, I look at *you* guys and I think, Why not? What am I so scared of anyway?

GABE: I don't know, what *are* you?

(Pause. Gabe is slicing zucchini. Beth helps him, watching how he does it. Karen hands Tom silverware.)

KAREN: Set the table.

TOM: *(Sets out cutlery, stops.)* What side does the fork go on?

KAREN: You're kidding.

TOM: No. *(He looks at Beth with mock-boyish helplessness.)*

BETH: Don't look at *me.*

KAREN: Left. Forks on the left, knives on the right.

(Beth cuts her finger accidentally.)

BETH: Oh, shit…

GABE: What.

BETH: Nothing. *(Sucks on her finger.)*

KAREN: What happened?

GABE: She cut herself, that's all.

TOM: She okay?

BETH: It's nothing. Really.

KAREN: *(Comes closer, sees the blood.)* Beth…

GABE: *(Turns on the water.)* Leave it under the water.

TOM: Have you got any Band-Aids or something?

BETH: It's nothing. God!

GABE: *(Re: the running water.)* Just leave it…

KAREN: *(Overlap.)* Uh, look under there.

(Tom looks. Karen gets a dish towel, gives it to Beth.)

Here. Put pressure on it.

BETH: Would everybody please…? I'm all right. Really. It's just a stupid cut.

KAREN: Are you sure? Let me see.

GABE: It's really not that bad.

KAREN: We just sharpened those knives; I should've warned you.

BETH: It's all right; it's not your fault. Forget about it, I'm fine.

(Holding the cloth against her finger, she moves out of the kitchen.)

GABE: *(Changing the subject.)* Look at that sky!

KAREN: Ooo!

(Tom finds Band-Aids and sits with Beth.)

BETH: Thank you.

(He wraps a Band-Aid on her finger.)

GABE: Come, let's go see.

(Gabe and Karen go out on the deck to admire the sunset; we see them looking off stage left and hear them ooing. Beth and Tom are alone.)

BETH: I'm so embarrassed.

TOM: Don't be.

BETH: I feel like such an idiot.

TOM: Why?

BETH: I was just trying to be a good little houseguest and it's like I end up in the emergency room...

TOM: Don't worry about it. Gabe and Karen's *job* is to make the rest of the world feel incompetent; it's their *job*.

(Beth laughs. They look at one another. A beat.)

GABE: *(From the deck.)* Hey, you've got to see this, you guys.

BETH: *(Calls.)* Be right there. *(To Tom.)* Coming?

TOM: Yeah, let me just...

(Gestures to the table he hadn't finished setting. She nods and goes out.)

BETH: *(Entering the deck.)* Oh, wow!

(Tom finishes setting the table.)

KAREN: *(To Gabe and Beth as she enters.)* Wait, I'll be right back; let me get the bruschetta...

BETH: *(Calls from the door.)* Could someone bring me my drink?

TOM: *(Calls.)* Okay.

(Karen fixes the plate of bruschetta. Tom finds Beth's drink. Then, standing very close to Karen, he lightly touches her hair. She isn't aware of it at first, then realizes what he's doing, stops and looks at him.)

KAREN: What.

TOM: You've gotten sun.

KAREN: I know.

TOM: It looks nice.

KAREN: Thanks. My hair always lightens in the summer.

(Silence as he resumes touching her hair. They look at one another.)

What are you doing?

(He doesn't respond; he continues fingering her hair. It's strangely charged for a moment. Karen, unnerved, brushes his hand away, busies herself.)

So, what do you think of Beth?

TOM: *(Equivocally.)* She's nice. She's intense. Better yet, what does she think of me?

KAREN: I don't know, I think she likes you.

TOM: Yeah? Then I like her.

KAREN: Uh, you're so deep.

(He laughs, touches her chin, turns her face to his. They look at one another; She looks confused, quizzical. Pause. Off, Gabe has said something to Beth that makes her laugh. Karen takes the plate of bruschetta and walks past him.) Excuse me.

(She goes out; Tom lingers inside, sips Beth's drink.)

BETH: *(In the doorway.)* Tom, hurry up. You're gonna miss the sunset.

(They look at one another. She extends her hand to him. Pause. Karen and Gabe's muffled voices, off. He smiles and goes to her.)

TOM: Okay…

(He gives her the drink. They join Gabe and Karen outside, looking off toward stage left. The screen door closes. The sunset is brilliant.) Oh, wow…!

BETH: Isn't that incredible?

TOM: It is. It really is.

(We hear their admiring sounds as the lights fade to black. End of scene.)

SCENE TWO

At rise: Karen and Gabe's garden patio and a bar/restaurant in Manhattan. Present day. Spring. A partly cloudy afternoon. Karen and Beth bring out a salad bowl and utensils and proceed to have a light lunch.

BETH: *(Entering, mid-conversation.)* When you promise your little girl you're gonna call at eight o'clock and eight o'clock comes and goes…

KAREN: Oh, no…

BETH: And *nine*, and *ten*…

KAREN: That's terrible.

BETH: Naturally she waits by the phone…

KAREN: Of course.

BETH: *(Continuous.)* …and asks me what *time* it is every two seconds. *He's* out somewhere with his *girl*friend, and *she's* leaving all these heartbreaking messages on his machine: "Daddy, where are you?"

KAREN: Oh, God…

BETH: That's what's so unforgivable. He just doesn't get it. "Tell Laurie I'm really sorry." I told him, "If you want to tell your daughter you're sorry for being a hopeless schmuck, call her when she's *awake* and tell her yourself!"

KAREN: Did you really say that?

BETH: Maybe I didn't say "hopeless" schmuck.

KAREN: Good for you. So did he call in the morning?

BETH: Uh huh. I'm trying to get the kids ready for school...*She's* exhausted, dragging herself through breakfast, *I'm* pissed, Sammy has to talk, too; they fight...You see how he continues to set these little bombs off long after he's moved out of the house?

(Karen shakes her head and picks at her food; Beth eats. Pause.)

KAREN: I'm telling you, this whole thing with you and Tom...You think you're on solid ground, then all of a sudden the earth cracks open and you're teetering on the abyss!

(Beth nods. A beat.)

You know? What I find so...*terrifying* about all this? Men seem to get by for years without really talking to you and then, one day, when they finally do, it's to tell you they're leaving.

BETH: You and *Gabe* talk...

KAREN: *(Equivocally.)* Yeah...

BETH: Of course you do. You communicate. You guys are not *like* everybody else; yours is a different story.

KAREN: Why?

BETH: You work together, you've made this lovely home together. Oh, come on, you're inseparable! He's incredibly involved with the boys...You're such good *friends*. That's so rare; do you know how rare that is? I always envied that about you.

KAREN: *(Surprised.)* Really?

BETH: Oh, God, yeah.

(Karen, still distracted, smiles. They eat in silence. Clouds pass. Birds fly overhead.

Meanwhile, Gabe enters the bar and sits at a table. A waiter silently takes Gabe's order and soon returns with a half-bottle of Pelligrino. Gabe has the self-conscious look of someone drinking alone who is trying not to appear self-conscious; he is waiting for Tom, who is late. He glances at his watch, sips, reads the Times, *looks around, glances at his watch again, checks his date-book.)*

KAREN: This is nice.

BETH: Mm. It is.

KAREN: You sure you don't mind eating al fresco?

BETH: Not at all; the sun feels great.

KAREN: I feel like I haven't seen you in ages...

BETH: I know. Talk about winters of discontent! Boy, am I glad *that* one's over; I thought spring would never get here.

KAREN: I was worried about you.

BETH: Aw...Really?

KAREN: I was; we both were. You disappeared on us.

BETH: I didn't mean to; I needed some time to myself.

KAREN: *(Nods.)* I know; that's what I figured. You needed time to...

BETH: Yes.

KAREN: I'm glad to see you looking so well!

BETH: Thank you.

KAREN: You do! You look wonderful!

BETH: Thanks.

KAREN: *(Continuous.)* I had visions of you hibernating, wallowing in despair, avoiding people...

BETH: *(Over "...people...")* No no, I'm doing much, much better now.

KAREN: I can see that. We respected your privacy, we didn't want to *descend* on you or anything...

BETH: I know, and I appreciate that.

KAREN: We began to wonder if you were *mad* at us or something...

BETH: Mad at you?! Why would I be mad at you?

KAREN: You stopped calling me.

BETH: Oh, Karen...

KAREN: When this thing first blew, you called all the time...

BETH: I know.

KAREN: *(Continuous.)* You'd stop by, and I really tried to be there for you...

BETH: You *were.*

KAREN: And then after a few weeks...

BETH: I thought you were getting sick of me.

KAREN: No! I didn't want to seem like a *ghoul* and call *you*...

BETH: You should have!

KAREN: But then *months* went by and I began to think that I must have *offended* you in some way...

BETH: Karen! No!

KAREN: Are you sure?

BETH: Karen, why would you have offended me?

KAREN: I don't know. You know me. *(A beat.)* You don't think, on some level, you blame me for this whole thing?

BETH: What?!

KAREN: Think about it: It was my idea to introduce you...

BETH: Oh, Karen, that's ridiculous. We were grown-ups, we knew what we were doing.

KAREN: I just wanted us to make our own extended family. That's all I wanted: a family.

BETH: I know...

KAREN: But it turned so sour. And I feel so responsible...

BETH: Oh, Karen...

KAREN: I set it in motion, I did, I brought about this unholy alliance. All this rancor and rage, the pain the kids are going through...

BETH: It was out of your control. That we came together was as much out of your control as our falling apart. You can't control everything, Karen, even though it sometimes seems you can. *(A beat.)* Tom was my destiny. He was. Let's face it, if you hadn't introduced me to Tom, I just would've found *another* schmuck who would've destroyed my life.

(Tom, looking tanned and fit in a smart summer suit, sunglasses hanging around his neck, breezes in and joins Gabe.)

TOM: Gabe!

KAREN: *(To Beth.)* Do you really believe that?

GABE: *There* you are.

(The men embrace; Tom's hug is more fervent than Gabe's.)

BETH: *(To Karen.)* Absolutely.

(The women resume eating in silence. The focus shifts to the men's table.)

TOM: Good to see you. God, I miss you.

GABE: Miss you, too.

TOM: Been here long?

GABE: A few minutes.

(They sit.)

TOM: Sorry about that. This meeting...

GABE: That's okay.

TOM: It's been weeks!

GABE: Months.

TOM: God, you're right. I'm so glad this worked out.

GABE: I had to be in the city anyway; our editor took me to lunch. Want some?

TOM: Thanks. *(Gabe fills his glass.)* How's Karen?

GABE: Fine.

TOM: Still pissed with me?

GABE: Uh…You could say that.

TOM: Boy, she really holds a grudge, doesn't she.

GABE: Well, this *is* sort of a biggie, though, you gotta admit. *(A beat.)* So, when'd you get to town?

TOM: This morning. Nancy came *with* me.

GABE: Oh, yeah?

TOM: She loves New York.

GABE: Uh huh. So, I guess you'll be going up to see the kids.

TOM: Actually, no, not this weekend.

GABE: Oh.

TOM: I'll have them *next* week. This is *her* turn; I'm not gonna mess with *that,* believe me. God forbid there's any change of plan…It's like Nuremberg.

GABE: *(A chuckle.)* Uh huh.

TOM: I promised Nancy a weekend in New York, just the two of us, *you* know, see a couple of shows…

GABE: Uh huh. How're they doing?

TOM: Who?

GABE: The kids.

TOM: Beth probably makes it sound like they're totally screwed up, right?

GABE: No…

TOM: *(Continuous.)* Like I *destroyed* them or something. But the truth is they're amazing.

GABE: Uh huh.

TOM: They really are.

GABE: Uh huh. And how are you?

TOM: I'm fine; I'm doing great.

GABE: You *look* great.

TOM: Thanks, I *feel* great. I lost a little weight…

GABE: I noticed. More than a *little.*

TOM: Nancy and I, we get up at six…

GABE: Wow. Six!

TOM: *(Continuous.)* Run three miles…

GABE: I don't know how you do it.

TOM: Come back, make love in the shower…

GABE: Uh huh.

TOM: And off to work. That's my new regimen. And let me tell you, it's totally changed my perspective on my day. Totally.

GABE: I'll bet. Must be those invigorating showers.

TOM: And she's got me eating really well: Nancy. I haven't been this fit in years. She wants to be a nutritionist.

GABE: Really. I thought she was a travel agent.

TOM: She is. I mean, she doesn't want to do that forever, she wants to go back to school and get a degree, *you* know.

GABE: Uh huh.

TOM: *(A beat.)* Don't prejudge her.

GABE: What?

TOM: You're prejudging her.

GABE: No, I'm not.

TOM: I know that tone…She's really really bright, Gabe.

GABE: I'm sure.

TOM: *(Continuous.)* Totally self-taught. You'd like her, I know you would.

GABE: I'm sure.

(Tom glances at the clock and pulls over a vacant chair. Gabe looks quizzical.)

TOM: She might be dropping by.

GABE: Huh?

TOM: Nancy.

GABE: Oh.

TOM: Said she might stop by to say hi. She's dying to meet you.

GABE: She is?

TOM: Yes!

GABE: Why?

TOM: Gabe, you're my oldest friend! I've told her so much about you.

GABE: Gee, I wasn't expecting to, uh…Today…?!

TOM: *(Over "Today…?!")* Don't worry. You'll love her. She knows a lot about food.

GABE: Oh, yeah?

TOM: She's incredibly knowledgeable about diet and stuff.

GABE: Uh huh.

TOM: You know that book *The Zone?*

GABE: Oh, yeah, I wondered if she might've…

TOM: She *swears* by it; she's got *me* reading it. The great thing about Nancy, I mean, one of the things that makes her so attractive, is how she—more than anyone I've ever known in my life—has been able to totally integrate the physical and the cerebral.

GABE: Hm.

TOM: She is so at home in her own body...See, I've never really felt that before. It's something you have to learn; a lover teaches you that, it's something you learn together. And Beth and I *never* had that, never. Well, you know Beth: I mean, let's face it, she's never been truly comfortable with her own body...

GABE: Really? Gee, I...

TOM: *(Continuous.)* So how could I expect her to be comfortable with mine? With Nancy, we'll be strolling along and she'll put her hand on my ass or something, just like that. It's perfectly natural, it's this energy that exists between us that we celebrate every chance we get.

GABE: Uh huh.

TOM: I mean, constantly.

GABE: A whole lotta celebratin' goin' on, huh?

(The scene returns to the women.)

KAREN: So, I guess you just *immersed* yourself in your work all this time, which was probably the smartest thing you could've done...

BETH: Well, actually, no; I haven't been in my studio in weeks.

KAREN: You're kidding.

BETH: I've had no desire to paint whatsoever.

KAREN: Oh, that'll pass...

BETH: No, I don't *want* to paint anymore.

KAREN: Why?

BETH: Right after Tom left...This *unburdening* took place. I looked at what I'd been doing with my life and it seemed so insignificant to me.

KAREN: *(Reassuring.)* No...

BETH: *(Continuous.)* I discovered I didn't need it anymore. Just like I didn't need Tom. I realized my painting was just an excuse not to deal with the realities of my life. It was this barrier I'd constructed, between me and the world.

KAREN: After all those years? All that hard work? But you're so creative.

BETH: So are you!

KAREN: No, I'm not; not like you.

BETH: Sure you are, you've got a great eye: Look at your house! And your cooking?

KAREN: No, I'm really very traditional, very much by-the-book. You've always been my idea of a free spirit.

BETH: It's not tragic, it's kind of thrilling, really. I can do anything. It's a relief not to have to go up to my studio in the morning.

KAREN: So what have you been doing with yourself all winter?

BETH: Well, therapy twice a week...

KAREN: Good.

BETH: And...I'm seeing someone.

KAREN: *(A bit taken aback.)* You are?

BETH: Uh huh.

KAREN: You little devil. Since when?

BETH: Since around Christmas.

KAREN: Really. And how's it going?

BETH: Actually, it's going wonderfully.

KAREN: Well, isn't that great!

BETH: It is. He's a wonderful man.

KAREN: What's his name?

BETH: David.

KAREN: Uh huh. How'd you meet him?

BETH: Actually, I met him years ago, like ten years ago or something.

KAREN: Oh, yeah?

BETH: He and Tom used to work together.

KAREN: No kidding. Another lawyer.

BETH: Yeah, right.

KAREN: Oh, well, you can't have everything.

BETH: Right. Anyway, he just happened to call a few months ago, for Tom...

KAREN: Uh huh.

BETH: *(Continuous.)* ...and then I filled him in on the whole story...

KAREN: Uh huh.

BETH: *(Continuous.)* And it turned out *he* was in the process of separating...

KAREN: Uh huh.

BETH: *(Continuous.)* So we met for a drink and, *you know,* it turned out we had a lot in common...

KAREN: Well, isn't it great that you're dating again!

BETH: Yeah.

KAREN: It certainly seems to agree with you.

BETH: Oh, it's been...

KAREN: I think it's great you're getting out and meeting other men. The hell with Tom. It's great to get your feet wet. I'm proud of you.

BETH: Well, actually, it's a bit more serious than that.

KAREN: What do you mean? *(A beat; she realizes.)* You're sleeping together? *(Beth nods.)*

Already? You're kidding.

BETH: *(Shakes her head, then, beaming.)* It's fantastic.

KAREN: Beth...

BETH: I'm sorry. I'm giddy. It's been so exciting. Stealing away when we can...When I was seventeen I had to tiptoe around my parents, now I'm tiptoeing around my kids.

KAREN: Gee, don't you think you should've waited a little bit? I mean, you're still feeling the fallout from Tom...

BETH: Oh, Karen...

KAREN: Don't you think you could've benefitted from being alone for a while? You haven't been alone in years.

BETH: I've *always* been alone; I spent my *marriage* alone.

KAREN: But to get *involved* with someone, right away?

BETH: I'm in love with him.

KAREN: What?

BETH: I'm in love with him. I am. Isn't this silly? This is like high school: I'm blushing.

KAREN: How could you be in love with him?

BETH: I *am*.

KAREN: *(Continuous.)* You've only just started seeing him.

BETH: Well, I *did* know him years ago.

KAREN: Through Tom.

BETH: Right.

KAREN: But that's different.

BETH: We went out with him and his wife a few times.

KAREN: A few times?!

BETH: I mean, it's not like he's a stranger. The preliminaries were out of the way.

KAREN: Okay.

BETH: There's a history there. There was already a kind of shorthand.

KAREN: But still: It's only been a matter of weeks...

BETH: Three-and-a-half months, practically.

KAREN: How could you be in love with him?

BETH: Why not? I fell in love with *Tom* that first weekend at the Vineyard.

KAREN: Yeah, and look where *that* got you. Sorry. *(A beat.)* I just think you
   have to be careful.

BETH: Karen…

KAREN: *(Continuous.)* You're very vulnerable right now.

BETH: Oh, please…

KAREN: I don't want you to get hurt. This is the rebound phenomenon: He's
   using you as a transitional object, or you're using him, or both.

BETH: *(Over "or both.")* It's not like that. I'm in love with him.

KAREN: How do you *know?*

BETH: I know. I'm gonna marry him. *(A tense pause.)* I shouldn't've told you.

KAREN: Of course you should have told me. I'm just concerned that…

BETH: *(Over "concerned that…")* David is not Tom. He's not. They're very different men. David has none of Tom's edge; Tom is dark and edgy, David
   is not, he's very…smooth, very steady. There's no hidden agenda with
   him. What you see is what you get. You know? He *talks* to me; he tells
   me what he's thinking. He lets me in.
   (A beat.)
   So much of my marriage to Tom was this dark little tango, this adagio
   dance. I don't want that anymore. I don't deserve that.

KAREN: *(Nods, then.)* I wish you well.

BETH: Thanks. *(Pause.)* He's great with the kids. You should see him with
   them. They're crazy about him. Particularly Sammy. He's all over him.
   Things were so gloomy, after Tom left, you have no idea…

KAREN: I know.

BETH: I never thought my kids would laugh again, I mean it, it was that grim.

KAREN: I'm sure.
   (Recognizing Karen's disapproving tone, Beth puts down her fork.)

BETH: Look, why do I even bother?

KAREN: What?

BETH: You think I'm crazy.

KAREN: I never said that…

BETH: I know what I'm doing, Karen. This is the man I was meant to be with.
   I really believe that. I had to survive Tom so I could end up with David.
   It was my fate.

KAREN: That may be, but, still, I wish you'd give it more time.

BETH: And let this moment pass? No way. I don't *want* to let this moment pass.

KAREN: Beth, I'm only…

BETH: *(Continuous.)* This is my opportunity for a *real* marriage, a *real* partnership. But you don't *want* me to have that, do you.

KAREN: *(Over "...do you.")* What an outrageous thing to say! Of course I do!

BETH: *(Over "Of course I do!")* I'm finally feeling whole, finally feeling like I'm on the right track, for the first time in my life, and what do you do? You undermine me! That's what you're doing!

KAREN: *(Over "That's what you're doing!")* I am not undermining you, I'm only thinking of what's best for *you.*

BETH: Oh; I see.

KAREN: Try being alone for a while. That's all I'm suggesting. Get to know yourself better.

BETH: Be alone? I should be alone? That's easy for *you* to say: You have *Gabe,* you have this *life...*

KAREN: Beth...

BETH: You know what *I* think? I think you *love* it when I'm a mess.

KAREN: What?!

BETH: You do. You love it when I'm all-over-the-place, which, let's face it, I'm very good at. I finally find someone who's like a, like an *anchor* and you don't want to hear about it!

KAREN: That is not true.

BETH: You *need* to think of me as a mess. It's the function I serve in your life: Poor Beth. If you ever have any doubts about your life, just take a look at *me:* Guaranteed to make you feel good about yourself...

KAREN: That really isn't fair.

BETH: Hey, it's just as much *my* doing as it is *yours;* I played the part: I was The Mess, The Ditz, The Comic Relief. You got to be Miss Perfect: Everything just right. Just the right wine, just the right spice; just the right husband, just the right kids. How was I supposed to compete with *that?*

KAREN: Nobody was asking you to compete with anything.

(A beat. Beth takes Karen's hand.)

BETH: We can't all *be* like you, Karen. God knows I've tried. No matter how much I stir, the soup still sticks to the pot, you know?

KAREN: Gee, I'm sorry you feel this way. I had no idea...

BETH: Karen...

(Karen slips her hand away. A long, awkward silence. Beth attempts light conversation.)

David's teaching me how to rollerblade.

KAREN: Oh, yeah?

BETH: I'm getting pretty good at it, too. We'll play hooky some afternoons and he'll take me out to, *you* know, along the canal?

KAREN: Do you wear kneepads and a helmet and everything?

BETH: Yes.

KAREN: 'Cause you could really hurt yourself on those things.

BETH: It's fun. You should try it. We'll give you and Gabe a lesson.

KAREN: Yeah, I can just see Gabe...

(They eat in silence.)

BETH: How *are* you and Gabe?

KAREN: We're good. We're fine.

(Beth nods. The men's scene resumes.)

TOM: *(Leaning forward.)* Gabe, this has been such an amazing adventure for me, you have no idea. I'm living the kind of sex life I never thought possible for someone like me. It's like I'm living a letter to *Penthouse.*

GABE: Gee, I can't wait to meet her.

TOM: The things she's got me *doing,* Gabe...I can't believe it myself! Nancy'll do anything. Anything. She is fearless. *I'm* the novice here. Man, the things she's shown me...

GABE: Lucky you.

TOM: Nancy has more imagination, more daring, more *wisdom* at twenty-six, than I'll ever have as long as I live. I mean, it just goes to show you how age is totally irrelevant. I'm a boy-toy at forty-three! I don't know what women have been complaining about all these years: It's *great* being the sex object. With *Beth,* sex was always up to me. It was never about her *want*ing me, it was never about *desire,* it was all about obligation. And then once the kids came...Well, *you* know how that is.

GABE: Uh huh.

TOM: Sex became one more thing on my list of things to do. You know? With Nancy, it's like sex is new again. It's like being eighteen with twenty-five years' sexual experience. We are *totally* in sync. She just has to stroke my fingers and I get hard, or give me a look, or laugh a certain way.

GABE: Do you two ever...*talk?*

TOM: Oh, yeah. Are you kidding? We talk all the time. Remember what that's like in the beginning of a relationship? All that talk, all that sex, all that laughter? Beth wouldn't let me talk. Did you ever notice that about her? *(Gabe shakes his head.)*
She'd cut me off all the time, like what I had to say wasn't important, or

like she was worried I might embarrass her or something. Nancy really hears me. She *hears* me.

GABE: Uh huh.

TOM: She saved my life, Gabe. She really did; she breathed life back into me.

GABE: *(Nods, then.)* Good. That's great.

(The women exit. Gabe sips his drink. Tom looks at him.)

What.

TOM: What are you thinking?

GABE: What do you mean?

TOM: Come on, Gabe, I *know* you, I know that *look*...

GABE: What. I'm just listening. You don't want me to say anything, right?

TOM: Oh, Christ...

GABE: No, isn't that what you told me, Tommy?

TOM: Come on...

GABE: *(Continuous.)* I'm supposed to nod and be supportive and keep my mouth shut.

TOM: *(Over "my mouth shut.")* I said that to you...when I was still very raw...

GABE: Oh. And you're not so raw anymore? Well, what are the rules, then? You've gotta fill me in here, pal, I've gotta know the rules so I don't step out of bounds.

TOM: Gabe...

GABE: Okay, you want to know what I'm thinking? I'm thinking: I hear you *talk*ing, Tom, I hear these *words* coming out, and you sound like a fucking *moonie* to me, Tom, you really do...

TOM: *(Over "...you really do...")* I'm trying to tell you...I was dying, Gabe! I was literally dying. You don't understand that, do you? I was losing the will to live, isn't that dying? The life I was leading had no relationship to who I was or what I wanted. Everything was about the kids! It's clear where *I* ranked in the scheme of things. I was out of town, every week, breaking my ass to race home, for what? So I could be a glorified gopher for my kids? She has them so over-scheduled, it's ridiculous. Ballet lessons, Suzuki...

GABE: But, Tom, that's...

TOM: *(Continuous.)* The constant logistics of "You pick up Sam and take him to lollypop tennis, I'll take Laurie to hockey practice..."

GABE: I know.

TOM: *(Continuous.)* This is what we'd talk about. No, really. This would pass for conversation in our house.

GABE: I know.

TOM: The dog finished me off. Oh, man, that dog. Sarge. It wasn't enough that we had two cats and fish and a guinea pig, no, Beth felt the kids *had* to have a dog because *she* had a dog. I'd spent my entire adult life cleaning up one form of shit or another, now I was on to *dog* shit. I should've gone into waste management. Just when Sam was out of diapers and I thought there'd be one less creature to clean up after...It never ends.

GABE: We've all made sacrifices to our kids. It's the price you pay for having a family.

TOM: How do you keep love alive when you're shovelling shit all day long? Let's face it, you either have a talent for it, or you don't.

GABE: A talent for what?

TOM: The whole domestic thing. You and Karen are amazing, are you kidding?

GABE: We don't have a talent for it, Tom, we just do it! It's part of the job description.

TOM: Yeah, but you have to *want* to do it. That's the thing: I never really wanted it. What was I thinking? It was completely against my nature. Settling down, having kids: It was just one more thing I did because it was expected of me, not because I had any real interest in it. Like law. I always felt, I don't know, *inauthentic* living this life.

GABE: What, you were a party boy trapped in the body of a family man? Tommy, I could swear I actually saw you *enjoy*ing yourself on a number of occasions in the last decade or so.

TOM: Well, sure. But, honestly, most of the time I was just being a good sport.

GABE: A good sport?!

TOM: You know what I mean...

GABE: *(Continuous.)* Wait a minute. You were faking it?! You mean to tell me that all those years—all those *years,* Tom!—the four of us together, raising our *kids* together, playing and traveling and hanging out...All the good times we had, the dinners, the vacations, the hours of videotape, you were just being a good sport?

TOM: No...

GABE: Then what, Tom, I don't get it. I was there, as well as you. This *misery* you describe, the agony. Gee, I thought we were all just living our lives, you know? Sharing our humdrum little existences. I *thought* you were there, wholeheartedly there. And now you're saying you had an eye on the clock and a foot out the door?!

TOM: You've got to stop taking this so personally.

GABE: How would *you* take it? You say you were wasting your life, that's what you've said.

TOM: *(Over "…that's what you've said.")* I don't mean you and Karen. I don't mean *you,* I'd never mean *you;* you're my best friend, I've got to be able to say this stuff to you. I'm talking about my marriage.

GABE: But it's not that simple, Tom. We were there. Karen and Danny and Isaac and I, we were all there, we were all a big part of that terrible life you had to get the hell away from—Isaac's totally freaked out by this, by the way—So when you repudiate your entire adult life…

TOM: That's not what I've done…

GABE: That's essentially what you've done. And I can understand how you might find it necessary to do that. It must be strangely *exhilarating* blowing everything to bits.

TOM: Gabe…

GABE: I mean it. You spend all of your adult life building something that's precarious in even the best of circumstances and you succeed, or at least you make it *look* like you've succeeded, your *friends* think you have, you had *us* fooled, and then, one day, you blow it all up! It's like, I watch Danny and Isaac sometimes, dump all their toys on the floor, Legos and blocks and train tracks, and build these elaborate cities together. They'll spend hours at it, they'll plan and collaborate, and squabble and negotiate, but they'll do it. And then what do they do? They wreck it! No pause to revel in what they accomplished, no sigh of satisfaction, no, they just launch into a full-throttle attack, bombs bursting, and gleefully tear the whole damn thing apart.

(Silence.)

TOM: *(Quietly.)* Well…

GABE: It all goes by so fast, Tom, I know. The hair goes, and the waist. And the stamina; the capacity for staying up late, to read or watch a movie, never mind sex. Want to hear a shocker? Karen is pre-menopausal. That's right: my sweetheart, my lover, that sweet girl with whom I lolled around on endless Sundays, is getting hot flashes. It doesn't seem possible. *(A beat.)* We spend our youth unconscious, feeling immortal, then we marry and have kids and awaken with a shock to mortality, theirs, ours, that's all we see, we worry about them, *their* safety, our *own,* air bags, plane crashes, pederasts, and spend our middle years wanting back the dreamy, carefree part, the part we fucked and pissed away; now we want that back, 'cause now we know how fleeting it all is, now we know, and it just doesn't seem fair that so much is gone when there's really so little left. So, some of us, try to regain unconsciousness. Some of us blow up our homes… And others of us…take up piano; I'm taking piano.

(Pause.)

TOM: I just want you to be my friend. That's all. I want you to be happy for me. Happy I turned my life around.

GABE: Sure, Tom. I'm happy for you.

TOM: *(Quietly.)* No you're not.

GABE: I'm not even sure it's happiness you want. Contentment suggests to me a kind of calm. And that, to you, apparently, is the *last* thing you want. You want to boogie. You want *intensity.*

TOM: What's wrong with wanting intensity?

GABE: Nothing. Hey, more power to you. If you can maintain things at that pitch…*(A beat.)* I must sound like a real bore to you, huh, Tommy?

TOM: No…

GABE: I'm really just a simple guy. I love my wife, I love my kids, I like what I do. I write about food. Really dullsville, huh? Karen and I, we love our boys, and we enjoy our garden, and taking our little trips, and we always love coming home to our little house.

TOM: Whatever works for you.

GABE: Thank you. *(A beat.)* I cling to Karen; I cling to her. Imagining a life without her doesn't excite me, it just makes me anxious. Maybe I don't get it every night, but hey, who wants it every night? I mean, besides you?

TOM: You're making *fun* of me because sex is still important to me?

GABE: I'm with you, pal, I just wonder how long you expect to maintain all that red-hot intensity. Intensity dies down eventually, you know, and becomes…something else, something ordinary. What happens then, you walk out and reinvent yourself all over again? What happens when your girlfriend decides she wants to have kids?

TOM: She won't.

GABE: How do you know?

TOM: Because I know she doesn't; we've talked about it.

GABE: But she's very young; twenty-six, right?

TOM: That's not that young.

GABE: Tom, twenty-six is very young.

TOM: But I told you: she's incredibly mature for her age.

GABE: Still, there's plenty of time for her to change her mind.

TOM: She's not going to. Believe me, she's the first to admit, she likes kids well enough, but she has very little interest in *having* them...

GABE: How can you be so sure?

TOM: Because I know her. And she knows herself.

GABE: Who knows themself at twenty-six?

TOM: *She* does.

GABE: Uh huh. *(Backing off.)* Okay.

TOM: You know, you can be so damn smug sometimes.

GABE: What?

TOM: You take this really superior tone, like you're above it all...

GABE: I do not.

TOM: You're not immune to all this, you know. Even you and Karen—*(Stops himself.)*

GABE: What.

TOM: Never mind.

GABE: *What.*

TOM: Come on, Gabe, I've heard you complain.

GABE: Well, sure, we all *complain,* Tom. That's what married friends do: We joke about sex and bellyache about our wives and kids, but that doesn't mean we're about to *leave* them. Marriages all go through a kind of baseline wretchedness from time to time, but we do what we can to ride those patches out.

TOM: Don't you ever just want to chuck it all?

GABE: Yeah. Sure. Of course I do.

TOM: Okay.

GABE: But the feeling passes. The key to civilization, I think, is *fighting* the impulse to chuck it all. Where would we be with everybody's ids running rampant?

TOM: You really see it like that?

GABE: I really do.

TOM: Boy, Karen really has you well-trained, doesn't she.

GABE: That's what *I* believe; Karen has nothing to do with it.

TOM: Look, all I'm saying is, don't do what *I* did. Don't shut your eyes. I was so steeped in denial and resignation. I know the signs, believe me. I'd hate for you to wake up at fifty and...

GABE: Why are you doing this? Huh? Why?

TOM: I'm your friend.

(Gabe nods. Pause.)

GABE: *We* had a deal, you know, not a marriage but something like it.

TOM: Yeah?

GABE: *(Nods, then.)* We were supposed to get old and fat together, the four of us, and watch each other's kids grow up and cry together at their weddings…

TOM: It's not like I'm *dead,* you know…

GABE: *(Looks at him, a beat.)* I guess I mean, I thought we were in this together. For life.

TOM: Isn't that just another way of saying misery loves company?

    (Gabe still looks at him. A beat.)

    I'm kidding.

    (Gabe's expression doesn't change.)

    Hey, I'll still be there. But it won't be with Beth.

    (Gabe nods, but he doesn't agree that Tom will be there. Tom misreads his sad look.)

    Don't feel sorry for me.

GABE: I'm not.

TOM: I'm a survivor. Remember that: I escaped.

    (Silence.)

    How's she doing?

GABE: Beth?

    (Tom nods.)

    Fine, I think. We actually haven't seen that much of her lately. Karen was supposed to have lunch with her today.

TOM: Oh, yeah? You meet David yet?

GABE: David?

TOM: *You* know, the guy she's seeing.

    (This is news to Gabe but he tries not to show his surprise.)

GABE: No, we, uh…

TOM: He's actually a very nice guy; I don't hold anything against him. You've got to hand it to him, hanging in there all these years, finally getting what he wanted.

GABE: What do you mean?

TOM: He really *fell* for Beth, you know, he was really in love with her. I'm sure she told you all about it.

GABE: *(Lying.)* Uh huh.

TOM: That's what's so weird. We could've broken up ten years ago, when they

had their *thing*. Maybe we should've. And now they're back together. Boy…
(Finishes his wine. Looks at the time.)
Well. I'd better go.

GABE: What about your girlfriend?

TOM: If she was coming, she said she'd be here by three at the latest. So I guess she must've chickened out.

GABE: Chickened out?

TOM: She was really intimidated about meeting you. She knows how important you are to me. *(A beat.)* I was actually a little nervous about this myself.

GABE: Why?

TOM: *You* know. It's been a while. Things have changed. *(A beat.)* Listen, I'll call you. Hey, how about, I'm seeing the kids next weekend, what if I…

GABE: Actually, we're gonna be away next weekend.

TOM: Oh.

GABE: My sister's in New Hampshire. We said we'd…

TOM: Uh huh. Well, next time, then.

GABE: Sure.

TOM: I really want you to meet Nancy. I'm telling you, you're gonna love her. We'll all go out to dinner. The four of us.
(Gabe nods and smiles.)
Well…She's probably waiting for me at the museum.
(Tom takes out his wallet.)

GABE: No, no, this is on me.

TOM: You sure?

GABE: Put it away.

TOM: Thanks. I'll get the next one.

GABE: That's right; the next one.

TOM: When's your train? I'll walk out with you.

GABE: No, I thought I'd stay for a minute. You know, gird myself for the ride home.

TOM: Well…
(Tom opens his arms to his friend; Gabe hugs him for the last time.)

GABE: Goodbye, Tom.

TOM: I feel so badly, we didn't get a chance to talk about *you*.

GABE: That's okay; nothing much to report. Same old. *You* know. So, take care.

TOM: You, too. I'll call you.

(Gabe nods. Tom starts to go.)

Say hi to Karen if you think she'd be glad to hear from me. I'll leave that up to you. And send my love to the boys. Tell Isaac everything's gonna be okay.

GABE: *(Nods, then.)* Bye.

(Tom waves and goes. Gabe's smile fades as he watches him walk away. He smiles and waves again; Tom has looked back one last time. Gabe stands there until he can no longer see him. He sits back down and ruminates for a moment. He finishes his drink. Then, he indicates to the unseen waiter that he'd like the check. Lights fade. End of scene.)

SCENE THREE

Lights up: Later that night. Karen and Gabe's bedroom. Neat, tasteful, comfortable, warm, inviting (in sharp contast to Tom and Beth's messy room); a beautifully-made bed with mounds of attractive pillows, neat piles of books, matching lamps. Gabe, in undershirt and boxers, begins to stack pillows.

KAREN: *(Off.)* Are you sure that's what he meant?

GABE: "When they had their thing." What else could that mean?

(Karen comes in from the bathroom wearing a nightgown. Together, they methodically strip covers, remove sheets and pillow cases, get fresh linens from a blanket chest and remake their bed before finally getting into it.)

KAREN: Maybe he was just trying to impugn Beth's character.

GABE: *(Over "...character.")* No no, there was nothing malicious about it. He was totally matter-of-fact, he alluded to it casually, *as if I already knew.* He assumed Beth had already told us herself.

KAREN: Huh. *(A beat.)* Ten years ago?

GABE: That's what he said.

KAREN: But that wasn't very long after they got married.

GABE: That's right.

KAREN: We saw them practically every weekend in those days, when would she have had time to have an affair?

GABE: I don't know, during the week?

KAREN: Beth and I talked constantly. That was such a happy time. For all of us.

GABE: I know.

KAREN: I didn't have a *clue.* Did you?

GABE: Not at all. But what do *I* know?

KAREN: There was nothing strange going on, was there? Do you remember any funniness?

GABE: No...

KAREN: Why didn't she ever tell me? She could've told me this afternoon.

GABE: She obviously felt she couldn't. She's spent all these months portraying herself as the wronged woman, she couldn't drop a bombshell like that. Her credibility would've been shot to hell.

KAREN: I'm one of her closest friends. Who would she have confided in if not me?

GABE: People don't usually go around talking about their affairs, do they?, otherwise they wouldn't be affairs.

KAREN: God, what does this say about our friendship? What were all these years *about?*

(Gabe shakes his head. They make the bed in silence.)

I *thought* it seemed a little too convenient, her white knight surfacing all of a sudden.

GABE: This changes everything, don't you think?

KAREN: I don't know...

GABE: Doesn't it? Doesn't it change your perspective on the whole thing?

KAREN: Maybe. Somewhat.

GABE: Only somewhat? She transgressed first.

KAREN: Yeah, but she stayed with the marriage. That's significant. He's shown no such integrity.

GABE: I don't know. How honorable is it to perpetuate a deception?

KAREN: It's a white lie.

GABE: That's a big white lie...

KAREN: I don't blame her for it.

GABE: You don't?

KAREN: No, the thing is, she stuck it out and tried to make it work.

GABE: So did he. He forgave her. He didn't have to.

KAREN: I still think he's behaved unconscionably badly.

GABE: Well, that's beside the point now, isn't it? It's totally irrelevant.

(They look at one another. Silence.)

KAREN: So what did you *say* when he let it slip?

GABE: Nothing.

KAREN: Nothing?!

GABE: I just let it roll right by, I didn't want it to look like he'd slipped *any*thing.

KAREN: God, Gabe, there you go playing dumb again!

GABE: Why, what would you have done?

KAREN: I would've said, "Wait a minute, back up: *What* thing ten years ago?"

GABE: You know what it was? Questioning it would have invited a whole new level of involvement and I just didn't have it in me.

KAREN: Why?

GABE: I sat there today, listening to him go on about his new life, and all this great sex, and how wonderful everything is, and, I don't know, I began to feel so sad.

KAREN: *(Sensitively.)* Oh, really, sweetie?

GABE: Tom and I have been friends for twenty-five years. We went through so many phases of our lives together, I took for granted that he'd always be there, that I'd always *want* him there. And today, I felt so detached from him...

KAREN: Really?

GABE: *(Continuous.)* I could feel myself pulling back, I could see him receding from view, getting smaller and smaller and smaller. And I realized...I don't love him anymore.

KAREN: Oh, honey.

GABE: I don't. Too much was said. I said too much, I learned too much...

KAREN: How did you leave it?

GABE: Oh, *you* know: The obligatory "we have to get together." He wants us to meet what'shername. Nancy.

KAREN: Oh, God, really?

GABE: Don't worry, it'll never happen.

KAREN: You really think so?

(He nods. Pause.)

GABE: I ordered a pork loin for dinner tomorrow night; remind me to pick it up in the morning.

(Karen nods. Pause.)

KAREN: When all this happened, I felt pretty certain that, in the end, at the very least, you'd still be friends with Tom and I'd still be friends with Beth. And now...

GABE: I know. *(Pause.)* He *looks* good...

KAREN: So does she. She's looking pretty again.

GABE: Must be all that incredible sex.

KAREN: Apparently.

(They get into bed. Each props up pillows and picks up books to read.)

GABE: You know?: Tom and Beth, and Beth and Tom? After all these months…Their breaking up and their reconstituting with new and improved mates, and the sturm and drang and revelations…One of these days normal life is gonna resume, you know, it *has* to, and then what? What'll be left once the smoke clears?

(She shakes her head. They read in silence. Karen is distracted, she puts down her book.)

KAREN: I had a dream the other night.

GABE: Oh, yeah?

KAREN: We were here, making love, and it was so simple and effortless, it was delicious. The way it used to be.

GABE: It still is.

KAREN: Sometimes; when it is.

GABE: What is that supposed to mean?

KAREN: Nothing, Gabe, you're missing my point.

GABE: I'm sorry. Go on.

(She shakes her head.)

Please. Tell me about your dream.

KAREN: *(A beat.)* Remember how natural and uncomplicated it used to be?

(He nods.)

All the time, every time?

GABE: Uh huh.

KAREN: We'd just find ourselves in each other's arms. We were there. We needed no bridges. That's all I'm saying. It was like that in the dream. We were here, in the dark, and it was wonderful, and then I realized, I sensed, in the dream, we weren't alone.

GABE: What do you mean?

KAREN: There were other people in bed with us.

GABE: Uh-oh, our parents.

KAREN: No no, not our parents. It was another couple, though, and they were sitting up in bed, alongside us, watching us, analyzing us, whispering in this on-going commentary, bickering with each other.

GABE: Well, that's easy: Tom and Beth.

KAREN: No, not Tom and Beth.

GABE: No?

KAREN: They were us.

GABE: What do you mean?

KAREN: *Both* couples were us. Two versions of ourselves, young and middle-aged, in the same bed at the same time.

GABE: Huh.

(Pause.)

KAREN: I don't know, it was an interesting dream.

GABE: Uh huh. It was.

(Annoyed, she returns to her book. Pause.)

KAREN: Is that all you have to say?

GABE: Uh…

KAREN: Any thoughts?

GABE: Well, uh…

KAREN: Anything?

GABE: I really don't know *what* to say.

KAREN: Great. Fine.

GABE: No! I mean, you're right, it is an interesting dichotomy. It is.

KAREN: *(Over "It is.")* Never mind.

GABE: Karen…

KAREN: Good night.

(She turns out her lamp, turns on her side.)

GABE: Hey. Honey…Honey, come on…

(Pause. She sits up again.)

KAREN: How come the minute the conversation turns to us you're struck mute?

GABE: Uh…

KAREN: Huh, Gabe?

GABE: I don't know…

KAREN: Why is that?

(He shrugs, shakes his head.)

We can sit here and go on and on about everyone we know and all the problems of the world and the minute I…You know?, for a guy who's pretty damn articulate about a number of things…Do you ever wonder about it, Gabe, do you ever wonder why that is?

GABE: Uh, yeah, sometimes…

KAREN: And?

(He shrugs.)

I tell you, I *confide* in you this dream I had…

GABE: Uh huh.

KAREN: *(Continuous.)* This revealing dream I had about us and you have nothing to say?

GABE: Well, sure.

KAREN: What. Speak.

GABE: *(A beat.)* It's...It obviously...I think it's about what happens to couples.

KAREN: What.

GABE: I think...it's the inevitable...evolution.

KAREN: Inevitable?

GABE: *(Considers this.)* Yes. I think it is.

KAREN: And what is it?

GABE: What.

KAREN: The evolution. Define it.

GABE: You want me to...

KAREN: Yes. Talk to me, Gabe. *Goddamn it, you have got to talk to me.*

GABE: Okay. *(A beat.)* It's...It's what happens when...when practical matters begin to outweigh...abandon. You know?

KAREN: Abandon?

GABE: Uh huh.

KAREN: Is that it? *(Gabe nods.)* Do they have to?

GABE: I think so. *(A beat.)* I *think* so.

KAREN: Why?

GABE: *(Shrugs.)* It's...I think it's...*You* know: Having kids...having to pay the mortgage...making the deadline...marinating the snapper...

KAREN: *(Tears in her eyes.)* Don't you ever miss me, Gabe?

GABE: *(Surprised by her sudden emotion.)* What?

KAREN: Don't you ever miss me?

GABE: Oh, God, honey, yes. Yes. *(He holds her. Softly.)* Sure I miss you. I miss you a lot.

KAREN: *(Almost childlike.)* How do we not get lost?

(Gabe shakes his head. He continues to hold her. He kisses her. They hold onto each other; they're both frightened. Silence. Soon he begins to play their intimate game from long ago.)

GABE: Uh oh.

KAREN: What.

GABE: You know what time it is?

KAREN: What.

GABE: It's that time again.

KAREN: *(Catching on.)* Oh, no...

GABE: Yup, I'm afraid so…

KAREN: Not tonight, Gabe, really…

GABE: It's time for me to scare you.

KAREN: Oh, no, Gabe, please don't scare me…

GABE: Sorry, kid, that's just the way it is…

KAREN: Please please don't?

GABE: It can happen any time now…

KAREN: Please, Gabe?

GABE: Any second.

KAREN: No…

GABE: Sorry, kid…

KAREN: No…Please…

GABE: A man's got to do what a man's got to do. *(A beat. Softly.)* Boo!
   (Startled, she gasps. They hold one another. Lights fade.)

END OF PLAY

Mr. Bundy
by Jane Martin

BIOGRAPHY

Jane Martin's *Jack and Jill* premiered in the 1996 Humana Festival of New American Plays, has been produced around the country, and won the 1997 American Theatre Critics Association award for Best New Play. Ms. Martin, a Kentuckian, first came to national attention for *Talking With*, a collection of monologues that premiered at Actors Theatre in 1981. Since its New York premiere at Manhattan Theatre Club in 1982, *Talking With* has been performed around the world, winning the Best Foreign Play of the Year award in Germany from *Theater Heute* magazine. Her other work includes *Middle-Aged White Guys* (1995 Humana Festival), *Cementville* (1991 Humana Festival), *Summer* (1984 Shorts Festival) and *Vital Signs* (1990 Humana Festival). Ms. Martin's *Keely and Du*, which premiered in the 1993 Humana Festival, was nominated for the Pulitzer Prize in drama and won the American Theatre Critics Association Award for Best New Play in 1994. Most of her work appears in a volume titled *Jane Martin: Collected Works 1980–1995*, published by Smith and Kraus.

HUMANA FESTIVAL PRODUCTION

Mr. Bundy premiered at the Humana Festival of New American Plays in March 1998. It was directed by Jon Jory with the following cast:

Cassidy Ferreby .... Margaret Streeter
Robert Ferreby .... Mark Schulte
Catherine Ferreby .... Stephanie Zimbalist
Jimmy Ray Bosun .... Norman Maxwell
Mr. Bundy .... William Cain
Tianna Bosun .... Peggity Price
Mrs. McGuigan .... Adale O'Brien

and the following production staff:

Scenic Designer .... Paul Owen
Costume Designer .... Nanzi Adzima
Lighting Designer .... Amy Appleyard
Sound Designer .... Martin R. Desjardins
Properties Designer .... Ron Riall
Fight Director .... Steve Rankin
Production Stage Manager .... Debra Acquavella
Assistant Stage Manager .... Heather Fields
Dramaturgs .... Michael Bigelow Dixon, Val Smith & Megan Shultz
Casting .... Laura Richin Casting

CHARACTERS

CATHERINE FERREBY: A woman of thirty-six. Well educated. A child psychologist.

ROBERT FERREBY: Her husband. Age forty. Works in an advertising agency. Volunteers weekends for AA.

CASSIDY FERREBY: Their daughter. Eight or nine years old.

MR. BUNDY: Their next-door neighbor. A man in his mid-to-late 60s. A retired teacher.

JIMMY RAY BOSUN: A truck driver in his mid forties.

TIANNA BOSUN: His wife. A woman in her early forties. A southerner.

MRS. MCGUIGAN: A neighbor. Sixty years old. She is raising her grandson whose parents passed away.

TIME & PLACE

Various locations in the middle of the country. The time is the present.

AUTHOR'S NOTE

The play is performed without an intermission.

Margaret Streeter and William Cain
in *Mr. Bundy* by Jane Martin

22nd Annual Humana Festival of New American Plays
Actors Theatre of Louisville, 1998
photo by Richard Trigg

Mr. Bundy

The play takes place on an empty stage surrounded, if possible, by a cyclorama. Into this space emblematic pieces of furniture are brought for each location. There are no walls and no complete rooms, though there might be a use for a free-standing rolling door. There is no attempt to hide the moving on and moving off of furniture during the monologues that bridge the scenes. Props are mimed except for a select few, central to the narrative. We begin with a chair, a television set and a bottle of cream soda beside the chair. The rolling door defines the front door. Catherine, a woman in her mid-to-late thirties, is discovered standing, in a freeze, holding the handle of her luggage-cart suitcase. Robert, her husband, a little older, stands several feet away looking at her. Cassidy, eight years old, is jumping rope in front of her parents' tableau.

CASSIDY: Don't listen to him sing;
   don't heed his call.
   It's the oogey-boogey monster
   over the wall.
   Don't throw him pennies,
   or feed him sweets,
   'cause you're just what
   the oogey-boogey eats.
   Don't open the cupboard
   if you need a cup,
   'cause the oogey-boogey's in there,
   and he'll eat you up!

(Cassie emphasizes the last line with a double or crossover jump. Then she runs off as the light emphasizes her parents and they break out of their tableau.)

ROBERT: *(After a pause.)* Oh boy.
CATHERINE: Hi.

ROBERT: Hello, Catherine. *(A pause.)* Can I hug you?

CATHERINE: Not yet, okay?

ROBERT: *(Nods.)* I am really, really glad. I am...really glad.

CATHERINE: Cassie's great. Wait'll you see her haircut. *(He smiles and nods. A pause. He walks over and embraces her. She stands with her hands at her sides. Finally she embraces him. They hold each other. They let go. She reaches up and takes him by the ears.)* Robert, you are such a jerk.

ROBERT: I know.

CATHERINE: *(Punches him in the chest.)* Don't be a jerk anymore.

ROBERT: I won't.

CATHERINE: *(Warningly.)* I don't forgive you. *(He nods.)* But I brought you some Switzers licorice. *(He takes it ruefully.)* And your new glasses are okay. *(Awkwardness sets in.)* I want to, uh...want to get this stuff put away before, uh, I pick up Cassidy at school.

(She moves past him with the suitcase. He stands for a moment and then speaks to us. She exits.)

ROBERT: What's forgivable and what's not and what's the difference? I was a jerk. "The quality of mercy is..." something, something. I don't even know if you can earn it? Maybe it just happens...like spontaneous combustion.

(He goes and sits down. The lights change. He is watching television. There is a bottle of cream soda by his chair. A doorbell rings.)

ROBERT: *(Surprised.)* Who is it?

JIMMY RAY: *(Offstage.)* Mr. Ferreby?

ROBERT: Who is it, please?

JIMMY RAY: You don't know me, Mr. Ferreby. I'm Jimmy Ray Bosun.

ROBERT: What is it you want?

JIMMY RAY: Got some info for you.

ROBERT: Who are you?

JIMMY RAY: It's about your little girl.

ROBERT: My little girl?

JIMMY RAY: Yeah.

ROBERT: Look, it's after nine at night. I'm in the book. Call me in the morning.

JIMMY RAY: I drive truck, buddy. I'll be three states away in the morning.

ROBERT: *(A pause. He opens the door.)* All right, state your business.

JIMMY RAY: *(Indicating it would be best if he came in.)* You got a convicted child molester livin' next door, pal. *(A moment.)* You want the info?

ROBERT: *(A moment.)* All right, come in.

JIMMY RAY: Nice place. I used to renovate.

ROBERT: So what's the deal, Mr....

JIMMY RAY: Bosun. You got a beer or somethin'? I been hitting it pretty hard.

ROBERT: No, I don't have a...

JIMMY RAY: What's that by your chair?

ROBERT: Cream soda. What is it you have to tell me?

JIMMY RAY: You got an abuser next door.

ROBERT: How do you know that?

JIMMY RAY: Well, I make it my business to know it. Lemme give you a card. *(Gets out wallet, hands him a card.)* You'll be glad I came down here, tell you that.

ROBERT: *(Looks at card.)* I thought you drove truck?

JIMMY RAY: Drive truck for my family, Mr. Ferreby. I do this for your family.

ROBERT: "Watch Dog."

JIMMY RAY: Yeah. Guys travelin' the country in the line of their work. Loose knit.

ROBERT: *(Indicating the card.)* The cross.

JIMMY RAY: Yeah. Christian guys.

ROBERT: And?

JIMMY RAY: We're gonna like stand here? *(Robert nods.)* Okay, whatever, so...sex abuser notification...so you should know these guys are on your block, right? Thing is, it varies real wide how effective that is. Some states, California, they get the work out real good, some places, they're real remiss. Buncha states actually draggin' their feet on it, if you can believe that. Okay, sometimes these scumbags move around a lot, hard to keep track on 'em. *(Points at the card Robert holds.)* "Watch Dog," we uh...we try to help out...notification, that falls down a lot.

ROBERT: You track sex abusers?

JIMMY RAY: Track 'em? Yeah, we kind of track 'em. You might say that.

ROBERT: And you're sure, absolutely, there's such a person in this neighborhood?

JIMMY RAY: Yeah, we got verification. We don't go off half-cocked or nothin' like that. He's out there waterin' his lawn, buddy, big as life you want to take a look. *(A moment.)* I saw a bike out front, how old is she?

ROBERT: Eight.

JIMMY RAY: Got three boys. Had a girl too.

ROBERT: What is he accused of?

JIMMY RAY: No sir, he's not accused, been convicted and served time.

ROBERT: For?

JIMMY RAY: Not likin' me too much, huh buddy?

ROBERT: I never said that.

JIMMY RAY: Ol' redneck rig guy. Feel a little out of place in the 'burbs. Folks, they usually figure out I'm here to help. Doesn't end up I'm standing out in the hall beggin' for a beer.

ROBERT: What, exactly, was he convicted of?

JIMMY RAY: Buddy, I think what you'll want to be doin' is get your neighbors in on this. They'd be real pleased you let them know. Best way's you put together a little neighborhood meeting, you know what I mean? We'll get this citizen moved along you catch my drift.

ROBERT: And tell them what for God's sake?

JIMMY RAY: It would be a real favor to me, buddy, if we didn't take the Lord's name in vain while we were talkin' this over.

ROBERT: Listen, I would like you to step back out on the porch, Mr. Bosman.

JIMMY RAY: Bosun.

ROBERT: Mr. Bosun. I'm going to give you my business card here…*(He gets it out.)* And if you have…hard documentation of your charges I would be extremely glad to see it. At which point I would make my own decisions about how to proceed. Thank you very much for your trouble.

JIMMY RAY: Wouldn't want to move too fast, right? Abrogate the scumbag's civil rights, somethin' like that? He was a high school teacher down at St. Alphonsus, Illinois, and what he would do is bring kids home, give 'em ice cream, videos, get 'em to play dress-up, Mr. Ferreby. Dress those boys up in girls' clothes, underwear, put lipstick on 'em, you know, have a little harmless fun such as that. Little later on he got picked up parked on a country road havin' oral sex with a kid and this whole thing, his whole modus operandi, well it came right out. Second offense, matter of fact. Down in New Mexico before that up to his tricks. Did three years, got out, went to movin' around, lo and behold he's out there right next door, big as you please.

ROBERT: But his offenses were with boys?

JIMMY RAY: Dressed 'em up as girls, see? Just a little hard to know which way his pin is bent, if you're on my wavelength here.

ROBERT: And you are suggesting?

JIMMY RAY: What's your line of work, Mr. Ferreby?

ROBERT: Marketing, why?

JIMMY RAY: You an' me, we're two different breed of cats you might say.

ROBERT: Meaning?

JIMMY RAY: Meaning, I'd cut his sorry balls off an' take him around to schools in a cage. Be real educational, but we live in what they call a civilized society. Don't they call it that? So, what you can do, buddy, is get your neighbors goin', your local TV goin', your Christian churches goin', run this guy right on off, 'cause I figure you love your kid, right?

ROBERT: Loving my child isn't the only issue here.

JIMMY RAY: Uh huh. Buddy, I travel the country on behalf of the Lord's innocent children who are given to us to guide and care for, and they are the only issue, my friend, far as I'm concerned. See, your beautiful little girl will not be harmed on my watch, that's not gonna happen, and if you take a good look at me, Mr. Ferreby, you will see that's not gonna happen.

ROBERT: Look...

JIMMY RAY: Now, buddy, I'm gonna send you down the documentation you lookin' for, along with a Watch Dog action sheet tells you one, two, three how to get this problem solved. When the time is right, or you run into a hitch, you give Jimmy Ray a call and we'll bring this to a *satisfactory* conclusion for all concerned. To a satisfactory conclusion is what I'm sayin' here. *(Looks at his watch.)* Gotta get back on the pedal. Like they don't pay me for what don't get delivered, right? Not in this lifetime. Thank you for hangin' with me on this thing. My wife Tianna would say I'm a better person for you not givin' me that beer.

ROBERT: I'm a recovering alcoholic, Mr. Bosun.

JIMMY RAY: Well who the heck isn't, buddy, I don't cast the first stone. *(He slaps Robert on the shoulder.)* God's will be done.

(He exits. Robert stands for a moment then looks at the card Jimmy Ray gave him. Lights change. Jimmy Ray moves downstage. Behind him the furniture is changed to a kitchen table and four chairs, representing the Ferrebys' kitchen. Mr. Bundy, a man in his sixties dressed in gardening clothes, sits drinking coffee. Catherine, Robert's wife, nicely dressed, sits with him as does their daugh-

ter Cassidy. It is a Saturday morning in the fall. They maintain a tableau until the end of Jimmy Ray's monologue.)

JIMMY RAY: Trouble is anymore people don't seem to know the difference between talkin' and doin'. I got a little land, not enough to amount to nothin', keep a few sheep. Guy down the road had this airedale dog he don't restrain. Dog got in with my sheep, you know, chased 'em around, one of 'em died right there like a heart attack. I told him restrain that dog…he's like some retired accountant. Happens another time, bites a couple sheep. I go down there, told him I told him twice that was all I was goin' to tell him. Next time I shot the dog dead, walked down there with the dog in my arms, ring the bell, he opens up, I hand him the dog. Just said, "I believe this is your dog." Dog he's got now, he restrains that dog. My idea is, you got to know when to stop talkin'.

(Light fades on Jimmy Ray. We are now in the Ferreby kitchen with Catherine, Cassidy and Mr. Bundy.)

CATHERINE: *(To Mr. Bundy.)* Coffee? More?

MR. BUNDY: Fine.

CATHERINE: Did you read today about that man who shot into the schoolyard in Kansas? *(He nods.)* Killed three children? Fifth graders. And then he said…he said he had sent them to heaven? As if, really, he had done them a favor? I mean I really think the world is a madhouse, and we're in a completely open area with the inmates. *(Picking up a nearly empty Pepsi can. She calls.)* Cassie!

CASSIDY: *(Off.)* What?

CATHERINE: Cassidy, how many Pepsis is that?

CASSIDY: *(Off.)* One.

CATHERINE: You didn't have one earlier?

CASSIDY: No.

CATHERINE: Then why is there an empty Pepsi in the garbage?

CASSIDY: *(Appearing. She is eight years old.)* It was in the fridge with one sip in it.

CATHERINE: You know the rules. What's that?

CASSIDY: Dad gave it to me.

CATHERINE: You've been eating that terrible white chocolate? That's why you're in a bad mood. What time is it, Mr. Bundy?

MR. BUNDY: Twelve forty.

CATHERINE: If you want something sweet, have a fig.

CASSIDY: I don't want a fig.

CATHERINE: Then forget the whole thing and read a book.

CASSIDY: I hate books.

CATHERINE: Was it this way when you grew up, Mr. Bundy?

MR. BUNDY: *(Reaches out and tickles Cassidy.)* You don't hate books.
(She jumps away.)

CASSIDY: Can I work on the train at Mr. Bundy's?

CATHERINE: *(An answer.)* Gymnastics. I don't know where Robert is, Mr.
Bundy. You could go down in the basement and see if you could find the
drill bits. You know where the closet is.

MR. BUNDY: I can...I can wait.

CASSIDY: Well, if Daddy isn't here, can't Mr. Bundy and I...

CATHERINE: Cassie...

CASSIDY: We're making a train with wheels that move and the smoke coming
out has the house number.

CATHERINE: Well, Mr. Bundy is an incredible craftsman.

MR. BUNDY: *(Pleased.)* Not so much.

CATHERINE: Your house number signs are so charming. You should take a
booth at the summer fairs.

MR. BUNDY: Not everybody likes such things.

CATHERINE: *(Seeing her nibble chocolate.)* Okay, pears and berries when we get
back.

CASSIDY: Please let me stay at Mr. Bundy's. Gymnastics is horrible.

CATHERINE: It's just the new teacher...

CASSIDY: She's yucky.

MR. BUNDY: *(Patting her hand.)* Come over after dinner.

CASSIDY: Now.

CATHERINE: Whoa, honey.

CASSIDY: Please Mommy. Then you wouldn't have to drive, and you could do
stuff. You always say you don't have time to do stuff. Mr. Bundy can
watch me.

CATHERINE: We take advantage of Mr. Bundy. *(To Mr. Bundy.)* Honestly.
Without you I couldn't have kept any of my case load.

MR. BUNDY: No one takes advantage.

CATHERINE: *(Looking out window.)* Thank God, here's your father. How late are we? *(Looks at Mr. Bundy's watch.)* Late. *(Checks her dress.)* Now what have I stained myself with? Cassie, go up and put your gym stuff on.

CASSIDY: The teacher is hopeless. You can't understand a word she says!

CATHERINE: *(To Mr. Bundy.)* She's from Bosnia, or Croatia. An ex-Olympian, I think.

CASSIDY: She goes like blah, blah, blah.

CATHERINE: That's an accent, go get your stuff.

CASSIDY: And she's got pimples.

ROBERT: *(Offstage.)* Catherine—

CATHERINE: We're in the kitchen. *(To Cassidy.)* Go on, Cassie, upstairs, he can take you. *(Cassidy exits.)*

ROBERT: *(Entering.)* Mea culpa, mea culpa, mea double culpa. *(He sees Mr. Bundy and stops.)*

MR. BUNDY: Afternoon.

CATHERINE: Are you all right?

ROBERT: Yeah but, first of all they gave me the wrong address…Oak Avenue. Not Oak Street, a little ten-mile differential, then this guy, a complete…oh, man, ummm, never mind…*(Hands her flowers.)* I know I am way late.

CATHERINE: No, okay, Cassie's getting…where did you get these?

ROBERT: From our front yard. *(Catherine laughs. To Cassidy.)* Cassie, do you have your stuff?

CASSIDY: *(Offstage.)* No.

ROBERT: Well get it, sweetie, we're late. *(To Catherine.)* The guy was…I couldn't walk out.

CATHERINE: He counsels for AA on the weekend.

ROBERT: Completely nuts.

CATHERINE: *(To Mr. Bundy.)* Alcoholics Anonymous.

MR. BUNDY: Oh, sure.

   (Robert stares at him.)

CATHERINE: *(Not understanding his look.)* Robert?

ROBERT: Listen, Catherine…*(To Cassidy.)* Upstairs now. *(Pushing her toward the door.)*

CASSIDY: Daddy…

ROBERT: Don't Daddy me, get the stuff.

CATHERINE: So?

ROBERT: Honey, they don't…don't have the people to pick up my hours, they…they lost…they're kind of in a bind…*(To Cassidy.)* Run, do not walk. *(She exits.)* Look, Mr. Bundy…

CATHERINE: Robert's hoping to cut down his weekend hours…

ROBERT: *(Overlapping.)* I, uh, listen…

CATHERINE: Lest we fail to recognize each other when we pass in the hall.

ROBERT: *(A look at Bundy. Back to Catherine.)* Look, could we get ten minutes?

CATHERINE: Honey, Cassie is…listen, thanks for the flowers. *(She smiles.)* Mr. Bundy wants drill bits.

ROBERT: What?

MR. BUNDY: Snapped a number nine.

ROBERT: Ummm…

CATHERINE: Could you look?

ROBERT: *(Looks at his watch.)* If I'm going to take…

CATHERINE: Cassie's still dressing.

ROBERT: *(Looks at Catherine, realizes it's not the time.)* Sure, okay, drill bits. *(Turns to go.)*

MR. BUNDY: I can do without.

ROBERT: No, no…hurry up, Cassie! I'll just…no problem…white box. *(He exits.)*

MR. BUNDY: Hard to find stuff.

CATHERINE: Well…your workshop is so well-organized.

MR. BUNDY: He uh…

CATHERINE: It's no bother.

MR. BUNDY: But uh…

CATHERINE: He's just frazzled. Cassidy! Now I'm going to have to run out…dumb stuff.

MR. BUNDY: *(Quickly rising.)* Oh sure.

CATHERINE: No, finish your coffee.

ROBERT: *(Re-enters.)* Drill bits. They don't uh…they don't have numbers on them.

MR. BUNDY: *(Looking.)* These are…sure, these are good.

ROBERT: Okay…great. So, uh, what, uh…Cassie!

CASSIDY: *(Offstage.)* Coming.

ROBERT: *(To Mr. Bundy.)* Look, we should…should talk.

CASSIDY: *(Offstage.)* Mom, where are my shoes?

CATHERINE: I am going to commit shoe-icide. Look in the bathroom! I need the advice of a child psychologist and I am a child psychologist. So we'll see you later, Mr. Bundy.

MR. BUNDY: Oh. Sure. *(He rises.)* These are just the thing. *(Starts to go.)* Tell Cassie after dinner.

ROBERT: After dinner what?

MR. BUNDY: Come over…if uh…

ROBERT: Cassie's busy after dinner.

CATHERINE: She is?

ROBERT: Yeah.

CATHERINE: *(To Mr. Bundy.)* Well, anyway, we'll see what's going on. And thanks for this morning.

MR. BUNDY: Oh, sure. *(To Robert.)* I'll get these back.

ROBERT: Right.

MR. BUNDY: These are the old ones.

ROBERT: Yeah.

MR. BUNDY: Good old ones. Can't find these. *(Awkwardly touches Robert's arm. Robert freezes. They stand there.)*

CASSIDY: *(Offstage.)* Found 'em.

CATHERINE: What time is it? That teacher is going to have a fit. Cassie! Bye, bye, Mr. Bundy. Cassie! *(Calling off.)* Come on, honey. *(To Mr. Bundy.)* Thanks. *(He goes, to Robert.)* What on earth?

ROBERT: What the hell is that guy doing over here?

CATHERINE: Shhh.

ROBERT: What do you mean, "Thanks for the morning"?

CATHERINE: Cassie loves him.

ROBERT: Yeah, well…

CATHERINE: The babysitter had hives. I had to do fruit-for-a-million for Cassie's school, he was nice enough…

ROBERT: Okay. I just don't think…

CATHERINE: *You* weren't here.

ROBERT: No…right, but…forget it. Later.

CATHERINE: Later what?

ROBERT: Okay, Catherine.

(*A pause.*)

CATHERINE: What's your deal?

ROBERT: I said okay. I'm just uncomfortable with him.

CATHERINE: In what way?

ROBERT: Catherine, I can't do this in…how about we skip gymnastics?

CATHERINE: We made a big thing about her going.

ROBERT: Okay, never mind, tonight.

CATHERINE: I just…we…you said you were going to tell them today, what…

ROBERT: They have nobody to replace me.

CATHERINE: *(Attempting a light tone.)* Hey, neither do we.

ROBERT: I want to be here. I do. But I have an obligation, they saved my life.

CATHERINE: I know. Robert, they saved you for us. They'll understand. Robert, please, please don't take this as a…as a threat, but…you know this. Swearing you would open up your weekends is one reason I came back.

ROBERT: I'll talk to them again.

CATHERINE: You have to tell them, not talk to them. You have to make up your mind it's important, otherwise…

ROBERT: I told you I'd go back to him, just lay off it.

CASSIDY: Are you fighting?

CATHERINE: No, honey.

CASSIDY: Then why is Daddy mad?

ROBERT: I'm not mad, honey.

CASSIDY: You are too.

CATHERINE: We're discussing, honey, sometimes that gets almost like mad.

CASSIDY: Do I have to go to gymnastics?

ROBERT: Yes, you are going to gymnastics.

CASSIDY: I want to finish the lawn train at Mr. Bundy's.

ROBERT: No. We're going. Let's go.

CASSIDY: No.

ROBERT: I don't like that tone of voice.

CATHERINE: Robert, if she really…

ROBERT: Come on, Cassie, it'll be fun. We can look in the Disney store afterwards.

CASSIDY: I'm not going. Mommy said I didn't have to.

ROBERT: We are going, Cassie.

CASSIDY: No!!

ROBERT: *(Picking her up.)* We're already late. *(She fights him.)* Ow.

CASSIDY: I don't want to. No!

ROBERT: Stop it.

CASSIDY: I won't stop it. I'm not going with you. You're poopy. You're a poopy daddy. Stop it!

ROBERT: We're going!

CASSIDY: You're hurting me! Let go of me! I want to get down!!

CATHERINE: Robert, for God's sake!

CASSIDY: Ow.

(Robert puts her down. Cassidy runs into her mother's arms.)

CATHERINE: That's not right, Robert.

CASSIDY: That teacher is jerky. I won't!

CATHERINE: *(To Robert.)* What were you thinking?

ROBERT: I didn't hurt her.

CATHERINE: *(Stroking Cassidy in her arms.)* It's okay, Cassie.

(Scene ends. We now go to Mr. Bundy's workshop, probably located in his garage. The kitchen table and chairs are moved off by scene changers. A work-bench is moved on. Cassidy sits on a crate nearby. During the scene change, Catherine talks to the audience.)

CATHERINE: Shaky. Look at that. *(A prayer without trimmings.)* Dear God, it's me, Catherine, and would you mind sending me a little equilibrium, because…ummm…I've been off-balance so long, it's hard to remember what balance is. *(A moment.)* Last week I saw a bumper sticker, it said "Harm not," and I thought, oh yeah, exactly, that's my ambition now…not to suffer harm and not to do it. Because I'm shaky. I can't handle it. And I want to be okay. Amen.

(She exits, and we are into the scene between Mr. Bundy and Cassidy.)

CASSIDY: Okay, "I'm looking over a four-leaf clover."

MR. BUNDY: You want sanding or you want singing?

CASSIDY: *(Begins the song.)* "I'm looking over a four-leaf clover that I overlooked before."

MR. BUNDY and CASSIDY: "The first leaf is sunshine, the second is rain, third is the lady who lives down the lane."

CASSIDY: Then what?

MR. BUNDY: "Someone that I adore."

CASSIDY: No, that's later.

MR. BUNDY: "No use complaining…" I don't know. Maybe rhymes with rain-ing.

CASSIDY: Why do people only know the first part of songs?

MR. BUNDY: If they know the first part. No more singing, just working.

(A pause. They work.)

CASSIDY: Knock, knock.

MR. BUNDY: Who's there?

CASSIDY: Old lady.

MR. BUNDY: Old lady who?

CASSIDY: I didn't know you could yodel. *(Mr. Bundy chuckles.)*

MR. BUNDY: *(Repeating.)* Old lady who.

CASSIDY: I want to do something.

MR. BUNDY: We sand, then we paint. Sand.

CASSIDY: I don't want to sand. I'll stand on your feet and you dance me.

MR. BUNDY: *(Working.)* No dancing.

CASSIDY: Can I get the dress-up box?

MR. BUNDY: Are we working here?

CASSIDY: Please!

MR. BUNDY: All right, all right.

CASSIDY: Yea! *(She goes to get it.)*

MR. BUNDY: For peace and quiet.

CASSIDY: *(Starts dragging a box.)* No, I did this box. Where's the other box?

MR. BUNDY: *(Points.)* Junk.

CASSIDY: *(Pulling other box over.)* I love this junk!

MR. BUNDY: You get fleas, it's your fault.

CASSIDY: I love fleas. *(She holds up a garment.)* What's this one?

MR. BUNDY: My grandfather's vest.

CASSIDY: *(Another one.)* This one?

MR. BUNDY: My mother's.

CASSIDY: It's too small.

MR. BUNDY: When she was a child.

CASSIDY: It's old.

MR. BUNDY: World War I maybe.

CASSIDY: What was that war about?

MR. BUNDY: Money.

CASSIDY: I have twelve dollars.

MR. BUNDY: Twelve? That's good.

CASSIDY: What's this?

MR. BUNDY: A barber's strop.

CASSIDY: Can I put this on?

MR. BUNDY: It's old and rotten.

CASSIDY: I'll be careful.

MR. BUNDY: It's just junk. *(He nods.)* Sure.

   (She immediately takes off her t-shirt but leaves her play shorts.)

CASSIDY: Don't look.

MR. BUNDY: I won't look.

CASSIDY: You're still looking.

MR. BUNDY: I was thinking. *(He sands.)*

CASSIDY: Was she rich?

MR. BUNDY: She lived in downtown Los Angeles. If we had that land we'd be rich.

CASSIDY: Was she pretty?

MR. BUNDY: She was ugly as a stone.

CASSIDY: She was not.

MR. BUNDY: She was. Her grandfather had horses. She teased them with a broom, she got kicked in the face. Many, many bones broke like that. *(He snaps his fingers.)* In those times they couldn't fix it. She always wore a veil, even when she would cook. One time the veil caught fire. I didn't care if she was ugly. Nobody cared except her.

CASSIDY: Was she nice?

MR. BUNDY: My mother? *(A slight laugh. The only time we see him laugh.)* Sure, she was nice sometimes. Everybody is nice sometimes. Even me.

CASSIDY: *(Finished, it's big on her.)* You can look. Am I pretty?

MR. BUNDY: Very pretty.

CASSIDY: No, really?

MR. BUNDY: Okay, okay.

CASSIDY: I can't reach. Button me.

MR. BUNDY: Come over here. *(She does.)* Turn around.

(She stands in front of him, facing out as he buttons the dress. The lights fade. As the scene is changed back to the breakfast table, a blond woman in a showy summer dress enters and talks to the audience during the change. She is Tianna, Jimmy Ray's wife.)

TIANNA: Oh yes, honey, I got the hair, you know I got the hair. That's right. Those bad diet pills kickin' in, suitcases out from under my eyes, shoot, darlin', look me over! Hey, I was at death's door, no kiddin'. Flat out I was, I'm tellin' you the truth. I tried to kill myself three times. I was that bad off, yes ma'am. But now even Jimmy Ray says I'm lookin' prime, and you don't get a compliment from Jimmy Ray that easy. Ladies, you know why I'm here. I lost a child just like every one of you here tonight, God bless us an' God help us, but I'm back an' I'm standin' here up front in my shiny hibiscus lipstick, an' you wanna know how the pieces got put back together, right? Well, my three sweet boys, sure. Jimmy Ray, my rock, my anchor, sure. My Lord and Savior, for dead sure. But what really brought me back was just how, pardon my French, pissed off I really was. See, I figured out I had a right to be angry, and a right to do somethin' about it. That rage is how I patched up my broken heart, and it's how you're goin' to start on yours tonight. Hey, I know what you've suffered, I know the loss sits in your heart like a stone, but listen to me, you got to take your personal tragedy an' turn it into your life's work, because there is such a thing as blessed revenge, honey, an' I'm gonna pass out some instructions right here on how to get it.

(We are now back in the kitchen with the Ferrebys who are in the midst of heated discussion.)

CATHERINE: This is…awful. This is awful.

ROBERT: I know.

CATHERINE: We don't need this.

ROBERT: What should we do?

CATHERINE: Cassidy…

ROBERT: Right.

CATHERINE: I don't see any…do you? In her?

ROBERT: No.

CATHERINE: It's not in her behavior, not in her drawings, not in her moods.

ROBERT: Okay.

CATHERINE: What are we going to do? I can…okay, I can watch Cassidy…I can…we don't know the guy who brought this. You never saw him before in your life, and we have no idea what his real agenda is!

ROBERT: Right.

CATHERINE: Can we buy this? I can't buy this. In terms of Cassidy, this is…okay, it's high school boys…when was it…can you read this date? This is a mess…

ROBERT: But he's next door…

CATHERINE: Yes, Mr. Bundy has been next door for two years. Nothing has happened, nobody has complained, he's been making lawn ornaments.

ROBERT: I think you're defensive because you let her go over there…

CATHERINE: No…

ROBERT: You didn't know, we lost our two best babysitters in one month, he seemed harmless, we're under...you know...stress...

CATHERINE: What I thought was...

ROBERT: We didn't think.

CATHERINE: I certainly did.

ROBERT: We had no reason to think...an hour here, an hour there, hey...

CATHERINE: What is your point?

ROBERT: Catherine, no matter what goes on between us, I have never, for the briefest moment, imagined Cassie wasn't your priority. Never, never, never. But there is a guy next door now who has harmed children...done them grievous harm, Catherine, we have to satisfy ourselves that no hint of this is in the wind here.

CATHERINE: If I thought...

ROBERT: Exactly. I don't think there has been harm, but I am going to watch my daughter's face while she tells me there hasn't. Better still, because I trust you absolutely, you are going to watch and I know you could see a flicker, or the flicker of a flicker. And then we are both going to know that there has been no harm. Then we are going to lay down some ground rules and then we can stop.

CATHERINE: *(Lifts documents.)* And open up what, Robert?

ROBERT: Catherine...

CATHERINE: All right, let's do it.

(He goes. Catherine sits. Mr. Bundy moves down into a solo light while we wait for Robert to return with Cassidy.)

MR. BUNDY: *(He holds a lawn sign jigsawed out of plywood in the shape of a locomotive with the word "Ferrebys" on it and the house number "42.")* I do a... a locomotive, this one...and uh...I do kitties, puppies, the kids like those, they...tugboats, lions...the manes on the lions, they're uh...oh, pretty hard on a jigsaw. I like the lions though. I uh...I give...guess you'd call those lawn signs...I give 'em to people, I don't sell 'em. Tell the truth, I do it to have the kids around. I've lived several places, always ends up the kids, they uh...when I'm doing my lawn signs. You know, makes me... makes me feel good. I taught kids. I understand kids...well, they uh, they pep you up late in life. *(Wipes eyes with a handkerchief.)* Got a...watcha-callit...tear duct problem. Lot of old folks, they get that. But a...but a... nice thing about kids, you make a mistake, something like that, with kids, well say, they forget about it. Next day it's like it never happened...whatever it was, all forgiven. Grown-up people, well in my experience that's not a quality they have.

(A pause.)

So a...that's...that's my lawn signs...kids they like 'em real well. Couldn't get along without the kids...I guess that's it.

(He exits as Robert re-enters with a sleepy Cassidy in his arms.)

ROBERT: We are very marginally awake.

CATHERINE: Hi, Cassie.

CASSIDY: Hi, Mommy.

ROBERT: *(Putting her on Catherine's lap.)* Here, sit with your mom.

CASSIDY: What's wrong?

CATHERINE: Nothing's wrong, sweetheart.

CASSIDY: Is it a tornado?

ROBERT: No, it's not a tornado. Do you want some juice? *(Cassidy shakes her head.)* Fruit loops?

CATHERINE: Daddy is joking.

CASSIDY: I want to go to sleep.

CATHERINE: Me too.

ROBERT: I have to ask you a couple of questions, honey, just for a minute.

CASSIDY: In the night?

CATHERINE: You know Daddy.

CASSIDY: Okay, juice.

(Robert goes to get it.)

CATHERINE: How is your spider bite?

CASSIDY: Itchy.

CATHERINE: You want something on it?

(Cassidy shakes her head no.)

ROBERT: *(Returning.)* Juice, honey.

CASSIDY: What questions?

ROBERT: Quick ones.

CASSIDY: What ones?

ROBERT: Have you ever hurt yourself at Mr. Bundy's?

CASSIDY: *("Are you kidding?")* Daddy?

ROBERT: Mr. Bundy ever hurt you, honey?

CASSIDY: I hurt myself on the glue gun once.

ROBERT: But he never hurt you?

CASSIDY: Why would he hurt me?

CATHERINE: He wouldn't.

CASSIDY: Can I go back to bed?

CATHERINE: In one second. *(She looks to Robert.)*

ROBERT: *(To Cassidy.)* Honey, ummm, while you were over there, has umm...over with Mr. Bundy...was there...nothing ever scared you?

CATHERINE: *(Seeing that Cassidy is confused.)* Has he ever touched you anywhere private, honey?

CASSIDY: You mean down there?

CATHERINE: Anywhere private?

CASSIDY: This is stupid. No, he hasn't.

ROBERT: Hugging or...just physical...physical stuff.

CATHERINE: Robert...

CASSIDY: *(Squirming out of her mother's arms.)* This is yucky. It's dark. *(Robert reaches out for her.)* No.

ROBERT: Come here, sweetie.

CASSIDY: Has he ever touched you?

CATHERINE: Cassie, it's fine. You said no.

CASSIDY: That's so stupid. I want my bed. *(Starts to go.)*

ROBERT: Can I have a hug.

CASSIDY: He didn't. That's yucky. *(And she's gone.)*

ROBERT: She may not go over there.

CATHERINE: Stop, Robert. Agreed. I'm going up.

CASSIDY: *(Offstage.)* Mommy?

CATHERINE: Coming honey.

(She goes. The lights change. The tables and chairs are cleared leaving a bare stage. During the change, Robert speaks.)

ROBERT: I haven't had a drink in twelve years. Before Catherine. I was a bad drunk, a mean drunk. I woke up once in some motel with a gun, .22 pistol, on the nightstand. No idea where I was or...where it came from. I was a...was a graphic artist at that time. TV was on...religious cable or something...Evangelicals...shoot, it was Falwell, Jerry Falwell, and I...I stayed there and watched that for ten hours. Took that in. Long time. Some spirit entered me. Then I ordered pizza and uh...called AA, and they came and got me. Since then I have to be careful to assign meaning, to make things important enough to me to stay sober. I have to remember to like my work. I have to remember that I love Catherine. Sometimes things, they still lose meaning. I know I love Cassie though. That's always clear. I tell some of the drunks that if there's one thing you're really clear about, you'll be okay. Telling them, that makes me remember.

(We're now in a mall parking lot, maybe there's a section of yellow parking lines on the floor. Catherine enters with shopping bags. Someone calls to her from offstage. It is Tianna.)

TIANNA: *(Offstage.)* Mrs. Ferreby? *(Catherine looks, she doesn't see anyone.)* Mrs. Ferreby, honey? *(Tianna appears.)* Oh my goodness, it's warm...*(Touches her forehead with a handkerchief.)* I'd have to say this isn't glow, this is plain ol' sweat.

CATHERINE: It's warm.

TIANNA: Looks like you shopped up a storm, darlin'. Oh, I do too. But I got to tell you I'm in recovery from shoppin'. I just got to keep my grabby little hands out of the malls by main force 'cause I'm a shopping fool and no kiddin'.

CATHERINE: I'm not sure we've met.

TIANNA: 'Cause you'd remember me, huh? Well I got my own style...even I don't like it sometimes. Well, hi, I'm Tianna Longest. Like a long man's tie, Tianna. I think my bad-boy husband Jimbo's friends with your Robert. I'm right, it's Robert? *(Catherine nods yes.)* I think they're workin' on a little project. You want a wet wipe? I think I got wet wipes.

CATHERINE: No thank you, I think I'm all right.

TIANNA: And you're Cathy, ain'tcha? Ooooh, pretend I didn't say that. I'm on a campaign with that word...and I've been doing good since last summer, I have.

CATHERINE: Yes, I'm Catherine.

TIANNA: Well, I know what you are goin' through on this next door thing, and there is nobody in this world can sympathize like I can.

CATHERINE: I'm sorry, you said your name was Longest?

TIANNA: Married name's Bosun, but I use my own name for my consultin' business.

CATHERINE: Was there something you wanted to talk to me about...or...I'm about to...*(Looks at watch.)*...pick up my little girl at a birthday party.

TIANNA: You're kiddin', it's her birthday.

CATHERINE: No, a little friend's.

TIANNA: That is always so cute! You slipped out, huh? I always slip out too. Get a few precious minutes on my own.

CATHERINE: *(Looks at watch again.)* I might even be a little late.

TIANNA: Well, I could ride along if you wanted...of course I don't know if you're comin' back by here?

CATHERINE: What is it you want?

TIANNA: Oooh, that's chilly. Don't be chilly, darlin', don't do that.

CATHERINE: I'm sorry but...

TIANNA: Now, you're going to think this sounds crazy, but I'm here to save your life, honey. Make precautions for savin' it. See, Cathy, you can't tell it by lookin' at me, but there's...somethin' dead somewhere in here...inside here...an' I don't want you feelin' what I feel, darlin'. I don't want you to feel this. *(Catherine looks at her for a moment and then turns to move to her car.)* My little girl was raped. She was five years old. Raped, sodomized, then he killed her, darlin', wrapped her up in a dry cleaner bag, he...he was a convicted abuser they let out to live down the road from me. *(Catherine turns back.)* My bad-boy Jimmy Ray an' me hadn't heard from you, we were gettin' real worried.

CATHERINE: Oh my God.

TIANNA: Oh sweetie, there's no use sympathizin' with me. There's just no use in it. There just isn't any kind of band-aid you can put on it you know what I mean.

CATHERINE: When did it happen?

TIANNA: Pretty near nine years now comin' up.

CATHERINE: I'm so sorry.

TIANNA: An' he's still there on death row. Yeah, still goin' on. He's workin' on some advanced correspondence degree from the University of California but Jimmy Ray an' me we think we'll get him executed pretty soon now.

CATHERINE: What was her name?

TIANNA: Cathy, honey, if I tell you her name I'm gonna cry all over this parking lot an' ruin my real nice makeup.

CATHERINE: I didn't mean...

TIANNA: Don't you worry. We got to go on come what may. Now the thing is we got to put our pretty heads together on your little problem, don't we now?

CATHERINE: You're talking about Mr. Bundy?

TIANNA: Mr. Bundy, uh-huh, I sure am.

CATHERINE: Well it's…it's taken care of really.

TIANNA: Well, how is that?

CATHERINE: Cassidy's not spending time there anymore. We took that step.

TIANNA: *(Encouraging.)* Well that's so good! Good for you!

CATHERINE: Robert felt…

TIANNA: That's a real good start, but we were wonderin' if you'd got the neighbors together, anything like that?

CATHERINE: Mrs. Bosun, we didn't think it was necessary to…

TIANNA: Tianna.

CATHERINE: Tianna…Mr. Bundy's…transgression, according to the things…documents your husband sent were quite long ago. Years ago. And they weren't violent…they were sex crimes but there seems to have been no repetition…

TIANNA: Uh-huh.

CATHERINE: And his…interest…never seems to have been little girls. I believe teenaged boys were involved.

TIANNA: Oh, you never know but, am I wrong, doesn't the neighbor on the other side of…Mr. Bundy…have a teenage boy? Am I mixed up?

CATHERINE: Well…

TIANNA: Then there's those two twin boys further down, the Kellerman boys, I believe they're in seventh grade and, of course, that boy won State High School Golf, but that must be, oh, two blocks or so, I guess.

CATHERINE: How do you know that?

TIANNA: Oh, darlin', we got to be real…thorough…we take up this burden.

CATHERINE: Then why come to us?

TIANNA: Well it would be safest to start next door we thought…see, directly concerned.

CATHERINE: He's an older man now, Mrs. Bosun, Tianna, he's in his sixties and he apparently, from your materials, has been, you know, completely straight arrow since his prison term thirteen years ago.

TIANNA: Honey, you're talkin' all about him an' just nothin' about your little girl.

CATHERINE: You know that is, uh, we don't really know each other, certainly not well enough to make judgments or uh, or accusations…

TIANNA: Oh, now, you got me all…

CATHERINE: I love her, Mrs. Bosun. I love her and I want her safe, but when she is safe I want her to learn people can change, people can make mistakes and people can be forgiven.

TIANNA: Uh-huh. Well, there's just so many views on a thing like this. An' I bet your feelin', like mine, is where many are affected, all should have a voice. You know, a democratic kind of thing. 'Course too, it's a big old country, there's a lot of places Mr. Bundy could go to. Move along if he felt like it.

CATHERINE: Move along?

TIANNA: Just move, honey.

CATHERINE: Whether or not he's dangerous?

TIANNA: Well, why would he want to be where he's not wanted?

CATHERINE: Who has said that?

TIANNA: Nobody's had the opportunity, darlin'. Plus I believe he's…well, gone to movin' around in the past.

CATHERINE: Look, Tianna, I am…or I was a, you know, child psychologist, and, uh, there was a young boy, my client, and uh, it was uh…clear…he shouldn't be released back to his parents' "care," and so…representing the State I fought that…hard…in court, and the parents, the parents…sometimes this boy had to be restrained…claimed I had, struck the boy during our sessions…and I had not…had not…and this, uh, went on for…endlessly for…eighteen months…in hearings…before it was decided in my favor. So I am sensitized…to these charges.

TIANNA: But, see, honey, you didn't hit the boy.

CATHERINE: I did not hit him, no.

TIANNA: Darlin', I don't believe you did. But it brings up the point that people get concerned, rightfully concerned, I can tell you that. With my little girl, I have asked a thousand times down on my knees why somebody didn't let me know there was danger, darlin'. And I've come to believe that is not a question for my Lord, it's a plain ol' question for my local police. Now the lady on the other side, Mrs. McGuigan, Jimmy Ray let her know and I would call her concerned.

CATHERINE: Other people know? I think that is…Tianna, I can't even begin to imagine what you have suffered and are suffering. I think you are an amazing person. I could never be so strong, I know I couldn't. And that you are…take the time to…devote yourself to this cause…well, I see many admirable things in that but, and please don't take this as…any lack of respect, but I think Robert and I can handle this…speak to Mrs. McGuigan privately…be on the lookout for any…anything. I guess what

I'm trying to say is that this is, we feel, a neighborhood matter to be handled by people in the neighborhood.

TIANNA: Lucy. That was her name.

CATHERINE: Your daughter?

TIANNA: From "Lucy in the Sky with Diamonds." You remember that? *(Catherine nods.)* She was...I miss her every day of my life. I miss her right this minute. An' my belief, darlin', is that the "neighborhood" is all the little girls and boys...all of them...so I help out there in that neighborhood. I promised my Lucy I'd do that. *(Dabs at her eyes.)* Cry me a river! Lordy, I have given these eyes a workout! I'm surprised I still got 'em. My, oh my. *(Pulls together.)* My own fault. So Cathy darlin', your sweet little girl she's probably the last one left at that party, an' you can blame it on me.

CATHERINE: *(Looking at her watch.)* I completely lost track.

TIANNA: Honey, she's just eatin' too much cake.

CATHERINE: I should...I can call on the cell phone.

TIANNA: Well, good then...listen, Jimmy Ray an' me, we'd like to come down Wednesday, nothin' formal, nothin' big, meet with you two and Mrs. McGuigan, she's real nice, try to get all this ironed out so we can get out of your business.

CATHERINE: I don't even understand why we're part of your equation. If you're bound and determined to do this, why don't you and your husband go ahead and do it?

TIANNA: Honey, we just can't be everywhere. We can't. An' Jimmy Ray, he says he's a bad one to do it 'cause he's just way too angry, poor man, an' he knows, an' he'll say this isn't an act of revenge, darlin', it's a precaution people have to take for their children. All I'm askin' is would you be kind enough to let me have my say on Lucy's behalf. Just an hour of your time, that's all I'm askin'.

CATHERINE: Well I...

TIANNA: Five thirty be real good for Jimmy Ray an' that darned truck, which might as well be his wife if you want to know the truth.

CATHERINE: I suppose we could try.

TIANNA: Well, you try *real* hard, you cute thing, 'cause we're gonna be here with bells on, an' it's real close to a nine-hour drive with my motion sickness. Lord have mercy! Now you trust me it's going to be for the best, honey. There's not too much in this life I know, but I know that. I'm going to bring you down some of my coconut cream pie if you'll just stick a pot of coffee on, maybe even squeeze in some girl talk. You just stick with Tianna on this one, honey. You won't be sorry.

(The lights fade.)

(Mrs. McGuigan speaks first from audience, then steps into a special as the scene is changed into the Ferrebys' living room, represented by a sofa, a coffee table and two chairs.)

MRS. MCGUIGAN: The country's gone to hell, and it's the parents' fault. Plainly put, I don't know where the common sense is. You don't have to let the kids see those movies: bang, bang, bang, crash, crash, crash, sex, sex, sex. Hollywood doesn't have a gun to your head. You don't have to buy them cars at sixteen, you don't have to let them date at fourteen, you don't have to let them smoke and drink and come home at one A.M. And most of all you do not have to blame every darn thing but yourselves as if it's the teachers' fault or television's fault or the liberals' fault or the government's fault. You're like a bunch of second graders…it's Jimmy's fault, it's Letitia's fault, it's Wally's fault, it's anybody's fault but my fault! What in the world is going on here? You pull up your socks, mister! You raise those kids like you know is right. Don't take any baloney from them, be up when they get home at night, insist they treat other people with respect or get their butts whipped or their cars taken, and they won't have to say "no" to drugs. These parents are just too self-centered to do what they should. It's not a popularity contest or a part-time job or the babysitter's responsibility. Boy, they make me mad! This isn't exactly brain surgery, you know, just do it. And if the parents did the job we wouldn't need all these social services or Christian kooks getting into our business selling us their righty, lefty values and two-bit armageddons. Don't you go blaming anything else. Your kid is your damned fault, and that's flat!

(She moves into the Ferrebys' living room and sits on the sofa with the Bosuns. Robert and Catherine are in the chairs.)

ROBERT: You've been very quiet, Mrs. McGuigan.
MRS. MCGUIGAN: When it's time to make noise, I'll make noise.
TIANNA: We just want you to speak up an' give us what-for if you want.

MRS. MCGUIGAN: My opinion is I don't like the idea of the man, but I can't say I dislike him in person.

JIMMY RAY: There is a real clear law in this state says he has to register with the police within fourteen days of taking up residence, and the police have a further responsibility to notify those in proximity of his criminal record immediately and with dispatch. Now these officers have just been bumbledickin' around.

TIANNA: Pardon his French.

CATHERINE: What about his right to privacy?

JIMMY RAY: He doesn't have a right to privacy.

CATHERINE: Legally?

JIMMY RAY: Legally, he has no right to privacy. He wanted his privacy he should have kept his hands off those kids.

CATHERINE: What happened to those kids?

JIMMY RAY: Okay, we don't have that follow-up.

CATHERINE: And we don't know if he has registered with the police?

JIMMY RAY: That is one-hundred-percent correct. Now I've had considerable experience on this thing…real considerable, thirty, forty of these creeps cross this country an' I tell you, Missus, the point is not has he registered, the point is putting organized community pressure on the police department to inform the neighborhood of his presence because once that neighborhood gets goin' he will pack up and get gone so fast you'll see a yellow streak all the way to the Mexico border.

CATHERINE: For what?

ROBERT: Catherine…

JIMMY RAY: For what?

TIANNA: Now Jimmy Ray…

CATHERINE: I thought you paid for the crime when you served the time. I thought that was the social contract.

ROBERT: This particular crime…

JIMMY RAY: *(Riding over.)* See, there's a real high percent…

CATHERINE: Yes, exactly…

JIMMY RAY: *Real high.*

CATHERINE: During the first five years…

JIMMY RAY: Ma'am…

CATHERINE: No, it's my profession. High recidivism early…

JIMMY RAY: What it is…

CATHERINE: But after all these years…

JIMMY RAY: We don't know…

CATHERINE: Let me finish please…

JIMMY RAY: This boy has several years where we don't know…

CATHERINE: Let me finish!

TIANNA: Honey, you go right ahead now.

CATHERINE: This is thirteen years after his release with no repetition and the statistic is less than a two-percent chance of another sex crime. Way less than two percent. The man is over sixty years old and uses a cane. We can't afford to generalize here. You have to take it case by case. Mr. Bundy did what he did…

JIMMY RAY: Let's call it by its name…

CATHERINE:…in 1985.

JIMMY RAY: Sexually forced children…

CATHERINE: Thirteen years ago…

JIMMY RAY: To sexually service him…

CATHERINE: And it's time he was forgiven.

JIMMY RAY:…and that man was a teacher.

CATHERINE: Yes…

JIMMY RAY: A teacher. He didn't just meet those boys in an alley somewhere, he took advantage of his position in a classroom to turn them homosexual.

ROBERT:	CATHERINE:
Now wait a minute…	That is patently absurd.

JIMMY RAY: Because I investigated that…

ROBERT: Ridiculous.

JIMMY RAY:…up, down and sideways and those boys had no homosexual activity up to that point.

TIANNA: Jimmy Ray talked to everybody…

ROBERT: That much is mythology, Mr. Bosun…

JIMMY RAY: What's that, buddy?

CATHERINE: You just don't…

ROBERT: Wait, honey.

CATHERINE:…is so absurd that I can't…

ROBERT: Wait.

CATHERINE:…listen to this.

ROBERT: *(To Jimmy Ray.)* Homosexuality does not work that way. You don't turn somebody to it…

JIMMY RAY: Was a case on the Internet…

(Catherine has to leave her seat in frustration.)

ROBERT: Excuse me...

JIMMY RAY: Heck, you probably...

ROBERT: Just let me...

JIMMY RAY: This other teacher, see...

ROBERT: Can somebody else talk here? You say the boy was in drag...he gave them dresses? Well, the hemline didn't turn them homosexual. For God's sake, if we've learned anything, we've learned it isn't environmental.

JIMMY RAY: You keep the Lord's name...

TIANNA: *(Stopping Jimmy Ray and addressing Robert.)* Darlin', you're not blaming the boys, are you?

CATHERINE: Thirteen years ago...

ROBERT: I am certainly not blaming...

TIANNA: See, he's not blaming the boys, Jimmy Ray.

CATHERINE: Tianna, I'm not sure this whole thing...

TIANNA: These are good folks, they know who the victims are...

ROBERT: Yes, as a matter of fact...

TIANNA: No sir, he's not puttin' it on the victims!

ROBERT: Oh brother.

JIMMY RAY: I got some business to do here, Tianna.

CATHERINE: I'm not saying it's right, but he paid for that. I'm saying it's over. He did what he did...

TIANNA: What's over, darlin'?

ROBERT: I think we should...

JIMMY RAY: It is not over! I'm gonna tell you one time it's not over. You see my wife over there?

TIANNA: Now don't, Jimbo...

JIMMY RAY: Last night I wake up, she's out of the bed, down curled up on the kitchen floor cryin'...

TIANNA: Shoot, darn it...

JIMMY RAY: Had some half-done colorin' book she found of our little girl's, an' she's collapsed on the floor...

TIANNA: This man is a good husband...

JIMMY RAY: So don't sit here in your fancy house...

TIANNA: Now, Jimmy Ray...

JIMMY RAY:	CATHERINE:
With your import rugs...	That is not the point...

TIANNA: You got to...

JIMMY RAY: An' tell me what's over!

TIANNA: …shut up now.

JIMMY RAY: *(Moving away.)* Heck with you.

TIANNA: *(She gives a little laugh.)* Goodness me, did I say that? You're all gonna think I'm a witchy woman, which I'm not. Now I think we're havin' a real good discussion…real heartfelt…gettin' all points of view…'cept Helen here is held back. You got to put your ideas forth, darlin'. I bet you got some strong ideas.

ROBERT: It's getting a little late here.

TIANNA: Now you hold on, you bad boy. Come on, Helen, I got these bulls in a corner momentarily.

MRS. MCGUIGAN: I don't have too much to say.

TIANNA: See, that's a white lie.

MRS. MCGUIGAN: Mr. Bundy has been very nice to me. A good neighbor day-in, day-out. Helped me replace a very heavy garage door. I'm the boy's grandmother, you know, and a single person, his father and mother…well, we won't go into that. Mr. Bundy, well he's always ready to help out, fix things, always brings over his tomatoes, pies he makes. This other thing…my grandson Allen, I'm raising him, he's in his senior year…always lifting weights…plays all sports. Too many for his grades if you ask me. I don't believe anybody is going to turn him anywhere if that's the conversation here. On the other hand, I believe once you've done these things…well I'm not at all sure it's something a neighborhood can take in, it's just too…this may not be a Christian point of view…it's just too hard. It's such an emotional thing. Once everybody knows…well, it won't be too logical. I like the atmosphere so much the way it's been. Some people say it's not real life it's so nice here. I'd have to say I don't mind a bit doing without real life when I come home. I feel I've been through a lot. I need the quiet. Maybe Mr. Bundy should move on. I'm not sure.

TIANNA: See that's such a good point. You put that so well, you really did. Isn't that a good contribution, Jimmy Ray? Now this man Mr. Bundy, despite the fact he has this mark of Cain, he's been making a real effort from what you say…

JIMMY RAY: Tianna…

TIANNA: Well, all those years now like Cathy says. He could just make his own decision to move on, not go through this whole thing getting sour as Helen points out…

CATHERINE: It doesn't have to get sour…

TIANNA: That's right, he could be talked to private, honey. I would be glad to take that on as my part. They say a little sugar makes the medicine go down. I believe he might move right on as a neighborly thing, and nobody would have to be the wiser.

CATHERINE: I doubt he has a place to go. If he did...

TIANNA: Now, I believe...

CATHERINE: *(Riding over.)*...he would be there.

TIANNA: Well, honey...

CATHERINE: He's been living next door to us for two years. He has never bothered your grandson, has he?

MRS. MCGUIGAN: Well, I don't believe he'd bother Allen.

CATHERINE: He has been with my daughter alone in his house many, many times, and no harm done.

ROBERT: We had two babysitters, but...

CATHERINE: *(Riding over.)* There have been no sex crimes in this area.

JIMMY RAY: Well...

CATHERINE: Within a wide area. He's been a good neighbor. There is not a shred of evidence that would lead us to conclude he had to be privately or publicly told to move on. Now I think this should be laid to rest with thanks to the Bosuns for their time and information. You can count on our being watchful, but other than watchfulness there is nothing to act on here.

JIMMY RAY: The man who raped and killed our Lucy, he had no record with little girls though he had previously harmed teenagers. He raped Lucy several times over six hours in a...an old gas station. Strangled her on a cement floor, threw her in the trunk of his car, took her back where he had a power saw, did the rest of what he did...*(Reaches in his coat.)* sometime during all that he must have stepped on her glasses...*(He puts the glasses on the coffee table.)* See it turned out...Charles DeYoung...Charles Gabriel DeYoung to quote his full name...well prior to Lucy he had confided to a couple people he had this rape record...served time but like this here the cops overlooked to notify...didn't have a taste for it, that department, it later came out...and the people he told, well they didn't tell no one. Had their reasons I don't doubt. So I have...Tianna and me...come to have a real firm belief in notification. Insiders, outsiders, whatever. *(A moment.)* Could be this Walker R. Bundy, to quote his full name...well, there is differences between him and Mr. DeYoung. *(To Catherine.)* Like you said about his age, all the different things. You can get him outta here private if you're willing to take that chance. I figure I'll give you three days to do that, but I want to make this clear…There is no place for these people next door anywhere. I find 'em, I'm gonna move 'em on for eternity. I will give them no rest and no roof. I will cast them out. Because any place I know they are I would be just too likely to come there and harm them and the Lord tells me I shall not kill, and I can't afford to be too tempted. I kid you not. You move him on or I'll move him on. It's going to happen one way or the other. *(A moment.)* Time to go, Tianna. *(She rises.)* We'd like to thank you for the fellowship. Thanks for the time in your home. *(He picks up the glasses.)* Only time I cried was when I saw these glasses. Ain't that somethin'? Go on, Tianna. *(Turns back.)* I'll be in touch.

(The lights go down but not out. As they come back up, Robert and Catherine are alone. It is minutes later.)

CATHERINE: I don't think this is right. Why didn't you say something?

ROBERT: I did say something.

CATHERINE: That gay isn't environmental?

ROBERT: He was using that to leverage Mrs. McGuigan.

CATHERINE: I'm talking about his using neighborhood pressure to get Mr. Bundy out of here.

ROBERT: I don't know where I am on that.

CATHERINE: You're kidding me?

ROBERT: No, I don't know.

CATHERINE: Robert…you had an affair, should they move you on? Out you? Run pickets in front of the house and pass out leaflets?

ROBERT: Come on, Catherine…

CATHERINE: No, turn it around. My dad had two drunken-driving arrests in the eighties. He still drives, isn't that a neighborhood issue?

ROBERT: Obviously not the same…

CATHERINE: Why not? He caused a very serious accident. The woman he hit had a child in the car. He still drinks, he still drives. Wouldn't everybody here be safer if we moved him on to Florida?

ROBERT: Okay, okay, we're both upset…

CATHERINE: Did it ever cross your mind that he could sue us?

ROBERT: He'd never get away with it.

CATHERINE: Are you kidding? He'd…

ROBERT: He'd have to be suicidal.

CATHERINE: In this day and age?

ROBERT: He'd lose.

CATHERINE: Robert, think about it...

ROBERT: But we have this child...

CATHERINE: Are you patronizing me?

ROBERT: ...you love better than anything fifty feet from this guy.

CATHERINE: Yes, I do love her and he's not interested in little girls.

ROBERT: Interested enough to have her over there every spare minute.

CATHERINE: Older people like children, Robert.

ROBERT: They do, yes. Listen, you remember when those kids used to climb our wall to get up on the garage roof? Nobody ever fell, but you were the one who insisted we pay eight hundred dollars to take down the wall. So, the real question, you know, the heart of it is, why take any chance with this guy at all.

CATHERINE: Because...I don't know.

ROBERT: Then let's not, okay?

CATHERINE: Because I know him. Because he drinks coffee here. I don't know. Because it's not right to do harm to someone who drinks coffee in your kitchen.

ROBERT: Catherine...

CATHERINE: No, no I...there's no...because sometimes you have to take chances to stay human...or...because I know he's...maybe because I'm too fragile to do harm right now.

ROBERT: You're not fragile, you're rock.

CATHERINE: Is that what you see? Oh, Robert...never mind, look...Mr. Bundy isn't a wall we can tear down...hold on...it's easy to move to extremes here, really, it can be seductive...feels really...active to make assumptions that...Robert, he has lost those drives or controlled them.

ROBERT: Catherine, there is no way in this world to be sure of that.

CATHERINE: He's demonstrated it.

ROBERT: He may still do it and he hasn't been caught.

CATHERINE: Nobody condones what he did thirteen years ago, but you can't run a society with life sentences for every crime, Robert.

ROBERT: He takes little trips, where does he go?

CATHERINE: He has to live somewhere.

ROBERT: Maybe he drives fifty miles and hangs out in the malls.

CATHERINE: So the moral imperative is to move him on to somebody else's mall?

ROBERT: Don't give me that. That's not how you react. There is nobody...nobody fiercer than you are about protecting your family...nobody.

CATHERINE: Then why am I not concerned, Bobby? We may both work but you know I'm the basic safety net for Cassie. I screen the babysitters, I check out the camps, I'm the one who has coffee with Mr. Bundy. Why should your view prevail now?

ROBERT: Because of what I feel, okay? I don't agree, in this case, to take any risk whatsoever with Cassie. Bundy be damned. I don't agree, okay?

CATHERINE: Honey, not taking risks is one thing, riding him out of town on a rail is another.

ROBERT: And both those things make Cassie safer.

CATHERINE: It's overkill, Robert, until all these people are put on an island, we have to cope. We can't just ruin his life to get a statistical edge.

ROBERT: He already ruined his life.

CATHERINE: Where are you coming from? Who drags me to church every Sunday? Who tells me we don't need prayer in the schools but we do need Christian ethics taught in the classroom? Forgiveness is a central Christian precept. Bobby, I am back in this house on that principle. I am busy forgiving you as we speak. Do you want to be forgiven?

ROBERT: No fair.

CATHERINE: Do you?

ROBERT: Yes, I do. You know I do.

CATHERINE: Well, so does Mr. Bundy, Robert, so what do we do now?

ROBERT: Beyond what I may feel here, or you may feel here, the fact is that Jimmy Ray took this out of our hands.

CATHERINE: No he didn't.

ROBERT: He gave us three days to get Bundy out of here before he saw to it it became a community issue. He will go to the papers. You saw his eyes. He'll go door to door.

CATHERINE: And if he does that?

ROBERT: Yes? What is that supposed to mean?

CATHERINE: Then we would convince the neighborhood to leave him alone.

ROBERT: You...what?! Do you...people aren't going to listen on this issue. This isn't the International Debate Society...

CATHERINE: I never said...

ROBERT: ...with points for style and research. Catherine, people fear and hate these guys, and with good reason.

CATHERINE: And sometimes that's wrong.

ROBERT: And sometimes...listen, what you suggest is the quickest way imaginable to become the biggest pariah in a hundred-mile radius.

CATHERINE: Robert, how can you...we're not talking about reputation here. We have several responsibilities.

ROBERT: Oh, my God. Can we get real here, okay? We bought a house we can't afford so we could have the neighborhood and the school district. I work in an advertising agency that is downsizing, and my job is to baby corporate clients whose personal politics are a little to the right of Vulcan the Barbarian. They should see me on local TV fronting for this issue? How would you like us to be moved on to another town?

CATHERINE: So it's not worry about Cassie, it's economic?

ROBERT: *(Slapping the table.)* Don't you dare say that to me!

CATHERINE: You said it.

ROBERT: You know exactly what I mean!

CATHERINE: Yes, unfortunately.

ROBERT: That guy is a sociopath...*(She throws up her hands.)*...no morals, no judgment, he proved it!

CATHERINE: Whatever.

ROBERT: And no, it's not economic, it's Cassie. The time she's spent over there makes my skin crawl, but all that...all that aside, you stood in this room and agreed with me that it was off-limits for her, and I saw her over there yesterday!

CATHERINE: Yes, I did agree, but that house has a slide and swings. She wasn't in the house. You won't even buy her a swing set. As a matter of fact, your chief argument was she could use the one over there. When I saw she'd gone over there I called her back. Why don't you come home on Saturdays and you can watch her!

ROBERT: *(Boiling.)* I don't want her over there, do you hear me? You see that she doesn't go over there, is that clear? I shouldn't even have to bring this up. Now you see it doesn't happen.

CATHERINE: I don't know who you think I am, but I don't take instructions.

ROBERT: Do not let Cassidy go anywhere near there.

(A pause.)

CATHERINE: Bobby, I am going to go over and talk to Mr. Bundy. I am going to tell him what we know about his past, and I am going to tell him there is likely to be trouble. I'm going to suggest he agree, in writing, to stay away from neighborhood children of any sex and age, and should he transgress that agreement we will have Jimmy Ray and Tianna make his life the living hell they suggest. I will then communicate this information to the Bosuns, and ask them not to proceed further. If they do I will organize support for Mr. Bundy, and what you do at that point is entirely up to you. I hope you will join me, but I have no "instructions" for you. I loved you once, and I came back here because I thought I could love you again. I think that's what we've been working on and hoping for. *(A moment.)* I understand what you feel, truly I do. It's just not what I feel. I wish it was. *(A pause.)* So, anyway, I think I should go over and see Mr. Bundy. *(Pause.)* It would really mean a lot to me if you would come with me. *(Pause.)* Robert?

ROBERT: I'll come with you.

(They look at each other.)

CATHERINE: Thank you.

(The lights fade and while they change to the furniture representing Mr. Bundy's living room, Tianna steps into a spotlight.)

TIANNA: Hey, I'm not getting fancy here, y'know, but, girlfriends, it probably comes down, don't you think, to whether there is such things as good an' evil? I mean, I'm no preacher now, shoot no, but I feel like we just got to come down on some side of that fence. Because evil, well if there was such a thing as that, well I don't think you can forgive evil, can you? Sure they got theologians, such as that, been working all this, but for simple folks...I don't mean dumb now...well, you know how I'd put it, darlin'? I'd say, honey, when you read the paper, some of these things people do, don't you just think "that there is evil"...like the word just attaches itself...you just can't explain it any other way. And the things you use that word on aren't any kind of a thing you can understand out of your human experience. These are acts you couldn't do, nor could anybody you know or ever met do those things, and yet they are done. They are done. So I believe that it does exist and, down where our instincts are, we know that. People who do evil, we can't recognize them as human, and this "evil" is beyond explanation, beyond forgiveness, an' beggin' your pardon here, they got to be stamped out or driven back to that darkness from which they come. Because once evil is the name of a thing, I say give it no quarter. 'Course as I say, I'm a simple person with simple ideas. *(She looks down at her hands.)* Got real nice finger polish though, don't I? Been likin' the red/brown tones, but I'm tryin' to get up the nerve to do 'em blue.

(The lights come up on Catherine, Robert and Mr. Bundy in his living room. He is filling their kitchen glasses with lemonade.)

CATHERINE: So the thing is, Mr. Bundy, the thing is, we...we know now you have a...criminal record.

ROBERT: We didn't go looking for it.

CATHERINE: Nothing you did...someone outside brought it to our attention.

MR. BUNDY: Oh no.

CATHERINE: I'm sorry, I know it was a long time ago.

MR. BUNDY: I prayed to God against this.

CATHERINE: I know that you...

MR. BUNDY: I'm on my knees every day that I could live this down...for all these years.

ROBERT: *(Seeing the tipping pitcher.)* You're spilling the lemonade.

(He looks nonplussed as it continues to spill.)

CATHERINE: The lemonade, Mr. Bundy.

MR. BUNDY: Oh. I'm sorry.

CATHERINE: Are you all right?

MR. BUNDY: All right?

CATHERINE: Why don't you sit down, Mr. Bundy?

MR. BUNDY: You see, I wanted to have myself castrated. I looked into that.

CATHERINE: Mr. Bundy, don't.

MR. BUNDY: No, I suppose you are not interested in my regrets.

CATHERINE: Mr. Bundy...we have to talk about this, I'm sorry.

MR. BUNDY: I should clean up the lemonade.

CATHERINE: I'll do it.

MR. BUNDY: This carpet...

CATHERINE: It's all right.

MR. BUNDY: Stupid.

CATHERINE: Mr. Bundy, you've probably been wondering why Cassie hasn't been over.

MR. BUNDY: She is a beautiful child. I would never harm a child.

CATHERINE: This is hard. This is so hard.

ROBERT: Do you want me...

CATHERINE: No. No, it's all right. We told her she couldn't, Mr. Bundy. It's as much for your sake as it is for hers. It would be...I would still be pleased if you came over for coffee. *(Robert shifts position. Mr. Bundy notices.)* Mr. Bundy, there is some chance of this becoming public knowledge. *(Mr. Bundy sits with a hand over his face.)* Not from us. I do think there might be a way...to head that off.

MR. BUNDY: You can see some things are still in boxes. I've moved nine times in thirteen years. It's pretty hard. I uh...well, probably I deserve to be humiliated like they do but, my uh...nerves are...pretty bad now...pretty bad and uh...I don't know if you...know my age? *(They nod.)* So uh, I get...very nervous about things. I was hoping not to move again so soon. One time they filled up my car with feces. They spray paint...things...on my house. Killed a dog, my dog, one time. Cocker spaniel dog my sister gave me.

ROBERT: Could you go to your sister, Mr. Bundy?

MR. BUNDY: I don't believe she could afford to be...singled out...where she lives.

CATHERINE: I don't think you have to move, Mr. Bundy. I'm not in favor of that. *(She hands him a piece of paper from a file folder.)* I wondered perhaps if you would feel you could sign this? *(He reads it.)* You know if you...if you could, I think we could use it...um...to defuse anything, well, that came up. But if you...

MR. BUNDY: Damn children...these...damn children! I'm not...I don't harm them! *(Robert rises.)* I'm sorry. I'm sorry. God help me. *(A pause.)* I uh... yes, whatever you want...I could sign this. I'm surprised you offer...any kind of help. They would...they would drive me out though anyway. They need to do it. See? My hands shake now. Like the crying. I'm not in control of it. *(Puts his hands in his pockets.)* I would ask if you could give me till the eighteenth. All my sister's money is in this house. I don't know if you know I work weekends at the uh...the clothing outlet on Route 62...they pay every two weeks. I would need that money when I go.

CATHERINE: Where would you go, Mr. Bundy?

MR. BUNDY: Can't say. Somewhere else. Get some boxes. List the house. I don't know. I guess it doesn't matter where I go. I wouldn't be there too long.

CATHERINE: Mr. Bundy, I think you have paid. I don't think you need to pay anymore. You are welcome to live next door to me. My husband feels it is inappropriate for you to see Cassie. I don't know…perhaps I do too. He feels it strongly and I would have to honor that. Because she cares for you, I think we should address that with Cassie with you there. *(Seeing Robert's expression.)* I do, Robert.

MR. BUNDY: I don't believe I can go through this. To stay. I've been…having some irregular heartbeat. Nervous uh…nervous conditions. *(Wipes his eyes.)* I cry quite a bit over…over I don't know what. I don't…I can't listen to them shouting outside the house anymore.

ROBERT: Perhaps then, the best thing…

CATHERINE: If you had to go through it…if it came to that…I believe, after all these years there would be people here who…would feel this should stop now. Myself…people from our church…some of the people in the neighborhood…

ROBERT: Catherine, I believe I'll go back over to the house. I…

CATHERINE: *(Continuing to Mr. Bundy.)*…and after awhile they wouldn't shout anymore, and you could be done with it. I would encourage you to see if we couldn't put an end to it.

(Pause.)

ROBERT: I'll be there when you finish.

CATHERINE: Please stay.

ROBERT: Good-bye, Mr. Bundy.

MR. BUNDY: Oh. Yes.

CATHERINE: *(To Robert.)* Just stay one minute. Mr. Bundy, I know these are hard choices but…

ROBERT: *(By the door, has bent over and picked something up.)* What is this? What the hell is this?

CATHERINE: What is what?

ROBERT: This is the uh…the twirly thing, you know, that uh…that flying toy…the spinning fairy whatsit…from uh, from that thing I brought home to Cassie…you know the thing…come on, Catherine…the toy I brought Cassie two days ago.

CATHERINE: It could be from anything.

ROBERT: It's not from anything…it's the propeller part from that thing I bought Cassidy. She's been in here in the last two days.

CATHERINE: All right, calm down.

ROBERT: *(To Mr. Bundy.)* Has my daughter been in here? I made it clear a week ago…

CATHERINE: We'll talk at home.

ROBERT: No, we won't talk at home! Listen, Mr. Bundy, I don't want my daughter in here! I don't give a rat's ass about your nerves or your...palpitations, I don't want Cassidy anywhere near you, okay? I don't care what kind of pals you are with Catherine, I don't care how many years it's been, if my child knocks on your door you tell her, in no uncertain terms, she is not welcome. I can't believe this. I'm going to say this so everybody clearly, clearly understands it. If I ever find out you have spoken to my daughter, other than to send her home, I am going to hurt you, you understand, do you harm...*(To Catherine.)* Don't touch me...and break up your house, smash all these things I see, these things I see here, and drag every newspaper I can find right down here to your front door. Does that seem clear enough to you? *(To Catherine.)* Do you not listen to me? *(To Bundy.)* She was over here two days ago, and she better not ever, God help you, be over here again! *(He slams out.)*

CATHERINE: *(To Bundy.)* Are you all right?

MR. BUNDY: *(Shaking his head.)* I uh...I uh...

(They stand. Neither can speak. Robert, who has been moving since he left, walks by Jimmy Ray leaning against a building. Bundy's furniture is being cleared. The lights dim on Bundy and Catherine, who exit.)

JIMMY RAY: Hey, buddy. *(Robert stops and looks at him. He looks down and then back up.)*

ROBERT: What do you want?

JIMMY RAY: Been waitin' on you.

ROBERT: I work right over there.

JIMMY RAY: Yeah, I know, I didn't want to embarrass myself dressed like I am.

ROBERT: What is it?

JIMMY RAY: I said I'd be in touch. You want a cigarette? *(Robert shakes his head "no.")* You on the non-smokin' committee? *(A thin smile.)* Who runs your family, boy?

ROBERT: What are you talking about?

JIMMY RAY: There ain't squat goin' on is what I'm talkin' about. Bundy just sits there. What are you, pussywhipped?

ROBERT: Good-bye, Mr. Bosun. *(He starts off.)*

JIMMY RAY: Your kid said to give you this note from her teacher. Somethin' about parents' night, somethin' like that. *(Holds it out. Robert takes it and opens it.)*

ROBERT: Where did you get this?

JIMMY RAY: I went down to see your girl, ask her a few questions.

ROBERT: You went…no…you talked to Cassie at her school?

JIMMY RAY: Yeah, I dropped by.

ROBERT: Are you…you have got to be…I don't think that was any of your business.

JIMMY RAY: Me either, pal…

ROBERT: That's right…

JIMMY RAY: I think it was your business…

ROBERT: Hold it…

JIMMY RAY:…but you didn't take care of it so I had to make it…

ROBERT: Hold it.

JIMMY RAY:…my business.

ROBERT: *(Finger in his face.)* Don't you ever…

JIMMY RAY: *(Uninflected.)* Don't go there, man…*(An explosive moment.)* Don't go there, Bobby-Bobby. *(The potential passes.)* Now you want to know what I know, or you don't care?

ROBERT: What?

JIMMY RAY: *(Reaching out to his lapel.)* You got something stuck to your coat there. You remember how when Bundy abused those boys, he got 'em to put on women's clothes?

ROBERT: Yes.

JIMMY RAY: He dressed your girl up too.

ROBERT: No.

JIMMY RAY: Yeah, he did.

ROBERT: How do you know that?

JIMMY RAY: She told me.

ROBERT: In what way dressed her up?

JIMMY RAY: Had her undress, Bobby, had her put on some special little outfit he had an idea she should wear.

ROBERT: Why?

JIMMY RAY: Don't believe she said "why."

ROBERT: And then what?

JIMMY RAY: I figure that's your question to ask.

ROBERT: *(To himself.)* Goddamnit.

JIMMY RAY: Lord's name.

ROBERT: He had her undress?

JIMMY RAY: So she said.

ROBERT: *(Controlled.)* Is that all of what you have to say to me?

JIMMY RAY: You're a piece of work, man.

ROBERT: I think we're done now.

JIMMY RAY: Where are you, buddy?

ROBERT: Get out of my face.

JIMMY RAY: I think you're about three bricks shy of a load, pal. What kinda man are you foolin' with your daughter's life? You ought to be ashamed of yourself. You don't get him outta there, you're gonna be real, real sorry. I don't know where you're at, I don't know why you aren't takin' care of your family and, to tell the truth, I don't think you got any balls. When all this comes down it's gonna be straight up your fault. Oh yeah. Oh yeah. Batter up, man. Up to you, Bobby, big time. *(Starts off.)* Don't forget parents' night.

(He leaves. The lights come down. Cassidy steps into a spot. Behind her they reset the kitchen table and chairs.)

CASSIDY: Mr. Bundy told me that you should never go with a strange person and if they try to…the bad person…to pull you, you should yell and say, "You aren't my father. You aren't my mother!" Which is pretty stupid because nobody ever pays attention to kids anyway. Anne Marie said she tried it when she was with her daddy in the mall and everybody just laughed or smiled, or didn't even look when he carried her out. He was really mad, too. Why would anyone want to hurt a kid anyways? It's so stupid.

(The lights come up in the Ferreby kitchen. Cassidy and Catherine are seated at the table. Robert is on his feet talking to the child.)

ROBERT: It's not stupid. I want you to look at me, Cassidy. I said look at me!

CATHERINE: Don't scare her.

ROBERT: There are times to be scared. There are times when it is sensible and useful. Now you went over there when we told you very clearly you should not.

CASSIDY: No.

ROBERT: Don't lie to me, Cassidy.

CASSIDY: I didn't.

ROBERT: You went over there a day later.

CASSIDY: Just to play on the swings.

ROBERT: Was your mother watching you?

CATHERINE: Robert...

ROBERT: Did your mother know you went over there?

(Cassidy looks at her mother.)

CATHERINE: It's all right, honey.

CASSIDY: Just to play on the swings.

ROBERT: *(To Catherine.)* You knew.

CATHERINE: There is no reason she can't play outside there.

ROBERT: There is every reason but the simplest reason is we agreed she shouldn't.

CATHERINE: That isn't what we agreed.

ROBERT: How do you have the nerve to say that to my face?

CASSIDY: I don't like it when you fight.

ROBERT: We're not fighting, Cassidy.

CASSIDY: You are too.

ROBERT: I want you to be quiet, Cassidy.

CASSIDY: Oh fine. *(She turns away from him.)*

ROBERT: Were you watching her on the swings? After you sent her over there...

CATHERINE: I didn't send her over there.

ROBERT: Did you watch her, Catherine!

CATHERINE: What's the matter with you?

ROBERT: Because if I can't trust you to watch her, then maybe there should be someone else here.

CASSIDY: I don't want someone else.

ROBERT: I told you to be quiet!

CATHERINE: Now you're scaring both of us.

ROBERT: What is the matter with *you?* What is the matter with both of you? She didn't just play on the swings. Your mom and I told you that for grown-up reasons it was dangerous.

CASSIDY: Swings aren't dangerous.

CATHERINE: To be fair, Robert, what we said was...

ROBERT: There were a lot of things we didn't say because of you.

CATHERINE: *(Going to get Cassidy out of her chair.)* Come on, Cassie.

ROBERT: Not yet.

CATHERINE: Come to Mommy.

ROBERT: Are you deaf, I said not yet.

CATHERINE: I think we should cool off now.

ROBERT: I want to know now, Cassidy, if you went in the house? And I want to know, clearly, if your mother knew you went in the house.

CASSIDY: Okay, yes.

ROBERT: "Okay, yes" what?

CASSIDY: For one minute.

ROBERT: Cassidy…Catherine, yes or no, did you know?

CATHERINE: Is this your…I don't know what…tough guy act?

ROBERT: Give me a straight answer!

CATHERINE: And are you more concerned about what she did in the house or whether you've been obeyed?

ROBERT: I'm not here to consider the fine points, Catherine, it seems to me I've made myself pretty clear. We agreed she wouldn't go in the house, and she was in the house.

CASSIDY: I wanted my train.

ROBERT: What train?

CATHERINE: The lawn decoration they'd been making together for weeks.

ROBERT: *(Punching the air in frustration.)* You let her go in there!

CATHERINE: No Robert. The furnace man showed up, so I said it would be all right to ring the bell and get the train.

ROBERT: Do you not take me seriously?

CATHERINE: That's an entirely different conversation. We can have that conversation later. Because of the furnace I might have been gone five minutes.

ROBERT: Five minutes?

CATHERINE: All right, seven minutes, eight minutes.

ROBERT: That is completely irresponsible!

CATHERINE: *(Explosive.)* And you are completely off the wall.

CASSIDY: No fighting! No fighting!

(Robert stops her with his hands on her shoulders.)

ROBERT: Honey…

CASSIDY: Let go of me! *(She struggles.)*

ROBERT: Stop it, Cassidy.

CASSIDY: You are mean. Let go!

ROBERT: Sit in the chair. *(Trying to break free, she accidentally hits him in the face and is momentarily free. In reaction, he lifts her roughly off her feet and overfirmly puts her back in the chair.)* Don't hit me!

CATHERINE: Leave her alone, Robert. *(She starts for the chair.)*

ROBERT: *(Warning her off.)* I'm talking to her.

CATHERINE: *(Trying to take his hands off Cassidy.)* Not like that.

ROBERT: I'm not hurting her.

CASSIDY: Mommy!

CATHERINE: You are hurting her! *(She tries to pull him away.)*

ROBERT: Get off me, Catherine.

CATHERINE: Just leave her alone.

ROBERT: *(As he pushes her away.)* I am talking to her.

(With the momentum of the push, Catherine missteps and falls to a sitting position on the floor.)

CASSIDY: Mommy!

(She runs to Catherine. Cassidy is intercepted by Robert who puts her back in the chair.)

ROBERT: Your mommy is all right.

CATHERINE: Stop it!!!

ROBERT: What did you do in the house?

CASSIDY: The lawn thing.

ROBERT: And what else?

CATHERINE: *(Rising.)* Get out of the room, Robert.

ROBERT: What else! Do you hear me!

CASSIDY: I asked him if I could play dress-up.

ROBERT: No!! Look at me!

(Catherine fiercely shoves him away from Cassidy. He stands there shaking, trying to prevent himself from going after her. She takes a step toward him to comfort him.)

CATHERINE: Robert…

(He bolts out of the room, upsetting a chair. Cassidy is crying. Catherine goes to her and cradles her. During the following, the kitchen set is struck and an armchair representing Mr. Bundy's living room is brought on.)

CATHERINE: It's okay, sweetie, it's all right, Cassie.

CASSIDY: Daddy hurt you.

CATHERINE: He didn't hurt me, I tripped.

CASSIDY: I hate him.

CATHERINE: No you don't.

CASSIDY: It was scary.

CATHERINE: I know it was. *(Getting up.)* Let's go up, I'll read to you.

CASSIDY: Hold me.

CATHERINE: I want to hold you. *(She takes Cassidy up in her arms in a standing position.)*

CASSIDY: I hate him.

CATHERINE: *(Singing.)* "I'm looking over a four-leaf clover that I've overlooked before…"

(Catherine continues to sing, taking Cassidy off. Simultaneously, we are now in Mr. Bundy's living room. There is a single armchair, and he is sitting in it reading a woodworking magazine. There is an insistent knock on the door. He puts down the magazine and starts to get up. Another knock, he opens the door, and Robert is there. Robert grabs Mr. Bundy furiously by his shirt front and drives him back to the center of the room.)

MR. BUNDY: Wait…
(Robert hits Mr. Bundy full in the face. Mr. Bundy's hands go to his face. Robert grabs him by the hair and knees him in the groin. Bundy moans and bends over in pain.)
ROBERT: Never…never, never touch her, creep.
(Robert grabs him and straightens him up.)
MR. BUNDY: Please, no…
(Robert hits him twice more in the face, and Mr. Bundy collapses to the floor.)
ROBERT: Never! Do you hear?!
(He kicks him.)
MR. BUNDY: Please. Please.
(Robert pushes him down, gets astride him and bangs his head on the floor.)
MR. BUNDY: Animal!!
(Catherine enters.)
CATHERINE: Robert…*(Robert punches Mr. Bundy in the face again.)* Robert, in Christ's own name! *(Robert stops. He looks at her uncomprehendingly.)* Oh, my God, Robert. *(Robert gets up. His hands are covered with Bundy's blood. Bundy still moves slightly.)* Help him. *(Cassidy appears behind Catherine. Robert looks at Bundy, then looks at his hands. He wipes them off on his pants. Catherine sees Cassidy and pulls her in so her face is hidden and she can't look.)* Please help him.

(Robert stares at her. Lights down. A light up on Tianna elsewhere. During her speech, Bundy's chair is struck and we go to the Ferreby bedroom where we will see Catherine pack.)

TIANNA: All right then, Jesus Christ tells us to turn the other cheek and repay evil with good, but that's not about our kids. See, they are too tender and the evil too hard. This is where the humanists and such have got themselves confused, my friends. For our children we must be as a pride of lions and strike a blow, not turn away. For anyone who harms a child has broken covenant with the tribe and become anathema. And those who are anathema must be destroyed.

(She exits as the lights come up on Catherine packing. Her clothes are in piles on the bed. Three already-packed suitcases are on the floor. She packs into a fourth suitcase on the bed. Robert enters.)

ROBERT: Please don't go.

CATHERINE: *(Packing.)* My sister's work number and home number are on the sheet in the kitchen. She and Cassie left around lunch-time. I'll be getting there pretty late, and then Cassie and I will take off for a few days.

ROBERT: Please don't go.

CATHERINE: I went down to the hospital. He's off the critical list.

ROBERT: Forgive me.

CATHERINE: The movers will be here in a few days, there are people packing him up. Oh, packing. I packed all Cassie's Barbie stuff but the car is full. I addressed the box. It's in the garage. I'd appreciate it if you sent it on.

ROBERT: We don't know what he did.

CATHERINE: He did nothing.

ROBERT: We don't know.

CATHERINE: What are you, Robert? Are you sorry?

(A pause.)

ROBERT: What will happen to us if I answer that? Can you take my answering that? *(They look at each other.)* I guess I'm sorry for me. *(She looks down. He goes to her.)* Catherine.

CATHERINE: No.

ROBERT: *(Tries to lift her chin to look at him.)* Look at me.

CATHERINE: I said don't. *(Turns away.)*

ROBERT: *(Tries to turn her.)* Just look at me.

CATHERINE: I don't need to.

ROBERT: For one second.

CATHERINE: No!

ROBERT: *(Forcing her to turn.)* How much is that asking?

CATHERINE: *(Slaps him hard. A moment. They look at each other.)* Damn it.

ROBERT: Hey…

CATHERINE: I can't believe this!

ROBERT: It's okay.

CATHERINE: It's not okay. You…

ROBERT: I'm not hurt…

CATHERINE: All this time…Cassie, Mr. Bundy, Tianna, I wanted to stay…not this. Where did you think I was? You think I wasn't frightened for Cassie? You think it didn't cost me anything? Sometimes I wanted Bundy on the moon, in a cage, anywhere but next door to me. When you had the affair I fantasized coming back and setting fire to the house, but it seemed…important not to go there, not to be that. It was easy to hit him, Robert, easy…and it was easy for me to hit you, and we both did it, and now we are what we never wanted to be. All for nothing. Just part of this whole apocalyptic thing that seems to be rolling downhill. The one thing…*the one thing* I didn't want to be part of!

ROBERT: The guy destroyed children for pleasure. What part of the equation is that?

CATHERINE: *(Closing her suitcase.)* I have to go, Robert.

(They stand separated, in silence.)

ROBERT: What am I going to do without you and Cassie?

CATHERINE: *(Simply.)* Cassie doesn't want to see you, and I don't want to live with you.

ROBERT: I'll do whatever you want. What do you want?

CATHERINE: *(Putting the suitcase on the floor.)* I don't want her to learn what you have to teach her. That's what I want.

(She takes the suitcase out. The lights go down but not out. We hear bus announcements for various parts of the country. A waiting bench is brought on in one area and Mr. Bundy, bandaged and in a neck brace, sits on it. Tianna enters with microphone from another direction.)

TIANNA: I want to see Charles DeYoung fry, I do. More than that, I want eye contact with him, because I want to see the moment when the light goes out. It's my right to be the last thing he sees, so he knows I do not forgive him.

BUS ANNOUNCEMENT: Twelve-forty bus for Dayton boarding door nine. One o'clock Greyhound for Albuquerque with stops in Springfield, Tulsa and Amarillo door six. Also at one P.M., San Francisco Express, door change to fourteen. Door fourteen.

(Bundy takes out his ticket and looks at it.

He unzips the bag in front of him on the floor and takes out a "get well" card obviously made by a child and looks at it. He pulls out the dress that Cassie tried on in his workshop.

He puts the dress and the card back in the suitcase, zips it and rises to go. He picks up his suitcase and walks down toward the audience. During the final bus announcement, the scene changers clear the stage of furniture.)

BUS ANNOUNCEMENT: Buses for Tampa, St. Petersburg, Orlando with intermediate stops, please proceed to door ten…door ten for all Florida destinations. Please do not leave luggage unattended in any part of the terminal.

(Mr. Bundy stands in a single light awkwardly holding the suitcase. Elsewhere on stage, Cassidy jumps rope.)

CASSIDY'S VOICE: Don't throw him pennies
 or feed him sweets,
 'cause you're just what
 the oogey-boogey eats.
 Don't open the cupboard
 if you need a cup,
 'cause the oogey-boogey's in there,
 and he'll eat you up.

(The lights fade on Mr. Bundy and Cassidy.)

END OF PLAY

Like Totally Weird

a full-length one-act

by William Mastrosimone

To Jonathan and Jason

BIOGRAPHY

William Mastrosimone, a resident of Enumclaw, Washington, made his playwriting debut with *The Woolgatherer* (1992 L.A. Drama Critics Award for Best Play), followed by *Extremities,* which premiered at Actors Theatre of Louisville in the 1981 Humana Festival (New York Outer Critics Circle Award for Best Play in 1982-83, John Gassner Award for Playwriting) and later became a feature film. *Nanawatai!* opened in Norway, later becoming the film *The Beast* (1988 Roxanne T. Mueller Award for Best Film, Cleveland International Film Festival). *Sinatra* received a 1992 Golden Globe Award for Best Mini-Series while *The Burning Season* received an Emmy nomination, a Humanitas and an Environmental Media Award (1995). Other films include *With Honors* and *Escobar* (HBO). Other plays include *Tamer of Horses* (1987 L.A. NAACP Award for Best Play), *A Tantalizing* (1982 Humana Festival), *Shivaree* (Warner Communications Award), *A Stone Carver, The Undoing* (1984 Humana Festival), *Sunshine, Cat's Paw, Burning Desire* and *Benedict Arnold.* He holds a M.F.A. from Mason Gross School of Arts, an Honorary Doctorate of Humane Letters from Rider College, and is a 1989 recipient of the New Jersey Governor's Walt Whitman Award for Writing.

HUMANA FESTIVAL PRODUCTION

Like Totally Weird premiered at the Humana Festival of New American Plays in March 1998. It was directed by Mladen Kiselov with the following cast:

Kenny	Kevin Blake
Jimmy	Chris Stafford
Russ Rigel	V Craig Heidenreich
Jennifer Barton	Kim Rhodes
Voice of Chauffeur	Craig Michael Robillard

and the following production staff:

Scenic Designer	Paul Owen
Costume Designer	Nanzi Adzima
Lighting Designer	Greg Sullivan
Sound Designer	Michael Rasbury
Properties Designer	Ron Riall
Fight Director	Steve Rankin
Stage Manager	Charles M. Turner, III
Assistant Stage Manager	Juliet Horn

CHARACTERS

RUSS RIGEL: actor, screenwriter, director, producer.

JENNIFER BARTON: actress.

KENNY, 16, and JIMMY, 15: Valley kids. Behavior: In body language, both need constant action—nervous hands, legs and feet. They need to move all the time. Life has to be an action movie. Boredom is their greatest bane.

VOICE OF A CHAUFFEUR

TIME AND PLACE

Beverly Hills Gardens, California. Now.

SETTING

A fabulous home: An upper level. A staircase leading to the ground floor. A niche holds two Oscars. Sofa. Open archways leading to various parts of the house.

COSTUME NOTE

The boys are walking billboards. Their clothes are advertisements of Russ Rigel movies. They wear baggy layers of clothing, sneakers that light up, sunglasses, baseball hats on backwards. They have skateboards. Kenny wears a t-shirt that reads: "Primordial Rage." Jimmy sports a t-shirt that says: "Dominator."

AUTHOR'S NOTE

The play is presented without an intermission.

Chris Stafford, Kevin Blake, Kim Rhodes and V Craig Heidenreich
in *Like Totally Weird* by William Mastrosimone

22nd Annual Humana Festival of New American Plays
Actors Theatre of Louisville, 1998
photo by Richard Trigg

Like Totally Weird

The age demanded an image
of its accelerated grimace.
—Ezra Pound

Lights down on the audience. Lights up on two Oscars. The audience hears the audio portion of a film scene. The film scene begins with the sound of a gunshot.

DIRK: *(V.O.)* Well, well, well, well, well. What's the world comin' to when my own partner points a nine at my head? How'd you find me?

LANCE: *(V.O.)* I followed the body bags. Assume the position. I'm taking you in, Dirk.

DIRK: *(V.O.)* Badge over friendship, eh? All the coffee and donuts, all the times I saved your ass, all adds up to zero, eh?

LANCE: *(V.O.)* I got a job to do. What do you want from me?

DIRK: *(V.O.)* All I want is the look on your face of the bud I used to know.

LANCE: *(V.O.)* You were a cop's cop, Dirk. I looked up to you. But this time you went too far.

DIRK: *(V.O.)* I cleaned up the scum in this town.

LANCE: *(V.O.)* Save it for the jury.

DIRK: *(V.O.)* Do you have to cuff me?

LANCE: *(V.O.)* C'mon, Dirk, you know the routine.

DIRK: *(V.O.)* I got six reasons you should let me slide on this one, buddy.

LANCE: *(V.O.)* What six reasons?

(Gunfire from two pistols. Then sudden quiet. After a moment, the two men groan in pain.)

DIRK: *(V.O.)* Can't believe you fell for that…Looks like we both sprung a leak, buddy.

LANCE: *(V.O.)* Where'd I hit ya?

DIRK: *(V.O.)* Lungs…Nice shot…You?

LANCE: *(V.O.)* I'll live. *(Sound of sirens.)* Here comes my back-up.

DIRK: *(V.O.)* No way they're gonna collar me, Lance…Can't ya do me one last favor, buddy? I can't reach my piece or else I'd do myself. Put one right between my eyes, buddy.

LANCE: *(V.O.)* C'mon Dirk. You can't ask me that.

DIRK: *(V.O.)* I need a prison like a hole in the head. Tell 'em I resisted. You'll get a citation.

LANCE: *(V.O.)* Close your eyes.

DIRK: *(V.O.)* Buenas noches, baby.

(Sound of one gunshot and Lance sobbing.)

(The light burgeons to fill the entire living room. On a magnificent coffee table, an empty champagne bottle, two glasses, and a Golden Globe Award. A sequined gown on the sofa. The room is adorned with works of art—all depictions of human beings and gods. A pair of matching high heels trails up the staircase. A tux jacket hangs over the railing. Enter Kenny and Jimmy, arrested by the splendor, goofing on the art, exploring every inch. At one point Jimmy puts his sunglasses on the table. He picks up a cigarette lighter in the shape of a gun. Pulls the trigger. Fire flicks out of the barrel.)

KENNY: This is like so cool.

(Kenny goes for the Golden Globe.)

JIMMY: Majorly cool! Kenny! The dress she wore last night. *(Jimmy picks up the gown. Kenny snatches it away, sniffs the remnants of perfume.)* Rock on. Do Jennifer Barton.

KENNY: No, no, no.

JIMMY: C'mon, c'mon.

(Kenny holds the dress up to his body with one hand, clutching the Golden Globe to his bosom with the other hand, pretending to be an actress receiving the award. Jimmy becomes his cheering section.)

KENNY: "Oh, wow. I didn't realize this thing was so heavy…Could this be some kind of mistake? I'm so unprepared for all this. I didn't write a speech. I'd like to thank all those who made me what I am. Thanks to my mother and father and little brother, Brendan. And my director, my friend, my lover, and my mentor, Russ Rigel, for believing in me…"

RUSS: *(Offstage.)* The jinni's out of the bottle. There's nothing anybody can do. So sue me! Sue me!

(Kenny and Jimmy take cover as Russ enters talking on a portable phone.)

RUSS: How big's your pecker, m'man? You're talking to the man with the top-grossing picture in North America. So sue me! And I'll counter-sue and own the fillings in your kids' teeth. *(Hits phone button.)* Sandy, who's next? Start stacking the calls. Are we clear? Go…What's up? I'm shooting a picture, got a picture in pre-, another in post-, busier than a one-legged man in an ass kicking contest. I want nothing to do with a low-budget picture. What do you mean why? How can I steal two million from a mil-lion-dollar picture? You're a dinosaur, David. You can't think in millions anymore. Ever since the big boat sank, we have to think in billions. Don't call me till you have a billion-dollar idea. *(Pushes button.)* Sandy? Next… Tom, why can't I have Joe for a production rewrite?…Tom, you're full of shit. I had pizza with Joe two nights ago at Spago and he said he's very available…I don't want Griffis…You have time? A) Griffis never had a picture with a decent gross; B) He dresses from Banana Republic; C) He can't write his name in the mud with a fucking stick. And it has nothing to do with the fact that he didn't thank me at the Academy Awards three years ago. Tom: A) I want Joe; B) You stand in my way, my footprints are gonna be on your chest; C) Have a nice day. *(He finds and ponders Jimmy's sunglasses. Hits button.)* Sandy? Where are you? This is not Kansas, Sandy. Here in L.A. we try and stay awake during business hours. Who's next? Go…Hello, Michael. Look, enough foreplay already. I need an answer…What would you say if I told you Julia's ga-ga over the script? Sorry, Michael, my assistant just beeped me. My mother's going into surgery right now. Hang on. *(Hits button.)* Sandy, speed dial Julia. Go… Julia, Russ…Why is it I can't get you out of my mind? Here I am, sitting at my desk, tears running down my face, halfway through a new script. The female lead is you, you, you. Well it's an inter-galactic *Romeo and Juliet*. She's an alien who—I'd rather tell you face to face at lunch tomor-row. I'll pick you up. Looking forward. Love you. *(Hits button.)* Sandy, you in a fucking coma? When I hang up on Michael in about thirty sec-onds, I want Glen then Adam. Are we clear? Go…Sorry to make you wait so long, Michael. Oh, she's fine. Just needed a little TLC. Quadruple bypass. Anyway, I need a memo you've got the financing in place…

Michael, what are you bringing to the party? I have a commitment from Julia. Now I need one from you...Look, Michael, Universal's calling me at home on Sunday for this project so fuck you forever or until I need you, whichever comes first. *(Hits button.)* Sandy? Earth to Mars? When Michael calls back I want you to "slip" that I'm on with Universal. Are we clear? Put him on...Go. Glen, listen: need you to ghost another script treatment on the way over. A) Must be on my desk in ten days without fail; B) Classic romantic structure: boy meets girl, boy loses girl, boy gets girl back again and finds out—ready for this?—girl is an alien; C) Make it fit Julia like a glove. Are we clear? Let's breakfast in the a.m., talk plot points and bucks. You come through for me, buddy, you're gonna direct the next one. *(Hits button.)* Sandy, sorry to interrupt your nap. Go... Adam, how's that new baby? Did the clothes fit her?...Jennifer and I sent over a box of stuff...I'll have Sandy track the package. Anyway, Adam, loved your treatment but I'm sorry to tell you I've got a very similar boy-meets-alien-girl in development. Matter of fact, due for delivery in ten days. More proof that you and I've got the same antennas and we just pluck the same ideas out of the air. Gotta run, but look, buddy, I wanna be in business with you. Send me more stuff and kiss that baby for me. *(Hits button.)* Sandy, find a baby shop in Beverly Hills yesterday. Have them send a thousand dollars worth of baby stuff for an infant girl right now, tonight. Who's on? What'd he say when you dropped Universal? Go...Michael, I can't apologize for my passion. I think we can put this thing back together if you'd just trust my integrity. Then let's make it contingent upon Julia's involvement. Love to your wife. Catch you on the sixth hole tomorrow. *(Hits button.)* Sandy, what are you on? Whatever it is, tell your doctor to decrease the dosage. Get me somebody to talk to. I'm free for ten minutes.

(Exit Russ. Kenny and Jimmy come out of hiding. Kenny takes a puff of Russ' cigarette.)

KENNY: *(As Russ.)* "Sandy, speed dial Julia. Go...Julia, Russ...Why is it I can't get you out of my mind? Here I am, sitting at my desk, tears running down my face—"

(They hear Russ and go back into hiding. Enter Russ. His tone, bearing, accent is suddenly quasi-British.)

RUSS: You know, Liz, I'd venture that Jennifer won over the seasoned pros because she has that elusive quality called dazzle...Off the record?...Of course we're serious...I give her jewelry all the time. I'm not partial to rings...Mind holding, Liz? *(Hits button.)* Sandy, ring Jennifer in the master bedroom. I need her right away. Entertain Liz with your irresistible charm while I take the next call. Who's up? Record the call...Heidi, I'm on the fly. Thursday next week I will be entertaining three Japanese gentlemen who require three goodwill ambassadors with unusual to exotic talents. Are we clear? Keep it warm for me, baby.

(Enter Jennifer Barton by way of the staircase in a robe.)

JENNIFER: Sweetheart, did you want me?

RUSS: All day long. Liz wants to feature you in her column tomorrow.

JENNIFER: Aww, Russ, I'm in a stupid funk.

RUSS: Stupid funk was invented to keep losers down and make psychiatrists rich. Jen, it's a million dollars free advertisement.

JENNIFER: But I'm all interviewed out. Bone dry.

RUSS: *(He takes her in his arms, dances her to the phone.)* Liz is a friend. You burp on the phone, she'll write to be or not to be. C'mon.

JENNIFER: Any second the fraud police'll burst in the door and take it back. Look at my competition. Susan, Geena, Emma. I can't hold a candle to them, Russ.

RUSS: Translation: you're scared of heights.

JENNIFER: C'mon, honey, be honest with me. They're great. Really great. They've made lots of movies. Classy movies. What have I done?

RUSS: They already won their awards. People want fresh faces. The elevator to the top has stopped. End of journey. You have arrived. Deal with it. Enjoy it. Because five years from now you'll do *Seagull* brilliantly and lose to a newcomer. Then you'll have lots of time for a self-indulgent funk.

JENNIFER: How do I play her?

RUSS: She likes anecdotes.

JENNIFER: I need a jump start.

RUSS: The day you barged in my office. Just don't hype her. And she likes humility with a touch of arrogance.

(He hands her the phone, pushes a button.)

JENNIFER: Hi, Liz...Thank you so much...I'm still waiting for somebody to pinch me. To be well thought of by one's peers is an honor—but can't compare to waking up in the morning and seeing the Golden on the coffee table...How? Well I went to a cattle call and saw everybody looked like me so I snuck in Russ' office and said, "Stop looking. There's nobody else who can play this role but me." And he said, "How would you feel about being photographed with your clothes off?" I said, "As long as I have a good script to hide behind." He gave me the role right on the spot...Well I guess you might say it's a marriage of the minds...Well, one thing at a time. For now it's just the minds...Well I'm in Russ's next movie *Ragnarok* and then we hope to adapt *Seagull*...Anton Chekhov...C,H,E,K,H,O,V. *(Russ taps his wristwatch.)* I'm really sorry, Liz, but our car just pulled up...Darling, what is it tonight? *(She holds the phone such that Liz can hear Russ' answer.)*

RUSS: Fund-raiser for physically handicapped kids.

JENNIFER: Oh, tonight? Jean Paul Gaultier. Thanks, Liz. Bye.

RUSS: You're a pro—when you can do it under pressure. We should go soon.

JENNIFER: Ten minutes. *(She hands the phone to Russ and ascends the stairs.)* Hey...you're the best.

RUSS: I know.

(Exit Jennifer.)

RUSS: *(Hits a phone button.)* Who's next up? What do you mean they hung up? Translation: you let them hang up, you limp-dick, closet fudge-packer. You wanna be in The Biz, get interesting! Learn to do a grease job. Hold all calls. I'll call you from the limo and return calls then. Are we clear? *(Russ hangs up, starts to leave, sees Kenny, then Jimmy.)* Who are you? *(Kenny and Jimmy just stare.)* You the groundskeeper's kids? Answer me! You're not allowed in the house. Tell your father to get his sorry ass in here. You hear me? Get out and stay out. *(Jimmy starts to go. Kenny stays.)* Hey, Shithead, I'm talking to you.

(Russ moves towards Kenny who pulls his gun. Russ stops. Kenny shoots the ceiling. Russ freezes as plaster sprinkles down. Kenny launches into the movie scene.)

KENNY: *(As Dirk.)* "Well, well, well, well, well. What's the world comin' to when my own partner points a nine at my head? How'd you find me?" *(Silence. Jimmy tosses the cigarette lighter to Russ.)*

KENNY: *(As Dirk.)* "Well, well, well, well, well. What's the world comin' to when my own partner points a nine at my head? How'd you find me?"

JIMMY: *(Prompting Russ.)* "I followed the body bags." He wants to do the scene with you.

RUSS: What?

JIMMY: You know, the shoot-out scene in *Primordial Rage*.

KENNY: *(As Dirk.)* "Well, well, well, well, well. What's the world comin' to when my own partner points a nine at my head? How'd you find me?"

RUSS: I don't know Lance's lines.

KENNY: But you wrote the movie!

RUSS: But I played Dirk. You're not the groundskeeper's kids?

JIMMY: No, we're just like fans.

RUSS: Fans.

JIMMY: We know all your movies. We saw *Primordial Rage* seventeen times.

RUSS: Wonderful. What do you boys want here?

JIMMY: Can I like have your autograph please?

RUSS: You want my autograph?

JIMMY: Yeah.

RUSS: I pay security bills up the ass and I got kids in my house with a loaded pistol. Of course you can have my autograph.

KENNY: Hey! I've seen this before! Is this the stairs in the movie where Dirk and Tara—?

RUSS: Yes, that scene was filmed here.

JIMMY: That's so cool. *(Russ finds a pen. Jimmy offers his arm.)*

RUSS: What's your name?

JIMMY: Jimmy. Could you sign it on my arm?

RUSS: *(Signs on Jimmy's bare skin.)* To Jimmy.

JIMMY: My biggest fan.

RUSS: My biggest fan. There ya go, Jimmy.

JIMMY: Cool. When's *Primordial Rage* gonna come out on video?

RUSS: Eight, nine months. I have a copy I can give you.

JIMMY: Really?

RUSS: Up in my office. Be right back. *(He starts to go up the stairs. Kenny cocks the gun. Russ stops.)*

JIMMY: I wouldn't.

RUSS: Okay. What's your name?

JIMMY: He's Dirk today.

RUSS: Like my movie character.

JIMMY: Yeah. Sometimes he wakes up as Dirk and he's Dirk all day long.

RUSS: What can I do for you, Dirk? *(Kenny tosses Jimmy the cigarette lighter gun and they both launch into the movie scene.)*

KENNY: *(As Dirk.)* "Well, well, well, well, well. What's the world comin' to when my own partner points a nine at my head? How'd you find me?"

JIMMY: *(As Lance.)* "I followed the body bags. Assume the position. I'm taking you in, Dirk."

KENNY: *(As Dirk.)* "Badge over friendship, eh? All the coffee and donuts, all the times I saved your ass, all adds up to zero, eh?"

JIMMY: *(As Lance.)* "I got a job to do. What do you want from me?"

KENNY: *(As Dirk.)* "All I want is the look on your face of the bud I used to know."

JIMMY: *(As Lance.)* "You were a cop's cop, Dirk. I looked up to you. But this time you went too far."

KENNY: *(As Dirk.)* "I cleaned up the scum in this town."

JIMMY: *(As Lance.)* "Save it for the jury."

KENNY: *(As Dirk.)* "Do you have to cuff me?"

JIMMY: *(As Lance.)* "C'mon, Dirk, you know the routine."

KENNY: *(As Dirk.)* "I got six reasons you should let me slide on this one, buddy."

JIMMY: *(As Lance.)* "What six reasons?"

(In slow motion they pretend to fire at one another—Kenny, with the real gun, Jimmy, with the cigarette lighter—reacting to every pretend hit. Both boys pretend to die in slow motion. We see they have rehearsed this scene many times.)

KENNY: *(As Dirk.)* "Can't believe you fell for that…Looks like we both sprung a leak, buddy."

JIMMY: *(As Lance.)* "Where'd I hit ya?"

KENNY: *(As Dirk.)* "Lungs…Nice shot…You?"

JIMMY: *(As Lance.)* "I'll live. Here comes my back-up."

KENNY: *(As Dirk.)* "No way they're gonna collar me, Lance…Can't ya do me one last favor, buddy? I can't reach my piece or else I'd do myself. Put one right between my eyes, buddy."

JIMMY: *(As Lance.)* "C'mon, Dirk. You can't ask me that."

KENNY: *(As Dirk.)* "I need a prison like a hole in the head. Tell 'em I resisted. You'll get a citation."

JIMMY: *(As Lance.)* "Close your eyes."

KENNY: *(As Dirk.)* "Buenas noches, baby."

(Jimmy puts the cigarette lighter gun to Kenny's head, pretends to shoot.)

RUSS: Very nice.

(Kenny and Jimmy jump and yell joyously.)

JIMMY: Just like the movie, huh?

RUSS: Good, solid work.

KENNY: Who's better, me or him?

RUSS: Hard to say.

KENNY: You think I got potential?

RUSS: Definitely. I'll have my assistant take your names and numbers and set up an audition.

(Kenny picks up the phone before Russ does, tossing it to Jimmy, back and forth playfully.)

RUSS: What do you need, Dirk? *(Kenny tosses the cigarette lighter to Russ.)*

KENNY: Do the scene with Jimmy.

JIMMY: Cool!

RUSS: You know, guys, I'd love to do the scene but I'm a little pressed for time right now.

KENNY: So how are the grosses this week?

RUSS: Bonkers.

KENNY: Hit break-even yet?

RUSS: We should be in the black this weekend.

KENNY: Cool. You pissed at that TV guy who gave your movie a bad review?

RUSS: Which one?

KENNY: The fat guy.

RUSS: Didn't see it.

KENNY: Jimmy, be the fat guy. I'm the skinny guy.

(Jimmy stuffs a pillow under his shirt. They both sit and launch into the movie review.)

JIMMY—THE FAT GUY: *Primordial Rage* is a piece of trash.

KENNY—THE SKINNY GUY: You're just an old fuddy-duddy who doesn't appreciate the artistry—

JIMMY—THE FAT GUY: Maybe ten years ago you could talk about Russ Rigel's artistry, but now he's doing bodybag movies. This man is a cancer on the body of Hollywood.

KENNY—THE SKINNY GUY: It's just fun! Does everything have to be high cinematic art?

JIMMY—THE FAT GUY: I estimated over two hundred killings in two hours. Is that what you mean by fun?

KENNY—THE SKINNY GUY: Two hundred? I think you forgot one.

(Pulls his pistol and mock-fires at Jimmy who pretends to fall dead with an ugly scream.)

KENNY: Don't worry, dude. I took care of fat boy for you.

RUSS: What do you mean took care of fat boy?

KENNY: Gave fat boy a call and some advice.

RUSS: Like what?

KENNY: *(Uses pistol as phone.)* "Another bad review might not be good for your health." Don't worry. I called from a phone booth.

RUSS: I really appreciate your zealousness, but—

KENNY: Anything for The Quad.

JIMMY: The Quad like totally rules!

RUSS: Sorry? The Quad?

JIMMY: *(Bows before Russ, kissing his shoes.)* Quadruple threat. Actor, Writer, Director, Producer.

RUSS: *(Pleased.)* The Quad.

KENNY: The Quad rules!

JIMMY: Kenny, do the speech, man.

KENNY: No, no, no.

JIMMY: C'mon! Do the speech! You gotta see this, Mr. Rigel!

(Kenny gives the gun to Jimmy, whips on Russ' tux jacket, picks up a Golden Globe and launches into an imitation of Russ at the award ceremony on TV the night before. Jimmy applauds.)

KENNY: *(As Russ.)* "Thank you, thank you, thank you so much! I love this town. I love the lights at night and the smog by day. I love its scarcity and its abundance. I love the magic that brings moviegoers by the millions in a dark room to feel, breathe, know, experience worlds beyond their own. Thank you for giving us the indescribable joy of knowing we touched you. Long live the magic. *(Jimmy cheers. Russ applauds.)*

RUSS: So you saw me hosting the Golden Globes last night.

KENNY and JIMMY: Duh!

RUSS: You have a phonographic memory. You got it word for word. Okay, guys, we have to go now.

KENNY: One quick question?

RUSS: Quick.

KENNY: Who makes the decision like if a character should like, you know, die in your movie?

RUSS: I do.

KENNY: You alone?

RUSS: I'm The Quad.

KENNY: Why'd you kill Dirk in the movie?

RUSS: I don't have time for this, okay?

JIMMY: I think we should go now. Thank you very much, Mr. Rigel.

RUSS: You're very welcome, Jimmy.

(Kenny holds up a picture of a young boy.)

KENNY: Who's this?

RUSS: My son.

JIMMY: How old's he?

RUSS: Fourteen.

KENNY: Live here?

RUSS: No.

KENNY: With his mother?

RUSS: No. Lives at school.

KENNY: Where?

RUSS: New Zealand.

JIMMY: Whoa. The other side of the world.

KENNY: Why doesn't he go to school here?

RUSS: I don't want him around this town.

KENNY: What do you mean?

RUSS: It's not a good place to raise kids.

KENNY: Who raises him in New Zealand?

RUSS: Jesuits. Strict.

(Jimmy picks up another picture.)

JIMMY: You know the President? Kenny, he's playing golf with the President.

RUSS: He's a friend. It was nice talking to you guys. Take care.

KENNY: You're not like pissed we walked in your house?

RUSS: Not at you. At those security clowns at the end of the street I pay to keep the public out. How'd you get past 'em?

JIMMY: We came down from Mulholland through the cactuses.

KENNY: We can't go now. Our friends won't ever believe we like met you. They'll say it's a fake autograph.

RUSS: Then why don't you take the Golden Globe for a momento? *(Puts Golden Globe on railing.)* And take an Oscar. Take two. They're small. Then they'll have to believe you. *(Takes Oscar out of niche.)*

JIMMY: Cool! When'd you win all these?

RUSS: Long time ago. This one for *Whisper,* and this one for *Hunger And Thirst,* Best Performance and Best Original Screenplay.

JIMMY: That what the fat guy meant?

KENNY: Never heard of those movies.

RUSS: They're more like art movies.

KENNY: Boring!

JIMMY: Boring!

(They have a "Boring" contest, i.e. repeat "boring" as fast as they can face to face till one of them falters, Kenny wins.)

RUSS: You guys are just too much fun. Okay? Happy?

JIMMY: Won't you like miss them?

RUSS: Hey, I have a few and I'm gonna win some more.

KENNY: Can I like have a picture of you?

RUSS: No. Okay, guys, we had a few yuks, but I really need to go now.

KENNY: Go where?

RUSS: I'm presenting awards to physically challenged kids.

KENNY: Crips?

RUSS: Handicapped kids, yeah.

(Kenny thrashes around the room like a "crip" drooling and talking from the side of his mouth unintelligibly. Jimmy cracks up. Kenny takes a vase out of a niche, tosses it to Jimmy. They play catch with it.)

RUSS: We need to be real careful with that, Dirk. It's two thousand years old. Christ walked the earth when the potter made that vase. *(Kenny tosses the vase to Russ—he catches it.)*

KENNY: Psych! Ever notice when somebody's gonna get iced in one of your movies the camera goes in for a close-up and that music starts. *(He mimics the music as he forms a frame of film with his hands like a director against Russ' face.)* And the dude gonna get iced, he's like whoa.

RUSS: Can I ask you a favor, my friend? Could you please not point that thing?

KENNY: Do brains really splatter like in the movies when you pop somebody in the head?

RUSS: I wouldn't know. It's all special effects.

KENNY: Ever notice in all your movies there's a gun to somebody's head?

RUSS: Oh?

KENNY: Yeah, and the camera circles around the guy with a gun to his head—

JIMMY: And you can see the sweat oozing out of his pores.

KENNY: And this look on his face—

JIMMY: Like whoa, man—

KENNY: I looooooooooove the scene in *Dominator* when the hit man's gun goes off by accident.

JIMMY: Aww, man, that was soooooooooo cool!

KENNY: And the kid in the back seat his brains splatter all over the car.

JIMMY: And they had to clean it up!

KENNY: Dude, how'd you think of that?

RUSS: It just sorta popped into my head. We need to wrap it up, gentlemen. Bottom-line this thing for me.

JIMMY: Like what do you mean?

RUSS: What are you looking for? Let's do business so I can be on my way. Coke? Heroin?

JIMMY: We just say no to drugs.

KENNY: Love that CLOSE-UP in the movie—*(Circling Russ like a cinematographer pointing the gun, mimicking music.)* When the girl smuggles in the drugs and the camera looks down the barrel of the hit man's gun.

RUSS: Okay, okay, okay, guys, drop the bullshit! Give me a number.

JIMMY: What kind of number?

RUSS: I've got some cash upstairs. You have a number in mind?

KENNY: Number?

RUSS: If you could just tell me what you want, believe me, I can make it happen. What do you want from me?

KENNY: Why'd you kill Dirk in the movie?

RUSS: What?

KENNY: You killed a good dude, man.

(Jimmy finds an ornate box filled with expensive chocolates.)

JIMMY: Whoa, man! Candy! May we?

RUSS: Help yourself.

(Suddenly they're both eight-year-olds.)

KENNY: All the ones in tinfoil!

JIMMY: All dark chocolate!

KENNY: All milk chocolate!

JIMMY: You have more than me!

KENNY: Do you have any gummy bears?

(Enter Jennifer dressed to kill descending the stairs.)

JIMMY: Wow!

JENNIFER: Sweetheart, you didn't tell me we had guests. Hi guys.

RUSS: This is Jimmy—

JENNIFER: Hello, Jimmy. I'm Jennifer—

JIMMY: I know who you are. *(Takes her proffered hand.)* Never wash that hand again.

(Jennifer sees Kenny's gun.)

RUSS: Jen, we have a little situation here.

JENNIFER: Uh-huh.

RUSS: Our friend here, well, he's got a lot on his mind.

JENNIFER: Uh-huh. How do you all know one another?

RUSS: These gentlemen are big enthusiasts of my work. They sorta dropped by for my autograph. They kind of invited themselves in.

JENNIFER: So you don't know one another?

RUSS: No. And right now we're trying to figure out what exactly would satisfy and reward their efforts.

JENNIFER: And you are? *(Proffering a hand to Kenny; he doesn't take it.)*

KENNY: *(He lifts his t-shirt to reveal another t-shirt underneath with Charles Manson's likeness. As Charlie.)* "The son of man. Some call me Man-son."

JIMMY: I think you should say hi to Charlie.

JENNIFER: Hi, Charlie. How's it goin'?

KENNY: *(As Charlie.)* "Bored."

JENNIFER: Bored?

KENNY: *(As Charlie.)* "Bored, bored, bored, bored, bored, bored, bored."

JIMMY: Can I like have your autograph?

JENNIFER: Of course, sweetheart.

JIMMY: Sign the back of my hand, please. Man, nobody's gonna believe we met Jennifer Barton.

RUSS: I'll get my video camera upstairs. Let's do a video together. How could your friends not believe that?

JIMMY: Rock on!

RUSS: Be right back. *(Starts up the stairs but stops by some weird feeling.)* Okay?

KENNY: Whatever.

RUSS: Jimmy? What do you advise me here?

JIMMY: I don't know.

RUSS: You don't know.

JIMMY: Whatever.

RUSS: Whatever.

JIMMY: Whatever. *(Russ goes back down the stairs.)*

KENNY: Man, you wanna go upstairs awful bad. You have a secret button up there?

RUSS: Secret button for what?

KENNY: There's buttons by the front door.

RUSS: The alarm system's off.

KENNY: What's all that?

RUSS: Intercom.

KENNY: Don't!

RUSS: I'm just showing you the buttons. Take it easy.

KENNY: What's K?

RUSS: Kitchen.

KENNY: S? Security?

RUSS: Swimming pool.

KENNY: P for police?

RUSS: Paddock. Stables.

KENNY: MB?

JIMMY: Mega-Basher!

RUSS: Master bedroom.

(Kenny laughs monstrously like Mega-Basher, a video-game combat character, and does a weird triumphant dance accompanied by Jimmy's imitation of a TV ballyhoo doing a commercial.)

JIMMY: He's bad! He's mad! He's the undefeatable man-masher known as— Mega-Basher...*(Echo effect, repeat.)*...Basher...Basher.

RUSS: Dudes, look, we have to present awards at a live TV function tonight. Our limo driver's gonna be knocking on the door any second now.

(Kenny goes after Jennifer as Mega-Basher. She doesn't flinch.)

JENNIFER: Mega-Basher's a pussy.

(Kenny stops his dance abruptly.)

KENNY: How do you know about Mega-B, you're like old.

JENNIFER: You better stop playing hooky from charm school. I kicked Mega-B's ass,

KENNY: Mega-B's unbeatable.

JENNIFER: If you're a spazz.

JIMMY: Whoa!

RUSS: Jen.

KENNY: Mega-Basher is designed unbeatable by some sucky little dweeb video-game manufacturer to drive us nuts.

JIMMY: Nobody at school ever beat Mega-Basher. Ever. Ever.

JENNIFER: Well maybe you don't know how to fight Mega-B.

KENNY: I know every combo and I never beat Mega-Basher.

JENNIFER: Combo knowledge is not the ability to street fight.

JIMMY: If you got past Mega-B, you must've seen inside of the Sacred Temple.

JENNIFER: Yup.

JIMMY: What's it like?

JENNIFER: There's no words for it. It's like so—*(Makes a sound to indicate superlative.)*

KENNY: Graphics that good?

JENNIFER: Rad.

JIMMY: Cool.

KENNY: You got witnesses you beat Mega-B?

JENNIFER: My little brother.

KENNY: Brendan.

JENNIFER: How do you know his name?

JIMMY and KENNY: Duh!

JENNIFER: Oh, you saw my acceptance speech last night.

JIMMY and KENNY: Duh!

JENNIFER: Only time Brendan ever talks to me is when we're teamed up in Mega-Basher.

KENNY: Where's he?

JENNIFER: Home with my folks.

KENNY: I wanna hear it from him.

JENNIFER: They live in Pennsylvania.

KENNY: So?

JENNIFER: It's a three-hour time difference.

RUSS: So what? Then it's nine o'clock there. Call him.

JENNIFER: You know I don't speak with my folks.

KENNY: Why?

JENNIFER: It's personal.

RUSS: You're calling Brendan, not your folks.

KENNY: Just dial. I'll talk.

RUSS: Maybe Jennifer should in case her parents—

KENNY: I'll talk. *(Kenny hands the phone to Jennifer. She hits the buttons and hands it back to Kenny.)*

KENNY: *(A perfect gentleman.)* Hi, I'm sorry to call so late but may I speak to Brendan about homework?…Kenny…Thank you. *(To Brendan.)* Hey, Brendan, whuz up, man? Kenny. I'm a friend of your sister's. Hollywood. Listen, Brendan, Jennifer says she beat Mega-Basher…How?…why wouldn't she tell?…But you saw her?…She didn't cheat or anything?…So how's it over there? Like how many McDonald's you have? *(Cups phone, to Jimmy.)* One McDonald's!—How many malls? *(Cups phone.)* One mall!—How many movies in the cineplex? *(Cups phone.)* What's a cineplex!—We have a cineplex with like eighteen movies! You got cable? How many channels? *(Cups phone.)* We got thirteen hundred!—You come out here, man, look us up. We'll show you around this town. Hey, thanks, man. *(He hangs up.)* How'd you beat Mega-B?

JENNIFER: What do we get?

KENNY: Like what do you mean?

JENNIFER: If I give up the secret of Mega-B, like what do you give us?

KENNY: Like what do you like want?

JENNIFER: We need to go.

KENNY: How'd you beat Mega-B?

JIMMY: I think you should like tell him.

JENNIFER: I think he should like answer my question.

KENNY: I'll let you know.

JENNIFER: That's not good enough.

KENNY: I let you go, I got nothing to do for the rest of the night.

RUSS: Stay here and watch us on TV. Kick back and relax.

KENNY: You sure are a hospitable man.

JENNIFER: Okay?

KENNY: Cool.

JENNIFER: Do we have a video game here?

RUSS: No, but I could have Sandy rush one over.

KENNY: He's just dying to get on that phone. How'd you beat Mega-B?

JENNIFER: Okay. At the beginning of the game, which character did you pick?

KENNY: *(Karate pose and scream.)* Rouser!

JIMMY: *(Karate pose and scream.)* Serpentine!

JENNIFER: That's why you dorks never beat Mega-B. You chose physical fighters. You have to choose Dakka.

JIMMY: Dakka? He's like a *monk!*

JENNIFER: A *warrior* monk from remote Tibet. Remember what spirit possesses his soul?

JIMMY: Tiger spirit!

JENNIFER: That's right: Mega-Basher is a man whose genes were spliced with a tiger. Tiger versus tiger. Mega-B can't be defeated solely by physical force. You have to checkmate his spirit. But don't even think about getting inside the Sacred Temple until you master the control pad. You gotta, gotta, gotta, gotta, gotta have the multi-hit combos down cold. All the moves gotta be second nature because it's ultimate fighting. You can't just stand there with kicks and punches when Mega-B comes at you.

JIMMY: Mega-B comes at you from every direction! By the time you block his kick, he throws five punches. Claws and punches come so fast you don't even have time to react!

(Kenny imitates Mega-B's insane laugh.)

JENNIFER: You gotta master the combo breaker, especially the jump-in auto doubles. *(She acts out the combat with Kenny.)* Okay, you're Mega-Basher, I'm Dakka the Tibetan Monk. Okay. You swim the river of blood. You zigzag up the bank to avoid the lava flow. Out of nowhere, Mega-B stands in your path.

(Kenny imitates Mega-B's laugh.)

JIMMY: I hate that laugh. It's so humiliating when Mega-B pulls off your head and reaches down your throat and pulls out your heart and eats it while it's still beating and then he lets out this huge burp. And throws you down into the Void with that insane laugh.

JENNIFER: What's the first thing Mega-B does?

JIMMY: Sweeps low!

JENNIFER: Yes! *(Jennifer imitates Mega-B's insane laugh.)* Mega-B sweeps low. You block low, you're open to top attack. That's why you gotta employ the combo-breaker. He comes in for a top attack—C'mon dudes, memorize this!—*(They repeat and imitate her karate.)* BLOCK, BLOCK, UPPERCUT, STRAIGHT PUNCH, UPPERCUT, BLOCK, BLOCK, SWEEP, DUCK, DUCK, KICK, KICK, FIERCE KICK, FIERCE PUNCH, SIDE KICK TO THE CHIN. Down goes Mega-B! Now you are truly worthy of entrance into the Sacred Temple.

KENNY: How's he die?

JENNIFER: Mega-B?

KENNY: Yeah! How's he die?

JENNIFER: Oh, it's so cool.

KENNY: Show us.

JENNIFER: But I'm all dressed up.

RUSS: Oh, I think you should give it a shot.

JENNIFER: Okay, here goes…

(She acts out the fight, yelling, pretending to be hit, laying it on thick, she roars in anger, then in pain, finally dying with a whimpering meow like a video game monster as Jimmy, Kenny and Russ cheer. Various house lights go on.)

KENNY: What's that? What's that? Who else's here?

RUSS: The lights are on a timer.

KENNY: Who's here? Who's in this house?

RUSS: Nobody, nobody. It's a timer. Six o'clock.

KENNY: Go look.

(Exit Jimmy.)

RUSS: Relax, relax.

KENNY: Whenever anybody relaxes in your movies, that's when they get it. You hit a button, didn't you?

RUSS: Don't have a button. But if I did, I wouldn't touch it. Tell you why. I know about joyrides. I know about forbidden fruit. I know about breaking all the rules. Makes you feel alive. But it's gotta come to an end. This is the end. Let's wrap it up for tonight and have lunch tomorrow.

KENNY: But you're having lunch with Julia tomorrow.

JENNIFER: Julia?

RUSS: Okay, then we'll get together for dinner.

JENNIFER: You promised me you wouldn't call her anymore. How does he know that?

RUSS: She called me about a project. Can we discuss my past another time, please? What do you say, m'man. I'll have my limo pick you up say around seven?

KENNY: You would really do that? You're not pissed I shot your ceiling?

(Russ and Jennifer start for the door.)

RUSS: Conversation piece.

KENNY: You won't press charges?

RUSS: For what, giving me a good story to tell on a talk show?

KENNY: I'm having a real bad day. The air pockets popped in my Nikes and I got no bounce when I walk. My mom buys Pop-Tarts *without frosting.* Now we got nowhere to go tonight.

RUSS: Here's some cash. Go to the movies.

KENNY: Saw everything.

RUSS: See you around midnight.

KENNY: Rest in peace. *(Russ and Jennifer stop.)*

RUSS: Can we go?

KENNY: I never said you couldn't leave.

RUSS: No, you didn't exactly say it...

KENNY: It's a free country.

RUSS: When you say it like that, m'man, I get the feeling you might do something.

KENNY: Like what?

RUSS: Don't play with me, my friend. Take what you want, okay?

KENNY: My mommy told me never take candy from a stranger.

RUSS: Fly in my Viper. Cruise Hollywood Boulevard in my Rolls. Bust out in my Harley.

KENNY: I don't need your junk, dude.

JENNIFER: We had a deal. I gave you the secret of killing Mega-B, showed you how Mega-B dies. You said we could go.

KENNY: Go.

RUSS: We're leaving.

KENNY: Good luck.

(There is a silent stand-off. Jennifer goes down the stairs, lights up a cigarette. Russ follows. Enter Jimmy.)

JIMMY: You gotta come see this, Kenny! There's like a glass room with a jungle inside. All weird plants and vines and parrots and a waterfall!

KENNY: So?

JIMMY: Know that parrot in *Primordial Rage?*

KENNY: The one Dirk nukes in the microwave?

RUSS: It's the same parrot. His name's Long John Silver.

KENNY: How can it be the same? Dirk nukes it in the movie.

RUSS: Special effects.

KENNY: You telling me the parrot didn't really explode?

RUSS: You can't explode a magnificent bird just to make a movie.

KENNY: *(Makes a face and gesture that shows his extreme displeasure.)* That fries me, man.

JIMMY: Oh shit.

KENNY: Ask anybody on the street, You see *Primordial Rage*? First thing out of their mouth: Whoa, man, the parrot scene is like so—*(Can't find the word so he screams and demonstrates the idea.)* That's why we went back to see your movie seventeen times. Just to hear the parrot squawk in the micro, man. We made you number one at the box office. We counted for seventeen people each. Think how many other dudes like us across the country. The world. And now you wrecked it, man. Wrecked it all. On top of that, I came all this way and you're nothing like Dirk. Nothing. Then I find out you're the one who decided to off Dirk, a good cop, a cop just trying to clean up this town. I mean like that fries me, man, that deep fries me.

RUSS: What makes you think Dirk died?

KENNY: 'Cause I saw the movie!

RUSS: You're wrong. Dirk survived.

KENNY: Duh! Nobody survives a talon bullet in the head!

RUSS: M'man, the movie's through the roof and that's just domestic. You think I'm gonna kill a box-office draw and throw away a sequel?

JIMMY: There's a sequel?

RUSS: The public demands a sequel. That's why I shot the last scene three ways: A) Dirk dies; B) He survives the gunshot and escapes; but I chose C) His situation is ambiguous, we're not sure if he dies or not. You say you saw my movie seventeen times. Go see it again. This time—pay attention! After Dirk's shot, the camera goes in for a close-up. His eyes are still open. He blinks. Once. One blink tells us he's still alive. You wanna see it? I got the tape in my office. We'll watch it in the screening room. I'll show you. The sequel script's up in my office, too.

KENNY: So how's it go, the sequel?

RUSS: The movie opens with Dirk covered in bandages. We find ourselves in a CIA recovery center. Deep underground. Location: top secret. We hear doctors mutter medical terms we don't understand. Cerebellum. Cerebral cortex. Blah blah blah. We come to learn that they're discussing Dirk's condition.

JIMMY: Is this gonna like wreck my enjoyment of the movie?

KENNY: How many times have I told you not to talk during movies?

JIMMY: Too many.

KENNY: Do a Daisy.

JIMMY: C'mon, man.

KENNY: Do a Daisy.

JIMMY: In front of people?

KENNY: You got something wrong with your ears?

JIMMY: Not in front of them.

KENNY: You're boring me. Do a Daisy.

(Jimmy rolls around on the floor yelping like a wounded dog. It builds to a crescendo as the dog dies. Jimmy gets up.)

KENNY: Doctors discussing Dirk's conditions. Go on.

RUSS: We learn that the talon bullet of which you spoke has passed clean through Dirk's brain. It destroyed the section in the medulla oblongata that controls his sense of right and wrong.

KENNY: So what's that mean?

RUSS: Dirk is now a pure killing machine.

KENNY: But that's what he was before.

RUSS: Yeah, but now he doesn't feel bad about it. Doctors discuss whether they should let him die. Without a sense of right and wrong Dirk might turn out to be another Hitler.

KENNY: Who?

RUSS: A very bad guy.

KENNY: Like what he do?

RUSS: Murdered thirteen million people.

KENNY: Wow.

RUSS: So word comes from the top: keep Dirk alive.

KENNY: Word from who?

RUSS: The President. They remake him electronically. One of his eyes is a laser. They surgically implant a microprocessor in his brain the size of your pinky fingernail. His index finger they turn into the barrel of a gun. His whole arm is one big clip with a thousand rounds.

JIMMY: Whoa!—Sorry.

KENNY: There was a movie like that.

RUSS: We'll do it better.

KENNY: Does Tara know there's a chip in Dirk's brain?

RUSS: Tara thinks Dirk's dead. She lays flowers on his grave every week. Can't see anybody else. Nobody compares to Dirk. CLOSE-UP on Tara's hand as she lays a rose across the tombstone. A shadow blankets her. She looks up. It's Dirk. She bursts into tears. CUT TO her place. They make love like prehistoric beasts.

KENNY: Don't make sense. If he's a pure killing machine, why's he need her?

RUSS: That's the thing: the part of the brain that controls love—still works. It's a struggle between the brain that he was born with versus the one they implanted.

KENNY: What's stronger? The microthing or love?

RUSS: We're getting to that. Dirk and Tara covered in sweat, melded in love, both on the verge of an orgasmic explosion. CUT TO CIA headquarters control room. A technician flicks a switch. CUT TO a satellite in outer space deflecting the signal to earth. BACK TO Tara and Dirk a nanosecond away from consummation when the radio signal activates the microprocessor. Dirk pulls away from Tara.

KENNY: But Dirk loves her.

RUSS: Yes, but his love is not strong enough to resist the radio wave.

KENNY: Wow. But what's Tara think?

RUSS: She... *(Beat. Looks to Jennifer.)*

JENNIFER: This isn't the Dirk she knows. Something's terribly wrong.

KENNY: *(Touches her face.)* Tara must be devastated.

RUSS: Dirk is torn between his love for Tara and the radio wave that beckons him to undertake the mission.

KENNY: Then what?

RUSS: BACK TO CIA headquarters. They see something is wrong. They increase the intensity of the radio wave. BACK TO Dirk and Tara. The radio wave pulls him out the door. They program him to take on all the L.A. gangs—a rampage like never before seen in cinematic history.

KENNY: That's not Dirk! Nobody controls Dirk! Dirk's better off dead than have some computer dweeb flicking a switch! Dirk was only the coolest, awesomest cop that ever was—and you killed him! Translation: your sequel's bullshit! It's all bullshit!

RUSS: You obviously feel strongly about the characters. I'd like you to sit down with my people and talk ideas.

KENNY: Yeah, and why would you want my ideas?

RUSS: I dig your demographics.

JENNIFER: He's saying you seem to know what kids want.

RUSS: You are the heartbeat of your generation. I'd like to have you sit in meetings, tell my people what you'd like to see up on the big screen.

JIMMY: Cool.

KENNY: Boring.

RUSS: You're a winner. You've got passion. Most people go home and bitch about the end of a movie. You try and do something about it. I don't want some unimaginative flunky who stops at the security gate. I want the genius who doesn't need anybody's permission and goes around 'em. I want the guy who don't flinch and don't give an inch. I want you in my rolodex and I want you on my payroll.

KENNY: Like how much?

RUSS: Enough to give you a rod from here to Arkansas. What do you think you're worth? Let's negotiate.

KENNY: I don't know how.

RUSS: I'll teach you. We can learn a lot from each other.

KENNY: I'm listening.

RUSS: First lesson: everybody's a whore. Only question is: what are they a whore for?

KENNY: You a whore?

RUSS: The biggest.

KENNY: So what are you a whore for?

RUSS: You're like me. Go for the jugular. You see m'man, when you know a person's dreams, what they want to do, what they want to be, what they want to have, then you know what they're a whore for. Then you have them in your pocket.

KENNY: So what are you a whore for?

RUSS: That's for me to know and you to find out.

KENNY: What am I a whore for?

RUSS: I haven't figured you out yet.

KENNY: What's Dirk a whore for?

RUSS: Dirk's not real.

KENNY: Dirk's real, dude. And Dirk's no whore. Nobody buys Dirk. Is that why you killed Dirk? Cause he's better than you? As my hero once said, "It's time to make some vertical people—horizontal."

RUSS: I wanna talk to Charlie.

KENNY: *(As Sandy, using gun as a phone.)* "I'm sorry, Mr. Manson stepped away from his desk. Can I help you?"

JIMMY: That's what your secretary said every time we called your office.

KENNY: We made you, and you couldn't even take our call?

RUSS: I get five hundred calls a day! Let me talk to Charlie!

KENNY: *(As Sandy.)* "Does he know what this is regarding?"

RUSS: Regarding a mutually beneficial arrangement.

KENNY: *(As Charlie, shirt up.)* "What's up, babe?"

RUSS: How can we get to a happy ending here? What's the deal?

KENNY: *(As Charlie, shirt up.)* "I don't make deals. I make demands."

RUSS: Love your style, Charlie…Love a guy who plays for all the marbles. You and me, we're men of the world. We understand one another. We understand the laws of life. You're top of the food chain or you're somebody's lunch. But if you look hard enough, there's always a quid pro quo. That's my religion. So let's put our heads together and make this a win-win negotiation.

KENNY: *(As Charlie.)* "What comes out of the end of your gun? *(Flicks the cigarette lighter.)* Fire? Know what comes out of the end of mine? A .357 dum dum. Looks like the negotiation's over." *(Kenny makes a camera with one hand, circles Russ like a cinematographer, pointing his gun with the other.)* CLOSE-UP on The Quad! And you know what that means!

RUSS: Kenny, Dirk, Charlie, whoever you are at the moment—Could you please point that somewhere else? *(Kenny points gun at Jennifer.)* Not there. *(Kenny points it back at Russ.)* Jimmy, what do you advise me here?

JIMMY: I'm not sure.

RUSS: My friend, that thing could go off by accident and ruin the rest of your life.

KENNY: What rest of my life, my friend? I could get it in a drive-by on the way to school. I could flip somebody off on the freeway and get it. Or we all could get it when the Big One comes. CLOSE-UP on The Quad!

JENNIFER: Kenny, what would your parents say?

JIMMY: Do your mom! Do your mom!

KENNY: *(As his mom.)* "Oh, Kenneth how many times have I told you not to shoot people in the head? You just give neighbors something else to talk about. When your father is the school principal, people expect better behavior."

JIMMY: Do your dad! C'mon! Do your dad!

KENNY: *(As his dad.)* "Now, Son, do you think this kind of behavior will get you into a good college? I'm sorry. A new pair of Nikes is out of the question." *(As himself.)* I'm the only one with last-year's Nikes! I'll be the freaky geek at school! CLOSE-UP on Dad! *(Mimes shooting his dad in the head.)* But Mom would be so unhappy without Dad. CLOSE-UP on Mom. *(Mimes shooting mom.)* And the crims are gonna go, Don't mess with that dude, man, he offed his mamma and papa and that big Hollywood producer and his bimbo. Erik and Lyle are gonna say, You outdid us, dude. You are the man! And Charlie's gonna say: *(Shirt up, as Charlie.)* "Proud o' you, Son." *(Shirt down.)*—And he carves a swastika in my forehead. And I say, Now I'm gonna make ya proud, Dad. And the warden comes and says, Here's your choice, boy: lethal injection, gas chamber, electric chair. And I say, All three. And they strap me down in the electric chair and give me lethal injection while I'm inside a gas chamber. And they hit the switch and turn up the gas. *(Sitting in the electric chair.)* And you should see the look on their faces when they see me undead. And they all piss their pants when I walk out the prison. Guards get up and aim their shotguns—BAM! BAM! BAM!—But nothing can stop me. People move out my way. Word spreads I'm unkillable. People try and be nice and hope I don't get pissed off. Whatever I need, I take. I need money, I go in a bank and take it and nobody says shit because I'm the king of the world. I need clothes, I take em. I go see *Primordial Rage*, I just walk in and sit down and I say, Rewind the movie. Let me see the shootout scene again. And they do it. I snap my fingers. They bring me pepperoni pizza and a frosty Coke. And nobody says shit to me about school 'cause I am king of the world. What I say goes. *(As Charlie.)*

"That's my boy!" *(Shirt down.)* 'Cause I'm king of the world. And when I see a beautiful girl, I say I wanna see your tits, and she lifts her blouse 'cause I am king of the world. Who am I?

JENNIFER: King of the world.

KENNY: Who am I?

RUSS: King of the world.

KENNY: Who am I?

ALL: King of the world!

KENNY: *(His eyes lock with Jennifer's.)* Who am I?

JENNIFER: You're king of the world.

KENNY: You know what that means.

> *(Long pause. Jennifer looks to Russ for help. He turns away. Long pause. Deliberately, delicately, Jennifer reveals her breasts to Kenny, but not to audience.)*

KENNY: They were bigger in the movie.

JENNIFER: What can I say? The cinematographer is god.

KENNY: I saw you take your clothes off seventeen times.

JENNIFER: You didn't see me. You saw my character.

KENNY: *(As Dirk.)* "Why didn't you tell me you once had a thing with Lance?" C'mon. Be Tara. Do the scene in the movie. *(As Dirk.)* "Why didn't you tell me you once had a thing with Lance?"

JENNIFER: *(As Tara.)* "It wasn't much of a thing."

KENNY: *(As Dirk.)* "Lance is my partner. Next time we're on a bust, I kick in a door, bullets go flyin', I'm gonna be wonderin' where my partner's head's at. A distraction like that can kill a man. You shoulda told me."

JENNIFER: *(As Tara.)* "I knew if I did I'd lose you."

KENNY: *(As Dirk.)* "A partner's a sacred thing to me." Go up the stairs like in the movie.

JENNIFER: What for?

KENNY: Go up the stairs like in the movie.

JENNIFER: Why can't we just do the scene here?

KENNY: 'Cause I wanna do the whole scene.

JENNIFER: We can't do the whole scene.

KENNY: Why not?

JENNIFER: You know why not.

KENNY: No, I don't. Why not?

JENNIFER: Because it ends in sex.

KENNY: So what? It's your character, not you. *(As Dirk.)* "A partner's a sacred thing to me."

RUSS: Let me make a call. In twenty minutes I could have the most beautiful women on earth in here. How many you want?

KENNY: How would you play this, Dad? *(As Charlie.)* "Still thinks you're a whore. Time for a close-up, son."

RUSS: Jimmy?

JIMMY: I would like agree with him.

KENNY: *(As Charlie.)* "Now we're gonna see if you got the juice, son."

RUSS: Can Jennifer and I have a moment of privacy?

KENNY: What do we get?

RUSS: What do you want?

KENNY: Do a Daisy.

RUSS: What do you mean?

KENNY: You know what I mean. *(Russ looks to Jimmy.)*

JIMMY: Be a dying dog.

(Russ does a Daisy as Jimmy did earlier. Kenny and Jimmy laugh.)

KENNY: Dirk would never do a Daisy. Not for anything.

(Exit Kenny and Jimmy.)

RUSS: You okay?

JENNIFER: I don't think I'm going to make it.

RUSS: Of course we'll make it. We just need to use our heads here. The way I see it, we have a choice between extremely bad and ultimate bad. I suggest we take extremely bad and go along with him.

JENNIFER: Bullshit.

RUSS: Jen.

JENNIFER: No.

RUSS: Listen.

JENNIFER: No.

RUSS: Take him upstairs—

JENNIFER: Forget it.

RUSS: And get my Uzi. Get my Uzi.

JENNIFER: Where is it?

RUSS: In the nightstand. Bottom drawer. False compartment. It's loaded.

JENNIFER: Like the one I used in the film?

RUSS: Exact same one. You have to take the safety off first. Then do him.

JENNIFER: He's just a kid.

RUSS: He's a homicidal maniac who happens to be a kid. Don't get all warm and fuzzy over this fucking loony tune. Drop him before he drops us.

JENNIFER: I don't know if I can do that.

RUSS: You did it in the movie.

JENNIFER: That was a performance.

RUSS: Semantics. In the movie you aimed an Uzi and people dropped. Do the movie.

JENNIFER: Okay.

RUSS: Why am I not convinced?

JENNIFER: This is real.

RUSS: Real unreal.

JENNIFER: Suppose I don't get the chance to get the Uzi.

RUSS: Suppose we're headlines tomorrow? We'll be forgotten in 24 hours. You see what you're doing? Sabotaging yourself. Loading yourself up with doubts. Put it in your mind to do one thing. Then do it.

JENNIFER: You're not hearing me, Russ. Suppose something goes wrong and I can't get it.

RUSS: Jen, Sandy's expecting a call from me. When he doesn't get it, he'll know something's wrong. Until then we have to play the cards we have.

JENNIFER: What's that mean?

RUSS: Make him happy.

JENNIFER: Make him happy.

RUSS: It's all about hormones. Once he gets off, it's over.

JENNIFER: For him. What about me?

RUSS: Jen, I understand about your feelings, but we have to smell the coffee here. I'm trying to pick the best thing for you.

JENNIFER: Ever since the day I drove out here, three thousand miles in my old clunker, that's all this business is about.

RUSS: Put it in your memoirs—if you're lucky enough to write 'em.

JENNIFER: That's all it's about. Does it ever stop?

RUSS: See that bullet hole up there? Better in plaster than in somebody's skull. Okay?

JENNIFER: What makes you think it won't come to that anyway? Would you do it for me?

RUSS: What's that have to do with the price of eggs?

JENNIFER: I just need to know. You're asking me to be a blow-up doll in some maniac's sick fantasy.

RUSS: It's a performance. It's a scene. Tara makes nice with Charlie.

Testosterone's coming out his ears. All he wants is the softness of a woman. The loveliness of a woman. Her voice. The touch of her skin. It means more than you can know. Don't even try to fathom it. It goes beyond anything you can imagine.

JENNIFER: If you knew me, you would know I can't do that.

RUSS: You did with me the day you walked in my office.

JENNIFER: Sorry?

RUSS: Lucky for us it turned into something beautiful. You did it before. Why can't you do it now? Now it's about living or dying. What's to consider?

JENNIFER: All I wanted was maybe a few soft words, some small comfort before I—"make him happy." But that was too much to ask of you. You just turned every tender moment we ever had into shit.

(Enter Kenny and Jimmy.)

KENNY: It's time.

JENNIFER: Look, you saw a movie. It made you feel something magical. You wanna feel it again. You wanna get all caught up in the magic again. *(Kenny pulls her up the stairs.)* Russ. Russ. Wait. Maybe you have a sister...Maybe there's a girl you like. How would you feel if this happened to her?

KENNY: *(As Dirk.)* "Why didn't you tell me you once had a thing with Lance?"

JENNIFER: *(As Tara. Beat.)* "It wasn't much of a thing."

KENNY: That's not how you said it in the movie.

JENNIFER: *(As Tara.)* "It wasn't much of a thing."

KENNY: *(As Dirk.)* "Lance is my partner. Next time we're on a bust, I kick in a door, bullets go flyin', I'm gonna be wonderin' where my partner's head's at. A distraction like that can kill a man. You shoulda told me."

JENNIFER: *(As Tara.)* "I knew if I did I'd lose you."

KENNY: *(As Dirk.)* "A partner's a sacred thing to me."

JENNIFER: "I thought we had a sacred thing, too."

(Kenny pulls her up the stairs. Jimmy shows the gun to Russ.)

JIMMY: You have to sit there and not move because I have instructions.

RUSS: What instructions?

JIMMY: You move, I have to do the execution scene in *Dominator*.

RUSS: How do you feel with my girlfriend being raped up there?

JIMMY: Kenny said no talking.

RUSS: Kenny said. Kenny said. Okay, now, here's the deal, Jimmy. I'm gonna stand up and I'm gonna come over there and you're gonna give me the gun.

JIMMY: Please don't.

RUSS: Here I come.

JIMMY: I think you better sit.

(*Jimmy cocks the gun. Russ sits.*)

RUSS: I think you're right.

JIMMY: No more talking, please.

RUSS: Hey, shit-for-brains, you know how much trouble you're in right now?

JIMMY: This is just any old day to you but to us it's like the coolest thing we ever did.

RUSS: Or ever will. You both are gonna end up ruined for the rest of your lives.

JIMMY: Maybe they won't catch us.

RUSS: They catch everybody.

JIMMY: Not in *Dominator*. The kid gets the girl and the money and escapes to Mexico.

RUSS: That's a movie! What are you, fourteen, fifteen?

JIMMY: Almost sixteen.

RUSS: At fifteen I ran my father's business better than that drunken bastard did. Sold popcorn and soda, did homework while I ran the projector, swept and mopped under the seats, cleaned the toilets, dropped receipts off at the bank, went to school the next morning. Where are you at fifteen? You'll never see the age of twenty.

JIMMY: So who wants to get old and boring?

RUSS: You're not cut out for this. You're not like that piece of shit. What are you doing with him? He makes you roll like a dog.

JIMMY: I got beat up everyday at school until Kenny and me became friends. Kids don't even look at me now cause they know he's...I'm sorry, you can't talk anymore.

RUSS: Just tell me why you came here.

JIMMY: The mall was dead.

RUSS: The mall was dead?

JIMMY: Yeah.

RUSS: The mall was dead. The mall was dead so you and Kenny took some hostages. Jimmy, like this is not even a fucking answer. Why'd you come here? Think.

JIMMY: Like I don't know what you mean.

RUSS: Jimmy, how many meanings can this have? Why'd you come to my home?

JIMMY: Oh, why we came here. My mom is like totally duh cause she forgets to leave me money for the weekend, leaves me a note on the fridge: "Do the best you can, see you Sunday night, Love Mom," 'cause she met this guy with a Harley and they ride around every weekend 'cause my dad like found out he was gay and went to live in San Francisco but at least he's not in a bad mood anymore. But he like calls me on my birthday. So where was I? Oh, why we came here. Oh, yeah. So Mom like works two jobs so I hardly ever see her but once she like had the flu and made me pancakes and we talked for like over a half-hour. Why'd I just tell you that? Oh, why we came here. Me and Kenny didn't have any money so we had to stay home and watch TV and saw you—what's that show where the weird guy goes into rich people's houses?

RUSS: *Lives of the Rich and Famous.*

JIMMY: Yeah. And they showed a picture of your house from a helicopter, right? So we jumped on our skateboards and hitched a few bumpers up to Mulholland and recognized your house and came down through the cactuses.

RUSS: But why the gun? Why's he come here with a gun? Why's he carry a gun?

JIMMY: There's a lot of nuts out there.

RUSS: Really?

JIMMY: Won't say how he gets it past the metal detector in school. He's afraid of a drive-by shooter. No more talking. I really mean it.

RUSS: You gonna get dirty for him? You shoot me, you'll be tried as an adult. And nutbag will only get charged with Breaking and Entering in juvenile court. You call that friendship? I call it bullshit. Do a Daisy? What the hell is that?

JIMMY: You wouldn't understand.

RUSS: Jimmy, I'm a very understanding person.

JIMMY: You won't say anything?

RUSS: Jimmy, I didn't get to this place in life because I'm untrustworthy.

JIMMY: Like we're having a battle of our fender-strats in the garage. And our neighbor, Mr. Rand—lives between us—comes over and says, Turn down those amps or I'll call the police, and that's the wrong thing to say to Kenny. So Kenny takes some hot dogs out of the fridge and lures Mr. Rand's poodle, Daisy, up in the hills of Monrovia. You sure you won't tell?

RUSS: Jimmy, you have my word.

JIMMY: You know the scene in *Dominator* where the hit man is trying to get out the window—?

RUSS: Yeah.

JIMMY: When the Doberman grabs his leg?

RUSS: Yeah.

JIMMY: Kenny pretended the poodle was the Doberman.

RUSS: Oh no.

JIMMY: And he did the scene.

RUSS: Oh no.

JIMMY: Shoved the pistol down Daisy's throat. Boom.

RUSS: Jesus.

JIMMY: But Daisy didn't die right away. She made this really, really, really bad sound…you know, she did a Daisy. And I'm like whoa! She looked at me like I did it to her. I knew her since I was five. And she kept biting at her side where the bullet came out and blood was coming out and I got all weird and Kenny said if I ever told, he would do my Golden Retriever, Redness, and then me. That's why he makes me do a Daisy. To remind me. But he's a good friend. I should've never told you.

RUSS: Good friend? Jimmy. He's your best friend. But he's sick. He needs help. You care about Kenny? Of course you do. Let's help him out of this. Let's rescue him. I'll pay all the psychiatric bills. Someday when he's all better, he'll thank us for saving his life.

JIMMY: I just don't wanna talk about this anymore, okay? He always knows when I'm lying 'cause it's all over my face.

(We hear a great commotion upstairs—breaking glass, etc. Enter Jennifer running down the stairs.)

RUSS: What's this? What's this? Are you okay?

JENNIFER: Don't worry about it.

JIMMY: Where's Kenny?

JENNIFER: Trashing the bedroom. Don't touch me!

RUSS: Jimmy, you're the only one who could end this. End it for you. End it for us. You have the power here. Look at her. She's been humiliated and raped.

JENNIFER: Nothing happened.

RUSS: What?

JENNIFER: You heard me.

RUSS: You talk him out of it?

JENNIFER: Skip it.

RUSS: Give me a clue.

JENNIFER: It must've been his first time. It was over before it started. Then he went berserk.

(Enter Kenny descending the stairs. He wears a tux jacket, buttoned, smoking a cigar. Hands Jimmy a set of bondage handcuffs on a three foot chain decorated with a pink ribbon. Kenny takes the gun from Jimmy, opens the revolver, loads it.)

RUSS: It wasn't loaded? The gun wasn't loaded?

JIMMY: Why didn't you tell me it wasn't loaded?

KENNY: If you knew, you'd act weak.

RUSS: Nice one.

KENNY: Thank you.

RUSS: Perfect.

KENNY: Did she say anything about me?

JIMMY: Yeah.

KENNY: What?

JIMMY: Stuff.

KENNY: What stuff?

JIMMY: Just stuff.

KENNY: About me?

JIMMY: Yeah.

KENNY: About upstairs?

JIMMY: Yeah. *(Kenny puts the gun to Jennifer's head.)* Duh! It was all cool stuff.

KENNY: Like what?

JIMMY: She said it was like in the movie.

KENNY: She said that?

JIMMY: Was it? *(They high-five.)*

KENNY: *(Smashing the vase.)* Don't look at me!

JENNIFER: Sorry.

KENNY: Look somewhere else.

JIMMY: I wanna go home now.

(The doorbell rings.)

KENNY: What is that? Who is that?

RUSS: Kenny, I swear. It's the limo.

KENNY: I think you pushed a button!

RUSS: There's no button. But you can bet your ass by tomorrow night there will be buttons all over this house!

JIMMY: Kenny, he never left his place, honest.

RUSS: It's our limo.

KENNY: Go look.

(Exit Jimmy.)

RUSS: Let me get rid of him.

KENNY: What button?

RUSS: V. Vestibule.

KENNY: Or vice squad.

(Enter Jimmy.)

JIMMY: It's a guy in a suit. There's a stretch limo in the drive.

(The doorbell rings again.)

KENNY: F.B.I. negotiator. *(Moving like a cop, cautiously, covering every angle with his gun.)* The SWAT team has us surrounded.

RUSS: Sorry. It's the limo driver.

KENNY: We'll see. Nobody talk.

RUSS: Kenny, if we don't answer, he'll think something's wrong, call my office, and they'll call the police. Let me get rid of him.

KENNY: All you have to do is say one thing, one thing.

RUSS: I understand.

(Doorbell rings.)

KENNY: Go, go, go.

(Russ speaks into intercom.)

RUSS: *(On intercom.)* Yes?

CHAUFFEUR: *(On intercom speaker.)* Limo for Mr. Rigel.

RUSS: *(On intercom.)* Mr. Rigel's gone.

CHAUFFEUR: *(On intercom speaker.)* But we had a six-thirty pick up.

RUSS: *(On intercom.)* Mr. Rigel drove himself to the function, thank you. Have a good day.

CHAUFFEUR: *(On intercom speaker.)* But I'm on time.

RUSS: *(On intercom.)* No. You're thirty minutes late.

CHAUFFEUR: *(On intercom speaker.)* It's six twenty-seven. I'm three minutes early.

RUSS: *(On intercom.)* No. Limos are traditionally thirty minutes early. A six-thirty pickup means the limo should be here at six o'clock. But seeing you weren't here as per usual, considering he was doing a live broadcast with a specific satellite link-up, Mr. Rigel drove himself to the function. That's what I meant earlier by the terse expression, Mr. Rigel's gone.

CHAUFFEUR: *(On intercom speaker.)* May I ask to whom I'm talking with?

RUSS: *(On intercom.)* Mr. Rigel's assistant.

CHAUFFEUR: *(On intercom speaker.)* My boss is gonna ask me for a name.

RUSS: *(On intercom.)* Sandy. Have a good day.

CHAUFFEUR: *(On intercom speaker.)* Sandy, I'm really sorry but you know, we live in a town with merging rush hours. Some dipsy-doodle gets stopped for a broken tail-light and rubberneckers back up traffic for ten miles on the 405.

RUSS: *(On intercom.)* Most illuminating. Have a nice life. And tell your employer you've lost the Rigel account.

KENNY: Go see.

(Exit Jimmy.)

RUSS: Okay?

KENNY: You're good.

RUSS: What?

KENNY: Beyond good. You're a genius. Chauffeur tells security, Rigel's not in. Some guy Sandy said he drove himself. Security says, Bullshit. Rigel never left. They call the SWAT team.

RUSS: You're dreaming.

KENNY: You're amazing. Chauffeur tells his boss the Rigel account is lost. Boss calls Sandy. Boss tells Sandy the chauffeur was turned away by a guy named Sandy. Sandy calls the SWAT team. Whoa. You're too cool.

(Enter Jimmy.)

JIMMY: He's gone.

KENNY: Go in the master bedroom. You can see the security gate. Tell me if the chauffeur stops and talks to the guards. Quick!

(Exit Jimmy.)

KENNY: You wanted him to recognize your voice. That's why the more you talked, the more he knew it was you. Is that what you wanted to do?

RUSS: I'm not that smart.

KENNY: You win Oscars.

RUSS: Oh, please.

KENNY: You think security's gonna come save you?

RUSS: You slipped 'em. How good can they be?

KENNY: You better hope they don't come. *(Shirt up. But now, crudely taped over Manson's face is a photo of Russ. Kenny mimics Russ in tone, cadence, attitude, and body language.)* "Are we clear?" *(Shirt down.)* Don't you want to say hello to The Quad? *(Shirt up.)*

RUSS: Hello.

(Enter Jimmy.)

JIMMY: The chauffeur stopped at security.

KENNY: How long did he talk?

JIMMY: Just for a second. Maybe just thanks.

KENNY: Bor-ing!

JIMMY: Bor-ing contest!

> *(They have a "Boring" contest. Kenny wins, dances triumphantly and laughs like Mega-Basher.)*

JIMMY: I wanna go.

KENNY: Go?

JIMMY: C'mon, we had our fun.

KENNY: You mean it?

JIMMY: Yeah. We just came to say hey, not all this.

KENNY: You're right. Man, the things ya gotta do just so people listen.

RUSS: No hard feelings from either one of us.

KENNY: *(To Jennifer.)* Really?

JENNIFER: Yes.

KENNY: Really, really?

JENNIFER: Yes.

KENNY: I had to know if it was like the movie. So it's cool?

JENNIFER: Yes.

KENNY: Cool. So I have potential, right?

RUSS: Tons.

KENNY: Who would know better than you? Maybe someday I'll win an Academy Award. I'll mention your name.

RUSS: Appreciate it.

KENNY: My parents'll pay for your old flowerpot and the hole in the—

RUSS: No, no, no. It's nothing.

KENNY: Cool. Thank you.

JENNIFER: For what?

KENNY: For the secret of killing Mega-B. *(Starts to go. Stops.)* Before I go I want to say…CLOSE-UP on The Quad! CLOSE-UP on Quad's bimbo.

RUSS: What do you want from me? If it's in my power, it's yours.

KENNY: I wanna see you cry like you did in the movie.

RUSS: That was a computer-generated tear drop.

KENNY: You didn't really cry? Aww, man.

JIMMY: Kenny! I'm hungry! I wanna go!

KENNY: Soon as we eat something. I feel like some chocolate chip cookie dough.

RUSS: What do we have in the fridge?

JENNIFER: Nothing. We're hardly home. Microwave popcorn?

KENNY: Can we bring the microwave in here?

RUSS: Why?

JENNIFER: No. It's built into the wall.

RUSS: There's a portable micro in the poolhouse.

KENNY: Have Sandy drop off McDonald's.

(Kenny throws the phone to Russ.)

RUSS: What's your pleasure?

KENNY: Two double bacon cheeseburgers, large fries and jumbo coke.

JIMMY: Me, too.

KENNY: By the time the french fries get here, they better be hot, firm and crispy, not cold, limp and soggy.

RUSS: *(On phone.)* Sandy, Russ…Get a pencil…Don't worry about it…Take this down exactly…Four double bacon cheeseburgers.

JIMMY: Hold the pickle.

RUSS: Hold the pickle on one. Two large fries, two jumbo Cokes. All this at my house yesterday. Sandy, I know what tonight is and I said don't worry about it. Now, find the nearest McDonald's and—Yes! McDonald's! And get that stuff from A to B like it meant job or no job. Cancel your date. Read your job description! You have no life when I need you. Sandy! Let's wake up and get on the same page here. Now listen! When those french fries arrive, I want them hot, firm and crispy, not cold, limp and soggy. Are we clear? I don't know. You're a five-figure trouble-shooter. Solve it. Stick it between your legs. Turn your car heater to the max. You wanna lecture on thermodynamics? Now let's make up our mind to do this to perfection because, Sandy, I cannot overstate the magnitude of this seemingly pedestrian request. So put a jet up your ass and go, go, go! *(Hangs up.)* Okay?

KENNY: You haven't been very nice to Sandy. Call him back. Apologize.

RUSS: *(On phone.)* Sandy, Russ. I'm sorry that I spoke to you in a contemptuous manner. *(Egged on by Kenny's gestures.)* I want you to know how much I value your devotion to me. *(Kenny gestures. Russ cups the phone.)*

KENNY: Give him a raise. Double.

RUSS: *(On phone.)* Sandy? Starting Monday I'm doubling your salary. *(Egged on.)* And after you deliver the french fries take a week off. With pay. Use my place in Hawaii. Take care, buddy. *(Hangs up.)*

KENNY: Dirk would never apologize. You bore me! We need some entertainment until the food comes.

RUSS: There's a wide-screen TV upstairs. CD's. Pool table. Swimming pool. Tennis courts.

KENNY: Jimmy, go get the microwave in the poolhouse. Put Long John Silver inside. Then bring the microwave in here. *(As Russ.)* "Yesterday."

JIMMY: What for?

KENNY: Duh!

JIMMY: *(Seeing Russ' picture.)* Where's Charlie?

KENNY: Gone.

JIMMY: Where?

KENNY: Didn't say.

JIMMY: Comin' back?

KENNY: Don't know.

(Exit Jimmy.)

RUSS: What's on your mind?

KENNY: I wanna do the parrot scene in the movie.

RUSS: Why?

KENNY: It'd be fun to see.

RUSS: Fun?

KENNY: Wanna hear the bird squawk.

RUSS: Let me run the movie for you on a twenty-foot screen. Hold the remote. Play it back. Freeze the frame.

KENNY: Duh! I wanna see it with my own eyes! Duh!

RUSS: Duh! It's all photographic tricks! Duh!

KENNY: Duh! It's only like the coolest weirdness that ever weirded me out in my whole life! Duh!

RUSS: Duh! It's all phony! Duh!

KENNY: Duh! How could it be phony when it made the audience go berserk! Duh! Some girl threw up a hot dog on my Nikes. That's not phony! Duh! *(As Russ.)* "A) Let's wake up and get on the same page here. B) Are we clear? And C)…" *(Shirt down.)* Duh! Duh! Duh!

RUSS: Duh contest! For Long John's life!

KENNY: C'mon, dude! *(Kenny and Russ have a "Duh" contest. It's vicious. Russ wins.)*

KENNY: You win! So you get to push the button!

RUSS: What do you really want from me?

KENNY: All I want is the look on your face when you push the button.

RUSS: Ask for something real and you'll get it.

KENNY: *(As Russ. Shirt up.)* "What's more real than classic romantic structure: boy meets parrot, boy nukes parrot, boy sees parrot explode."

RUSS: That's sick.

KENNY: Then why'd you put it in the movie?

RUSS: Because it's unthinkable!

KENNY: No it's not. You thought of it.

RUSS: Not to have anybody do it.

KENNY: Why not?

JENNIFER: Because he's a man of principle: rape his fiancée but don't hurt his parrot.

RUSS: Go tell your analyst.

(She goes to strike him. He just stands there. She restrains herself, lights a cigarette, puts on headphones and listens to music privately. Enter Jimmy carrying a microwave oven. Inside we hear the squawking parrot, its long tail feathers hanging out the door.)

JIMMY: Kenny! It talks! The parrot talks!

KENNY: How long does it take to nuke a parrot?

RUSS: Do one of the other parrots.

KENNY: *(As Russ. Shirt up.)* "Drop the bullshit! Give me a number!"

RUSS: I don't remember.

KENNY: Okay, so let's try thirty seconds!

JIMMY: Duh! That's what it takes to like warm up a burrito.

(Kenny punches in the numbers on the microwave.)

KENNY: Three, zero...

RUSS: I want to talk to The Quad!

KENNY: *(As Russ. Shirt up.)* "What're you bringing to the party?"

RUSS: Name it.

KENNY: Why'd you kill Dirk?

RUSS: Okay. The test audience wanted Dirk dead. They felt he had to pay the price for all the gore. The ratings people threatened to take away my PG-13 and slap an R on me. Financing threatened to pull the plug.

KENNY: And you gave in?

RUSS: I told you, I'm a whore.

KENNY: I want you to know how I feel. Push it, whore.

RUSS: You know I can't do that. Jimmy! Talk to your buddy.

JIMMY: If I was you, I'd like push it.

RUSS: C'mon, guy, you're joking, right?

KENNY: *(As Joe Pesci.)* "What am I, a fuckin' clown? I'm here to amuse you? Push it."

JENNIFER: Russ, push it.

RUSS: Shut up!

KENNY: *(As DeNiro.)* "You talkin' to me? Are you talkin' to me?"

RUSS: You bested the best. Not many people can say that. Mazel tov. You've got a big piece of me in the oven, m'man. You know what it cost for the climate control up in Long John's sanctuary? Mimics the rain forest. Everyday I'm up there feeding him fresh organic mangoes. All the other parrots, they're females for m'man. *(Breaking down.)* Sometimes I can't sleep. I'm up there with Long John till dawn. Not many could understand. Look at the plumage. It's Picasso. It's Mozart.

KENNY: It's toast. *(As Russ.)* "How big's your pecker, m'man?"

RUSS: Please. Don't make me do that.

KENNY: *(As Clint Eastwood.)* "Go ahead. Make my day."

JENNIFER: Push it!

KENNY: Push it!

KENNY, JENNIFER, JIMMY: *(Repeat.)* Push it!

(Kenny puts the gun to Russ' head. Russ pushes the button and breaks down in horror as the microwave starts to hum. The bird squawks. Kenny pulls Jimmy into a dance around the microwave.)

KENNY: *(Repeat.)* Boom chucka chucka chucka boom chucka chucka chucka boom!

(Kenny works himself into a frenzy. Jimmy joins in the chant. Improvise as the bird begins to shriek as it is cooked alive. Russ collapses on the sofa. The microwave door explodes open with a puff of smoke. Silence.)

KENNY: You're right. It was better in the movie!

RUSS: Oh God. *(Jimmy vomits in a corner.)*

KENNY: Hot lunch is now being served! There must be stuff we didn't think of. Jimmy, get another boom chucka chucka chucka boom!

JIMMY: It's like too weird for me.

KENNY: We need another boom chucka chucka chucka boom.

JIMMY: I'm sick.

KENNY: Bor-ing!

JIMMY: I can't help it.

KENNY: What would Dirk do now? *(Re: bondage handcuffs.)* These from the movie?

RUSS: The same.

KENNY: Cool. *(Repeat)* Boom chucka chucka chucka boom chucka chucka chucka boom. *(To Russ and Jennifer.)* Hands up! *(Kenny threads the handcuffs through the railing, attaches one manacle to Russ' hand, the other manacle to Jennifer's. He pops the key in his pocket. Jimmy continues to be sick.)*

RUSS: What are you doing?

KENNY: Maybe we're gonna do the bondage scene.

JIMMY: Aww, no, Kenny, c'mon. Didn't they suffer enough?

KENNY: I now pronounce you man and wife. *(To Jimmy.)* Hey, Daisy, I'm doing this for you. You don't seem to appreciate all the trouble I go through to entertain you.

JIMMY: I do. I do. But I wanna go home now.

KENNY: Okay, let's go.

JIMMY: What about them?

KENNY: I'll take care of them. We can't leave on foot. We need some wheels. What do you want, the Rolls, the Viper or the Harley?

JIMMY: I don't care. Let's just go.

(Exit Kenny.)

JENNIFER: Jimmy, thank you for what you did before.

JIMMY: Yeah, I lied to my best friend.

RUSS: You don't have a best friend. But Kenny does.

JIMMY: Just shut up.

RUSS: Kenny trust you?

JIMMY: Yeah.

RUSS: Why'd he not leave the gun with you?

JIMMY: Maybe he's got good reasons.

RUSS: He doesn't trust you. Because you're weak. You're a pussy. You crack under pressure.

JENNIFER: Leave the kid alone.

RUSS: Stupid little jerk-off. Don't you realize after he does us he's gonna do you because you'll crack under interrogation the way you're cracking now?

JIMMY: I'm not cracking.

RUSS: You already cracked when you vomited. Your vomit gave you away, Jimmy. You're sick to your stomach because you're sick in your heart because Kenny's sick in the head.

JIMMY: One more word and I'll holler and he'll come down here and this place'll look like one of your movies.

RUSS: Boo. You don't have the guts to holler, you little fuck. You can just about wipe your ass. I am offering you a way out right now. Right now. This second. The offer's not good two minutes from now. So when you're looking at the world for twenty years through a keyhole in your new career as some gorilla's girlfriend in the big house, I guarantee you'll be thinking of me. You'll be thinking of this moment. You'll be the sorriest piece of shit in the sewer of humanity because you had a chance and didn't take it.

JIMMY: I didn't even want to come here.

RUSS: He bullied you. I understand. I get pushed around all the time.

JIMMY: You can't say no to him when he's all pumped up.

RUSS: You don't have to say no to him. All you have to do is go in the kitchen. Dial 911. Tell 'em you're at my house. Your voice will be recorded. That will count for something in a court of law.

JIMMY: But I didn't do anything!

RUSS: You held me at gunpoint.

JIMMY: The gun wasn't loaded.

RUSS: In the eyes of the law, same difference, loser. You get on that phone right now, I defend you to the last.

JENNIFER: I'll keep him to that promise, Jimmy.

RUSS: I own this town. I own people in D.C. I can cut you a deal. *(Jimmy doesn't move.)* You deserve everything Kenny does to you when I tell him you told me about Daisy.

JIMMY: You promised me.

RUSS: *(Seizes Jimmy, pulls him onto the couch.)* Grow the fuck up, will you? What do you think this is, the fucking Boy Scouts? You betrayed your good friend Kenny. You're a back-stabber. You're Judas. And if I know that maniac, he'll drop your dog for that in a heartbeat. Now get your ass in that kitchen, you slimy mall rat, and get on that phone.
(Russ shoves Jimmy towards the door. Exit Jimmy.)

JENNIFER: Who are you?

RUSS: A survivor. Who are you?

JENNIFER: I never saw you till now.

RUSS: How do you do? Nice to meet you. Have a nice day.

JENNIFER: I can't believe you'd dump me and then cry over a stupid bird.

RUSS: That stupid bird saved my life.

JENNIFER: Put it in your memoirs.

RUSS: You're too wrapped up in your own hurt to understand.

JENNIFER: Russ, I don't want to understand.

RUSS: Afraid you might learn something about me and have to forgive me? We both could be dead in two minutes. I want you to know. Because I need your forgiveness…Directing my first picture. Amazonia. I take sick. Fever, hundred and six. Dry heaves. Delirium. Can't move. Sores break out all over my body. Oozing, pussy, throbbing sores. It's Biblical. Doctor doesn't have a clue. The studio takes me off the picture. It's the rainy season. Nothing flies in or out. Roads are three feet of mud. They can't evacuate me. Line producer sticks me on a straw mat in a grass hut among these Stone-Age savages who eat roots and monkeys. True story. Only thing in the hut is a squawking parrot on a perch. Clipped wings. And I'm dying. For the first time in my life I feel my soul squirm inside. Feel it tug away from my dying flesh like a helium balloon. Ready to dump me just like the studio. I cry out. Nobody hears me. And then the bugs come. Drawn to the pus. Bugs like you've never imagined. Bugs swarm over me. Sipping at my sores. I'm too weak to swat them away. I cry out. Nobody hears me. But the parrot. Hops off its perch. Hops all around me. Eats the bugs. Parrots don't eat bugs. This one does. For me. At that moment I know there is not one being on this earth who really cares for me. But for this parrot. I give the head monkey-eater my Rolex for the bird, bribe I don't know how many custom agents, and take my rare feathered friend stateside. True story.

JENNIFER: Why'd you never tell me that before?

(Enter Jimmy.)

JIMMY: He smashed all the phones. Phone in the kitchen. Phone in the dining room. Phone in the—

RUSS: That shows what he thinks of you, Jimmy. We're chained. We can't get to a phone. He smashed all the phones because he doesn't trust you. He's gonna do you right after he does us, Jimmy.

JIMMY: Aww, man. I wish I was dead.

RUSS: Kenny may give you that wish. But I'm with you.

JIMMY: Like what do you mean?

RUSS: I care about you. I wanna help you.

JIMMY: Why?

RUSS: I just do.

JIMMY: Yeah, people like say stuff and then they never, you know, whatever.

RUSS: But I'm Russ Rigel. I'm not a halfway guy. I wanna take care of you. *(Silence.)* C'mer. *(Jimmy shakes his head no.)* C'mer, Jimmy. *(Jimmy turns his face away.)* Look at me. *(Russ opens his arms.)* You have two friends over here. *(Jimmy slowly moves towards Russ.)* C'mon. *(Russ takes Jimmy in his arms. Jimmy bawls like a baby.)* It's gonna be okay. Nobody's gonna touch you. Not Kenny. Not anybody. 'Cause you're gonna stand up to him.

JIMMY: You know I can't.

RUSS: I saw you stand up to him.

JIMMY: When?

RUSS: When you two guys did the scene from the movie. *(Jimmy stops crying.)* I saw you. Right here. Right in front of my eyes. You were a whole other person. You were Lance. The look in your eye scared me. You walked different. You looked twelve feet tall. See, Jimmy, you don't know how strong you are. You seem like a nice sweet kid from Monrovia. But under the skin, you're a fucking tiger.

JIMMY: You think?

RUSS: I don't think. I know it. I saw it. Right here in my living room. If you can be a tiger in the scene, you can be one in life.

JIMMY: But he's got a gun.

RUSS: You have a bigger gun.

JIMMY: What do you mean?

RUSS: What if you had an Uzi?

JENNIFER: Russ, are you crazy?

RUSS: Shut. Your. Mouth.

JIMMY: I'm scared.

RUSS: How scared will you be when you have to watch your Golden doing a Daisy?

JIMMY: Aww, man.

RUSS: Lance was scared, too. Remember the scene when the police chief tells Lance to bring in Dirk? What'd Lance say at first?

JIMMY: *(As Lance.)* "Get somebody else."

RUSS: *(As Police Chief.)* "You know his mind, Lance. You can find him. Bring him back." Remember? Master bedroom. Nightstand. Bottom drawer. False compartment. Beautiful thing about an Uzi is you don't have to aim. Just spray 'em. Loaded with a full clip. Little red switch. The safety. Just flick it on and you're in business. *(As Police Chief.)* "Lance, you have to bring in Dirk."

JIMMY: *(As Lance.)* "Get somebody else, chief."

RUSS: *(As Police Chief.)* "You're the only one. You know his mind. You can find him. I don't care how you do it. I'm closing my eyes on this one, Lance."

(Exit Jimmy.)

JENNIFER: And what do we do when the bullets start flying?

RUSS: Duck.

JENNIFER: You're still him.

RUSS: Jen.

JENNIFER: Let go.

RUSS: Listen to me.

JENNIFER: Not until you let go.

RUSS: I need you now. And you need me. *(He lets her go.)*

JENNIFER: This may be the luckiest day of my life. I don't need anything from you anymore. If I see tomorrow, I quit the picture.

RUSS: You cause me a financial disaster, I'll get a body double, kill off your character, and nobody'll hire you to go out for coffee. Professional suicide.

JENNIFER: Sue me.

RUSS: Think you'll go back and do shoestring plays in Harrisburg? You can't quit.

JENNIFER: Why, is there somebody you have to fuck to get out of the business?

RUSS: You can't quit. You're just another pretty L.A. girl with a mediocre talent. I had the faith, the vision, and the fortune to put you up on the screen and make you a bankable commodity.

JENNIFER: And who is that up there? She's made up of lights and shadows and camera lenses and make-up. She's a mess of body parts. Three days it took us to shoot that bedroom scene. A scene that made me no longer welcome in my parents' home. Three fourteen-hour days for a two-minute scene. Because you can't ever do what's been done before. And it's all been done ten thousand times. How many ways are there for lips to kiss? How many ways are there for two bodies to be lost in passion? You made her, yeah, but I wouldn't have the commodity Jennifer Barton over for dinner. Or the lowlife that created her.

RUSS: Jen, I think we could put this thing back together.

JENNIFER: What?

RUSS: I never tell you how important you are in my life. I mean, you don't know. Just coming home, finding you here. Finding you in sweats on the stair-stepper. Watching you sleep. I get a rush. This place is a shack without you. You made it a home. I never had that. I can't imagine not having you in my life.

JENNIFER: You make me sick. I'm gonna work real hard at it, real, real, hard, and little by little, I'm gonna get you out of my system. And one day you'll be Russ Who.

(Enter Kenny.)

KENNY: Where's Jimmy?

RUSS: He went looking for you.

KENNY: I told him not to leave here. Why's nobody ever listen to me?

(Enter Jimmy from the top of the stairs. He carries an Uzi and wears sunglasses and is dressed in a long raincoat and fedora from Russ' wardrobe.)

KENNY: Where'd you get that? Let me see.

JIMMY: No.

KENNY: Whoa.

JIMMY: *(As Lance.)* "Assume the position, Dirk. I'm taking you in." *(He repeats.)* "Assume the position, Dirk. I'm taking you in."

KENNY: *(As Dirk.)* "Badge over friendship, eh? All the coffee and donuts, all the times I saved your ass, all adds up to zero, eh?"

JIMMY: *(As Lance.)* "I got a job to do. What do you want from me?"

KENNY: *(As Dirk.)* "All I want is the look on your face of the bud I used to know."

JIMMY: *(As Lance.)* "You were a cop's cop, Dirk. I looked up to you. But this time you went too far. You turned this town into a river of blood."

KENNY: *(As Dirk.)* "I cleaned up the scum in this town. I didn't expect a medal but I never thought my own partner would hunt me down. Do you have to cuff me?"

JIMMY: *(As Lance.)* "You know the routine."

KENNY: *(As Dirk.)* "I can give you six reasons you should let me slide on this one, buddy."

JIMMY: *(As Lance.)* "What six reasons?"

(They both fire at the same time. The stage is full of noise and smoke. There is a running gun battle. Russ and Jennifer take cover behind the coffee table.)

KENNY: Cool! We're in the movie! We're in the movie!

(Jimmy falls shot in the leg.)

RUSS: Aww, man, my leg! My leg!

KENNY: You almost got me! How's it feel to be shot?

JIMMY: Somebody help me! Mom! Mom!

KENNY: Bor-ing! Let's do it again!

JIMMY: I can't, Kenny! My leg!

RUSS: Jimmy! You do the scene, you little sonofabitch! Do the scene, Jimmy!

(Kenny helps Jimmy to his feet on the stairs. Kenny returns to his original place. As he turns—)

KENNY: *(As Dirk.)* "Well, well, well, well, well..."

(Jimmy sprays him with the Uzi. Both kids fall wounded.)

KENNY: Wanna do it again?

JIMMY: Somebody help me!

(Kenny sits up, back against the wall. He picks up an Oscar, holds it up victoriously.)

KENNY: I would like to thank the Academy...and all those who made me what I am...

(Kenny slumps over dead, Oscar still in hand.)

RUSS: I won! Ha ha! I won!

JIMMY: Kenny? Are you kidding? Kenny? Wake up, man! C'mon, man.

JENNIFER: Jimmy?

JIMMY: My leg! It's on fire!

RUSS: Jimmy, get the key in Kenny's pocket.

JIMMY: I can't.

RUSS: Do it! Now! Go, go, go!

(Jimmy crawls to Kenny.)

JIMMY: It hurts.

RUSS: Shut up and get the key. And the phone.

(Jimmy pulls pieces of the broken phone out of Kenny's pocket. Faint sound of sirens.)

JIMMY: It's broke.

JENNIFER: They're coming, Jimmy!

RUSS: Get the key! Hurry!

JIMMY: I can't, I can't. I just can't.

RUSS: Don't you tell me that, goddamit! Do it! Just do it!

JENNIFER: Jimmy? Jimmy?

JIMMY: Yeah?

JENNIFER: How bad are you hit?

JIMMY: Bad. I can't move my leg.

JENNIFER: Reach for me, Jimmy.

JIMMY: I can't.

JENNIFER: Try.

JIMMY: I am.

JENNIFER: C'mon. Yeah. Good. Good.

(Russ snatches the key from Jimmy's hand. Jennifer pulls Jimmy close, puts his head in her lap.)

JENNIFER: I am so proud of you.

JIMMY: Aww, man.

JENNIFER: You're the bravest guy I ever knew.

JIMMY: Aww, man, I did my best friend.

RUSS: What are you talking about? You're a hero, Jimmy.

JIMMY: Am I gonna live? Am I gonna live or die?

(Sirens rise in crescendo.)

JENNIFER: They're coming, sweetheart. They're gonna fix you up and you're gonna be alright.

JIMMY: Did I do good?

RUSS: You were fabulous! They're coming! We're gonna do this town. Go places. Wait till you see Cannes. The Grand Palais. The parties. The women. The buzz in the air. First we'll do the talk shows.

JIMMY and JENNIFER: What?

RUSS: They're here! Hang on, kid. The rollercoaster is ready to roll! Your name is gonna be big in this town.

JIMMY: What do you mean?

RUSS: What do I mean? Duh! There's a movie in this!

(Lights fade to black.)

END OF PLAY

Meow
by Val Smith

BIOGRAPHY

Val Smith is the author of numerous plays which have been published and produced nationally. Her first full-length drama, *The Gamblers,* was a finalist at the Eugene O'Neill National Playwrights Conference, won the Playhouse on the Square's Mid-South Playwrights Competition, and was produced at American Stage Theatre in New Jersey in 1992. Her second full-length, *Ain't We Got Fun,* was commissioned and produced by Actors Theatre of Louisville in the 1993 Brown-Forman Classics in Context Festival—The Roaring Twenties. She is the recipient of awards from the Kentucky Women's Foundation and the Kentucky Arts Council. Her most recent full-length, *Marguerite Bonet,* was a finalist for the 1997 Francesca Primus Prize and received a workshop production at Florida Stage. Ms. Smith wishes to thank the Pleiades Theatre Company for their kind participation in the development of *Meow.*

HUMANA FESTIVAL PRODUCTION

Meow was first performed at the Humana Festival of New American Plays, in March 1998. It was directed by Frank Deal with the following cast:

Pat	Stephanie Zimbalist
Linda	Peggity Price
Waitress	Sara Sommervold

and the following production staff:

Scenic Designer	Paul Owen
Costume Designer	Kevin R. McLeod
Lighting Designer	Greg Sullivan
Sound Designer	Mark Huang
Properties Designer	Mark Walston
Stage Manager	Juliet Horn
Dramaturgs	Amy Wegener, Megan Shultz
Casting	Laura Richin Casting

CHARACTERS

PAT: Early forties. Married. Has a teenage daughter.
LINDA: Late late thirties. Divorced.
    Both are attractive, intelligent middle-class women. Both are friends and have worked in the same office for years.
WAITRESS: Early twenties. Attractive. Exudes 'tude.

SETTING

A booth in a restaurant. The restaurant is a few blocks from the office where both women work. It's the kind of place where office workers congregate after hours to catch a drink before going home. They don't stay for dinner because, let's face it, the food is bad. The atmosphere is ferns and ceiling fans and quaint stuff on the walls—in other words, a "manufactured" neighborhood bar feeling which never for a minute fools anybody that the place isn't a franchise.

TIME

Friday. An hour after work.

Stephanie Zimbalist and Peggity Price
in *Meow* by Val Smith

22nd Annual Humana Festival of New American Plays
Actors Theatre of Louisville, 1998
photo by Richard Trigg

Meow

A table in a restaurant. At rise, Linda is nursing what's left of a whiskey sour. The Waitress has recited a long, long list of specials.

WAITRESS: Finally…there's our red-snapper grilled in…herbed butter and topped with a peanut and ginger sauce served with…special Jamaican-style gratin potatoes and the vegetable medley—

LINDA: Jamaican-style?

WAITRESS: —gratin potatoes. Yeah. *(Beat.)* They're potatoes that are kin-dahhh—

LINDA: Gratinized?

WAITRESS: Yeah!

LINDA: So you haven't had them.

WAITRESS: Randy the busboy says they're really good. *(Beat.)* A'course Randy'll eat anything.

LINDA: I'll just stick with a whiskey sour. And a Merlot for my friend.

WAITRESS: Done with the Happy Hour won tons? *(Moves to take them.)*

LINDA: *(Moves to hang onto them.)* Nahhht quite! *(Pause.)* You know, these were so yummy, could we have another batch?

WAITRESS: 'Kay. *(Beat.)* So. You don't want dinner…
(Pat enters and sits down.)

PAT: *(Overlapping.)* Maybe they've got some good specials…

WAITRESS: Well…*(Clears throat. Here we go again.)*…there's our breast of chicken rolled in polenta…

LINDA: *(Interrupting.)* Thanks, thank you! That won't be necessary…

PAT: No?

LINDA: *(To Pat.)* Trust me. *(To Waitress.)* We're on a strict semi-liquid diet. *(Hands the Waitress the menus.)* But thanks. *(Pause.)* Oh, and don't for-get…*(The Waitress is gone.)*…our drinks. I get the feeling that—like Shane—her work here is done. *(Beat.)* How's Dan?

PAT: Not home yet. Left another message. Gawd, poor dog is gonna be hop-ping from leg to leg. And from leg to leg.

LINDA: Dan usually work this late?

PAT: I keep tellin' him he's gotta negotiate something like normal hours. You're so lucky. You don't have a dog to feed, or a husband you have to check in with, or a teenage daughter you have to delude yourself is at her girlfriend's house baking cookies.

LINDA: Yeah. *(Beat.)* I'm so stoked we're gonna be working together on this investment retreat.

PAT: Hawaii! A *budget!*

LINDA: Are you kidding me?

PAT: They're giving *us* money! Can you believe it!

LINDA: Somebody must have died at main office.

PAT: Whoohooo! Look out! Yes!

PAT and LINDA: —Together again!

(They laugh wickedly and clink glasses. A beat.)

LINDA: Did I tell you? That damn Sheila broke the copier again.

PAT: She only uses the thing four times a year. She breaks it every single time. How is that possible?

LINDA: Oh, and she's refined her technique. Now she doesn't even have to touch it. Now all she has to do is stand by it. And I mean it *totally* breaks. Not a simple paper clog. Oh no. There you might have hope. Sheila breathes on it, call in the surgeons. Everybody has to trek downstairs with their stuff and take a number. Gawd, it's *such* a pisser. She approaches, I hear myself saying, "Sheila! Let *me* do that for you!"

PAT: Hmmm. Maybe it's a—tactic.

(Linda considers this.)

LINDA: No. I don't think Sheila's smart enough for a—tactic.

PAT: *(Pause.)* Do you like Sheila?

LINDA: Do I like Sheila? *(Pause.)* Do I like Sheila. To be truthful, I don't think much about Sheila. Unless she wants to use the xerox machine.

PAT: You know how some people just—rub your fur the wrong way. Sheila does that to me.

LINDA: Oh yeah? What's she do?

PAT: She doesn't have to do anything. She just bugs the hell out of me.

LINDA: Yeah. Yeah-h-h-h. Plus she's this big around. *(Thumb and forefinger.)*

PAT: You think that's it?

LINDA: Isn't it?

PAT: *(Pause.)* Is this what they call being retro?

LINDA: Oh yeah.

PAT: I don't know why Sheila pisses me off.

LINDA: Yes, you do. She's young and she's thin and she's a big doof. She breaks the xerox machine.

PAT: Maybe she affects me like she does the copier. Maybe she gives off microscopically destructive vibrations.

LINDA: Just be thankful you don't have Beth Silver in your section. You want to talk somebody rubbing your fur the wrong way. Ughhhh.

PAT: What?

LINDA: What do you mean what? I told you about Beth Silver. The spandex mini-skirts. To here. You sit across from her at a meeting, you feel like her gynecologist. The guys love it.

(The waitress crosses, drops menu and retrieves it. The two women take it in.)

PAT: I'll bet they do.

LINDA: No surprises there.

(The Waitress moves off as Linda tries to wave her down for the drinks.)

PAT: *(Beat.)* Are we bitter?

LINDA: My, we're in a philosophical mode tonight. Bitter. Naturally. But we have a right to be.

PAT: I always feel weird trashing other women.

LINDA: Yeah? Since when?

PAT: I don't even *know* Sheila—

LINDA: You don't have to *know* Sheila to know Sheila. There's nothing to know. *(Beat.)* And with Beth—well, there you know more than you *want* to know. The woman is an anorexic collagen-injected wench-bag. *(Pause.)* Got a kickin' fine stylist though.

PAT: Lin-dah.

LINDA: What? That's not catty. That's truthful.

PAT: *(Beat.)* I mean, what we're doing here is so much a sign of the disenfranchised, I can't tell you.

LINDA: Whoa-ho-ho!

PAT: I mean it. What are we actually doing here?

LINDA: We're dishing.

PAT: We're venting.

LINDA: Exactly.

PAT: Exactly! I mean, we could concentrate our attacks upwards, at the actual source of our anger. But what do we do? We funnel our frustrations down the pyramid. At those less powerful—women we barely know—or across the pyramid, at each other—

LINDA: I hate to ask this, Pat, but...did you like, read a book or something?

PAT: I'm serious. I've been thinking about this a lot lately. For instance, take—ah—well, take my daughter. Joannie's drop-dead gorgeous—

LINDA: —She is—

PAT: —She's gorgeous—and smart, and sweet. And here I am. Approaching the middle of my life—

LINDA: —Wow. And I thought we were the same age—

PAT: —yes, the low, low, low end of our forties—and I am being made increasingly aware that I'm no longer the fresh young thing I once was. The figure's dumpy—

LINDA: No way!

PAT: Yes, Linda, way. No amount of exercise or dieting can stem this slow, relentless, downward slide of decay.

(Waitress crosses again on "slow, relentless, downward slide." Linda tries to flag her again but she's gone. Pause.)

LINDA: Two words, Pat. *(Beat.)* Plastic. Surgery.

PAT: Now, see—why? Why should I keep some—some scalpel-wielding huckster in three-hundred dollar loafers and a cigar boat in Florida just because I want the illusion of turning back the clock? Why not just keep buying different mirrors? Or, or, better still, why isn't how I *actually* look good enough?

LINDA: Why?

PAT: Yes! Why?

LINDA: In four words? Beth. Silver. Gets. Promotions.

PAT: *(Beat.)* That is so—twisted!—That is so revoltingly—disgustingly—

LINDA: Archaic Sexist Chauvinistic Crapola?

PAT: Yeah!

LINDA: And yet, ya know, so inescapably *there.*

PAT: Not to mention it's unfair to Beth Silver.

LINDA: Sorry. Something must have flown in my ear.

PAT: Well, how will Beth Silver ever know whether she got her upgrade because of her brain—or because of her skirt?

LINDA: A better question might be, does Beth Silver care? Have a won ton before I hoover them all.

PAT: But, really, think about where all this leads, Linda. My own daughter, for god's sakes. My own daughter who is *fifteen* years old! Now, how is *she* competition?

LINDA: Kids that age can be real turds.

PAT: No! It's the culture! It's a culture wherein the second, as a woman, you turn forty, your stock plummets. Blammo. Off the board. Might as well be Brown-Williamson: No wonder we're all so insecure. And it isn't gonna change until we change it!

LINDA: Right on. I am woman. Hear me roar.

PAT: I have a husband who loves me—we've had our problems, who hasn't—I have a good job, I have a great kid, I have my health. So why waste energy tearing into other women who happen to be younger or thinner?

LINDA: Or both. *(The younger, thinner Waitress appears with a Merlot and a Manhattan. She puts the drinks down and starts off. Linda takes a sip.)* WHOA THERE, ROADRUNNER! *(The Waitress returns. Linda smiles at her.)* Beep-beep. *(Pause.)* I didn't order this.

WAITRESS: *(Pause.)* 'Kay. No prob.

LINDA: I *hate* Manhattans. That's a Manhattan.

(The Waitress picks the drink up and sniffs it, puts it back down.)

WAITRESS: Whadya order?

LINDA: I ordered a whiskey sour. And we were hoping for won tons.

WAITRESS: 'Kay.

PAT: *(Jumping in.)* I understand. I used to waitress. You get busy—

WAITRESS: Oh tell me. Man, it's like *E.R.* back there—

PAT: Really?

WAITRESS: —Flu. Yeah. We got two servers out. The chef and the busboy are taking turns hurlin' in the bathroom—

LINDA: Okayyy! I hate to break up the Department of Health survey but might it be possible to get my whiskey sour? Forget the won tons.

PAT: Linda.

WAITRESS: *(Long pause. Cool stare.)* 'Kay. No prob.

LINDA: You can take—

(But Waitress exits without the Manhattan.)

PAT: *(Beat, as she notices Linda's expression.)* What?

LINDA: "I used to be a waitress…I understand…" Pat. The woman has a wind tunnel where her brain should be.

PAT: Oh, and isn't it easy to pick on food-service personnel?

LINDA: All I want is what I ordered. How does that make me a villain?!

PAT: *(Overlapping.)* She got the order a little scrambled doesn't mean she's a ditz. Harried perhaps. Ditz—not.

LINDA: Okay. *(Beat.)* If I complain to the manager, am I going up the pyramid?

PAT: Linda.

LINDA: If the manager is a woman, am I still going up the pyramid? Or am I going down the pyramid? Or am I really going across—

PAT: Linda!

LINDA: I just want to know—what's the book? "Running With—" what? Hamsters?!

PAT: Admit it, you're jealous of how she looks.

LINDA: What?! I am not! I'm complaining because she's lousy at her job!

PAT: Oh? Young and thin. And a ditz. *You* pointed it out.

LINDA: I don't believe this! Okay. Okay. *(Beat.)* Are you jealous of me?

PAT: What's that got to do with anything?

LINDA: You heard me.

PAT: No, I'm not jealous of you.

LINDA: How do you know this altercation that we are having is not just an excuse, a—a—way of disguising your own attack across the pyramid?

PAT: I'm not attacking you. You're my friend.

LINDA: And you've never been jealous of a friend? Never, ever?

PAT: *(Doubtful.)* No.

LINDA: Not even the time I got that bonus for processing the most—?

PAT: You earned it. I was happy for you!

LINDA: Never. Ever.

PAT: *(Beat.)* Well. Okay. Maybe. In the past.

LINDA: *(Great news.)* Really? When?

PAT: A few—isolated—moments. They were there. Then they were gone. I didn't feel good about them. Can't even remember them—

LINDA: Try.

(A beat.)

PAT: Christmas party at our house. Three years ago.

LINDA: Oh, yeah. *(Pause.)* Yeah?

PAT: You had on that green dress—

LINDA: Yeah. The one that made me look like I had cleavage. I loved that dress.

PAT: You looked nice.

(A beat.)

LINDA: That's it?

PAT: Yeah.

LINDA: Me in the green dress? That's it?

PAT: Dan said he thought you—he said you looked sexy.

LINDA: Oh. *(Pause.)* Dan said that.

PAT: Yeah.

LINDA: Oh. *(Pause.)* Well. *(Pause.)* Nice of him.

PAT: He was right. You did.

LINDA: Yeah, I did. *(A beat.)* You did too.

PAT: No, I didn't.

LINDA: Sure you did.

PAT: I didn't. You don't even remember what I was wearing.

LINDA: Um, wasn't it the gold number with the—sleeves—

PAT: No! I couldn't *fit* into that. I wore a tent made out of purple velvet.

LINDA: *(A bad memory.)* Oh, oh yeah.

PAT: Oh, who cares!

LINDA: Yeah, who cares! *(A beat.)* Wow. Christmas. Yeah. Boy, were we hammered that night. You passed out in the den. Wow. I'd almost forgotten. *(Laughs. A beat.)* So. Did Dan say anything else?
(A beat.)

PAT: Linda!

LINDA: What?

PAT: Geez! What else would Dan have to say? *(Beat.)* Linda? *(Beat.)* What else would Dan have to say?
(A long moment. Pat stares at Linda. Linda shrugs, avoids Pat's gaze. After a moment, Pat swats Linda's arm.)

LINDA: Ow! What?

PAT: You are so devious.

LINDA: Okay.

PAT: You had me buying it!

LINDA: Yeah?

PAT: You know you did—

LINDA: Oh, I know. Give me "up, down, across the pyramid." Geez, Pat, where do you come up with this stuff?

PAT: Just been on my mind. For awhile. *(Beat.)* Hey. I know how much you despise Manhattans but *(Picks up her glass to toast.)*—?

LINDA: Sure. *(Raising her glass.)* To us.

PAT: To us. *(They clink glasses.)* Together again.
(Lights go to black.)

END OF PLAY

Resident Alien
by Stuart Spencer

For the Jane Hoffman Players
—You know who you are—

BIOGRAPHY

Stuart Spencer of Brooklyn, New York, is the author of numerous plays, including *Water and Wine* (published by Smith and Kraus) and *Blue Stars* (published in *Best American Short Plays of 1993-94*). His plays *Sudden Devotion* and *Go To Ground* have been produced in New York at Ensemble Studio Theatre, where he is a member. As a screenwriter, he has been commissioned to write films for Campbell Scott and for the director George Camarda, and has recently completed an original screenplay, *For You, Anything*. He is currently at work on a playwriting textbook called *Tools of the Playwright*. He teaches playwriting in private classes at the Playwrights Horizons Theatre School and at Sarah Lawrence College. He also teaches dramatic literature at Sarah Lawrence College and at New York University. He is a member of the Dramatists Guild and is a fellow of the Edward Albee Foundation.

HUMANA FESTIVAL PRODUCTION

Resident Alien was first performed at the Humana Festival of New American Plays in February and March 1998. It was directed by Judy Minor with the following cast:

Michael	William McNulty
Priscilla	Carolyn Swift
Ray	Brad Bellamy
Alien	V Craig Heidenreich
Hank, The Sheriff	Brian Keeler
Billy	Corey Thomas Logsdon

and the following production staff:

Scenic Designer	Paul Owen
Costume Designer	Nanzi Adzima
Lighting Designer	Amy Appleyard
Sound Designer	Martin Desjardins
Properties Designer	Ron Riall
Stage Manager	Juliet Horn
Assistant Stage Manager	Charles M. Turner, III
Dramaturg	Michael Bigelow Dixon
Assistant Dramaturg	Meghan Davis
Casting	Laura Richin Casting

CHARACTERS

MICHAEL

PRISCILLA

RAY

THE ALIEN

HANK, The Sheriff

BILLY

All characters are in their thirties, except Billy, who is about 12.

TIME AND PLACE

Various locations in and around a small town in Wisconsin. The present.

STAGE

The stage setting should be minimal, fluid enough that the scenes can change easily and quickly.

NOTE

Selections from the following are included in this text:

Fear and Trembling by Sören Kierkegaard, translated by Alastair Hammay.

"Fly Me To the Moon," music and lyrics by Bart Howard.

SPECIAL THANKS

John McCormack, Artistic Director of the All Seasons Theatre Group, Chilton Ryan of the Theatre Artists Workshop of Norwalk, and to the Sarah Lawrence College Theatre Department for arranging early readings of this material.

Also to Scott Williams for his invaluable services as friend and artist.

Brad Bellamy, Corey Thomas Logsdon, V Craig Heidenreich,
Brian Keeler and Carolyn Swift
in *Resident Alien* by Stuart Spencer

22nd Annual Humana Festival of New American Plays
Actors Theatre of Louisville, 1998
photo by Richard Trigg

Resident Alien

ACT ONE
SCENE ONE

A farmhouse in Wisconsin. Late at night.

On stage are Michael, Priscilla and Ray. Michael sits in a chair. Priscilla and Ray circle around him.

MICHAEL: He wanted to go to the quarry. I said, "No, Billy, it's too close to bedtime." He said, "Please? I want to see the sunset. It's summer. I don't have to get up for school."

So I said, "Fine. We'll go to the quarry."

So we're walking through the woods, and it's already dark in there, even though the sky is blue. And we get to that clearing—you know, where the trail heads off to the left there? And there was this light. Above, and behind us. Then it started to move towards us—this light—and we ran down the trail, but it followed us.

Then we saw it, right in front of us, on the ground. And the light changed color and focused, like a narrow beam, pointing right at Billy. And I yelled, "No! Take me! Take me!" But I was frozen in place. I couldn't move! And Billy walked right towards it, like a trance.

And then…it was gone. One second, it was there. The next…nothing. And I was alone.

At least I thought I was alone. They left someone. One of their own. He said, "We took your friend." I said, "Where did you take him?" He said, "Don't worry. He'll be fine."
(Priscilla walks up to him, confronting him.)

PRISCILLA: Bullshit.

RAY: Okay, okay! Now hold on here. Okay Michael, so—that's all just fine. So, where is he now?

MICHAEL: I just told you, he's in the ship.

RAY: Not Billy—this guy they left. This alien.

PRISCILLA: Why are you asking him where the little green man is?!

RAY: Because maybe we could talk to him.

PRISCILLA: Ray, there is no little green man.

RAY: You don't know that. Michael, if they left someone, then where is he?

MICHAEL: I...I don't know. He left. He's not here.

PRISCILLA: He left? Where did he go?

MICHAEL: He didn't say. He said not to look for him.

PRISCILLA: And you didn't, I suppose.

MICHAEL: I'm not going to do anything he said not to. They have Billy.

RAY: But if he knows where Billy is...

MICHAEL: He's in a spaceship!

PRISCILLA: Fine. We're calling the sheriff.

MICHAEL: Go ahead. Call the sheriff. It's not going to do any good.

RAY: *(To Priscilla)* He's right about that. If it's aliens, there's not much the sheriff's going to be able to do.

MICHAEL: They took him away and he's not coming back until they decide.

PRISCILLA: Michael, you have bullshitted me before // and you're not going to bullshit me again...

MICHAEL: *(Overlapping at //.)* Bullshat.

PRISCILLA: What?!

MICHAEL: "Bullshat" would be correct.

PRISCILLA: *(To Ray, suddenly at a loss.)* You see what I'm dealing with?!

MICHAEL: You're a literate woman, Priscilla. I don't know why you pretend you're not.

PRISCILLA: You are not dragging me into a fight about the past tense of shit. No! I'm sorry! I refuse!

RAY: All right now, Michael. Come on here. You don't really believe this.

MICHAEL: It's not a question of believing. When something happens to you— when it happens present tense, first person—then it's not like you either believe or you don't believe. It's just a matter of what happened to you. If you're in a car accident and you break your left arm, you don't go around afterwards saying, "Now I believe in car accidents." You just say, "I was in a car accident. That's what happened to me."

PRISCILLA: Well, guess what? I don't believe Billy was kidnapped // by a bunch of aliens in a…

MICHAEL: *(Overlapping at //.)* Borrowed.

PRISCILLA: Borrowed?

MICHAEL: It's the preferred term.

PRISCILLA: You see? He's been reading up on the stuff! You have a history, you know. It wouldn't be the first time you made things up, invented stories, imagined things that aren't true.

MICHAEL: I never "imagined" things!

PRISCILLA: You displayed an inability to distinguish between reality and fantasy! The shrink said that, not me!

MICHAEL: I was there! I saw it!

PRISCILLA: Oh yes, you always concocted stories, Michael, but at least it was always something original!

MICHAEL: Priscilla, this happened!

PRISCILLA: I'll take you into court if I have to.

MICHAEL: You do what you have to do. You always did.

PRISCILLA: You've taken advantage of my good nature too many times, Michael! I am Billy's legal custodian. You only get to see him because I say so!

MICHAEL: I can't help what the people in spaceships do!

RAY: Okay, okay. Listen you two. It's time to saw this off. I got to get up and go fishing early.

PRISCILLA: You're not going fishing, mister.

RAY: I told Roger I was going to meet him up to Machickanee Flowage.

PRISCILLA: *(To Michael.)* If my son isn't on my doorstep first thing tomorrow morning, I'm calling the sheriff's office and I'm going to have you arrested. Is that clear? So you'd better go back out to the quarry, stick out your little green thumb, flag down that spaceship, and get them to beam Billy back down to earth before his mother throws one hell of an interplanetary fit.

(She exits.)

MICHAEL: They don't beam people. That's TV.

RAY: See if you can't fix it, huh? I got enough problems as it is.

(He exits. The door to the laundry opens and a man enters. He has a slightly greenish tinge to his skin.)

ALIEN: Which one were you married to?

(Lights out.)

SCENE TWO

The same, somewhat later, still night. The Alien sits at the table, awake, bored stiff. Michael has fallen asleep, his head on the table. He wakes up with a start.

MICHAEL: Uh.

ALIEN: Sleep must be very boring.

MICHAEL: Actually it can be quite interesting.

ALIEN: Pretty slow going from this end. You do it a lot?

MICHAEL: Every night.

ALIEN: Oooo baby. Sure hope you got cable.

(Michael gets up and goes to the window.)

MICHAEL: It's almost daylight.

ALIEN: Yes.

MICHAEL: So they'll be back soon.

ALIEN: Did I say that?

MICHAEL: You said they'd be back before sunrise.

ALIEN: Did I?

MICHAEL: Wait a minute. They won't be back before sunrise?

ALIEN: Oh, they'll be back before sunrise. Maybe not this *particular* sunrise.

MICHAEL: I trusted you!

ALIEN: I'm sorry if you misunderstood // but I…

MICHAEL: *(Overlapping at //.)* Nobody misunderstood! You said they'd be back before sunrise!

ALIEN: It's all for the best. You'll see.

MICHAEL: The best? It's for the best my son isn't coming home?

ALIEN: He might be having a great time up there. You don't know.

(Beat.)

MICHAEL: Well, how much longer?

ALIEN: I don't know.

MICHAEL: They don't tell you?

ALIEN: They never tell me anything.

MICHAEL: Are we talking days? Weeks? Months? What?!

ALIEN: Oh days, days. At the very most, a week. Or two.

MICHAEL: I wish you'd just tell me the truth.

ALIEN: Well I don't know. That's the truth. Sometimes it's short, sometimes it's long. But they always put the people back where they came from.

Always. Really. Now please, won't you sit down? *(Michael resists at first but finally gives in.)* Here. Drink your coffee.

(Michael stares into his coffee.)

MICHAEL: It's cold.

ALIEN: You don't like cold coffee?

MICHAEL: No.

ALIEN: Boy, things sure are different down here. We like our coffee cold. Also funny you drink coffee to wake up. We drink cocktails when we want to wake up. When we drink coffee it's to get us all wacky-wacky. Mind if I smoke? *(He takes out cigarettes and lights one.)* Smoking helps control our libido.

MICHAEL: What's wrong with your libido?

ALIEN: Somebody on the last planet had this great phrase: Like a bull in springtime. And I should warn you, we don't distinguish between gender.

MICHAEL: You have sex with anybody?

ALIEN: Well, not anybody. But someone good-looking such as yourself— *(Michael flashes him a worried look.)* Relax, I'm smoking. It's fine.

MICHAEL: Just tell me one thing.

ALIEN: Of course.

MICHAEL: Why did you take him?

ALIEN: We prefer the term "borrow".

MICHAEL: Oh right. I feel so secure about my only son when you say you only "borrowed" him. My compliments to your language experts. They've obviously been reading George Orwell.

ALIEN: *1984.* Good movie.

MICHAEL: It's also a book.

ALIEN: Yeah, but once you see the movie, it sort of spoils it.

MICHAEL: The question is: why?

ALIEN: I think I lost you.

MICHAEL: Why did you take him?

ALIEN: Borrow him.

MICHAEL: Why?

ALIEN: Some obscure test to investigate some statistical aberration in some previous test that is part of some longer, on-going survey that's part of some endless study of some tiny little behavioral quirk. You know what these people are like: inquisitive, tenacious little minds. So annoying.

MICHAEL: Billy's not in any danger, is he?

ALIEN: Well that's a relative question. No pun intended. *(Michael doesn't crack a smile.)* See, you're his relative and…never mind.

MICHAEL: Is he in danger?

ALIEN: Let me put it this way. He walks to school everyday, right?

MICHAEL: Yes.

ALIEN: Is that dangerous?

MICHAEL: Of course not.

ALIEN: Well, but—getting hit by a car. A random lunatic. Child molesters.

MICHAEL: Of course there's some danger. There's some danger in getting up in the morning.

ALIEN: There you go. Couldn't say it any better.

MICHAEL: You don't even know, do you.

ALIEN: Hey, I'm support team, okay? I don't know the details.

MICHAEL: I thought you were part of some scientific mission. I thought you were an advanced race.

ALIEN: Advanced race, yes. But I work in the kitchen. I'm a busboy.

MICHAEL: Then what are you doing here?

ALIEN: Shore leave.

MICHAEL: This is insane.

ALIEN: I thought maybe you could show me the good hangouts.

MICHAEL: Shore leave? Is this common?

ALIEN: No. It's strictly forbidden. They'd kill me if they found out.

MICHAEL: Kill you?!

ALIEN: Well, no. But they would make me do dishes all the way home.

MICHAEL: So you know nothing.

ALIEN: No.

MICHAEL: You're useless.

ALIEN: I think I have a few skills.

MICHAEL: But essentially, you're useless. My boy is kidnapped // and…

ALIEN: *(Overlapping at //.)* Borrowed.

MICHAEL: My boy is kidnapped, and you're just here to party down.

ALIEN: You could have done worse. I didn't have to come back. I could have just walked off and left you on your own. How would you have liked that?

MICHAEL: Better than this!

ALIEN: You don't mean that.

MICHAEL: Oh yes, I do.

(The Alien stamps out his cigarette.)

ALIEN: Okay. Have it your way.

MICHAEL: Where are you going?

    (The Alien takes a swig of coffee.)

ALIEN: To find myself a good time.

MICHAEL: You can't.

ALIEN: Why not?

MICHAEL: It's five o'clock in the morning. Everything's closed.

ALIEN: That's all right. I can wait. *(The Alien goes to the door.)* We'll see how you like it when I'm not around.

    (He exits. Michael stares after him. Lights out.)

SCENE THREE

The same. The next morning. 8:30 A.M.

The Sheriff waits while Michael is dressing for work. He listens to the radio playing the triumphant, joyous end of the First Movement of Beethoven's Seventh Symphony. It sounds tinny and thin on the radio. The music pauses for a moment.

SHERIFF: I just stopped by to…*(The music continues, then finishes.)* I just stopped by to…

MICHAEL: Shh!

RADIO ANNOUNCER: That was Beethoven's Seventh Symphony, conducted by // Herbert von Karajan of the Berlin Philharmonic…

MICHAEL: *(Overlapping at //.)* What?!

SHERIFF: What's wrong?

MICHAEL: God, I hate it when they do that. I give money to them, besides.

SHERIFF: What did they do?

MICHAEL: There's another three movements for cryin' out loud! *(To the radio.)* Play the whole damn symphony or don't play it at all! *(He flicks off the radio.)* And you could knock.

SHERIFF: *(Forced cheerfulness.)* 'Morning.

    (Michael starts to put on his K-Mart uniform.)

MICHAEL: What time is it?

SHERIFF: Time for some of that good coffee you make.

MICHAEL: It's all gone. I need the time, please.

SHERIFF: What's the matter, lose your watch?

MICHAEL: I stopped wearing watches—they only reminded me I wasn't on time.

SHERIFF: It's 8:28.

MICHAEL: You mind if we get to the point? I'm late for work.

SHERIFF: Well, Priscilla called about some sort of problem with Billy.

MICHAEL: There's some sort of problem all right. He's in a spaceship at the moment. As soon as he's back on earth, you can tell her I'll send him right over.

SHERIFF: Now, Michael—Billy is her child too. This is no way to deal with...whatever.

MICHAEL: I am sick of you always taking her side! What about me? Do I come across as such a runaway marble? Huh?

SHERIFF: Yes, you do.

MICHAEL: Sure, "That Michael—fancy books, fancy radio station." I know what everybody says.

SHERIFF: We'd just like to know where Billy is.

MICHAEL: I told you where he is.

SHERIFF: In a spaceship.

MICHAEL: Yes.

SHERIFF: Is there a phone in this spaceship?

MICHAEL: What?

SHERIFF: So maybe we could talk to Billy?

MICHAEL: You know, I'm just guessing—but I bet there isn't.

SHERIFF: Well, a radio then. Some sort of communication device. *(He flips his hand open a la Star Trek.)* You know—"Kirk to Enterprise." That kind of thing. So we could make sure Billy's okay. It'd take a load off Priscilla's mind, I can tell you.

MICHAEL: If there was some way to talk to Billy, don't you think I would have done it?

SHERIFF: So you haven't talked to him.

MICHAEL: No!

SHERIFF: And you're not planning on it in the near future.

MICHAEL: If I could I would, and I can't!

SHERIFF: All right, okay. Just a thought.

MICHAEL: Look, do you mind? You don't keep K-Mart waiting if you know what's good for you.

SHERIFF: Well, I've got a couple more questions. *(Michael gestures impatiently for him to continue.)* Priscilla said you mentioned someone else.

MICHAEL: He's not here.

SHERIFF: So there was another person with you.

MICHAEL: It's one of them. An alien. A busboy alien.

SHERIFF: What's he doing down here?

MICHAEL: Taking some time off. He's AWOL.

SHERIFF: An AWOL alien busboy. I never heard of that.

MICHAEL: Well, he's not your science fiction alien. He's a real alien and he has a real life. Not an interesting one necessarily, but a life.

SHERIFF: Where is he?

MICHAEL: *(Beat.)* I don't know.

SHERIFF: No idea?

MICHAEL: No.

SHERIFF: He just left, just like that? Not a word?

MICHAEL: That's right.

SHERIFF: Any guesses which way he was heading?

MICHAEL: Look, they're an advanced race, okay? I don't pretend to know what one of them might be thinking. They're very subtle, very brilliant.

SHERIFF: I thought he was a busboy.

MICHAEL: Well, I'm talking about potential.

SHERIFF: And I'm talking about where he went. Does he drive a car?

MICHAEL: I seriously doubt it.

SHERIFF: So he's hitchhiking.

MICHAEL: Maybe, but I don't think anybody's going to pick him up.

SHERIFF: Why not?

MICHAEL: He has green skin.

(The Sheriff lets this register—a big impact.)

SHERIFF: Trinkle.

MICHAEL: Are you all right?

SHERIFF: Mrs. Trinkle. High School.

MICHAEL: Yeah…?

SHERIFF: Yearbook staff.

MICHAEL: Right. Senior English.

SHERIFF: Good times. Good years.

MICHAEL: You know, you don't look so good.

SHERIFF: All of a sudden, it's right there—I don't even know why…*(He tries to think for a second, but gives up and shrugs.)* It's gone.

MICHAEL: Little Proustian moment I guess.

SHERIFF: Yeah, I guess so...what?

MICHAEL: Nothing—good times. Good years.

SHERIFF: Seems like a long time, doesn't it.

MICHAEL: It is a long time. Be nice to go back, though, wouldn't it.

SHERIFF: We always thought a lot of you, Michael. Always thought you were the one going somewhere. That you were going to get out into the big world.

MICHAEL: You don't lose your provincialism by leaving the provinces. This is my big world, right here.

(He indicates a book on the table. The Sheriff fingers it.)

SHERIFF: *Fear and Trembling.* Sören...

MICHAEL: Kierkegaard.

SHERIFF: Any good?

MICHAEL: It's a page-turner.

SHERIFF: Don't you think you'd be better off leaving, though? Going off to Chicago, Minneapolis, New York? Someplace where people could...appreciate you?

MICHAEL: So what's this? The part in the movie where the sheriff is saying "get out of town"?

SHERIFF: Actually, the sheriff is saying stay right where you are until this whole thing is over. Then get out of town. Find another town—where you can be happy, where you fit in. For yourself, I'm talking.

MICHAEL: Sure, no problem. Just one thing.

SHERIFF: What's that?

MICHAEL: Show me the town.

(Lights fade on them.)

SCENE FOUR

A roadside bar. Lots of different beer signs and a jukebox that doesn't work quite right.

Ray is behind the bar. The Alien sits on a barstool, nursing a tap. Something about the lighting of the bar makes his skin look like it's a normal color. 10:30 A.M.

Ray is placing a bottle of beer on the bar in front of the Alien. There are two empty bottles already there.

RAY: One more?

ALIEN: No, no.

RAY: Go on, go ahead.

ALIEN: I think I had enough.

RAY: Don't you worry. I'm trained to know when to cut you off, and you're nowhere near the limit yet.

ALIEN: You think so?

RAY: I know so.

ALIEN: I'm just not sure I ought to.

RAY: Go on.

ALIEN: You really think I should?

RAY: Absolutely.

ALIEN: No...

RAY: Just go ahead.

ALIEN: All right.

(The Alien takes a deep swig. The sound of a car pulling into the lot outside. Ray goes to the window.)

RAY: That'd be the Sheriff.

ALIEN: *(Stands up, trying to look calm.)* Sheriff?

RAY: He come by to talk to the wife.

ALIEN: Are you sure?

RAY: Oh yeah. She and her ex are goin' through some trouble on account of he kidnapped their boy and said it was aliens that did it. You know, one o' those typical things. *(He looks through the window. He waves and talks— doesn't yell—through the window even though the Sheriff obviously can't hear him.)* Yup, he's goin' right around to the back door. Hey. How ya doin'? *(Meanwhile, the Alien is visibly putting this all together in his head. Ray comes away from the window. The Alien polishes off his beer. Ray opens another beer for him.)*

ALIEN: Kidnapped by aliens.

RAY: Can ya top that?

ALIEN: How's she taking it?

RAY: Not so good. He's done this before, of course, but he never said it was aliens before. I'd say that was the part that got her wound up.

ALIEN: I feel so bad.

RAY: How come?

ALIEN: Well, I just do.

RAY: Oh. I see. Well, that's darn nice of you.

ALIEN: I wish there was something I could do.

RAY: Well, when Priscilla's like this, she's in her own world. You'd have to be from another planet to get through to her.

(Beat.)

ALIEN: Interesting. Care to join me?

RAY: Oh no. Not policy.

ALIEN: I figured you were the owner.

RAY: Well, yeah, I am. But the wife is management. Final word is mine but management pretty much runs the show. She says when I drink behind the bar, the books don't balance at the end of the day.

ALIEN: And neither do you, I bet.

RAY: Eh?

ALIEN: Balance at the end of the day.

RAY: Oh dang. That's a good one. I got to tell Priscilla that. You're quick on the comebacks, ain't you. You and Priscilla'd get along great. She's quick on the comebacks too.

(The Alien has been staring at him.)

ALIEN: Please have a drink.

RAY: Well, no, I shouldn't, no.

ALIEN: I hate to drink alone.

RAY: I understand, but no…

ALIEN: It's a lonely feeling.

RAY: I can appreciate that. But no. Really.

ALIEN: Go ahead. You have this one.

RAY: No, I better don't. I don't handle it so good this early.

ALIEN: Just the one, please?

RAY: I don't think so.

ALIEN: It's so lonely.

RAY: I understand that, but I…

ALIEN: Please? Just one.

RAY: Nope. Can't. Sorry.

ALIEN: Please?

RAY: Okay.

(Ray takes a drink. Lights blackout.)

SCENE FIVE

The office in back of the same bar. Time is continuous from the previous scene. The Sheriff stands in the doorway, while Priscilla confronts him.

PRISCILLA: Do you know what Michael said to me two months ago? He had Billy for the afternoon and Billy threw a fit because Michael wouldn't let him watch his favorite TV show. And Michael told me if I couldn't keep Billy away from garbage like that, he was going to take matters into his own hands. His words: "take matters into his own hands."

SHERIFF: What's the show?

PRISCILLA: *The New Adventures of Hercules.*

SHERIFF: That's not so bad.

PRISCILLA: Of course it isn't.

SHERIFF: Michael ought to like that one. Sort of like a little bit of classical literature there.

PRISCILLA: And then the other one about the woman—Xerox, or Xanax, or Xantac or...

SHERIFF: *Xena: Warrior Princess.*

PRISCILLA: That's it.

SHERIFF: Now there's a problem. There's a lot more sex and violence in that *Xena: Warrior Princess.*

PRISCILLA: There's no sex in *Xena: Warrior Princess.*

SHERIFF: The way Xena's whatchamacallits come poking out of her breastplate? Are you kidding? I can't let my Ethan be watching that kind of thing. He'd lose control.

PRISCILLA: Well apparently you watch it.

SHERIFF: Priscilla, I'm a grown man.

PRISCILLA: You're missing the point, Hank.

SHERIFF: I think you're missing Michael's point.

PRISCILLA: What are you going to do about this?

SHERIFF: We've searched the whole woods and there's no sign of Billy.

PRISCILLA: Of course not. Michael wouldn't leave him in the woods. But I know what he might have done.

SHERIFF: What's that?

PRISCILLA: Drove Billy down to Sheboygan and left him with his Aunt Daisy.

SHERIFF: Then why don't you go down there and get him?

PRISCILLA: Because I'm not playing this game with Michael again. He did this same thing last year. It took me three days to figure it out and when I finally did I ended up on a two-hour car trip to Sheboygan, listening to him lecture me about my bad taste in TV shows. So this time, I'm putting it in the hands of the authorities. That's you, by the way.

SHERIFF: I'm happy to go pay Aunt Daisy a visit.

PRISCILLA: And if he's not there, I want you to arrest Michael.

SHERIFF: Priscilla, I think we can give it a day or two before that happens.

PRISCILLA: This is why I stuffed envelopes for your campaign? So you could tell me to wait a day or two?

SHERIFF: If we give him some time, he might just come around on his own.

PRISCILLA: I've got news for you, mister. Sheriffs get voted in and Sheriffs also get voted out. And I've got dirt on you, don't forget that.

(She collects her checkbook, purse, etc. and prepares to go out.)

SHERIFF: There's no dirt on me.

PRISCILLA: You drive that county car when you go fishing up to Wabeno. *(Sheriff reacts.)* Didn't think I knew that, did you. That's against regulations. I could use that in a campaign.

SHERIFF: What point are we trying to make here, exactly?

PRISCILLA: I have a son who is missing.

SHERIFF: You just said he's in Sheboygan with his Aunt Daisy.

(She is ready to go.)

PRISCILLA: Maybe. Now, by the time I get back from the wholesaler, I want the poop on this. However you do it, that's up to you.

SHERIFF: Priscilla...

PRISCILLA: At least bring him into your office.

SHERIFF: And do what?

PRISCILLA: Put the pressure on, for cryin' out loud!

SHERIFF: I already did that.

PRISCILLA: Hank, now listen. You set a mean speed trap, nobody can touch you on kittens in trees. But the Spanish Inquisition you are not. Can't you see that he's—

(Ray enters.)

RAY: Priscilla, we got any Blackberry Flavored Brandy in the storeroom?

PRISCILLA: You're interrupting, Ray.

RAY: Well, we got a customer wants Blackberry Flavored Brandy.

PRISCILLA: You've been drinking, haven't you.

RAY: I ain't been drinking.

PRISCILLA: I smell it on your breath, you weasel.

RAY: I ain't been drinking.

PRISCILLA: If you drink up our profits, I'll take that shotgun off the wall and kill you. Do you understand me?

RAY: *(To the Sheriff.)* I hope you heard that. That's evidence.

PRISCILLA: Correction…I will divorce you, strip you of all your worldly possessions right down to your jockey briefs, wait until January, and then throw your bare-assed sorry-looking self into the snowbank. Then I will take the shotgun and kill you. Are we clear?

RAY: You don't scare me for one second.

(Ray exits.)

SHERIFF: You two seem to be doin' a lot better. I was concerned there.

PRISCILLA: Don't worry your pretty little head about me.

SHERIFF: Well sometimes I do.

PRISCILLA: You had your chance, big boy. It's a little late for regret.

SHERIFF: Priscilla, I'm not talking about that.

PRISCILLA: You'd better not be!

SHERIFF: That was a very long time ago.

PRISCILLA: Not long enough!

SHERIFF: Priscilla, it was Junior Prom.

PRISCILLA: The heart knows nothing of years, Hank. It knows nothing of miles. It was a moment ago, it was as close as you are to me. And it was Homecoming.

SHERIFF: Well, I'm sorry.

PRISCILLA: Me too. If you hadn't // dumped me…

SHERIFF: *(Overlapping at //.)* I never dumped you.

PRISCILLA: You most certainly did.

SHERIFF: You're the one who broke it off.

PRISCILLA: Because I would not be humiliated by watching you ask Amy VanderHooven to Homecoming.

SHERIFF: You weren't even speaking to me.

PRISCILLA: Not after you asked Amy VanderHooven!

SHERIFF: Priscilla, this is ancient history.

PRISCILLA: You're right. Yes. So let's do current events: your job. That's all I ask. You darn well do your job.

(She exits before he can say anything. The lights change.)

The bar. Some time has passed. The Alien still sits on his bar stool. Ray is considerably drunker than before. Ray sings karaoke.

RAY: "Fly me to the moon!
　　And let me play among the stars!
　　Let me know what spring is like
　　On Jupiter and Mars!
　　In other words, hold my hand
　　In other words, darling…
　　(The system goes dead and the music stops. Ray continues.)
　　…kiss me!
　　Fill my heart with song…"
　　—wha' happened?
　　(The Alien applauds wildly.)

ALIEN: Bravo! Eccellente! L'ho Amata! Dovresti cantare per tutta la vita!

RAY: Hey, you speak good Spanish.

ALIEN: Grazie.

RAY: Come to think of it, y'kinda have that olive compleshion. Ya got some Mexican in ya?

ALIEN: Mind if I ask you something?

RAY: Yeah, sure. I got to siddown though…*(Ray comes around the bar and sits on the other bar stool.)* Okay, shoot.

ALIEN: This whole situation with your wife and the missing kid and everything. It's got me thinking. I think we've got a classic kind of an ethical problem here.

RAY: Wha's that?

ALIEN: It's a moral dilemma.

RAY: I know whadda friggin' ethcal problem is. Whadisa problem, is whad I'm tryin' to say. Whatcha got on your mind—go 'head. Jes' say it.

ALIEN: Suppose some…friends of yours, someone close to you…

RAY: I don' have any friends. Everybody hates me.

ALIEN: Well your wife then.

RAY: She hates me too. Everybody hates me.

ALIEN: Well, someone you love—even if they don't love you.

RAY: I love my mother. Oh God I love her. She's dead.

ALIEN: Okay, suppose your mother committed a crime.

RAY: But she's dead.

ALIEN: It's hypothetical.

RAY: Oh. Okay, I'm with ya.

ALIEN: Let's say she kidnapped someone.

RAY: My dead mother.

ALIEN: And you were her accomplice. You helped her.

RAY: Oh that's good.

ALIEN: Not directly, but you allowed it to happen. You provided certain services which allowed the kidnapping to proceed. And this was very upsetting to people. The kidnapping. But suppose she had led you to believe that it was for a good cause. That in the long run, the fact that she had kidnapped someone would make the world a better place.

RAY: Yeah.

ALIEN: Although you don't really know how it would make the world better. But you're pretty sure it would. She said that it would.

RAY: She.

ALIEN: The kidnapper. Your mother.

RAY: Oh yeah. I' sorry. Go 'head.

ALIEN: So the question is, would you feel morally responsible for all those people being upset? Even if you're only an accessory. In other words…

RAY: *(Singing.)* "In other words…!"

ALIEN: Would you choose to believe your mother, who claims it's for the greater good? Or would you sympathize with the family of the kidnap victim and try to help her—them in some way?

RAY: You wanna know what I think?

ALIEN: Yes. I'm asking.

RAY: You gotta help 'em out.

ALIEN: Really.

RAY: Oh yeah.

ALIEN: How?

RAY: Bring 'em some canned goods.

ALIEN: Canned goods.

RAY: That 'n a nice bottle of Blackbery Flavored brandy. But we're outta that.

ALIEN: Provide comfort.

RAY: Yup.

ALIEN: That's exactly what I was thinking. You've got a beautiful soul.

RAY: You're darn tootin' I do.

ALIEN: Come here.

RAY: Wha?

ALIEN: Grazie molto. Sei stupido, ma molto gentile.

(The Alien embraces and kisses a stiff Ray. Lights change.)

SCENE SEVEN

K-Mart, Michael's place of work. Michael is stacking toy flying saucers onto the shelf. The Sheriff hands him boxes.

SHERIFF: Priscilla is happy in her new life, Michael. One of these days you have to accept that.

MICHAEL: She is not happy with him.

SHERIFF: Priscilla's as happy as Priscilla gets. She's not an easy woman to please.

MICHAEL: I pleased her.

SHERIFF: Well, apparently—no.

(Michael climbs down off the stepladder.)

MICHAEL: I was good for her.

SHERIFF: She divorced you.

MICHAEL: Ultimately, yes, but we had some good years.

SHERIFF: You did not.

MICHAEL: Well—months, anyway.

SHERIFF: Everything always comes back to Priscilla in your mind. You're fixated on her. You've got to let go of that anger.

MICHAEL: Did she tell you that?

SHERIFF: She didn't have to. Now look, I want to clear up a couple things before I head to Sheboygan. Did you threaten to take Billy if he, uh...*(The Sheriff consults a notebook.)*...if his home environment didn't get better?

MICHAEL: Did she tell you that?

SHERIFF: Yes or no?

MICHAEL: I meant Ray. She knows that.

SHERIFF: What's wrong with Ray? He's a solid guy.

MICHAEL: He's a moron.

SHERIFF: He's a typical, regular guy.

MICHAEL: Exactly. He's a moron.

SHERIFF: For example.

MICHAEL: Billy arrives for the weekend, goes right to the television set and flips on this show called *The New Adventures of Hercules.* I'm sure you never saw it. It's stupid. Anyway. I say to him, "Oh no, we're not watching *The New Adventures of Hercules,* not on my time."* But Billy says Ray told him that *The New Adventures of Hercules* is just like reading classical literature—only the TV is better because it's all acted out in front of you. Inside, part of me dies. The other part, of course, is going to dismember Ray.

SHERIFF: All the kids watch that stuff, Michael.

MICHAEL: This is my son—my flesh and blood, a boy who walked to the CD player when he was five years old and put on Beethoven's Seventh Symphony all by himself. That same boy is pleading to watch *The New Adventures of Hercules.* It's obscene!

SHERIFF: Well at least it wasn't *Xena: Warrior Princess.* There's too much sex and violence on that one if you ask me.

MICHAEL: Sex and violence is not the issue, Hank.

SHERIFF: It is for my Ethan. You should see what happens when Xena comes out in that breastplate with her whatchamacallits all stickin' out.

MICHAEL: Hank, you're missing the point.

SHERIFF: Well I think you're missing Priscilla's point.

MICHAEL: That Hercules show takes a timeless myth that penetrates to the core of our collective psyche, rips out every shred of meaning, and gives us back the empty shell. The myth of Hercules is about guilt and courage and innocence and rage—and sex and violence for that matter, but real sex and real violence. It's about what they mean. That TV show is about a guy with big muscles and long hair!

SHERIFF: Well sex and violence wasn't the same thing in the old days.

MICHAEL: What are you talking about?

SHERIFF: Not like sex and violence today.

MICHAEL: Are you kidding?! What about *Anna Karenina?*

SHERIFF: I don't know her and I don't know what kind of TV she likes // but I...

MICHAEL: *(Overlapping at //.) Hamlet* then! We had to read that in high school! *A Streetcar Named Desire! Crime and Punishment!*

SHERIFF: Okay I get the...

MICHAEL: *The Iliad! The Odyssey! The Bible!*

SHERIFF: Michael, okay.

MICHAEL: Sex and violence galore!

SHERIFF: Okay, I get it.

MICHAEL: You don't get it.

SHERIFF: I'm not a total rock-head, Michael. I get it!

MICHAEL: It's all Ray's fault—she wasn't like this when she was with me!

SHERIFF: All right, that's about enough. I'm taking you down to the station.

MICHAEL: The station?

SHERIFF: You need some time to cool off. Now come on. Let's go.

MICHAEL: You've been waiting for this for twenty years, haven't you! Ever since I started seeing Priscilla, ever since the time I stayed home from bowling to watch *Live From the Met*.

SHERIFF: Are you coming with me now?

MICHAEL: No.

SHERIFF: Please?

MICHAEL: No.

SHERIFF: Michael, I'm asking you please.

MICHAEL: Well, are you asking me or telling me?

SHERIFF: I'm asking you.

MICHAEL: Then no. How do you like that?

SHERIFF: Michael, just come down to the station.

MICHAEL: No.

SHERIFF: I don't want to arrest you.

MICHAEL: Why not? You're the sheriff.

SHERIFF: I don't want to do the paper work.

MICHAEL: Sorry then. Not going.

SHERIFF: *(Almost whining.)* Oh come on, Michael…?

MICHAEL: On one condition. When this over, when Billy's back, you promise me you'll read *Anna Karenina*.

SHERIFF: Oh for cryin' out…

MICHAEL: It's a good book.

SHERIFF: Michael…

MICHAEL: There was a time you would have done it, Hank. When you would have been curious, anyway.

SHERIFF: *(Slight beat.)* Okay. I'll give it a shot. After Billy is back.

MICHAEL: *(The slightest smile.)* You're gonna love it.

SHERIFF: I'm sure I will. After you.

> *(Michael exits, followed by the Sheriff. The lights cross-fade.)*

SCENE EIGHT

The bar. Ray is asleep—passed out—on the top of the bar. He snores. The Alien finishes off his beer and walks around to the back of the bar. He pours himself a big cup of coffee.

He's about to drink it when Priscilla appears behind him, coming in from the back with a carton of bottles.

PRISCILLA: And just what do you think you're doing?

ALIEN: Oh. I paid for this.

PRISCILLA: What am I, stupid? Get out from behind there.

ALIEN: You can ask him. I paid in advance. I'm covered.

PRISCILLA: Mister, don't mess with me. The Sheriff's a friend of mine and I've got a twelve-gauge back there. Now move it on out.

ALIEN: Under protest.

PRISCILLA: Under anything you want, just do it.

(He comes out from behind the bar. She goes behind it herself.)

ALIEN: When he wakes up, he's going to back me up on this.

PRISCILLA: I'll make a mental note of it.

ALIEN: You must be Priscilla. Ray here speaks highly of you.

PRISCILLA: Ray here drinks in the middle of the day.

ALIEN: So do I.

PRISCILLA: Some people can hold it.

ALIEN: It did seem to put him right out.

PRISCILLA: Any excuse to take a nap. That's my Ray. Mind if I make a suggestion?

ALIEN: Not at all.

PRISCILLA: Considering I just caught you in the act of what amounts to stealing, why don't you and I just remain strangers? The door's right there.

(Ray snorts in his sleep.)

ALIEN: I need to say two things. First, this is my fault and I'm sorry. Don't be angry with him. If you must be angry with someone, I'm the one.

PRISCILLA: So far, so good. And the other thing?

ALIEN: You're unhappy.

PRISCILLA: Yeah, well—you would be too, believe me.

ALIEN: Yes, Ray told me about Billy. But that's not what I meant. I meant something deeper. Something very basic.

PRISCILLA: My emotional condition is none of your concern.

ALIEN: But it is my concern. No man is an island, entire of itself; every man is a piece of the continent, a part of the main; if a clod be washed away by the sea, Europe is the less, as well as if a promontory were, as well as if a manor of thy friend's or of thy own were; any man's death diminishes me, because I am involved in mankind; and therefore never send to know for whom the bell tolls; it tolls for thee.

PRISCILLA: *(Fascinated, softening in spite of herself.)* Not local, are you.

ALIEN: No, but I like the neighborhood.

PRISCILLA: You ought to be meet my ex-husband. You and he'd get along great.

ALIEN: I'm not so sure about that. I sort of prefer women.

(She laughs out loud.)

PRISCILLA: So does he. *(Pause. They look at each other. She's unsure of herself but liking it.)* I thought you were leaving.

ALIEN: We were discussing your melancholy state of mind.

PRISCILLA: Just what exactly do you care about that?

ALIEN: I told you. I am involved in mankind.

PRISCILLA: Oh yeah. I'm impressed by the way. You know the whole thing. How did that happen?

ALIEN: No, let's talk about you instead.

PRISCILLA: Uh-unh. Me first.

ALIEN: I memorized it.

PRISCILLA: Why?

ALIEN: Your turn. Tell me your sorrows.

PRISCILLA: No. Why did you memorize it?

ALIEN: Because I had to. They made me.

PRISCILLA: They?

ALIEN: My…employers. It was part of a training program. They made us learn all kinds of stuff. I don't know what half of it means, to tell you the truth. Except for that one part. "I am involved." That part I get. *(Beat.)* Your turn.

PRISCILLA: Life stinks.

ALIEN: Expand.

PRISCILLA: You divorce your first husband and he kidnaps your little boy and won't give him back and the sheriff who dumped you just before Homecoming, and who you helped get elected to office, won't lift a finger to get him back. And you leave your second husband in charge of the family business for two hours and you come back to find him dead drunk with some strange man behind the bar acting like he owns the place.

ALIEN: Hey, I told you—I'm covered. Two hundred American dollars, in advance.

(He indicates two 100-dollar bills under Ray's head. Priscilla checks, finds the money, and pockets it.)

PRISCILLA: What do you do? Print it yourself?

ALIEN: No, other people do that for me.

PRISCILLA: Oh, rich kid, huh?

ALIEN: Rich enough to take you away from all this.

PRISCILLA: Yeah? Where would we go?

ALIEN: Where do you want to go?

PRISCILLA: I want to go wherever my kid is.

ALIEN: Oh.

PRISCILLA: Can't manage that one, can you.

ALIEN: No. Not really.

PRISCILLA: Didn't think so.

ALIEN: But I'm sure he'll be back.

PRISCILLA: Oh you are, are you.

ALIEN: Oh yes, he'll be back.

PRISCILLA: That's so comforting, coming from you, I can't begin to tell you.

ALIEN: All safe and sound.

PRISCILLA: What do you know? Huh?

ALIEN: I have a good sense of these things.

PRISCILLA: You don't know anything. You don't have a crazy ex-husband and you probably don't have kids either, do you. So what would you know about that? Huh? What would you know about those feelings? You don't know anything.

ALIEN: I'm sorry you're upset.

PRISCILLA: One thing I don't need is sympathy!

ALIEN: Yes it is.

PRISCILLA: No it is not!

ALIEN: Everybody needs sympathy.

PRISCILLA: I am not everybody. I am Priscilla Zuelke. *(Pronounced Zull-key. Rhymes with Full-key.)* I do not need anything, anytime, from anyone. All I need is my little boy back!

ALIEN: I know.

PRISCILLA: That's all I want!

ALIEN: It must be awful.

PRISCILLA: It is awful!

ALIEN: Of course it is.

PRISCILLA: You don't know. He's only twelve! He doesn't understand about divorces and custody battles and...*(She breaks down and cries.)*

ALIEN: Go ahead. Have a good cry. *(She cries. He strokes her shoulder.)* That's right. Let it out. Let it out.

PRISCILLA: Oh God! It's too much!

ALIEN: Yes, it is.

PRISCILLA: It's too much for one person!

ALIEN: It is, you're right. It isn't fair. *(He moves in closer and embraces her lightly.)* You've been very brave.

PRISCILLA: No, I haven't.

ALIEN: Yes, you're very brave. You've kept a very level head through all of this.

PRISCILLA: How would you know?

ALIEN: I've got eyes. I see how you are. You're very strong. You're very brave. But when it's too much, it's too much. A person can only take so much.

PRISCILLA: That's right. *(She stops crying.)* You're touching me.

ALIEN: Is it all right?

PRISCILLA: Well, no, not really.

ALIEN: Why not?

PRISCILLA: Because my husband is right there.

ALIEN: He's asleep.

PRISCILLA: People wake up.

ALIEN: Eventually.

PRISCILLA: No really. I...I didn't want this.

ALIEN: I know. You want your baby back.

PRISCILLA: Yes.

ALIEN: I can't help you there. But I can help you here.

PRISCILLA: Oh...

ALIEN: If you want me to.

PRISCILLA: I...I don't know...

ALIEN: I think you do know.

PRISCILLA: I think I do too.

(They kiss.)

PRISCILLA: Not here.

ALIEN: Yes.

PRISCILLA: No, there's an apartment upstairs.

ALIEN: I don't like apartments.

PRISCILLA: But my husband…

ALIEN: He won't wake up for hours.

PRISCILLA: How do you know?

ALIEN: I know. I know more than you think.

(He presses her against the bar and kisses her passionately. They sink to the floor, and begin to make love. Lights fade.)

SCENE NINE

The same, evening. Michael is at the front door. He sees Ray asleep on the bar.

MICHAEL: Hey. Wake up. Wake up. Ray, wake up.

RAY: Oh gawd…

MICHAEL: Come on. Wake up.

RAY: Pr'cilla's not here.

MICHAEL: I'm not looking for Priscilla.

RAY: Well, sh's not here.

MICHAEL: Will you please wake up?

RAY: I'm 'wake.

(But his eyes stay shut. Michael walks around the bar, pours a glass of water and throws it in Ray's face. Ray opens his eyes.)

RAY: Thank you.

MICHAEL: I thought you stopped drinking during the day.

RAY: This was social. I was pressured.

MICHAEL: Who?

RAY: Some drunk. Who else stands outside a bar at 10 o'clock in the morning?

MICHAEL: How did he look?

RAY: He looked like a drunk. That was some bad case of liver damage. Worst-looking skin I ever saw.

MICHAEL: Sort of…green?

RAY: I'd say more like yellow. Inside the bar here, he didn't look so bad—neon lights, you know. But outside in the daylight…whoo-ee. Scary.

MICHAEL: You're sure it wasn't green.

RAY: Liver damage don't make you green.

MICHAEL: But maybe this wasn't liver damage, Ray.

RAY: Hey, gimme some credit, would you? I know something on the subject, okay?

(He goes behind the bar and cleans himself up with a rag.)

MICHAEL: Where did he go?

RAY: I don't know.

MICHAEL: When did he leave?

RAY: I don't know.

MICHAEL: You mean, you passed out while he was still here?

RAY: When you pass out, you don't have much say over when.

MICHAEL: Did he say where he was going?

RAY: He just said he had to take off.

MICHAEL: Take off?

RAY: Yeah, get goin'.

MICHAEL: Well, did he say "get going," or did he say "take off"?

RAY: What difference does it make? He left, okay?

MICHAEL: It makes a lot of difference!

RAY: Well I can't remember.

MICHAEL: Well, the first time you said "take off."

RAY: Okay.

MICHAEL: So is that it? Is that what he said?

RAY: Yeah. Okay? That's what he said.

MICHAEL: You don't even know, do you?

RAY: No, I don't know! The rest of us aren't so perfect, Michael. I never went to college, I don't take notes!

MICHAEL: That's not what this is about!

RAY: Oh really? Then what's it about?

MICHAEL: That drunk was an alien! He's one of them!

(Slight pause.)

RAY: Oh boy oh boy.

MICHAEL: That's right "oh boy oh boy."

RAY: You're really cracked, ain'tcha?

MICHAEL: Didn't it occur to you even once? You sat there and listened to me last night talking about the aliens and how they took Billy, and this morning a green-skinned man shows up at your bar?

RAY: I know liver damage when I see it, and that was liver damage. It was yellow.

MICHAEL: Their skin is green.

RAY: Well, this guy, it was yellow.

MICHAEL: That's because you see the world through the light of an Old Milwaukee sign!

RAY: I took your wife, Michael. Okay? I'm sorry about that. But there's no need to get personal.

MICHAEL: You did not take Priscilla.

RAY: Well, she's married to me.

MICHAEL: You did not "take" her.

RAY: You still got a burr up your ass about that.

MICHAEL: Priscilla left me, Ray. You had nothing to do with it!

(He starts to leave.)

RAY: You never loved her.

(Michael stops.)

MICHAEL: I loved her.

RAY: Well you sure as heck never understood her.

MICHAEL: I understood her. Better than you ever will. Priscilla is music. There's a song inside her and someday she's going to sing it and believe me, the tune will not be Ray Zuelke.

(Michael exits. Ray calls after him.)

RAY: That's how much you know! There's no song inside Priscilla. She can't even carry a tune!

(From offstage we hear a lovely voice.)

PRISCILLA: "Fly me to the moon
And let me play among the stars…
(Priscilla enters from the back. She doesn't see him at first.)
Let me know what spring is—" *(She sees Ray.)* Oh. Hello.

RAY: I was just gonna…

PRISCILLA: Oh, look at your poor head. Here, let me help you.

RAY: Sorry I went overboard again.

PRISCILLA: Sit, sit.

(She takes the cloth from him.)

RAY: Priscilla, if you're winding up for the pitch, go ahead and let fly. I'm ready for it.

PRISCILLA: What pitch?

RAY: About how I fell asleep at the bar.

PRISCILLA: "Got drunk and passed out" you mean, don't you.

RAY: Yes, Priscilla.

PRISCILLA: Ray, from now on, let's both of us say what we mean and mean what we say. Okay?

RAY: Yeah, okay.

PRISCILLA: Head back.

(He puts his head back. She puts the cloth on his head.)

RAY: I know you're angry at me.

PRISCILLA: Ray, I'm not angry. The world is a beautiful place. Surprising. Unplanned. And if you let yourself be surprised, if you're unafraid, if you accept the possibility that anything is possible but that nothing is certain, then you can really live, Ray. We spend most of our existences turning away from that ecstacy, denying it, refusing it. Fearing it. It's too beautiful, it asks too much of us. But when we find it— Angry, Ray? I just can't find it in myself.

RAY: Priscilla.

PRISCILLA: Yes, Ray.

RAY: I'm goin' fishin' with Roger up to the Flowage.

PRISCILLA: That sounds lovely.

RAY: The Flowage, Priscilla, real early—and we won't be back 'til late.

PRISCILLA: Have a wonderful time. Arrivederci.

(She kisses him on the forehead. Lights fade.)

SCENE TEN

A clearing in the woods. The Alien sits, reading a book, occasionally glancing at the sky. Michael enters in a hurry. He stops abruptly when he sees the Alien.

MICHAEL: Christ!

ALIEN: Ah yes, the Messiah. Tell me, what's your take on it? Son of God? Or merely a very great prophet among many others?

MICHAEL: I've been looking for you.

ALIEN: Or doesn't it matter? Isn't his message the relevant issue?

MICHAEL: You're waiting for them, aren't you. They're coming back.

ALIEN: No comment.

MICHAEL: Why else would you be out here?

ALIEN: Michael, it would be better if you went home.

MICHAEL: I'm staying right where I am. If Billy's coming back, I want to be here. *(He sighs, annoyed, and sits down. He sees the book.)* What's that?

ALIEN: It's yours. Kierkegaard. I hope you don't mind.

MICHAEL: How do you like it?

ALIEN: I'm glad you asked. I'm still working on the first sentence, actually. *(He reads.)* "If there were no eternal consciousness in a man, if at the bottom of everything there were only a wild ferment, a power that twisting in dark passions produced everything great or inconsequential; if an unfathomable, insatiable emptiness lay hid beneath everything, what would life be but despair?" Now what does that mean, exactly?

MICHAEL: It means there has to be something else.

ALIEN: Expand.

MICHAEL: Something other than mere passion, mere feeling, mere animalistic drive. Life is not only the wolf howling at the moon without thought or consciousness. Life has meaning. Humanity has thought. We are aware, we're sentient. We think. We endow the world with meaning through consciousness. At least, that's what Kierkegaard hopes. We try to understand the moon. We try to understand our own howl. The point is not merely to howl, but to grapple with the nature of the howl. To comprehend it on some level.

ALIEN: I see. *(He closes the book and hands it to Michael.)* I guess I like more of a story.

(Beat.)

MICHAEL: It's going to be cold. I should have brought a jacket. Don't you get cold?

ALIEN: All the time.

MICHAEL: You don't look cold.

ALIEN: You get used to it.

MICHAEL: I guess it's always cold in outer space.

ALIEN: Yeah, and no one can hear you scream either. I saw that movie. Scared the crap out of me. Checked under my bunk for a month.

MICHAEL: How do you know all these movies, anyway?

ALIEN: The TV signal. It doesn't stop when it gets to your TV set, you know. It keeps going, out into space. Didn't you see *Contact?*

MICHAEL: No. *(Beat.)* So I'm not supposed to be here.

ALIEN: Not really, no.

MICHAEL: I was there when they took him, wasn't I?

ALIEN: That was a mistake.

MICHAEL: So they make mistakes.

ALIEN: Are you kidding? Why do you think we keep coming back? Because interstellar travel is such a treat? Because our thirst for knowledge cannot be assuaged? No. Because they can't get it right. That's why.

MICHAEL: I don't know what you've got to be so bitter about.

ALIEN: I was told I was going to participate in a great endeavor, a noble quest to learn, to communicate, to understand. And what do I end up doing? Bussing tables. For people who do not appreciate me. Who don't even like me. In fact, they loathe me. They despise me.

MICHAEL: Well, I don't despise you.

(The Alien stands up suddenly.)

ALIEN: Hold on! Hold on!…

MICHAEL: No really, I don't despise you.

ALIEN: You will when I tell you they're not coming.

MICHAEL: But they are coming.

ALIEN: No—they're not.

MICHAEL: Oh come on!

ALIEN: I'm sorry! I just got word. They changed their minds.

MICHAEL: Just when just got word? You have a radio?

ALIEN: It's not a radio.

MICHAEL: Well, what is it?

ALIEN: It's a doo-hickey.

MICHAEL: A doo-hickey.

ALIEN: A Telepathy Enhancement Device. A doo-hickey. They send messages and I listen.

MICHAEL: If you're AWOL, how do they know to be sending you messages?

ALIEN: They're not sending me messages. It's an open channel. I get everything.

MICHAEL: Well, I don't see any doo-hickey.

ALIEN: It's implanted.

MICHAEL: Where?

ALIEN: *(With his finger in his mouth.)* Ith in 'ere.

MICHAEL: Look, I want him back. I want my son back!

(Michael moves closer, grabbing the Alien.)

ALIEN: You'll get him back! Don't worry about it!

MICHAEL: When?!

ALIEN: Before sunrise!

MICHAEL: Which sunrise?

ALIEN: I don't know!

MICHAEL: Well, ask them!

ALIEN: How can I ask them?!

MICHAEL: Use the doo-hickey.

ALIEN: It doesn't work that way. You can't talk into it.

MICHAEL: What kind of radio is that, you can't talk into it.

(Michael threatens him physically again.)

ALIEN: It's not a radio, and it's one-way! They talk to me, I can't talk to them!

MICHAEL: You're lying to me!

ALIEN: Why would I lie!?

MICHAEL: Because it doesn't make any sense! What if you were in trouble? What if you needed help? What if somebody were going to kill you? Huh?

ALIEN: You wouldn't hurt me. You're bluffing.

MICHAEL: Wouldn't I?

ALIEN: You wouldn't hurt a flea.

MICHAEL: But you're not a flea, you're an alien. What if I were just pissed off enough—what if I wanted my son back just enough that I said I was going to murder you if you didn't get him back here?! What would happen then? Would your little one way doo-hickey turn into a two way doo-hickey? Well?! *(Pause.)* Well? Would it?

(Michael has him down on the ground now.)

ALIEN: No!

MICHAEL: I'll kill you.

ALIEN: You wouldn't!

MICHAEL: I will if I have to! I'm not lying!

ALIEN: Yes you are!

MICHAEL: Do they hear you now? Do they hear what you're saying? Do they hear what I'm saying? *(Into the void.)* Do you hear what I'm saying?!

ALIEN: No, they can't! *(Michael is still clutching him.)* Don't you get it, Michael? It's because I don't really matter. I'm extra. I'm the throwaway. If they lose me, life goes on. The mission goes on. That's who I am. You didn't get some cosmic Einstein, some messiah from another planet. You got me.

(Michael lets go of him and stands. He looks up at the sky.)

MICHAEL: They're really not coming.

ALIEN: Not tonight.

(Pause.)

MICHAEL: It's really cold.

ALIEN: Yup.

MICHAEL: Well, I'm going back.

ALIEN: To sleep?

MICHAEL: If I can.

ALIEN: Sometimes you can't sleep?

MICHAEL: Not if I'm wound up.

ALIEN: Are you wound up?

MICHAEL: You could say that. Listen, why don't you come back to the house. We could talk.

ALIEN: What is there to talk about?

MICHAEL: You could tell me about where you're from.

ALIEN: You don't want to know about that.

MICHAEL: How do you know?

ALIEN: It's boring. It's a boring place. They're all a bunch of boring self-important snobs. They're so Goddamn self-important it makes me want to puke.

MICHAEL: Do you have a god?

ALIEN: What?

MICHAEL: You said "Goddamn." Do you have a god?

ALIEN: Not a god: God. Everybody's got God. You've got God, don't you?

MICHAEL: Yes. I mean…not everybody, you know…believes.

ALIEN: But you've got God.

MICHAEL: Yes.

ALIEN: So who cares if anybody believes. Having God is the important part. People want to believe, they believe. If they don't, they don't. Not everybody believes in me but I'm still here, aren't I.

MICHAEL: You see, when you say something like that—it's so—

ALIEN: So what?

MICHAEL: I could have had you tracked down, you know. You could be in the slammer right now. And I could have shown this whole town that I'm not loony tunes. But I didn't because you—Come back to the house. We'll talk. I'll make you some coffee.

ALIEN: Cold?

MICHAEL: Cold.

ALIEN: It's a deal.

MICHAEL: Then come on. *(He gets up.)* We'll go talk about God.

(Michael gestures for the Alien to go ahead of him. The Alien exits. Michael is about to follow when he stops to look up at the sky. The lights fade. End of Act One.)

ACT TWO
SCENE ONE

A TV talk show set.

Michael sits on one chair, Priscilla in another. They're a few feet apart. The Alien stands off to one side, with a hand-held mike. He has that slightly unctuous tone of a talk-show host.

ALIEN: We're back with Michael and Priscilla, and the question we're trying to deal with today is: what do you do when your ex-husband says he didn't kidnap your little boy—aliens did! *(Over Michael's head a sign appears that reads "Says His Son Was Kidnapped By Aliens.")* But Priscilla his ex-wife, just isn't having any of it! *(Over Priscilla's head a sign that reads "Doesn't Believe A Word He Says.")* So, Priscilla—I have a question for you. Did he ever lie to you when you were married to him?

MICHAEL: I never lied to her.

PRISCILLA: This is my question.

MICHAEL: I never lied to her.

PRISCILLA: *(To the Alien.)* Would you tell him it's my turn?

ALIEN: Michael, please—you'll get your chance.

PRISCILLA: It wasn't that he lied, exactly.

MICHAEL: I never lied.

PRISCILLA: Let's just say he had certain problems perceiving reality.

MICHAEL: That is not true.

PRISCILLA: When we first got married, he told me that, when he was a little boy, he used to fly down off his roof.

MICHAEL: I never said that.

PRISCILLA: Yes you did Michael.

MICHAEL: I said it was like flying.

PRISCILLA: You always said, "I flew off the roof and went flying around the yard."

MICHAEL: Because that's how it felt. *(To the Alien.)* I built a home-made glider when I was a kid.

PRISCILLA: Sure, he tells you that. For years, I never heard the home-made glider part. All I ever heard was: "I flew off my roof."

MICHAEL: You used to love that story.

PRISCILLA: I used to love a lot of things about you until I found out you were a pathological liar. *(To the Alien.)* He used to make stuff up about our little boy too. Used to insist that Billy put on a Beethoven symphony when he was five years old, all by himself. Except the way Billy tells it, he thought he was putting on the soundtrack to *Beethoven*, that St. Bernard movie!

ALIEN: Okay, okay. But we're looking for something really, deeply strange about Michael. Can you dig down, try to really give us something good?

PRISCILLA: *(Slight beat.)* He once told me that he saw angels on the ceiling of the church.

MICHAEL: Because I did.

PRISCILLA: You did not.

MICHAEL: Yes I did.

PRISCILLA: No you didn't Michael.

MICHAEL: Yes I did. *(To the Alien.)* I saw them.

PRISCILLA: *(Throwing up her hands.)* Uh!

(The Alien holds up the microphone to the Sheriff, who is in the audience.)

ALIEN: Yes sir.

SHERIFF: Well I think Michael here is missin' Priscilla's point.

ALIEN: *(Going back to Michael.)* Thank you.

SHERIFF: *(To Michael.)* You got to let go of that anger. Hello Ethan!

ALIEN: *(Back with Michael.)* So Michael, you saw actual angels on the ceiling of your church.

MICHAEL: I certainly did.

PRISCILLA: Nobody else saw them. All anybody else saw was the reflections of the sun off the windshields of cars that were passing by outside.

MICHAEL: I saw the same thing—it's just that I saw something more. I saw what those reflections meant!

PRISCILLA: You see? He admits he never saw angels!

MICHAEL: Priscilla, it's a metaphor. *(To the Alien.)* She pretends she doesn't know things, but she does.

PRISCILLA: And he's condescending!

MICHAEL: Condescending?! Because I give you credit?

(The Alien goes to Ray, also in the audience.)

ALIEN: Yes sir, go ahead.

RAY: I got a question.

ALIEN: Go ahead.

RAY: My question is you don't know dick! Whaddya think of that?!

ALIEN: Thank you so much. *(Back to Michael.)* Michael, let me get this straight. You saw a metaphorical angel.

PRISCILLA: A normal person would say he made it up!

MICHAEL: That's right. Metaphorical.

ALIEN: But real angels are different than metaphorical ones, wouldn't you say?

MICHAEL: All angels are metaphorical. They are an expression of the deity.

PRISCILLA: You see how he gets? *(To Michael.)* You're a snob, you know that?

ALIEN: Priscilla, hold on a second...

PRISCILLA: *(To the Alien.)* That's exactly the way he talks to me all the time.

MICHAEL: Because you sell yourself short!

ALIEN: So you never saw a real angel. And you lied about that.

MICHAEL: I did not lie about it. I saw real angels.

ALIEN: But they were reflections of some kind of light.

MICHAEL: In my mind, they were real. And that's where angels are real—in your mind.

ALIEN: And the aliens, where are they? In the spaceship—or in your mind? Hold that thought, Michael. We're going to take a break. Back after these messages!

(The Alien exits.)

MICHAEL: Aliens are nothing at all like angels. Aliens are just people who come from other planets. They're perfectly ordinary people.

PRISCILLA: *(To Michael.)* You got caught. He's smarter than you.

MICHAEL: A lot of people are smarter than I am.

PRISCILLA: You got your tit caught in the ringer, Michael.

(She stands up to leave.)

MICHAEL: Where are you going? This is television! You can't leave!

PRISCILLA: So why don't you kidnap me!

(She leaves. Michael pursues her as far as the door. Throughout the next speech, the overhead signs lift out of sight, the lights change. Michael calls after her, frantically.)

MICHAEL: I did fly! What I did was the same thing as flying. You have no grasp of metaphor, Priscilla! A metaphor is not unreal, it's just a different kind of reality. A deeper, truer kind, as a matter of fact, but you need a little imagination to get to it. And that's what's wrong with you and everybody else in this town. Lack of imagination. Fantasy is good, it's healthy, it's normal. Every one of my shrinks have told me so! And if you knew the first thing about medieval theology, you'd know I was right about angels, too. They are a manifestation of the deity, and so are our thoughts, so don't tell me I'm crazy just because I happen to believe in levels of reality that you can't begin to appreciate.

(He realizes he's no longer on the TV set, but back in his own house. It's night. The Alien has re-entered.)

ALIEN: You okay?

MICHAEL: Yeah. Just a daydream.

ALIEN: You have intense daydreams, don't you.

MICHAEL: Yeah. Bad habit. Listen! What do you say we finish our Ibsen marathon? Huh? We still haven't read the last act of *John Gabriel Borkman*.

(Michael picks up a rather thick book.)

ALIEN: Gee, I thought I might go out, actually.

MICHAEL: You don't want to know what happens?

ALIEN: I have to tell you, I haven't really gotten, you know, uh, involved really, in John Gabriel Borkman's dilemma.

MICHAEL: Oh. Well, that's okay. I mean, I can finish by myself while you're gone. I'll let you know how it ends.

ALIEN: That'd be great. Good. Yeah, let's do it that way.

MICHAEL: Good, then. You go out. Have a good time. You going to get a drink, or some coffee?

ALIEN: Oh, coffee I think. They make a good stiff cup of coffee down at the truck stop.

MICHAEL: They don't mind about the, uh—?

(He indicates the skin.)

ALIEN: I went to the cosmetics counter at Penney's. Picked up a neutral pancake base, a little blush, a little powder. I'm all set.

MICHAEL: Sure, sure. Well that's fine. This'll be good. I'd kind of like to just be here by myself anyway, and...uh, so. Good.

ALIEN: Michael, I tried.

MICHAEL: I know you did.

ALIEN: I have listened to every string quartet of Ludwig Van Beethoven. I have stayed up with you reading the complete prose dramas of Henrik Ibsen. I have read the first twenty-three chapters of *Buddenbrooks*.

MICHAEL: *(Correcting his pronunciation.)* Buddenbrooks...

ALIEN: I have grappled with Marxist theory, was startled by the sensuality of Plato and braced by the astringent logic of Aristotle. But Michael, I want to listen to the Spice Girls. I want to flip through the new *Us Magazine*. I want to watch *Friends*. That's what I came down here for and I want it.

MICHAEL: You have to give it time. Civilization isn't easy.

ALIEN: It's been ten days.

MICHAEL: That's the blink of an eye.

ALIEN: But I come from a planet where everybody is just like you! An entire species of yous, people who spend all their time reading books or writing articles or devoting themselves to some highbrow artistic endeavor or making up little scientific projects, trying to figure out how they fit into the big cosmic plan. I figured I might get a vacation from them, pop out for a few hours, maybe a day. Hang around with some normal people. I'm not trying to be mean, Michael. I actually like you. It's oil and water, that's all.

MICHAEL: So your answer is go out and drink coffee all night long!

ALIEN: Well let's be honest, Michael. You've been harboring some serious hostility against me.

MICHAEL: What are you talking about?

ALIEN: I saw the explosives.

MICHAEL: Explosives?

ALIEN: In the laundry.

MICHAEL: Excuse me?

ALIEN: They're crude but dangerous, Michael. I know. We have gunpowder where I come from also.

MICHAEL: No, no, no. July Fourth is coming up.

ALIEN: Yeah, so?

MICHAEL: Those are fireworks.

ALIEN: I know about you people on this planet. I see the news. You start to get resentful and you have to blow somebody up.

MICHAEL: No, no. They're my fireworks. I'll show you.

(Michael starts to exit.)

ALIEN: No, no! Don't go in there!

MICHAEL: But they're completely harmless!

(Michael again starts to exit.)

ALIEN: Hold on! Hold on! Getting a signal! Ship's coming back! I gotta go!

MICHAEL: They're just for fun. You light the fuse, it goes up in the sky. Big noise! Lots of color!

ALIEN: *(He finally gets it.)* Wait a minute...July Fourth?

MICHAEL: Yes.

ALIEN: Fourth of July!

MICHAEL: Yes!

ALIEN: Fireworks!

MICHAEL: Yes.

ALIEN: Boy do I feel stupid!

MICHAEL: We go out to the backyard at sunset and set them off.

ALIEN: We?

MICHAEL: Billy. Billy is usually with me.

ALIEN: Oh. Sorry.

MICHAEL: It's fine. *(It isn't fine though; a beat.)* I just wish you wouldn't start yelling that the ship was coming every time you get tense.

(Beat.)

ALIEN: So you're not planning on doing me bodily harm.

MICHAEL: Of course not. I like you.

ALIEN: You really do?

MICHAEL: Of course.

ALIEN: I'm not anything you want me to be.

MICHAEL: No one is what I want them to be. But I could help you. You could become something. You've got the raw materials. You're not stupid.

ALIEN: Thank you I think but I...

MICHAEL: You're a very quick study.

ALIEN: Michael, no...

MICHAEL: You read, you understand.

ALIEN: Michael, please...

MICHAEL: You're sensitive.

ALIEN: Michael.

MICHAEL: You respond. Not everybody responds. You at least respond.

ALIEN: But I don't give a damn! I'm sorry but I'd better go. And I don't just mean tonight.

(Beat.)

MICHAEL: Where do you think you're going to go?

ALIEN: Well, that first day—when you were such a jerk—I made one very nice friend.

MICHAEL: Who?

ALIEN: Just someone I liked. A lot, actually. I've been thinking about her ever since—but everyday I kept figuring it was my last day here, so I didn't want to go back and stir up those feelings again. But the way things are looking, I might as well go find her, spend some time.

MICHAEL: You're going to go to look for a woman looking like that?

ALIEN: I picked up a very appropriate ensemble at the men's store today.

MICHAEL: I meant the skin, not the outfit.

ALIEN: This woman won't care about skin color—she's not that way.

MICHAEL: Well, you'd better get going if you're going to find her.

ALIEN: Not tonight—in the morning. Tonight I just want to get out to the truck stop, get some coffee and some nice, soothing flourescent lighting.

MICHAEL: Well, suit yourself. Have a good time.

(He picks up the book of plays and opens it.)

ALIEN: Thanks, I, uh…

(Michael's face is already in the book. The Alien exits. After a moment, he returns.)

ALIEN: Or…We could go outside and shoot off some early fireworks!

(Michael looks up at him soberly. Then with both hands he snaps the book closed with a loud clap. Lights out.)

SCENE TWO

K-Mart, later that morning. A Blue Light on the top of a pole. It's not on. Michael is up on a short stepladder poking around in the light. A toolbox is on the floor. The Sheriff is beside the ladder.

SHERIFF: What are you doing?

MICHAEL: I'm going to electrocute myself. I'm kidding. It's a broken blue light, Hank. K-Mart without an operational Blue Light is not K-Mart as we know it.

(The Sheriff holds the ladder.)

SHERIFF: I stopped by 'cause I got to thinking about our talk that first day after Billy was missing. When I remembered Mrs. Trinkle? What'd you call that?

MICHAEL: Proustian.

SHERIFF: Right. Something about that kept nagging at me. So I got out my old annuals. And I looked through them. And right there, in our junior year, we did a play. A Mrs. Trinkle original. You were in it. You remember what you played?

MICHAEL:…yes.

SHERIFF: What did you play?

MICHAEL: Hank, this is not relevant.

SHERIFF: What did you play, Michael?

MICHAEL: A Martian.

SHERIFF: And what color skin did you have in the play?

MICHAEL: Green.

SHERIFF: That's right. Color picture right there in the annual.

MICHAEL: Well Sherlock, you've done it again. Time to break out the cocaine and play the violin.

SHERIFF: Michael, cocaine is no laughing matter and neither is this.

MICHAEL: I never said it was a laughing matter.

SHERIFF: Now I'm going to ask you one last time. What did you do with Billy!?

MICHAEL: I didn't do anything.

SHERIFF: Michael…

MICHAEL: Sometimes, Hank, things just happen. Things are imposed. Things we don't want. This is one of those things, Hank. I did not want Billy taken, she did not want Billy taken, you did not want Billy taken. But Billy was taken. It's none of our doing. And there's nothing we can do about it. This is not about psychology or human will. It's the quintessential existentialist crisis, Hank: what do you do when you can do nothing? You fix the Blue Light. So that even if the world frustrates you, even if you have no place to go, and no one to go to if you did—even then, at least there will still be a Blue Light Special. At least that.

SHERIFF: That's real good. Real nice. Now I got some news of my own. If Billy's not back by six o'clock, I'm going to get a warrant for your arrest.

MICHAEL: (Throwing up his hands.) Of course you are.

SHERIFF: That's gonna mean jail, prosecution, the whole shebang. Maybe even prison.

MICHAEL: Naturally! What better way to deal with all your jealousies and resentments? I just wonder what you're telling me for. Doesn't sound like very good police work to me.

SHERIFF: It's lousy dang police work! It's called friendship! You don't believe that maybe, because you're too caught up in your own ideas about how I resent you. And no matter what I do, I can't make you see that's not it. I am jealous of you because you've got this way of seeing the world that's so much more complicated and interesting and weird than anything I could ever dream up. And I'm mad as heck at you because you won't get out of here and go someplace where people might see the world the way you do. (A little too loud.) Darn it, Michael, I do not resent you. I love you like a brother!

MICHAEL: (Beat.) I know that.

(The Sheriff takes off his watch and hands it to him.)

SHERIFF: Just so there's no confusion. Six o'clock, Michael. No later.

(The Sheriff leaves. Michael reaches down and flips the switch on the Blue Light. It turns on as the lights fade.)

SCENE THREE

Michael's house. Late afternoon. Michael enters in his K-Mart uniform. Priscilla enters from inside the house.

MICHAEL: Hello. Trespassing, I see.

(She folds her arms and studies him for a moment.)

PRISCILLA: There's a man living here. People have seen him through the windows.

MICHAEL: Yes and?

PRISCILLA: Michael, are you gay? Is that it?

MICHAEL: That's the alien.

PRISCILLA: I knew you were going to say that.

MICHAEL: I always said you were sharp, Priscilla.

PRISCILLA: You know, I've been very patient with you. I have not gotten hysterical—which I could have. I have not had you thrown in jail—which I could have. But if this…man has anything at all to do with Billy being gone—I don't care if he's from the moon or Milwaukee, there's going to be serious heck to pay.

(Ray enters, talking.)

RAY: I checked all through the attic, but I couldn't find anything else…well, well, well.

MICHAEL: What is going on here? Breaking and entering is a crime, you know.

RAY: We didn't break anything.

MICHAEL: That's not what it means, Ray.

PRISCILLA: All right now.

MICHAEL: He thought it meant that. Didn't you, Ray?

PRISCILLA: *(To Ray.)* You go on outside. I'll deal with this.

MICHAEL: You're married to the missing link. You realize that.

RAY: If I wasn't so darned even-tempered, I'd have to have it out with you.

PRISCILLA: Ray, go home. I want to talk to Michael.

RAY: Oh no. He ain't gettin' away so easy this time.

MICHAEL: Get away with what?

RAY: *(To Priscilla.)* Go on, show him.

PRISCILLA: It's fine, Ray, really. Just leave us alone.

RAY: Go on, show him what you found.

(Priscilla produces a fistful of makeup in her hand.)

RAY: Pancake and blush. Now that's kinky, I don't care what you say.

MICHAEL: When he goes out for coffee at night he wears makeup to cover the green skin.

RAY: He's some kinda kinky guy you met, and now you're cohabitating.

MICHAEL: He's from another planet!

RAY: Which one?

PRISCILLA: Ray, please…

RAY: Which planet? Don't think about it now. Which one?

MICHAEL: I…

RAY: Mars? Jupiter?

MICHAEL: …I don't know.

RAY: You don't know what planet he's from.

MICHAEL: No.

PRISCILLA: Ray…

RAY: You ever ask?

MICHAEL: No.

PRISCILLA: Ray, listen to me…

RAY: You never once thought to ask.

MICHAEL: No!

RAY: So you're shacked up with this guy, but you don't even know what planet he's from. Don't you want to know the kinda person you're having relations with? Huh? Mike?

PRISCILLA: Ray, go away. Now!

RAY: Fine. You want to side with the uh, what-do-you-call, "promiscuous homosexual agenda" here, you go right ahead. But you better know one thing. Every item on the shelf has got a price. Every last one.

(Ray exits.)

PRISCILLA: I didn't come here to snoop.

(She follows Ray as far as the exit, watching to make sure he's gone.)

MICHAEL: Well, you did a pretty good job of it.

PRISCILLA: Michael, I'm pregnant. *(Pause.)* I missed my period last weekend, so I took the home test and I…I don't know what to do!

MICHAEL: Well, Priscilla, it can't be that bad. I mean, you've got Ray // and even if he isn't…

PRISCILLA: *(Overlapping at //.)* It's not Ray's.

MICHAEL: How do you know?

PRISCILLA: Believe me, I know.

MICHAEL: So you've been—stepping out…

PRISCILLA: No! Once. Ten days ago. Right after Billy…*(She looks at him, doesn't want to start a fight.)*…was gone.

MICHAEL: Oh, really nice timing.

PRISCILLA: I was vulnerable! I was depressed and angry and very lonely. And this…person came along and made me feel like it was all okay. I don't know. It was like…magic. I can't explain. Michael, please, I'm coming to you because you're the only one I didn't think would judge.

MICHAEL: Who is he?

PRISCILLA: I don't know.

MICHAEL: You don't know his name?

PRISCILLA: He came into the bar one day, and one thing // led to another and I…

MICHAEL: *(Overlapping at //.)* Came into the bar…?!

PRISCILLA: Yes.

MICHAEL: The day after they took Billy?

PRISCILLA: I was confused, Michael. I felt so isolated. I was raw. He started quoting that Ernest Hemingway thing at me—for whom the bell tolls, that thing—and that's all I remember, basically. And I fell for it. He sort of reminded me of you, in a way.

MICHAEL: Me?!

PRISCILLA: You, but not you. Better than you. Different. Anyway we spent most the afternoon together. It was very strange, with Ray right there, passed out the whole time. But somehow, very right. The entire time I was with this man, I could feel myself changing, inside, deep inside— being rearranged, becoming the person I was always meant to be. I even stopped worrying about Billy. I didn't stop thinking about him, but I stopped worrying. Then we said goodbye finally. He told me he couldn't give me his number. I understood, of course. He never actually said he'd call, but of course I assumed—like the dupe that I am. *(She unconsciously touches her stomach.)* I have to have it, Michael. You know me, I couldn't not have it.

MICHAEL: What if you could find him?

PRISCILLA: What are you saying?

MICHAEL: I know who it was.

PRISCILLA: What do you mean? How could you know?

MICHAEL: I just do.

PRISCILLA: Well, who?

MICHAEL: You're not going to like the answer.

PRISCILLA: Michael, who is it?

MICHAEL: Just don't get mad at me.

PRISCILLA: I won't get mad.

MICHAEL: It's the alien.

PRISCILLA: Michael, we've had our problems. But I was always under the impression that when push came to shove we were still friends—that I could at least talk to you. Now listen to me: there are no aliens! Aliens did not take Billy. You are not living with an alien. An alien did not get me pregnant! This is the real world Michael, and in the real world there are no such things as aliens! Or angels! Or flying! Now if you have a shred of human compassion in you, I'm begging you—stop running away from reality, have a little gratitude for the fact that I left you, and for once in your life help me!!

MICHAEL: Oh my god.

PRISCILLA: What?

MICHAEL: *(An epiphany.)* I don't love you, Priscilla.

PRISCILLA: Well good.

MICHAEL: I don't love you.

PRISCILLA: I'm very glad.

MICHAEL: *(Clutching her back.)* I mean, I really don't love you.

PRISCILLA: Michael, I know that. Let go of me.

MICHAEL: I haven't loved you for years. I thought I did. All this time—I thought I loved you. Because there you were…so beautiful, so smart—don't roll your eyes—you are. And funny besides. I couldn't believe that someone like you couldn't be what I wanted. I kept thinking to myself—underneath all these intense feelings of hostility, she must be the woman for me. But now all of a sudden, it's so clear: I don't love you! I only loved what I wanted you to be! And I couldn't stand to see you go because I always thought somehow, someday you'd be that person. But you won't. I know that now! And I really don't love you!

PRISCILLA: Well, I…I don't love you either.

MICHAEL: I know. Isn't it great?

(He embraces her and she responds. They hold tight for a moment. She gently presses him away.)

PRISCILLA: All right. Great. Now, where is he?

MICHAEL: The alien?

PRISCILLA: Yes. Fine. The moon man. Just tell me where he is.

(The Alien has entered through the front door during the above, behind Priscilla's back. Michael points, she turns to see him. He smiles at her, touching her on the arm.)

ALIEN: Greetings earthling!

PRISCILLA: Eek!

(She grabs Michael.)

ALIEN: I'm sorry. Did I hurt you?

MICHAEL: Yes. You got close to her, then you left her. On this planet, that's all it takes.

PRISCILLA: You're…you're—

MICHAEL: He's the alien.

PRISCILLA: It's you.

ALIEN: Yes.

PRISCILLA: *(To Michael.)* You weren't making it up.

MICHAEL: No.

PRISCILLA: You were telling the truth. The whole time.

MICHAEL: Yes.

PRISCILLA: You don't have Billy.

MICHAEL: No.

PRISCILLA: He has Billy.

MICHAEL: No, the ones in the ship—they have Billy. This one's a busboy.

PRISCILLA: You're a busboy?

ALIEN: Yeah.

MICHAEL: He's an AWOL alien busboy.

PRISCILLA: *(Takes a step towards the Alien.)* You…asshole!

ALIEN: Is she talking to me?

MICHAEL: My guess is yeah.

PRISCILLA: *(Approaching him now.)* Where's my son?

ALIEN: *(Backing away.)* He's in the ship. He'll be back soon.

PRISCILLA: *(Pursuing.)* Soon isn't good enough, mister. I've been very patient about this.

ALIEN: I know. You've been wonderful.

PRISCILLA: You get those friends of yours on the horn and you get my boy back.

ALIEN: I can't.

PRISCILLA: Sorry—don't understand "can't." Not familiar with that word.

ALIEN: It means not able!

PRISCILLA: *(Grabs him and puts him in an arm lock.)* Oh really? And what if I took off your left arm and beat you over your head with the bloody stump? How would that affect your "not able"?

ALIEN: Michael, help me. She's hurting me!

MICHAEL: Priscilla, I already tried this. He can't. He's a busboy.

PRISCILLA: *(Lets go.)* I can't believe you're the same guy I let seduce me.

ALIEN: I wouldn't say seduce, exactly.

PRISCILLA: Do you think you might have told me you weren't human? That would be the considerate thing to do before sleeping with someone.

ALIEN: It never occurred to me. I didn't think it was important.

PRISCILLA: I'm having a baby, you jerk!

ALIEN: You are? I am? *(Michael nods yes.)* I'm going to be a father?

PRISCILLA: Yes!

ALIEN: *(To Michael.)* I'm going to be a father.

MICHAEL: Yeah, I heard.

ALIEN: I'm going to be a father!

PRISCILLA: Oh I get it. All your friends have been here, getting write-ups in those magazines you flip through in the checkout but have too much good taste to actually buy. And you just had to do the same. Well I am not going to be just another notch in your ray gun, buddy!

ALIEN: Listen, you had something to do with it too.

PRISCILLA: You sweet-talked me.

ALIEN: You wanted to be sweet-talked.

PRISCILLA: You took advantage of my vulnerability.

ALIEN: I soothed your raw, anxious nerves. I made you feel better.

PRISCILLA: Sure—then you dumped me.

ALIEN: But I'm back. I missed you.

PRISCILLA: Why should I believe that? You already lied to me once.

ALIEN: I never lied to you.

PRISCILLA: You were pretending to be something you weren't.

ALIEN: What? You mean, from earth?

PRISCILLA: Yes—your skin, for one thing.

ALIEN: That was the lighting in the bar, I had nothing to do with…wait a second. It's this "race" thing, isn't it. That's very important to you. I read up on it.

MICHAEL: You read something?

ALIEN: Fine, it was a video.

PRISCILLA: This is not about "race."

ALIEN: See, you have an idea on this planet that people belong to certain "races." Nobody else in the entire universe ever heard of this "race" thing, but here you completely obsess about it, even though at the same time you insist it's not in the slightest bit important. Our theory is—it's some kind of instinct to keep life complicated and difficult. Almost as if you didn't really want to be happy.

PRISCILLA: I'd love to be happy. I just want to know what I'm sleeping with.

ALIEN: Well, wouldn't we all. See, you don't realize it, but you people here—on Earth—you're the subject of a lot of studies. One of them is to figure out your mating rituals, which are very unusual—very intricate. Amazing levels of complexity.

PRISCILLA: They're not all that complicated.

ALIEN: A person has to be the right age, have the right politics, the right accent, they have to call God by the right name, have the right philosophical positions, the right kind of job, the right of kind of...whatdoyoucallit—"social standing." And then the really important one: gender . That one really blows my mind. I mean, who cares? Take your pick!

PRISCILLA: *(To Michael.)* He's kidding, right?

ALIEN: And the amazing thing is, you not only keep track of all these things but, once in while, you actually make a good match! It's remarkable, really—that you're able to find somebody you actually like after you're done eliminating all the people you've convinced yourself aren't right for you. But where I come from, we take a slightly simpler approach: you find somebody you like, and everything else—well, you work around it. *(To Priscilla.)* And I like you. Even if you are different. Because, well, maybe you noticed—there are some striking similarities between us. And even in the ways that we're different, there are some pretty great ways that we seem to, sort of, uh...complement each other.

PRISCILLA: You make it sound so easy.

ALIEN: It is easy. This, anyway. Things that are really complicated, well—what can you do. But things that are simple, why not leave them simple?

(Priscilla looks at Michael.)

MICHAEL: He's got a point.

PRISCILLA: We do throw up roadblocks, don't we?

ALIEN: And the bad part is when the roadblock shuts off a road that goes to a very nice place.

PRISCILLA: You're an alien.

ALIEN: *(Sympathetically.)* I know.

PRISCILLA: It's very hard to get past that.

ALIEN: *(Again.)* I know.

PRISCILLA: You're green.

ALIEN: And you're pink.

PRISCILLA: Besides which, you're going to get back on your spaceship, and go flying off into the wild blue yonder.

ALIEN: Well, I've been thinking about that. I really don't like it with them. I mean, I love them. But I can't stand them. You know what I mean?

PRISCILLA: *(Sneaks a glance at Michael.)* Oh yeah, I know.

ALIEN: And I've got a very good reason to stay.

(He goes to her.)

PRISCILLA: I'm a married woman.

ALIEN: You'll get a divorce.

PRISCILLA: Right. Okay. But I'm not going to marry you. I'm on a very bad trend and I want to break it. *(They start to kiss.)* What kind of baby are we going to have?

ALIEN: The usual. Part you, part me.

PRISCILLA: He won't be…malformed in some way…

ALIEN: Don't worry—they usually get your skin color. I realize that's important.

PRISCILLA: You make me sound prejudiced.

ALIEN: Yes, but I like you anyway.

(They kiss.)

MICHAEL: Well then! Welcome to the planet!

ALIEN: Hold on! Hold on!…

PRISCILLA: What's wrong?

ALIEN: Michael, wait a second…

PRISCILLA: What is it?

ALIEN: Quiet please! I'm getting a…They're on their way!

PRISCILLA: Who's on their way?

ALIEN: The ship. It's coming back!

(Lights out.)

SCENE FOUR

The bar. Ray behind the bar, the Sheriff playing a time-killing game of flipping on his hat. A large book sits on the bar.

SHERIFF: So what time is it now?

RAY: You just asked me that.

SHERIFF: That was a good half hour ago.

RAY: And what time was it then?

SHERIFF: 8:09.

RAY: That'd make it 8:39.

SHERIFF: Would you do me a favor and check?

RAY: I guarantee, it's 8:39. I got a very accurate internal clock. Fishermen all got very accurate internal clocks.

SHERIFF: They do?

RAY: Yup.

SHERIFF: Why is that?

RAY: So you know what time to get the heck home and have dinner.

SHERIFF: Would you check for me?

RAY: Look, I don't want to have to be going to check every two minutes now. This is ridiculous.

SHERIFF: As a duly elected officer of the law, I'm telling you to check the time.

RAY: Fine. *(Ray lifts his arm, pulls back his sleeve and checks his watch.)* It's 8:41.

SHERIFF: Your internal clock is slow.

RAY: No. The watch runs fast.

SHERIFF: Is that right.

RAY: So, you gonna go for him?

SHERIFF: Not yet. It's not time.

RAY: Well how much longer you gonna give him?

SHERIFF: Until it's time. Now mind your own business.

RAY: You know, a lot of us do lousy jobs we don't like.

SHERIFF: I realize that.

RAY: Don't mean we shirk our duty.

SHERIFF: I'm not shirking. I'm stalling.

RAY: What do you think's gonna happen? You think that alien spaceship's gonna bring Billy back?

SHERIFF: Possibly.

RAY: You don't believe in no spaceship.

SHERIFF: I believe in Michael. Anyway, a few hours won't make much difference one way or the other.

RAY: No, 'less he's heading for Canada. In which case he'd get about a third the way there.

SHERIFF: He's not heading for Canada.

RAY: You don't think so, huh?

SHERIFF: No, I don't think so. He's going to do the right thing and bring Billy back.

RAY: Yah?

SHERIFF: Yah.

RAY: You don't sound too sure.

SHERIFF: I'm pretty darn sure.

RAY: How 'bout a drink to help you decide.

SHERIFF: I can't drink. I'm on duty.

RAY: Come on, just you and me. Nobody's going to know.

SHERIFF: Same as you, Ray. Can't drink on duty.

RAY: Well, it ain't same as me tonight.

SHERIFF: How's that?

RAY: I'm gonna have one.

(Ray fixes a drink behind the bar.)

SHERIFF: I thought the uh…management didn't like that.

RAY: That was the old management. New management don't care what I do.

SHERIFF: What are you talkin'?

RAY: I fired the old management this afternoon.

SHERIFF: How'd she take it?

RAY: She don't know yet. But I figured since her and me were gettin' a divorce, it only made sense.

SHERIFF: You're getting divorced?

RAY: Yup.

SHERIFF: How did she take that?

RAY: She don't know that yet either. Gonna tell her when she gets home tonight. She'll get over it, though. Say what you like about Priscilla, she knows the price of peanuts. *(He takes a long drink. The Sheriff opens his book.)* Whatcha got there? *(The Sheriff shows him the book.)* Anna Kara-sumpin-er-other. Didn't know you went in for the romance novels.

SHERIFF: I promised Michael I'd take a crack at it. So here goes. *(Reading.)* "Happy families are all alike; every unhappy family is unhappy in its own way." *(They look at each other. Concern. That's cutting a bit too close to home.)* What time is it now?

RAY: 8:46.

SHERIFF: It's time.

(A beat. The Sheriff officiously heads for the door, followed by Ray—who is careful to take along his beer. Lights fade.)

SCENE FIVE

The clearing in the woods. Twilight. The Alien and Priscilla enter, moving. Michael lags behind a bit.

MICHAEL: Priscilla...slow down already!

PRISCILLA: I'm not going to miss the landing, Michael. I want to be there.

ALIEN: We're here. This is it.

(They all stop. The Alien checks the sky.)

PRISCILLA: Any sign?

ALIEN: Not yet. They're still pretty far out.

MICHAEL: Priscilla...

PRISCILLA: How you do know?

ALIEN: I have this doo-hickey. They send messages.

MICHAEL: Priscilla, he does this...

PRISCILLA: You mean like a radio?

ALIEN: Not really.

MICHAEL: Don't even try, okay?

PRISCILLA: But they're bringing Billy back, right? For sure.

ALIEN: Of course. That's why they're coming. And to get me, of course.

PRISCILLA: But you're not going.

ALIEN: Not if I can help it.

PRISCILLA: Not if you...! I thought you said you weren't leaving.

MICHAEL: Priscilla this is what // I'm saying...

PRISCILLA: *(Overlapping at //.)* You just said you were staying. You promised.

ALIEN: The thing is that they can be very...

PRISCILLA: Very what?

ALIEN: Determined.

PRISCILLA: What does that mean?

MICHAEL: Priscilla, he does this // every time he gets into a...

PRISCILLA: *(To Michael, overlapping at //.)* We're talking here!

ALIEN: If they want me back, they have their ways.

PRISCILLA: Well, there has to be something…

MICHAEL: Priscilla, listen to me. His favorite thing to do when he gets tense is to say the ship is coming.

ALIEN: I'm not tense.

MICHAEL: Of course you are.

PRISCILLA: Are you tense?

ALIEN: I'm not tense.

PRISCILLA: He's says he's not tense.

MICHAEL: He asked you to be his significant other and now he's having second thoughts and so he says the ship is coming. He does this, I'm telling you.

ALIEN: *(To Priscilla.)* I did say it before, yes. But they really are coming this time.

MICHAEL: Every day he said this to me.

ALIEN: Sometimes it was true. They'd say they were coming, then they said they weren't.

MICHAEL: You're the little alien who cried ship.

ALIEN: I can't help that. They kept saying, "Whoops! One more test!"

PRISCILLA: Tests? What kind of tests?!

ALIEN: You know those tests where you have a car going from Center City to Freemont at thirty miles an hour, and another car coming from Freemont to Center City at sixty miles an hour, and when do they pass each other?

PRISCILLA: They're giving him math tests?

ALIEN: I never said they were nice. *(To Michael.)* And they can't change their minds this time because they're low on gas. They'll only just get back home as it is.

MICHAEL: You see? Low on gas. He says things like that and we're supposed to believe him. *(To the Alien.)* Spaceships don't run on gas.

ALIEN: How would you know?

(The ship passes by overhead—noises and lights.)

ALIEN: Okay? Good enough? Now look—I don't want to go back. I want to stay.

PRISCILLA: Well, what are we going to do?

ALIEN: I don't know. We don't have much time. *(To Michael.)* Think of something!

PRISCILLA: We're going to have to hide you.

ALIEN: They'll find me.

PRISCILLA: How?

ALIEN: The doo-hickey. It sends a signal, like a beacon.

PRISCILLA: What if we took you back and put you in the basement? Would that work?

ALIEN: Only if it's lined in lead.

MICHAEL: What if they didn't think you were missing? What if we put somebody else on the ship, even if it wasn't you...I bet they'd just take off and head home.

ALIEN: Actually...yes, they probably would.

MICHAEL: Yes. Of course they would. That's what I'd do.

(Priscilla suddenly knows what Michael's thinking.)

PRISCILLA: Michael...?

MICHAEL: I'm going to do it.

PRISCILLA: You can't...

MICHAEL: Yes, I can. *(To Alien.)* Can't I.

ALIEN: Probably. It's pretty easy to fool them.

PRISCILLA: Michael, this is out of the question.

MICHAEL: No, don't you see? It's the answer to the question.

ALIEN: They won't even notice him. They never noticed me. Just act like you know what you're doing.

PRISCILLA: But he doesn't know what he's doing! Not in a spaceship!

ALIEN: It's easy. Just one, crucial thing: serve from the left, take from the right.

MICHAEL: I'm not getting on that ship so I can be a busboy.

PRISCILLA: You're not getting on that ship, period.

ALIEN: Okay. So, go right to the main control room and tell them what's up. They like it if you're direct.

PRISCILLA: What if they don't like it? What if they get angry?

ALIEN: They don't really get angry. Condescending yes, but not angry. Anyway, they'll like Michael.

MICHAEL: You think so?

ALIEN: A lot more than they ever liked me. Just get them going on Beethoven or something.

MICHAEL: They know Beethoven?

ALIEN: They loooove Beethoven.

MICHAEL: But how do I explain?

ALIEN: You won't have to. We use telepathy when we meet someone new. We think it's more polite.

MICHAEL: But I don't have telepathy.

ALIEN: Yes, you do. You'll see. It sort of kicks in when you need it.

MICHAEL: Okay, so where's the control room?

ALIEN: Well, when you get inside, you take a right. Not your first right, that's the bathroom. The second right, it's a four way.

MICHAEL: The second right.

ALIEN: And you go down the corridor about…I don't know…I'm really bad at distances, but let's say a hundred feet.

MICHAEL: A hundred feet.

ALIEN: Maybe a hundred fifty.

MICHAEL: A hundred fifty.

ALIEN: Wait a second! There's a water fountain. On your left is a water fountain.

MICHAEL: Water fountain. Good.

ALIEN: If you get to the water fountain, you went too far. So go back about twenty feet and take a right.

MICHAEL: Okay, second right, then right again.

ALIEN: Well, no. I mean, if you went past it and got to the water fountain and had to go back, then it's a right. But if you get it right the first time, then it's a left. And you're there! Simple. Right?

PRISCILLA: Michael, you're going to get lost.

ALIEN: You're going to make it.

PRISCILLA: Michael, you can't just go to another planet. People don't do things like that. This is your planet.

MICHAEL: Not really.

PRISCILLA: Michael, there are problems. I'll grant you that. You have a hard time fitting in, but this is your planet and you're staying right where you are!

MICHAEL: Sometimes people are born one sex and they spend their whole lives feeling like that's not the sex they were meant to be. So they change it. Maybe I was born on the wrong planet. Maybe I have to go.

PRISCILLA: Michael, these are very weird circumstances. You're all worked up. You haven't thought it through.

MICHAEL: I think about this every day of my life! Priscilla, don't you see? I don't speak the language. I don't understand the customs. I suffer from culture shock in the world of my birth. I'm like a refugee, a temporary resident, waiting for my visa application to go through so I can go home to the land where I belong. Now all of a sudden, somebody hands me a passport and all my papers, and says, "now or never." I'll miss you but I have to go. I want to go. And not just for me, Priscilla. For you too. This is the one, best gift I'll ever give you. He's perfect for you. He's decent and honest and loves you for who you are, and he'll love Billy just the same way, and best of all he loves prime-time television. And let's face it, I love Billy, and he loves me. But only because he's the most patient boy on earth. That Beethoven CD he put on when he was five? I knew he wanted the movie soundtrack. Take the gift, Priscilla. It's the only thing I've ever given you that you really wanted.

(They embrace. A bright light from offstage, sounds of a spaceship landing.)

ALIEN: They're coming down!

PRISCILLA: Michael, I'm worried. I can't help it.

MICHAEL: I'll send you a sign. How's that?

PRISCILLA: What kind of sign?

MICHAEL: I don't know. A signal. When you get it, it means everything's fine. Okay? Good-bye. *(He embraces her again.)* And uh—you too.

(He embraces the Alien and turns to go.)

ALIEN: Michael. Thank you.

(They lock gazes for a split second. The ship lands. The Alien ducks behind a log and Michael turns back to the ship as Billy appears.)

BILLY: Dad! Mom!

(Billy runs to them. They have a three-way embrace.)

MICHAEL: Are you all right?

BILLY: I'm fine.

PRISCILLA: Don't let me go. Are you all right? Talk to me.

BILLY: I'm fine.

PRISCILLA: Did they hurt you?

BILLY: No. But those math tests were really hard.

MICHAEL: How did you do?

BILLY: I aced 'em.

MICHAEL: That's my boy!

(The lights flash and swirl for a moment, then stop. Michael draws Billy to him. Priscilla knowingly retreats.)

MICHAEL: Listen, we've only got a second. There's been a...a kind of a change in plans.

BILLY: What do you mean?

MICHAEL: I'm not staying here with you. I'm going to get on the ship.

BILLY: Wow. Okay.

MICHAEL: You see, they left...*(He looks around but can't see the Alien.)*...well he's around here somewhere. One of their own. He's taking my place on earth and I'm taking his place on the ship.

BILLY: And they'll figure that you're the other guy.

MICHAEL: Do you think it'll work?

BILLY: Oh yeah, no problem. They're pretty spaced out.

MICHAEL: Billy, I just…can you understand? I want it to be clear—we won't ever see each other again.

BILLY: Wow. That is kind of a drag.

MICHAEL: It's a really huge drag.

(They embrace.)

BILLY: But Dad—wait a second! Once you get inside, they'll give you this doo-hickey. It goes right here in your tooth. *(He indicates.)* People send you their thoughts, and you can send yours too!

MICHAEL: You got a two-way doo-hickey?

BILLY: Oh yeah—if they like you, they make it a two-way. So when you get yours and I have mine, we can always be in contact with each other—anytime we want, just by thinking!

MICHAEL: Wow.

BILLY: Yeah, cool—huh?

MICHAEL: But Billy, can you understand why I have to do this?

BILLY: Oh yeah.

MICHAEL: You can?

BILLY: It's just like on this one *Star Trek.* These two guys were in the wrong universes from the beginning, and they had to get back to the universe they belonged in, even if that wasn't the universe they came from. Because the other universe was, like, where they belonged. And it's the same with you, basically. Except you don't have to do all this matter/anti-matter transponder stuff.

MICHAEL: That's right. That's it.

BILLY: You see? You always said *Star Trek* was junk, but sometimes it's just like life. Except *Star Trek* is a little more complicated.

MICHAEL: God, I hope you're right about that. *(Lights swirl and flash again, this time they don't stop.)* I love you.

(He grabs Billy and draws him close.)

BILLY: I love you too, Dad. You better get going. They're about to take off.

MICHAEL: I'm really going to miss you, Billy. I'll miss you a whole planet's worth.

BILLY: Me too, Dad.

(They embrace once more then pull away. Billy starts to exit.)

MICHAEL: Mind your mother. Unless you really think she's wrong. In which case, try to make the ethical choice.

BILLY: 'Kay, I will!

(Billy crosses to Priscilla. The lights flash, whirl, become blinding as Michael disappears into them. The Alien emerges from behind the log and takes his place at Priscilla's side.)

ALIEN: Hello.

PRISCILLA: Oh, I'm sorry, I…

BILLY: Hi.

ALIEN: I'm in love with your mother.

PRISCILLA: I hope that's all right.

BILLY: Sure, I guess so.

PRISCILLA: Are you sure?

BILLY: Oh yeah. I heard all about him on the ship—*(To the Alien.)* and you sound great.

(They do a "special" handshake. Spaceship lights and noises offstage as it starts to rise. They all look towards it. Softly, in the background, we hear music rising. Ray and the Sheriff enter at a run. Ray still has his beer with him. They stop, awestruck at the rising ship.)

SHERIFF: Michael!…Billy!…Michael! I told him to think about relocating, but holy cripes!

BILLY: Hey, do you hear that?

PRISCILLA: What the heck is that noise? It sounds like something's wrong…

ALIEN: No, there's nothing wrong. I recognize the CD…

(The music rises now. It's Beethoven's Seventh Symphony, First Movement.)

ALIEN: BILLY: Beethoven!

PRISCILLA: It's your father. It's his sign!

ALIEN: There he goes!

BILLY: They sure looove their Beethoven.

(Their heads slowly turn upwards to follow the ship over their heads, until they end up facing out to the audience. The music rises to a crescendo.)

PRISCILLA: Good-bye Michael!

BILLY: Good-bye Dad!

SHERIFF: Don't be a stranger!

ALIEN: Bye-bye! Bye-bye!

RAY: Hey, I think that's Sagittarius!

(Their hands reach out towards the audience to wave good-bye as the music climaxes and the lights fade to black.)

END OF PLAY

The Trestle at Pope Lick Creek

a drama

by Naomi Wallace

"Nothing in the world is single."
—Percy Bysshe Shelley

BIOGRAPHY

Naomi Wallace currently divides her time between Kentucky and North Yorkshire, England. Her plays include *One Flea Spare,* commissioned and produced in October 1995 by the Bush Theatre in London. It received its American premiere at the 20th Humana Festival at Actors Theatre of Louisville and was awarded the 1996 Susan Smith Blackburn Prize, the 1996 Fellowship of Southern Writers Drama Award, the 1996 Kesselring Prize and the 1997 Obie Award for best play. It was produced by New York Shakespeare Festival in March 1997. *Birdy,* an adaptation for the stage of William Wharton's novel, opened on the West End in London at The Comedy Theatre in March 1997 and on the West End in Athens, Greece at the same time. *Slaughter City,* which was awarded the 1995 Mobil Prize, received its world premiere in January 1996 at The Royal Shakespeare Company. *In the Heart of America* received its world premiere at the Bush and was subsequently produced at Long Wharf Theatre and in Dortmund, Germany. It was published in *American Theatre* magazine and was awarded the 1995 Susan Smith Blackburn Prize. Her plays are published in Great Britain by Faber and Faber and in the United States by Broadway Play Publishing and Smith and Kraus. Her film, *Lawn Dogs,* which was filmed in Louisville and produced by Duncan Kenworthy *(Four Weddings and A Funeral),* opened successfully in Great Britain in November of 1997 and won numerous film awards. A published poet in both England and the United States, Ms. Wallace has received grants from the Kentucky Foundation for Women, the Kentucky Arts Council and a 1997 NEA grant for poetry. Her book of poetry, *To Dance a Stony Field,* was published in the United Kingdom in May 1995. At present, Ms. Wallace is under commission by the Royal Shakespeare Company and Toledo Films. Ms. Wallace donated her royalties from the Humana Festival production of *The Trestle at Pope Lick Creek* to the Fairness Campaign in Louisville.

HUMANA FESTIVAL PRODUCTION

The Trestle at Pope Lick Creek was commissioned by Actors Theatre of Louisville and premiered in March 1998. It was directed by Adrian Hall with the following cast:

Dalton Chance	Michael Linstroth
Pace Creagan	Tami Dixon
Chas Weaver	Jonathan Bolt
Gin Chance	Marion McCorry
Dray Chance	Michael Medeiros

and the following production staff

CHARACTERS

PACE CREAGAN: a girl, seventeen years old.

DALTON CHANCE: a boy, fifteen years old.

GIN CHANCE: Dalton's mother, forty-one years old.

DRAY CHANCE: Dalton's father, a few years Gin's senior.

CHAS WEAVER: a jailer, early fifties.

SETTING:

1936. A town outside a city. Somewhere in the United States.

NOTES:

Accents of the characters should be as "neutral" as possible, an accent from somewhere in the U.S.

The sets should be minimal and not realistic.

Tami Dixon and Michael Linstroth
in *The Trestle at Pope Lick Creek* by Naomi Wallace

22nd Annual Humana Festival of New American Plays
Actors Theatre of Louisville, 1998
photo by Richard Trigg

The Trestle At Pope Lick Creek

PROLOGUE

Darkness. Then we see Dalton sitting on a stool upstage in a corner. His back is all we see. Beside him is a small candle. From the light of the candle, Dalton makes hand shadows. We can see the shadows but we cannot discern what they are.

DALTON: This is a. Horse. *(He makes another hand shadow.)* This is a swan. No. Not a swan, shit. A falcon. Yeah. A falcon. No. There's no claw. It's a duck. *(He makes another hand shadow.)* Now it's a turtle. There's the shell. But hell. It could be a fish. With a fin. *(Makes another hand shadow. Pace appears. She is there but not there. Standing behind Dalton.)*

PACE: That's not a fish, Dalton Chance. You should know better. That's a bird. A pigeon. The kind that live under the trestle.
(Dalton slowly turns and peers into the darkness. He doesn't see Pace, though she is visible to us. He calls softly.)

DALTON: Creagan? Pace Creagan? Is that you? *(Dalton stands up. He cries out to her.)* You go to hell Pace Creagan!
(Pace tips the candle over and there is darkness. End of prologue.)

ACT ONE
SCENE ONE

Months earlier, two youths, Pace and Dalton, run to meet under the trestle at Pope Lick Creek. Pace gets there ahead of Dalton. They have been running and are both out of breath.

DALTON: You had a head start!

PACE: Nah. You haven't got any lungs in that puny chest of yours. Listen to you rattle.

DALTON: *(Breathing hard.)* I'm not rattlin'.

PACE: Yeah you are. What've you got in there? A handful of nails.

DALTON: Twisted my ankle.

PACE: Yeah, yeah.

DALTON: So this is it, huh?

(They look up above them.)

PACE: Yep.

DALTON: It's not that high up.

PACE: Almost a hundred feet. From the creek up.

DALTON: Some creek. There's no water: it's dry.

PACE: Don't care; can't swim anyway. What time is it?

DALTON: Coming up to seven.

PACE: Exact time.

DALTON: Six forty-one.

PACE: She comes through at seven ten. Sometimes seven twelve. Sometimes she'll come on at seven nine for ten days straight and then bang, she's off three minutes. She's never exact; you can't trust her. That's what I like.

DALTON: How many times have you done it?

PACE: Twice. Once with Jeff Farley. Once alone.

DALTON: You're lyin'. Jeff Farley never ran it.

PACE: Nope. Never did. Tied his shoes on real tight, took two deep breaths, said "I'm ready when you are." And then he heard that whistle. Aren't a lot of people can hear that whistle.

DALTON: So you didn't do it twice.

PACE: I would of but he turned tail and ran.

DALTON: So how many times then? Just once?

PACE: Once. And that's once more than you.

DALTON: Yeah. Who was witness?

PACE: No one here to see me.

DALTON: You're lying.

PACE: Whatever you say.

DALTON: Did you run it or not?

PACE: Sure. Once.

DALTON: How come I don't believe you?

PACE: Me and you, we'll have witnesses. Philip, Lester and Laura Sutton will be here at seven o five.

DALTON: No. No way. You said just you and me as witness.

PACE: If you get scared and run, who's to say you won't lie and say I chickened too?

DALTON: You said just you and me.

PACE: It'll be just you and me. Up there. Down here in the creek bed we'll have the three stooges watching us. Keeping tabs. Taking notes. And you can be sure they'll check our pants when we're done and see who's shit.

DALTON: You know. You don't talk like a girl. Should.

PACE: *(Meaning it.)* Thanks.

DALTON: But you look like one. So I guess you are.

PACE: Want me to prove it?

DALTON: No.

PACE: How old are you?

DALTON: Sixteen. In a couple of months.

PACE: *(Nears him.)* Well, well. Almost a man. *(Pushes him backwards, but not too hard.)* Listen to me, Dalton Chance, two years my junior, and shut up. Here's what we're going to do.

DALTON: Just spell it out for me. Once and clear.

PACE: Okay. She's pulling eight cars at seventy tons apiece at eighty-five. Not a big one, as far as they go. But big enough. The engine herself's one hundred and fifty-three tons. And not cotton, kid. Just cold, lip smackin' steel. Imagine a kiss like that. Just imagine it.

DALTON: How do you know what the train weighs?

PACE: I looked her up. The year, the weight, the speed.

DALTON: So you can read.

PACE: Yeah, well. You and her are coming from opposite sides, right. You've got to time it exact 'cause you need to make it across before she hits the trestle. It's like playin' chicken with a car, only she's bigger and you're not a car. The kick is once you get halfway across, don't turn back and try to outrun her. You lose time like that. Just face her and go.

DALTON: So what if you know it's too close? You go for the side, right?

PACE: There's no side.

DALTON: Yes there is.

PACE: There's no side. Look at it.

DALTON: There's a side.

PACE: What's the matter with you? Look at the tracks. Look at them. There are no sides.

DALTON: So what do you do if you can't make it across before she starts over?

PACE: You make the cross. That's all there is to it.

DALTON: But what if you can't?

PACE: Remember Brett Weaver?

DALTON: That's different. He was drunk.

PACE: He was not.

DALTON: Yes he was. He was drunk.

PACE: Say that again and I'll punch you.

DALTON: The papers said he was drunk.

PACE: Brett wasn't drunk. He was just slow.

DALTON: Slow? He was on the track team.

PACE: That night he was slow.

DALTON: How do you know?

PACE: I just know.

DALTON: Well. I've had a look like I told you I would and I've decided: I'm not crossing.

PACE: I knew it. I knew it.

DALTON: Only a drunk or an idiot'd play that game. Not me.

PACE: You got the heart of a rabbit. A dead rabbit. And now you owe me a buck.

DALTON: No way. I never said for certain. I said maybe. And you said it was safe. You didn't say anything about there being no safety sides. You said it was a piece of cake.

PACE: It is a piece of cake. If you time it right.

DALTON: Forget it.

PACE: You're breaking the deal. Pay me a buck right now or else.

DALTON: I said no.

PACE: *(Pulls a switch blade.)* Then I'll hurt you.

DALTON: Put that away. You're warped. That's what everyone says at school: Pace Creagan is warped.

PACE: Then why'd you come up here with me? I'm not even your friend.

DALTON: No. You're not my friend. My friends don't pull knives.

PACE: You were starting to like me, though. I could tell. You said you'd run it with me.

DALTON: I said I might. I thought it could be fun. Warped people can be fun sometimes.

PACE: If you back down everyone will know.

DALTON: I don't care. I don't have a fan club.

PACE: Mary Ellen Berry is coming as witness too.

DALTON: No she's not.

PACE: I asked her to. And she knows you've got a fancy for her.

DALTON: Big deal. I asked her out. She turned me down. End of story.

PACE: She says you're too short.

DALTON: I'm not short.

PACE: I don't think she was talking height.

DALTON: I'm leaving.

PACE: Hey. I told her to give you a chance. She likes me. She listens to me. I told her you were going to cross the trestle with me. She said "oh." You know, like she was thinking things.

DALTON: What things?

PACE: You know. The way girls think things. One, two, three, about face. Change of season. Oh. She said "oh" like she was about to change her mind.

DALTON: Mary Ellen's popular. Why would she listen to you?

PACE: *(Shrugs.)* I once told her to take off her clothes and she did.

DALTON: And what does that mean?

PACE: It means I can run faster than she can so she does what I tell her to do. And she'll be here tonight. She's coming to watch us cross.

DALTON: You had a look at her? Naked? What's she like?

PACE: I'd say she's on the menu. Front, back, and in reverse. You'd like her.

DALTON: How would you know what I like? You're not good-looking.

PACE: Yeah. But that's got nothing to do with trains.

DALTON: So how close were you that time you crossed?

PACE: I'd say I had 'bout eight seconds leeway.

DALTON: Eight seconds. Sure.

PACE: A kid could do it. Look. We won't do it tonight, okay. We'll work up to it. Tonight we'll just watch her pass. Take her measure. Check her steam. Make sure we got it down. Then when we're ready, we'll run her. It'll be a snap.

DALTON: A snap. What if you trip?

PACE: Brett tripped.

DALTON: He was messed up. Even if he wasn't drunk. He used to hit himself in the face just for the fun of it. Brett was a loon. He'd hit his own nose until it bled.

PACE: Brett wasn't a loon.

DALTON: I saw Brett hit himself. I saw him do it.

PACE: It's none of your business.

DALTON: You were his girl.

PACE: We were friends. I never kissed him. And you're gonna run the trestle. One of these days.

DALTON: How come?

PACE: 'Cause if you don't your life will turn out just like you think it will: quick, dirty and cold.

DALTON: So this is going to change my life?

PACE: It's gonna change something. Tell me you don't need something to change.

DALTON: I might go to college when I graduate.

PACE: You're not going to college. None of us is going to college.

DALTON: I got the grades for it. That's what Mr. Pearson says.

PACE: And who's gonna pay for it? Look at your shoes.

DALTON: Huh?

PACE: Your shoes. If your Mom's putting you in shoes like that then you aren't going to college. *(Beat.)* Come on. Let's go up and watch.

DALTON: If I can't go to college, I'll just leave.

PACE: Some things should stay in one place, Dalton Chance. You're probably one of them.

(End of scene.)

SCENE TWO

Dalton, some months later, in an empty cell. He looks older now, dishevelled. He just stares. And stares. At nothing. After some moments, Chas, the jailer, enters. He seems friendly enough. Dalton doesn't acknowledges Chas's presence.

CHAS: On break. Thought I'd sit it out with you. The other guy, across the hall. He's looking for grass in his cell. Thinks he's a moose. Could be some other herbivore but every now and then he lets out this call and it sounds close enough to a moose. Yesterday, a bug. Some kind of a beetle, I think, with huge claws. He used his arms like pinchers. Opening and closing them. Opening and closing. For hours. Wayne was leaning in to give him some grub and the next minute he caught Wayne around the neck. Almost choked him to death. While I was prying him off he's making this sound. A beetle sound, I guess. Sort of like. *(Chas makes a beetle sound.)* Self respect: gone. Was the manager of the Plate Glass Company. A real Roosevelt man. Good to his men, though he laid them off. Then his head went pop one day and he started breaking up the plant. Glass everywhere. Wrecked half the place. Even the WPA says close it down. No one needs glass these days. Might want glass but they don't need it. Mr. Roosevelt, I say, want to buy some glass? *(Beat.)* What kind of a beetle was it, you think? Big pinchers. Opening and closing. How'd the visit go? I know your folks. Nice people. Sorry to hear your Daddy's still out of work. But who isn't? Well, I'm not. I'm still here. Could be somewheres else, like Spain shooting some whatyoucallem, but I might get killed and then bein' here looks better. I had a boy like you. You must have known my Brett at school. Big fellow. Fast runner? Moose's easier to identify. Distinctive. My break's about up. So what do you think, kid? How many years do you think you'll get? Or will they hang you? When they hang you the last thing you hear is your own neck break. And if you got a thick neck bone, a strong one, a young one, then it takes a while to break clean through, sometimes hours, and all the while you're dying you're hearing it snappin' and crackling and poppin', just like a stick on the fire. So what do you think?

(Chas gets no response so he shrugs and leaves the cell.)

DALTON: A stag beetle. That's what kind it was.

(End of scene.)

SCENE THREE

Dalton is trying to get the shoes off his mother's feet after she's come home from work.

DALTON: Yeah it does. I read it at the drugstore.

GIN: Just leave it.

DALTON: All your nerves're squashed up in the ball of your foot. Stop wiggling.

(Dalton gets one of her shoes off. She relaxes now as he massages her feet.)

GIN: How's the math going at school?

DALTON: *(Teasing.)* You've got seven toes.

GIN: Woman on the right of me, Barbara Hill, laid off Tuesday. Woman on my left, laid off today. Just waiting my turn.

DALTON: You've been there forever. They need you.

GIN: How is he?

DALTON: Quiet.

GIN: Yeah, quiet.

(Gin unwraps a small stack of plates. Looks at them. Then wraps them up again.)

GIN: It's getting harder to find the plates. Even the Salvation is running short. I don't want to use the ones my mother gave me. Might have to one of these days.

DALTON: It'll be okay.

(Dalton is finished with her feet. He begins to unpin her hair and then brush it. She lets him.)

GIN: You got anything better to do your afternoons than take care of an old mother when she comes home from work? You should be out with the boys. Yelling. Falling down. Doing fun things boys do. What do boys do for fun?

DALTON: You know the trestle up by Pope Lick? Well, I was with a girl there this afternoon, after school.

GIN: Hmmm.

DALTON: Name's Pace Creagan. We watched the train come through.

GIN: Boy got killed up there a couple of years ago.

DALTON: It's not a big train but it's big up close. And loud.

GIN: You kiss her?

DALTON: No way. She's not the kissing kind. Not pretty either.

GIN: Not that handsome yourself, Dalton.

DALTON: That's what she said.

GIN: I know the Creagans. They're all right.

DALTON: Even if I wanted to, and I'm not saying I do, I never really—you know, like how people do—kissed a girl.

GIN: Not much to it. Just open your mouth and start chewing. First time I kissed your father it was all wet and disgusting. By the second time I'd started to like him, and then it was like breathing water for air, that smooth.

DALTON: I don't know.

GIN: Neither did I.

(Dray appears. He sits in a corner with a stool. No one speaks for some moments. Dray just sits with his back to them. As they speak Dalton walks over and lights Dray's candle, casually; he does this all the time for his father.)

DALTON: I need some new shoes.

GIN: I know that.

DALTON: I'll get a job.

GIN: You've got school.

(Dray makes a hand shadow on the wall.)

GIN: And no one's hiring.

DALTON: You know, the train that comes through Pope Lick, the engine weighs one hundred and fifty-three tons. That's what Pace says.

(Dray makes another. Dalton watches his father. He moves to put his hand on his father's shoulder but his father looks at him, like a warning, so Dalton withdraws his hand.)

GIN: Trains. Yeah. Huge, sweatin', steamin', oil-spittin' promises when I was a girl. Always taking someone away, never bringing someone back. I couldn't get used to it.

DALTON: I'm going out. *(He kisses his mother on the cheek, then moves away.)* When you were fifteen. Like me, Mother. What did you want?

(Dray makes another.)

GIN: Someone to look me straight in the face and tell me flat out that I wasn't going anywhere.

DALTON: Yeah? Well then say it to me. Go on. Say it to me.

GIN: *(Quietly.)* Dalton.

DALTON: Say: Dalton, my boy. You're not going anywhere.

(Gin is silent for a moment.)

GIN: You're my child.

DALTON: *(Quietly.)* That doesn't make any difference.

(Dalton exits. Dray stops making hand shadows. He is still.)

GIN: *(Gin just looks at Dray's back.)* Touch me.

(Dray is still. He turns to look at her, then slowly looks away. End of scene.)

SCENE FOUR

Pace and Dalton at the trestle, a few days later.

PACE: We need to watch her for days and days. Studyin'. Studyin'. And then one night we'll run her.

DALTON: Sure. One night.

PACE: There's a simple reason we're biding our time. Waiting for the moment that counts: We don't want to die. Now repeat after me: We don't want to die.

DALTON: We don't want to die.

PACE: So we'll be patient.

DALTON: Yeah. Until Christmas. I'll be getting some new shoes. And then I'll hook a job. Move up.

PACE: That's against the laws of gravity. Besides, you can't move up when you've got no teeth.

DALTON: I've got teeth.

PACE: You won't in a few years.

DALTON: You've got no determination. No plan for the future.

PACE: Yeah, but I watch.

DALTON: Watch what?

PACE: Things. People. Tomorrow. Today. I've been watching. For years. And this is how things are. You and me and the rest of us kids out here, we're just like. Okay. Like potatoes left in a box. You ever seen a potato that's been left in a box? The potato thinks the dark is the dirt and it starts to grow roots so it can survive, but the dark isn't the dirt and all it ends up sucking on is a fistful of air. And then it dies.

DALTON: I'm not a potato.

PACE: Yes you are.

DALTON: No I'm not. Potatoes can't run. I can. And when we decide to do it, I'm gonna make it over that trestle before you're halfway across. Until then, I'm going home.

PACE: What time is it?

DALTON: Six fifty-one.

PACE: Tell you what. We'll have a practice first.

DALTON: What kind of practice?

PACE: A real kind. Almost. Just to warm up. Pop the bones. Roll the blood over. You know.

(Pace opens the paper bag she has with her. In it are a pair of boys pants. She starts to take off her dress, not caring a bit that Dalton is there.)

DALTON: Jesus.

PACE: Would you practice running the trestle in a dress? *(Dalton turns around.)* You can look if you want.

DALTON: No thanks. You're not my type.

(Pace continues changing.)

PACE: *(Casually.)* Why not?

DALTON: You're loud. Your hands are dirty. You stare. *(Beat.)* And you're not pretty, really.

PACE: You said that before.

DALTON: Well, it keeps coming back to me.

PACE: Anything else, kid?

DALTON: There'll be more once I get to know you.

PACE: I'm ready. *(Dalton turns around. Pace is dressed in pants and a shirt, perhaps her brother's. She throws the dress at Dalton.)* Smell it.

DALTON: No way.

PACE: Baby. *(Dalton smells the dress.)* Well?

DALTON: It smells nice. Flowery. Like a girl.

PACE: *(Cuffs him as she snatches the dress back.)* Want to know what I don't like about you, Dalton Chance? You're a good boy. A very good boy.

DALTON: So what's that mean?

PACE: It means someone, before it's too late, has got to break you in half. *(Sighs.)* I guess it'll have to be me.

(End of scene.)

SCENE FIVE

The present. Dalton in his cell, turned away from Chas.

CHAS: Her hands. Not natural. Never seen it before. She was crying when she left you. I gave her a cloth to wipe her face. She took it from me. Gave me a shock. Her hands. Says it won't come off. Happened with the chemicals. Says lots of them down at the factory have it. She asked me not to tell. Who am I going to tell? You? You already know; she's your mother. Now him over there, he doesn't know who's his mother. A turtle doesn't consider those things. Want to know how I know he's a turtle? *(Chas demonstrates a turtle, moving his neck in and out of his shell.)* I know what you're thinking: Could be a goose. I thought of that. But a goose doesn't do this—*(Chas moves his head slowly from side to side, then cocks his head to one side, opens his mouth and eats.)* A goose doesn't eat like a turtle. How you feelin', boy? What're you thinking? Still won't talk. Still won't talk. But they got it on record when they brought you in: Yeah, I killed her. That's what you said. Why didn't you lie? They don't have a witness. Four words. Just four words: Yeah, I killed her. But won't say why.

Won't say how. What kind of a game are you playing? Well, they'll find it out. They know about kids. I had a boy your age. Couple of years older than you. Not much to him. But he was my son. *(Beat.)* To think. He was just a kid like you. Scared of nothing. Yeah. Scared of nothing 'cause you are nothing. Half of you kids wanting to kill, the rest wanting to die. Wanting to die like it's a nice, cold drink and you're going to suck it down in one gulp and then get up and walk away from it. Right. Kids. Just want to eat, fuck and tear the ornaments off the tree. But only if you don't have to get out of bed in the morning to do it. The whole damn country's going to hell 'cause of your kind. *(Beat.)* You should have killed your own self instead. That's what they say. *(Beat.)* I loved my boy Brett. But I never could figure what he was. Something kinda small. Like a wheel, maybe. Something that spins in place in the dark. He had a gap in his heart. He was empty. I know; I was his father. Sometimes he'd ask me to embrace him. *(Shrugs.)* He was my son. *(Beat.)* So he'd be here, in my arms, sniffling like a baby. But there was nothing. I was holding him. He was in my arms. But it was like holding onto. Nothing. *(Beat.)* What's it feel like to be like that? Huh? What's it feel like to be that empty? *(Begins to take off his shirt.)* I'm going to have to hate you, I guess. There's not much choice. *(Chas stands over Dalton. Dalton is shivering and does not respond. Chas puts his shirt around Dalton.)* I'll bring you some dinner. You've lost weight. Hard not to do in here.

(End of scene.)

SCENE SIX

Pace, Dalton and Gin are sitting together. There is a strained feeling. Dalton wants things to be okay, nice.

GIN: Dalton made a clock for his science project. Didn't you, Dalton?
DALTON: That was last year. This year I made a scale. To measure things on.
GIN: A scale. That's right. I use it in the kitchen. To measure flour. It works really well. You want to try it, Pace?
PACE: I don't do much with flour.
GIN: Oh. *(Beat.)* But I'm sure you help your mother in the kitchen.
(Dalton speaks before Pace can answer.)

DALTON: Pace likes to sew. Don't you? *(Pace just looks at Dalton.)* She makes
her own clothes. Tell her you make your own clothes, Pace.

PACE: I make my own clothes. My mother's not what she used to be.

GIN: That's nice. I mean, about your clothes. What did your mother used to
be?

PACE: Hopeful. *(Beat.)* Thank you for the tea, Mrs. Chance. It was very sweet.

GIN: That's how we like it here. In our home.

*(They all sit in an awkward silence. After some moments, Pace places the
large bag she's brought on the table.)*

DALTON: Pace said she brought something for you, mother.

GIN: My, that's nice. You didn't need to, really.

PACE: I made it in science class. Like Dalton did.

*(Pace unwraps the bag to reveal a strange mechanical engine. It looks impres-
sive.)*

GIN: Oh. That's. Nice. What is it?

PACE: It's a beam engine.

GIN: I see...

PACE: The beam engine was the first practical working steam engine. It's simple: Fire here at the bottom heats the water, the steam forces up the piston and it's cooled, fast, by spraying cold water on the cylinder. This
turns the steam back to water and makes a vacuum in the space under the
piston.

GIN: Piston.

DALTON: It's a present, Mother.

PACE: You see, the pressure of air outside the cylinder then pushes the piston
back down again. And so on. The crosspiece joining the engine to the
pump gives it its name: "beam" engine.

GIN: This is a train you've got here?

PACE: An engine. But it's an older model.

GIN: Looks kind of small to me.

PACE: The original was bigger than both of us.

GIN: Well, start it up then.

PACE: Doesn't work. Did once. Second time, my father he was leaning over it
to have a look, caught his beard on fire. Third time: bang. Not a big one
but I got a piece of glass in my arm.

GIN: Sounds unpredictable.

PACE: It's the only thing I had of my own to give you. *(Beat.)* I didn't get a
good grade on it.

GIN: You're two years older than Dalton.

DALTON: Mother.

PACE: Almost.

GIN: He's been seeing a lot of you these past weeks.

DALTON: Can we have some more tea?

PACE: You ever hear of Cugnot, Mrs. Chance? Nicholas Cugnot. Made the first steam machine that moved. Crawled two mph before it blew up. That was in France. 1769, I think. The government put Cugnot in prison. Explosion didn't hurt anyone. Never understood why they put him in jail.

GIN: My son doesn't know a thing about trains.

PACE: I think they were afraid. Not of the machine, but of Cugnot. They'd never seen anything like that moved by steam. Just plain old water *(Makes the sound of steam.)* into steam. It must have changed them somehow. Just to see it. They couldn't forgive him.

GIN: What do you want with Dalton?

DALTON: Christ. We're just having tea.

GIN: Hush up. *(Dalton shuts up. He puts his head in his hands.)* We're a family here, Pace. A regular family. My husband, Dalton and me. Lots of trouble out there, lots of bad weather. But we take care of each other; nothing out there we need. I want you to know that.

PACE: You know the Union Pacific? They're gonna build the biggest steam locomotives in the world. The engine and tender'll weigh over five hundred tons. Colossal. They'll be 4-8-8-4 articulated locomotives with two sets of driving wheels, each with their own cylinders. *(Gin just stares at her.)* I'm sorry. Mrs. Chance. But me and Dalton. It's none of your business.

GIN: Cylinders, huh? Driving wheels. Articulated locomotives. If you're thinking to trick my son—

DALTON: I can't believe this...

PACE: Mrs. Chance, I'm not sweet on your son's locomotive system, if that's what you mean. We've never touched each other. I've got nothing to be ashamed of. Though I did tell him to take off his clothes once, down under the trestle.

GIN: To take off his—

DALTON: Pace !

PACE: *(Interrupts.)* Shut up, Dalton. *(Beat.)* And then once on the tracks. A hundred feet up. Wasn't a train in sight. It was kinda chilly that evening, but it was safe.

GIN: I think you better leave now.

PACE: He doesn't like me, really. He says I'm loud.

GIN: *(To Dalton.)* You took off your clothes?

PACE: He's your son. He does what he's told.

GIN: Why would you do such a thing? Anyone might have seen you.

PACE: Yeah. I did. And he's not like an engine at all. Nah. Dalton's pale. Real pale. No steam. How's he keep warm? Doesn't know the first thing about cylinders. And he's so light, what keeps him where he stands? On the tracks, slip, slip, slip. No traction. Now, the Big Boys, the new ones, they'll need near ten tons of coal per hour in their firebox. And the grate where the coal'll be burned is bigger than a kitchen. *(Ginny just stares at her.)* Imagine it. That's what we're coming to.

(End of scene.)

SCENE SEVEN

Dalton and Pace at the trestle.

PACE: Let's start here. On this tie.

DALTON: What tie? The track's up there.

PACE: Imagine it, stupid.

DALTON: Right.

PACE: See, this tie's marked with a red X.

DALTON: Maybe I want to start on this other tie.

PACE: Look. It's tradition, Okay. Besides, Brett made this X so let's use it. Now, you crouch down like this. Go on. Yeah. That's right. Like at a track meet. Point your skinny rear to the stars. Got it.

DALTON: I'll count down.

PACE: Now when you say "Go" we run like crazy to the other side. But don't check your feet. You'll trip if you check your feet. Just trust that your feet know where to go.

DALTON: I hear you.

PACE: You're playin' chicken with the train so you keep your eyes on the engine headed towards you. It'll look like she's real close but she won't be. If you start when I tell you to, you'll have enough time to make it across and have dinner before she starts over the trestle. Ready?

DALTON: Pace?

PACE: Yeah?

DALTON: My legs are shaking.

PACE: This is practice, Dalton. There's no train down here.

DALTON: My legs aren't so sure.

PACE: On the count of three. Come on.

DALTON and PACE: One, two, three—

DALTON: Wait!

(Dalton seems to be looking over an edge.)

PACE: Don't look. You'll lose your nerve.

DALTON: It's a long way down.

PACE: Why don't we just walk it. Give me your hand.

(Pace takes his hand and begins to walk him.)

DALTON: God we're high up.

PACE: *(Smacks him.)* Keep your eyes on the other side. Pretend that we're running.

DALTON: We are. I'm out of breath.

PACE: We're almost there. Yeah. Yeah. Grease those knees. And now you trip.

DALTON: What?

PACE: You trip.

(Pace trips him so he falls to the ground.)

DALTON: Hey! What the— You tripped me. Hey—

PACE: It might happen.

DALTON: Why'd you—

(Dalton tries to get up. She knocks him back down, hard.)

PACE: You might trip. Anything's possible. We got to be ready for it.

DALTON: But I wouldn't've tripped! You pushed me!

PACE: Don't get up. Just sit there. Like you tripped. Let's say I'm flaggin' behind and you look over your shoulder to see how I'm doing and you trip. And just as you trip you hear her coming around the hill.

(Pace makes the sound of a train whistle.)

DALTON: You sound like a kitten. It's like this.

(Dalton makes an even better and more frightening whistle.)

PACE: Yeah! And you can hear her cold slathering black hell of a heart barrelling towards the trestle and it sounds like this.

(Together they make an engine sound, surprisingly well.)

PACE: But you've twisted your ankle.

DALTON: Yeah. And I can hardly stand. It feels like my foot's coming off. *(Makes a painful gasp.)* I try to run but I can only hobble. And the train, she's just about to cross.

PACE: And then there I am. At your side.

DALTON: No. I'd slow you down and you know it. You just pass me by. *(Makes the sound of an arrow flying.)* Like an arrow. You've got to save your own skin.

PACE: Yeah, but I can't just leave you there.

DALTON: Yes you can.

PACE: You'll be killed.

DALTON: I'll be torn apart.

PACE: So I put my arm around your waist and start to drag you down the tracks with me. It's hard going. We've only got fifty feet or so 'til we're clear.

DALTON: But the train. *(Dalton lets out a terrible scream of a whistle.)* So you drop me.

PACE: No.

DALTON: You drop me and run. You run for your life.

PACE: No. I don't leave you. I—

DALTON: You make it across. Just in time. Alone.

PACE: I drag you with me.

DALTON: And as you clear the tracks, you feel the hurtling wind of her as she rushes by you, so close it's like she's kissing the back of your neck, so close she pulls the shirt right up off you without popping the buttons. *(Beat.)* And then? And then you hear me scream.

(Dalton lets out a terrible scream and at the same time Pace screams.)

PACE: I save you!

(They are silent some moments.)

DALTON: The train, she disappears over the trestle and on down the track. *(Beat.)* You, Pace Creagan, are standing there, breathing hard—

PACE: My heart jumping jacks, yeah, shooting dice in my chest. Snake eyes. But I'm alive. Alive!

DALTON: As for me, well, you know I'm dead. You're certain. But still you have to go back and have a look. To see what's left. Of course there's almost nothing left.

PACE: Yeah there was. There was a lot left.

DALTON: No. Just some bits of. Meat. And a track shoe. That's all. I'm mashed potatoes now. Just add some milk and stir. And you were right, Pace my friend. My life has changed. Completely. Only I'm not around to enjoy it.

PACE: He wasn't wearing track shoes.

DALTON: Hey. Take a look at my face. I'm talking to you: I'm dead.

PACE: Brett was wearing boots.

DALTON: And now maybe my Mom will be able to scrounge up some new shoes for the funeral. If she can find my feet.

PACE: *(Calmly.)* Shut up. Just. Shut up. Have you ever put a shell up to your ear?

DALTON: What?

PACE: A conch shell. One of those big ones. It's not the ocean you're hearing. Or even the blood in your head. *(Makes the sound of a shell over one's ear.)* That's the sound. You know it. And it's been going on for years. Even now you can hear it. Listen. It's this town. Our future. You and me. *(Makes the sound again.).* Empty. No more, no less. Just. Empty.

DALTON: I want to change my life. But not like this. I'm going home.

PACE: Wait.

DALTON: *(Leaving.)* Not this time.

PACE: Take off your clothes.

DALTON: Why?

PACE: Because you want to. *(Dalton begins to undress. Pace watches him. He's about to take off his underwear.)* Stop. There. Yeah. That's enough. *(They both watch each other. Pace moves closer to him, but not that close.)* Are you cold?

DALTON: A little. *(Beat.)* Well. Are you gonna touch me or what?

PACE: No. I just wanted. To look at you.

DALTON: Once you take your clothes off. Something is supposed to happen.

PACE: It already has. *(Beat.)* Get dressed.

(After a moment, Dalton slowly starts to get dressed. End of scene.)

SCENE EIGHT

Gin and Dray. He sits immobile. She uncovers a small stack of plates. She tosses one to him. Suddenly he comes alive and they are tossing a plate back and forth between them as they speak. They've done this before.

GIN: You got to get out.

DRAY: I'm movin'. You just can't see it.

GIN: At the WPA office. They're helpin' people find jobs.

DRAY: A handful.

GIN: That's better than nothing.

DRAY: I don't know.

GIN: I went by the Council. They got kicked out of the church basement. Got a room in the Watson storehouse. More like a closet than a room.

DRAY: The Council. They're not government.

GIN: No, they're not. Just people out of work. Tryin' to get things going. Lots of talk about the Plate Glass factory.

DRAY: It's closed down.

GIN: Talk about opening it up again. Building it back up. Running it themselves. Machinery's still there. Most of it. It's a mess but it's all still there.

DRAY: We've got what we need. The three of us. Under this roof.

GIN: I know that.

DRAY: Sounds like you're getting involved.

GIN: No. I'm not. I'm just listening.

DRAY: My father worked there when he was a boy. There'd be explosions now and then. He wore eye wear. A lot of them didn't. Once the glass hit him in the mouth. Long thin pieces of glass. He pulled them out his cheeks with pliers, like pullin' fish bones out a fish. (Beat.) That place doesn't belong to them, Gin. Sounds like communists.

GIN: People, Dray. Just people tired of not working. Tired of waiting for the WPA to hand out the jobs. Tired. Just tired. You know that kind of tired.

DRAY: Can't remember when I wasn't.

GIN: I remember. When you were a boy.

(Dray almost drops a plate, but catches it. He becomes more playful.)

DRAY: You lie, Miss Ginny Carol. I was never a kid.

GIN: Yeah you were. And so was I.

DRAY: Nah. That was just a fancy idea we had about ourselves.

GIN: You didn't bring me flowers like other girls got. You brought me tomatoes.

DRAY: You can't eat flowers.

GIN: And corn. You were nineteen.

DRAY: A bucket of frogs, too. I made you close your eyes and put your hands in it. You didn't scream like most of them did. You went dead pale. I thought I might have killed you. And then you did the damnedest thing: You kissed me. Not on the cheek, either. Smack on the mouth.

GIN: I was in shock. The frogs did it to me. *(Beat.)* You hardly kissed me back.

DRAY: I was in shock. Never had a girl put her tongue in my mouth before. We weren't even engaged. You took me to the storm shelter and took off your dress. You pushed me to my knees. I never kissed a girl there before. I never even thought it could be done. You went dead pale. That was the second time I thought I killed you. When you finally let me get to my feet, you had a clump of my hair in each of your hands, you'd pulled on my head so hard.

GIN: I wasn't tired back then. And neither were you.

DRAY: No, I guess I wasn't. *(Beat.)* There were two things I wanted when I was a boy: One was to land a good job at the foundry, the other was to have you turn me into a bald man by the time I was old.

GIN: You lost quite a bit of hair over the years. Though not lately, I'm sorry to say.

(Dray misses a plate and it drops and breaks. Silence.)

DRAY: It was mine, Gin. Nineteen years of it.

GIN: Yeah, and what did it give you? A bad arm, a broken collar, burns across your back so deep the bath water stays in them.

DRAY: That job was mine.

GIN: We're still here.

DRAY: Yeah. And you won't ever leave me.

GIN: I won't ever leave you, Dray. *(Silence some moments.)* I heard at work they were hiring a couple of men down at Turner's. You might—

DRAY: *(Interrupts.)* I was there this morning while you were at work. They hired three men. Three men. Fifty-two of us they left standing. There wasn't a sound. For the longest time we just stood there watching the door that'd been shut. All that disappointment. Fifty-two men. Fifty-two of us. And weighin' how much? None of us eating big these days. Most of us lookin' lean. Maybe…nine thousand pounds, all of us together. That much disappointment. *(Beat.)* And not a sound. *(Dray sits with the plate in his lap. They sit in silence some moments. Gin moves to touch Dray, to comfort him. Dray speaks gently to her.)* Don't touch me, Gin. I could kill you.

(End of scene.)

SCENE NINE

Dalton lying asleep on the floor in a blanket. He gets up. He is shirtless. He thinks he's alone. But Gin is standing over him; he starts.

GIN: Dalton.

DALTON: You're always alone.

GIN: He hardly leaves the house.

DALTON: You'd think this might be special circumstances.

GIN: He's restless. Without you home.

DALTON: He never looked me over when I was there.

GIN: You don't have to look at someone—

DALTON: From what I remember, he didn't look at you any more than he did at me.

GIN: Not long ago he used to hold me.

DALTON: Big deal. Holding someone's a cinch. You just open your arms, pop them inside, then open again and you're done. It doesn't cost. It's easy.

GIN: And the girl. What about her, then. To hold her.

(Pace appears. While neither Gin nor Dalton sees her, sometimes they sense, at different moments, that she is "there." Pace is playful.)

GIN: Was that "easy"?

DALTON: That's none of your business. *(Beat.)* I don't want you here.

PACE: Was that "a cinch"?

DALTON: *(Shouts.)* I didn't hold her! *(Now he is quiet.)* She held me. Pace did. But it wasn't that. Holding. Sometimes when I was with her, she wasn't there. Or when I was without her, she was there, but not there. Alone at night in bed, I could feel her breath in my ears. No.

PACE and DALTON: That's not it.

PACE: It wasn't just you and me.

DALTON: It was something more. Like at school. At school they teach you. To speak. They say it's math,

PACE: history,

DALTON: geometry, whatever. But they're teaching you to speak. Not about the world but about things. Just things: a door, a map,

PACE: a cup. Just the name of it.

DALTON: Not what a cup means, who picked it up, who drank from it,

PACE: who didn't and why;

DALTON: where a map came from, who fixed in the rivers, who'll take the wrong turn; or a door. Who cut the wood and hung it there? Why that width, that height? And who made that decision? Who agreed to it? Who didn't?

PACE: And what happened to them because of it?

DALTON: They just teach us to speak the things. So that's what we speak. But there's no past that way.

PACE and DALTON: And no future.

DALTON: 'Cause after you've said the thing, you move on. You don't look back. You never think to cross it, never stop and turn.

PACE: *(No longer playful.)* But you stopped, didn't you, Dalton? You stopped and turned.

DALTON: She laughed at everything that seemed right.

PACE: And you didn't turn back. *(Calmly.)* You son of a bitch.

DALTON: It wasn't just at night. In the day sometimes. Not her voice but the sound of her. I could hear it. Like water running in a pipe. Coal shifting in the grate. But that's not it. It was more like this. This cup. *(Dalton takes his drinking cup, calmly kneels and breaks it on the floor. His hand bleeds slightly. He sorts through the pieces.)* Look. This was sand and heat. Not long ago. Other things, too. Pieces and bits. And now. It's something else. Glass. Blood. And it's broken. *(He picks up a large piece, nears Gin.)* I could cut you open with it. *(Gin slaps him in the face. He's taken aback, put in his place.)*

DALTON: But that's what she did to me. Cut me open and things weren't just things after that. They were more. What they'd once been and what they could be besides. I was just a kid—

PACE: Like any other. You didn't care.

DALTON: I never even thought about it. But then one day I wasn't sure. She did that to me. She made me—hesitate. In everything I did. I was. Unsure. Look. It's not a cup anymore; it's a knife.

(Pace stands close to Dalton, but he cannot see her.)

PACE: I could cut you open and see my face.

DALTON: And it was true. I could touch myself at night and I didn't know if it was her hand or mine. I could touch myself. I could put my hand. I could. Maybe I was asleep. I don't know but sometimes I put my hand. Inside myself.

PACE: *(Whispers to him.)* And you were wet.

DALTON: I was wet. Just like a girl. It was. Yeah. Like I was touching her. Just to touch myself. *(Beat.)* It wasn't right.

(Silence some moments.)

GIN: Only time I ever knew things were right is when they were wrong. Everyone said your father was a mistake. After I made that one, and it worked out so well, I dedicated myself to making as many mistakes as possible in a lifetime. The only time I was ever sure who I was when I was wrong. *(Beat.)* I think you loved that girl.

DALTON: Yeah. Maybe that's why I killed her. Please. I want you to go.

GIN: All right.

(Pace suddenly kicks a piece of the broken cup. It skids between Gin and Dalton. Gin looks at the broken piece. Split scene: Dray is alone in another area. In the dark. He is making awkward movements about the room. Then we see he is dancing without music.)

PACE: There's your cup, kid. Drink from it.

(Then Dray sings and dances his song.)

DRAY: When I was still living, when I was a boy
I could sing like the water and dance like a toy.
My love she would kiss me 'til my mouth it was warmed.
There was no place on earth where we'd ever be harmed.

(End of scene.)

SCENE TEN

Pace and Dalton under the trestle.

DALTON: There's no one home at my house in the daytime. We could hang out there. Well, my Dad's at home but I'm not sure he counts as someone anymore. Ever since he got laid off at the foundry, he sits with the lights off. He's got a candle burning. Makes shadows on the wall with his hands. Spiders. Bats. You know. Rabbits.

PACE: I guess I'm supposed to think that's sad.

DALTON: You think about kissing me?

PACE: Kissing you where?

DALTON: I don't know. Here. In your yard. Or mine.

PACE: I mean where on you?

DALTON: My mouth. Where else?

PACE: Nope. We're friends.

DALTON: Like you and Brett were friends?

PACE: That was different. He was like my sister or something.

DALTON: Yeah. Yeah. Just forget it, okay. Pace Creagan isn't that kind of girl, anyhow. She pulls knives. She takes off her clothes. She pisses under the trestle.

PACE: Shits there too. I mean, why go all the way home?

DALTON: But she doesn't think about kissing.

PACE: Not on the mouth; that's common.

DALTON: Where else then?

PACE: I don't know. A place where no one else has kissed you, maybe. Everyone in the world has kissed you on the face, right?

DALTON: Keep talking.

PACE: If I ever kiss you, and I'm not saying I ever will, it will be someplace even you've never thought of before.

DALTON: You mean—

(Dalton looks down at his crotch, with a sort of reserved bravado.)

PACE: No way. You could trick me and piss on me. Look, if you want a kiss so bad, I'll give it to you, but you got to promise to take it wherever I want to plant it.

DALTON: If it's at least ten seconds long, I promise.

PACE: Agreed. Take down your pants.

DALTON: *(Suddenly afraid.)* No. Wait. You said it wasn't there!

PACE: It's not. Trust me. *(Dalton drops his pants.)* Turn around.

DALTON: Pace. I'm not sure—

PACE: *(Interrupts.)* Shut up, kid. We got a deal. *(Dalton reluctantly turns around. Pace stands behind him, then drops to her knees.)* Count. *(Pace puts her mouth just above the back of his knee. She kisses him there and holds it)*

DALTON: One, two, three, four, five, six...seven......... *(Pace slaps him and he continues counting.)* eight, nine, ten.

(Pace stands up. Dalton pulls up his pants. They look at each other.)

DALTON: Well. Yeah.

PACE: You happy now?

DALTON: Happy. Sure. I'm gonna run home right now and call up my friend Sean and tell him all about it. How it was great. How long it lasted. How far we went. "Sean, Sean, guess what? She tongued the back of my knee!" Is that what you did with your friend Brett? You kiss him like that too? *(Pace approaches him, then spits on him and wipes her mouth.)*

PACE: There. You can have it back. I wish I'd never done it.

DALTON: *(Starts to push her. He's pushing her hard backwards but she keeps her footing. The potential for violence to escalate is evident.)* Spit on me? You think you can do that? Who the hell do you think you are? Who the hell, Pace Creagan? What's so special about your kiss, huh? I could just take it, you know. I could just take it if I wanted to.

(Now Pace pushes back. Dalton hesitates. Pace raises her arm to hit him but then hesitates.)

DALTON: Go on. I'm your friend. Hit me.

PACE: I don't want to hit you. I want you to shut up. You liked it. I could tell. You're mad at me 'cause you liked it.

DALTON: I wanted you to kiss me on the mouth.

PACE: When you were counting. All the while. Couldn't you feel it? Where I was kissing you, it was on your mouth.

(They are quiet some moments.)

DALTON: What I said about Brett. It was stupid.

PACE: Yeah. It was *(Beat.)* But you were wrong the other day. That's not what a train does to you. It doesn't mush you up in neat little pieces. This train. She's a knife. That's why we loved her. Me and Brett. This train, you've seen her. So much beauty she's breathless: a huge hunk and chunk of shiny black coal blasted fresh out of the mountain. *(Beat.)* We had a good start. Me and Brett. We both could of made it. 'Course Brett, he was faster. I expected to be running behind. But Brett was worried. About me. He was stupid like that. He turned to look over his shoulder at me and he tripped. I thought he'd just jump up and keep going so I passed him right by. We'd timed it tight, and right then that engine was so close I could smell her. *(Beat.)* I thought Brett was right behind me.

DALTON: You left him on the tracks?

PACE: I thought he was running behind me. I could hear him behind me. He didn't call out. He didn't say wait up. I didn't know. Why didn't he call out? *(There is the real sound of a whistle in the distance.)* Not even a sound. Brett just sat there where he'd fallen. And then he stood up, slowly, like he had the time. He stood there looking at her, looking her straight in the face. Almost like it was a dare. Like: Go ahead and hit me. You can't do that to a train. You can't dare a train to hit you. 'Cause it will.

(Another whistle, closer this time.)

DALTON: This is stupid. Brett was alone up there. Nobody knows.

PACE: Just stood there like she could pass right through him for all he cared. Like he wasn't going to flinch.

DALTON: Let's get out of here, it's getting late.

(Dalton takes her arm.)

PACE: Let go of me.

DALTON: You're making this up.

PACE: Get off.

DALTON: You're out of your mind.

(Dalton tries to grab her again. She resists and he stumbles. There is the sound of a train rushing over the trestle above them. The sound is enormous. Then it disappears into the distance. He's cut his hand.)

DALTON: Shit.

PACE: You all right?

DALTON: No. Cut my hand.

PACE: Let me see.

DALTON: Just a scratch.

PACE: It's not how you think it is. The train, she doesn't mush you up. An arm here. A leg here. A shoe. No. She's cleaner than that. I walked back down the tracks after the train had passed. She cut Brett in two.

DALTON: Pace.

PACE: You know what I thought? Blocks. Two blocks, and maybe if I could fit the pieces back together again, he'd be. Whole.

DALTON: Will you shut your mouth. Please.

PACE: *(She rips a long strip of cloth from her dress, bandages his hand.)* Use this. Wrap it around your hand. It'll stop the bleeding.

DALTON: Thanks. *(Beat.)* You going home now?

PACE: I don't know. My mom made a loaf for my brother's birthday tomorrow. Maybe we could weasel some out of her tonight.

DALTON: Okay.

PACE: We're going to do it for real.

DALTON: Yeah. We'll do it. We'll make the cross.

PACE: Both of us. Side by side.

DALTON: That's right.

PACE: A steady run.

DALTON: As can be.

PACE: Does your dad really make shadow animals on the wall?

DALTON: Yep.

PACE: Can you?

DALTON: Never tried.

PACE: That's pretty neat. Not everyone can do that. I can't. *(Pace stands close to him, face to face for a moment.)* You won't take anything from me that I don't want to give you, Dalton. And that's a fact.

DALTON: All right. *(Beat.)* Hey, I'll race you down the hill.

PACE: Nah. I'm tired. *(Beat.)* Go!

(Blackout. We hear Dalton's voice in the dark, but as though it were coming from a distance away.)

DALTON: Hey, you— I'll catch you this time!

(End of scene.)

SCENE ELEVEN

In the semi-dark we see only the hands of someone. Two blue hands. They move about in the dark. They "play." As though someone were hesitantly trying out their glow in the dark. The hands walk along the stage like tiny people. Suddenly, they bump into someone they did not see. Now we see Pace standing there, looking down at her feet where Gin is on her hands and knees, looking up at her. Pace is in the same dress we saw in her earlier encounters with Dalton. The tear in the dress is larger. This is the only difference in her appearance.

GIN: Oh. Pace. *(Pace just watches Gin.)* I didn't see you. I was just. Trying to get used to this. It won't come off. They're lights, almost. It doesn't hurt. Well, it hurts 'cause I scrub them but it does no good. This color's here to stay. One morning I go to work and I come home with blue hands. They changed chemicals again at the plant. All sixteen of us in my section got blue hands. Some of the women, they were upset when it wouldn't wash off. But we had to see it as a wonder, too. During break, we turned off the lights and standing all together, some with our arms raised, others at our side, we looked like a Christmas tree in the dark, with blue lights. Then we all put our arms over our heads like this *(Demonstrates.)* and waved our fingers and we were a flock of crazy blue birds taking off. We started laughing then, and piling on top of each other, imagine it, and most of us women my age, and our hands were like blue snowballs flying this way and that. One of the girls, Victoria, she laughed so hard she peed right where she stood. Another one, Willa, she slipped in it and that had all of us roaring. *(Beat.)* Then Laura Townsend said we had all better think again 'cause we had the hands of dead women. Well, that put an end to the fun and we went back to work. The manager said it would wear off but it won't. We even used bleach. We'll have to get used to it.

Kind of ugly and kind of pretty both, isn't it? But hands aren't meant to be blue. *(Beat.)* You're almost a woman yourself, Pace . Hell, I don't blame him. My husband. We're not. Close. Do you know what I mean? Like we used to be.

PACE: You asked me what I wanted with your son.

GIN: I meant no harm, girl. A mother's supposed to ask.

PACE: I was going to be different. I don't know in what way. That never mattered. But different somehow. Do you know what I mean?

GIN: There's blood on your leg.

PACE: And Dalton would be there to see it happen. That's what I was getting him ready for.

GIN: What are you doing out so late? Where's Dalton?

PACE: He'll be home. He's still out at the trestle. *(Beat.)* He's not alone. He's with a girl.

GIN: Oh. Pace. I'm sorry.

PACE: I'm not. I was watching them. At first, I couldn't see them. It was dark. And there was this noise, like water rushing. Right through my head. But then I looked harder and I could see them. He stood over her. He was shaking her. But she wouldn't get up. And he was shouting. Shouting so loud. He wouldn't shut up.

GIN: Dalton wouldn't— No. Dalton's—

PACE: *(Interrupts.)* But she wouldn't answer him. The girl just turned her head. She hates him, I thought. And that made me glad. And then he stopped shouting. He gave up and put his head on her breast. *(Beat.)* And then, well. I saw it; he kissed her. He kissed her.

GIN: There'll be other boys, Pace—

PACE: And she let him. I never let Dalton kiss me, but she did. And then, I felt him kiss her. I felt it. He was kissing her. Kissing her. But his mouth was inside of mine. And I let him. I let his mouth be inside of me like that, even though I wasn't with him anymore.

GIN: *(Moves to comfort Pace.)* Come here, girl. I'm sorry.

PACE: *(Stepping backwards.)* Don't touch the back of my head.

GIN: Why not?

PACE: It's gone.

(We hear a door slam loudly.)

GIN: Dalton? Dalton!

(We hear the loud slamming of the door, like a cell. The slamming echoes. End of Act One.)

ACT TWO
SCENE ONE

It's dark in Dalton's cell but then a light appears. It's Chas. Dalton lies sleeping on the ground. Chas stands over Dalton, watching Dalton sleep.

CHAS: Least you could do is turn into a boat. A little one. No oars. I could guess it. I know water. *(Dalton moans in his sleep, like a child. Chas sings to put Dalton back to sleep.)*
Rocking on the sea, looking for my soul
Dead man's blood from an old boat hole.
Sail to the left, sail to the right,
Sail to the end in the cold moonlight.

Sleep of the dead. That's you. Creagan. Pace. Ring a bell? In the dead. Of night. What're you thinkin'? Are you there with her or somewhere else? *(Standing over Dalton, Chas begins to peel an apple. Chas lets the bits of peel fall across Dalton's face.)* Why do I spend my time on you, huh? Could it be I know our friend across the hall is on his way out of here? The poor man's got no wind in his cell. Still, he's doing this. *(Chas turns his head to the left and right like a weathervane.)* He's a weathervane tonight. *(Beat.)* I'm waiting for you to surprise me, kid. Turn your head, open your mouth, roll your eyes, swish your feet and I'll know it: You're a fish of sorts. Could you do that? Here? Change into something else completely? Or am I wastin' time, my time, when I could be over the sea fightin' with the Abe Lincoln, bullets and dive-bombers whistlin' and divin' and you here, sweet as baby's breath, sleeping and moaning over a dead girl. Is that right? Blue hands aren't right. Men without jobs isn't right. Mangled girl isn't right. And I'm sharing my apple. What are county jails coming to. *(Softly chants.)*

Apples, apples, buy a veteran's apples,
    sweet and hard as ruby rocks.
Five cents a piece, two dollars for a box
Apples, apples, buy an old man's apples.
Fought for his country, left on his back.
Won't you taste his apples, they're black, black, black?

Whatever you are my boy, I'll find you out. I won't sleep. And little by little, you'll stop sleeping too. *(The peels falling on his face finally wake Dalton and he screams himself awake. He sits up, not knowing where he is.)* Another one, kid. That's about three a night now. You're sweating 'til you stink. Hey. I got a good one. What's this? *(Chas gets down on all fours and acts out something contorted and disturbing.)* Come on. Make a wild guess. I'll give you a buck. And a hint: it's something you can't see, but it's there from the moment you're born 'til the moment you die. What is it? *(Chas repeats the act. This time it's more grotesque. He comes up close to Dalton, too close and Dalton backs away, frightened.)* Give up? *(Beat.)* It's your soul.

DALTON: *(After some moments.)* Go to hell.

CHAS: He speaks! He speaks! And what does he tell me? Go to hell. Go to hell. That's us in here, isn't it? Just you and me, hour after hour. So tell me. Tell me. Why'd you kill her? Think she was pregnant? Well, she wasn't. But they say you got a chance if you say you thought she was. Don't you want a chance, Chance? *(Beat.)* Why'd you kill Pace Creagan?

DALTON: Don't. Say her name.

CHAS: Pretty name. Strange. Strange girl too. Lucky she wasn't more of a girl. More of a girl, and they'd hang you for sure. That's what they're saying. Seen her parents since? No. But I have. Like two grey sticks, the man and the wife, so thin with grief they are. As they walk, the wind blows them from one side of the road to the other. You did that to them. You did that, boy. She was a kid. A box of grahams. You opened her up, took a handful and threw the rest away. *(Dalton gets to his feet.)* That's it, boy. That's it. Lets see some life in you. I know what's inside of you. I know what's inside. Don't think I don't know. Here? *(Chas throws the small knife down on the floor between them.)* There it is, boy. You can use it. Go on. Show me what you really are. What happened that night, huh? Lose your nerve? You tried though. We know that. Dress all torn up. She must have put up a hell of a fight. I bet you liked that. That's the way you kids like it. All that fightin' hoists your flag, gets you flappin'. Got you so edged, you couldn't hold it in. Couldn't wait. Shot your cum all over her dress but missed the target. Oh yeah. It was your cum all right. But Pace Creagan died a virgin. That's what the doctor says. *(Dalton moves away from Chas. After some moments, Chas picks up the knife. He speaks gently.)* You want to kill me, don't you?

(Dalton shakes his head "no.")

CHAS: I can see the hate rising out the top of your head like steam. Here, take this. Go on. *(Chas holds out the knife.)* You got to face up to what you are. You're a killer. A kid with a shell for a heart. A head full of black water. Everything sunk. Everything drowned inside you. *(Chas forces Dalton to hold the knife. Chas forces the knife up to his own throat. Dalton is passive. Chas whispers.)* Go on. It's what makes you whole.
(Chas laughs softly. Then suddenly Dalton shouts and forces Chas backwards. Dalton forces Chas to the floor with the knife to his neck.)
DALTON: I don't want to do it. You're just a man. *(It seems as though Dalton could kill Chas any moment.)* I can't even imagine it. Killing someone like you. With her. With Pace. I could imagine it. This what you want to hear? Okay, then. Like her parents, she was just a stick. I picked her up, carried her a little ways, and when I got tired I broke her—snap—in half. Threw the pieces to the side. Those are the facts. It was that easy. You want a reason? Okay: The only way to love someone is to kill them. *(Dalton releases Chas.)* God damn it I did what I was told, became what I was taught: a man with a little piece of future, 'bout as big as a dime. Only there wasn't one. There never was for most of us. That was the plan and it never was ours. But I bought that plan anyway 'cause it was the only thing to buy. Those are the facts. This isn't about who we are. This isn't about what we wanted. My country loves me. That's why it's killing me. It's killing my father. Those are the facts. Those are the facts of love.
CHAS: *(After some moments.)* You. You're not our children. We don't want you.
DALTON: What you were making earlier? That wasn't my soul. *(Beat.)* That was yours.
(End of scene.)

SCENE TWO

Gin stands with her mother's blue plates behind her back. Dray has cornered her.

DRAY: Give them to me.
GIN: Get out of this house and get your own. These were my mother's. I won't do it anymore. The Salvation was out. The woman there says to me, "What're you doing with all those plates, Ma'am." I said, "There's no food anymore. We eat them." I went down the road. I stopped at the

dump. Next thing I'm on my hands and knees, digging through garbage to find something for you to break. That's when I started laughing. Laughed so hard two rats flew out from under me.

DRAY: Just give me one.

GIN: Not one. Not two. Not ever again.

DRAY: Gin.

GIN: Go to the jail and visit your son. Get outside. Tear the bricks from the sidewalk if you have to. I don't care.

DRAY: I can't. I'm afraid.

GIN: Of what?

DRAY: That if I go out, they won't be able to see me.

GIN: Who? Who won't be able to see you?

DRAY: People. Out walking in the road.

GIN: Yes they will.

DRAY: They'll walk right through me. *(Dray slowly takes off his shirt, seemingly unconsciously, while he speaks.)* My mother used to tell me, "Dray. You are what you do." In the foundry, it's no rest and you've always got a burn somewhere. I never minded. I was doing. I was part of the work. Part of day. I was. I don't know. Burning. Freezing up. Inside that buzz. Melting down alongside thirty other men. But we were there. You could see us, and we weren't just making steel, we were. I don't know. We were. Making ourselves. We were. I was. All that. Movement. Movement. And now I do. Nothing. So. Then I am. What? Yeah. Nothing.

GIN: Go talk to them. They understand. They'll listen.

DRAY: I won't have anything to do with that Council. I know what they're up to. They're gonna take something that's not theirs. They're gonna break the law.

GIN: Yeah, well sometimes you break the law or it breaks you.

DRAY: Red thoughts, Ginny.

GIN: Yeah. My thoughts are red and my hands are blue.

DRAY: *(Dray begins to methodically rip his shirt into pieces as he speaks. This is a violent act, but somehow he does it calmly.)* They were running. Like all of us are. A few months back, up North. You know the story. *(Rips the cloth.)* A strike. Out on the street. Thousands of them. Doing something about it, *(Rips the cloth.)* like you say. Republic Steel brought the police out. Ten men were killed. All of them strikers. *(Rips the cloth.)* Papers said the strikers started it. Weeks later. It got around. They were running away. *(Rips the cloth.)* The bullets hit them in the back.

GIN: I never said I wasn't afraid.

DRAY: *(He's finished with his shirt, and is very calm.)* You can go ahead now. If you want.

GIN: Where?

DRAY: I don't know. *(Gin carefully, hesitantly touches his bare arm. Dray closes his eyes. She touches his chest.)* You're cold, Gin. *(She keeps touching him. Now his back.)*

DRAY: But it's nice. It almost burns. *(Beat.)* There. That's enough.

GIN: I don't want to stop.

DRAY: I don't want to either.

GIN: I want you to kiss me.

DRAY: I can't. I might hurt you.

GIN: I don't care.

DRAY: *(Gently.)* Get away from me. *(He's suddenly furious.)* I want you. Can't you understand that? I want you and it's choking me. Look at me: I don't know how to belong to my life. To be here. Not knowing where here is anymore. Am I here, Ginny? What you're looking at—is it me?

GIN: *(After some moments.)* I'm going into that plant with the rest of them. I'm going to work with glass. We're going to make it ours. But I'm a coward. If they come after us, I'll run too. But I won't live. Like this anymore.

DRAY: Do you want me to leave?

GIN: I want you to change.

DRAY: I can't.

GIN: I love you. So. I'll leave you behind.

(End of scene.)

SCENE THREE

Pace and Dalton. Pace is dressed in her brother's clothes. Dalton holds out her dress to her. She takes it, looks at it.

PACE: That's not my fault.

DALTON: Maybe it is. A person doesn't wait for nothing.

PACE: Some people do. Some people wait for nothing all their lives. You're one of those people.

DALTON: If they cut you open they'd find out why you smell so sweet: 'cause you're half dead already.

PACE: *(Examining the dress.)* You made it wet.

DALTON: I'm sorry. I didn't mean to.

(Pace throws the dress aside.)

PACE: Dalton Chance, when we're grown, I want to stand here with you and not be afraid. I want to know it will be okay. Tonight. Tomorrow. That when it's time to work, I'll have work. That when I'm tired, I can rest. Just those things. Shouldn't they belong to us?

DALTON: What do you want from me?

PACE: I want you to watch me, to tell me I'm here.

DALTON: You're here. You don't need me to tell you.

PACE: Yes I do. So watch me. Whatever I do. Take a good look. Make some notes. 'Cause one day I might come back here to find out who I was— and then you're going to tell me.

DALTON: I don't. Damn it. I don't know what you mean.

PACE: Look, it's simple—

DALTON: *(Interrupts.)* Stop it. Every time we meet, afterwards, it's like pieces of me. Keep falling off. It shouldn't be that way, Pace. Something's got to come clear. To make sense. I keep waiting. I can't do it anymore.

PACE: All right. Then tonight we'll run her.

DALTON: No. Not tonight.

PACE: Tonight.

DALTON: That's not what I'm waiting for. It's just a train.

PACE: Yeah. Well it's going somewhere. And it doesn't look back. Tonight, goddamn it. You'll run it tonight.

DALTON: No. Not me. That was just a game.

PACE: We've been working on this for weeks. You can't back down. It's time. I can feel it. Everything's quiet. Everything's waiting. Listen? Hear how quiet it is. That's us. You and me. Waiting for our lives.

DALTON: It's just talk, Pace. Just talk. This used to be fun. That's gone. You're gone. I don't know where but you're gone.

PACE: I could hurt you.

(Pace takes out her knife.)

DALTON: I'm not afraid of your knife. You could cut me open but I'd still leave.

(Pace jumps him and knocks him down. She sits on him.)

PACE: What's the matter with you?

DALTON: You said you'd change me. You did, goddamn it. You did change me. Now change me back.

PACE: I can't.

DALTON: Yes you can.

PACE: How? Just tell me how.

DALTON: I don't know. How the hell am I to know? I didn't do it. You did it.
You brought me here. You talked and talked. You put your hands inside
my head. You kissed me without kissing me. Tonight. Finally tonight.
But not like a girl should. You fucked me but I wasn't even inside you.
It's ridiculous. This isn't how I want to be.

PACE: How do you want to be?

DALTON: Normal. Like any other kid. And satisfied. Like I used to be. Just satisfied. And now. Now I want everything. I want everything to change.
You did this to me.

PACE: Say it.

DALTON: No.

PACE: Say it.

DALTON: No.

PACE: I hate you, Pace Creagan.

DALTON: Yeah. I do! *(Beat. He's quiet now.)* And there are times I've never
been happier; I can't forgive you for that. *(Pace touches his face gently, then
gets off of him. She starts to leave.)* Where you going? Pace. Hey. Pace.
(She leaves. End of scene.)

SCENE FOUR

Dalton in his cell, still on his back. Dray enters. He carries a small pillow.

DALTON: I was just going to sleep.

DRAY: Yes. I know it's late.

DALTON: Why did you come?

DRAY: Isn't it natural a father would come?

DALTON: You've hardly left the house in months.
(Dray holds out the pillow to Dalton.)

DRAY: I brought you your pillow.
(Dalton doesn't take it.)

DALTON: That's not my pillow.

DRAY: It's not?

DALTON: I haven't used it for years. The feathers are poking out of it. I used to wake up in the night and my face felt like it was full of nails.

(Dray runs his hand over the pillow. He finds a feather and pulls it out)

DRAY: Yeah. There's one. *(He finds another.)* Here's another.

(Dray continues to gently comb and search the pillow and pull out a feather here and a feather there, sparingly, as the scene continues. Dalton watches this strangely tender exercise. Dray looks at each feather he removes, then forgets it as he goes on to another. The feathers float unnoticed to the ground.)

DALTON: I don't sleep much in here anyway. *(Watching Dray pull the feathers.)* So are you going to roast it after you pluck it?

DRAY: Not as bad as I thought it'd be. Walking the street again.

DALTON: It's about time.

DRAY: 'Course I did have this pillow to hide my face in. You think anyone saw me?

DALTON: I hope not.

DRAY: There's something I want you to do for me.

DALTON: You think I killed her.

DRAY: I want you to touch me. *(Dalton does not respond.)* Does the thought. Disgust you?

DALTON: You haven't let me. In a long time. *(Dray advances. Dalton is suddenly furious.)* Stop right there. Don't, goddamn it! *(Beat.)* You think you can come. In here. *(Dalton rips the pillow out of Dray's hands and throws it aside.)* After all this time with this fucking pillow and everything's going to be okay? Yeah. It disgusts me. You disgust me. Like a little fucking kid sitting in your corner week after week waiting for the world to change. Well it changed, Father. At least for me. No. I don't want to touch you. What difference could that make now? To me, you're just a noise in the corner. I won't even notice when you go.

(They are quiet some moments. Dray does not move to leave.)

DALTON: Stay with me.

DRAY: I don't want to live like this.

DALTON: How?

DRAY: Unchanged. *(Beat.)* Your skin's warm. I can feel it from here. So close to me you smell of. Honey. I don't know. Gasoline. And somewhere behind it all something like, something like. I don't know. I don't— All my life I wanted to say something that mattered. I don't know why. *(Beat.)* I've got to get back now. Your mother's gone out. I must. Talk to her. It's getting dark. But the sun's still out. I don't know why. I came.

DALTON: To bring me my pillow.

(Dray sits down.)

DRAY: What do I do now?

DALTON: Go home.

DRAY: Yes. I must get back. At the edge. Not too far. That was our home. What happens when we die?

DALTON: How the hell should I know? You should be telling me that. I'm the one who's supposed to die. Christ, what's going on here? They're going to hang me. Do you understand? I told them I killed her.

DRAY: Did you kill her?

DALTON: I don't know.

DRAY: I think when we die, we just. Disappear. A few handfuls of nothing maybe. And that's it. What do you think?

(Dalton sits down beside him, but not that close. Dalton shrugs.)

DALTON: We just lie down and we don't get back up.

DRAY: Will it be terrible?

DALTON: Some people think there's a light. Some say it comes from above. I don't believe it. If there's anything at all, it'll come up from under the ground. Where we don't expect it. A light. A warm light and it'll cover us.

DRAY: What color is the light?

DALTON: Who knows.

DRAY: Red. I think it should be red.

DALTON: Yeah. Like the sun, when you look at it with your eyes closed. *(After some moments.)* I'll touch you now. If you want.

DRAY: I'm going to close my eyes.

DALTON: Why?

DRAY: So no one will see us.

(Dray closes his eyes. Dalton awkwardly rests his head on his father's shoulder. It is a small gesture. They sit this way together some moments. Then Dalton lifts his head away again. After some moments of silence Dray gets to his feet.)

DALTON: Wait a minute. I want you to show me how to make an animal on the wall. Any animal. I don't care what.

(Dray takes the pillow with him.)

DRAY: It'll take too long.

DALTON: I got the time.

DRAY: *(Looking at the small bunch of feathers on the floor.)* As though a bird had died here.

(Dray leaves.)

DALTON: Wait a minute. Wait.

(Dalton looks, surprised, at the floor around him. There feathers stir as though a breeze had passed through them. End of scene.)

SCENE FIVE

Dray meets Chas as he leaves the cell. They stop and stare at each other. Elsewhere onstage, a feather falls on Dalton, though now Dalton does not seem to notice. A few more fall as the scene progresses.

CHAS: Never stops talking about you. Thinks you're a hell of a guy. *(Dray doesn't respond.)* Way a son should. Just like mine.

DRAY: He's dead.

CHAS: Looks pretty lively to me.

DRAY: *(Interrupting.)* Yours. I mean.

(There is an awkward silence.)

CHAS: You're out of work. I've got this job.

DRAY: Your son was on the track team.

CHAS: I trained him. Out the old road to the cutoff in Eastwood.

DRAY: I've got to go.

CHAS: He says you do shadows.

DRAY: What of it?

CHAS: Hey. What's this? Your son never guessed it.

(Chas imitates a plane doing a perilous landing. No sound. Dray considers him carefully.)

DRAY: Baby elephant.

CHAS: Elephant? Like father like son. Wrong, but close. An aeroplane. Motor gone dead. Doing a dead-stick landing. In slow motion of course.

DRAY: Okay. This?

(Dray acts out a camel. With full conviction. Chas circles him, studying Dray's every movement. Dray seems to come alive in this charade, in a way we haven't witnessed before.)

CHAS: Nothing else but a camel, probably a dromedary.

(Dray stands stunned.)

DRAY: Yeah.

CHAS: Not bad at all. Can you do a windmill?

DRAY: I got to go.

CHAS: Wait, wait, we just started. I could teach you. I'm teaching your son.

DRAY: Save it for your own. Good-bye.

(Dray doesn't move.)

CHAS: I'm sort of practising. For him. You know?

DRAY: You're pretty good.

CHAS: He was asking for that pillow.

DRAY: It's not his.

(Dray leaves. We hear the sound of someone blowing air. As though they were blowing out matches, but more gently. End of scene.)

SCENE SIX

Pace and Dalton sitting together, a few feet apart. Pace is blowing on a small feather. We hear the sound of her breath in the silence.

Then Pace blows the feather into the air, and keeps it above her head, blowing on it, just a little, each time it descends. She lets it land on her upturned face.

Dalton watches this. Pace sees him watching her. She gives him the feather. He tries to copy her. He does so badly. Pace just watches. And laughs. They are enjoying themselves.

Then Dalton "gets" how to do it. He blows the feather up and keeps it in the air. Pace watches him. Then he lets the feather float slowly down between them.

They are both quietly happy. Because they are no longer alone. Because they are watching each other just being alive. End of scene.

SCENE SEVEN

Chas is sweeping up the feathers in the cell. Dalton's back is turned.

CHAS: What do you expect? A hotel or something. There's holes in the roof.

Sometimes they build a nest up there. It's the way of the world. They're moving you tomorrow. The trial'll start. It'll be the last of us. Empty cell. Might never get filled, then I'd have to find something else. Move to another jail. Might be no more criminals, not even a rich man who thinks he's a crab. Scuttlin' back and forth. Makes sweeping a devil's job. I can tell you. Still. *(Chas pokes the broom into Dalton's turned back.)* You gonna tell them the truth this time? Only witness was you. Huh, huh? No explanation. No defence. Look, kid. If you talk, if you give them something to make them think you're crazy or sorry or scared, they might not hang you. If you don't talk, they will. Those are the facts. *(Dalton doesn't respond. Chas tutts at him.)* A nice-faced boy like you. I had a nice-faced boy. *(Chas keeps poking Dalton in the back.)* There was no substance to him. I could knock you down and sweep you up like you were nothing but a scrap of dust.

(Suddenly Dalton turns and grabs the broom.)

DALTON: Hey. Guess what this is?

(Dalton slaps himself in the face. Then again. Then he starts to pull his own hair and hit himself, as though someone else is hitting him. He beats himself to the ground in an ugly, violent and awkward manner. Chas watches. Slowly he backs away. They are silent.)

CHAS: I've been good to you.

DALTON: Yeah. Brett was a nice boy. He used to hit himself. I saw him do it. Why was he like that? He was a fucking loon, that's why.

CHAS: Brett wasn't a loon. *(Beat.)* Sometimes. Well. I hit him. In the mornings, right before he went to school. Just about the time he'd start on a bowl of cereal. And a lot of the time, she'd be there. Pace. Your Pace. But I'd hit him anyway. Brett liked her to see it. After I hit him, Brett would take Pace aside and ask her if she saw it. Of course she saw it. She was standing right beside him! But Brett wanted to make sure. Then one morning I'm just about to hit him when he says, "Wait a minute, Dad. You've got a headache so you just sit back down and take it easy. I'll take care of it." So Brett hauls off and hits himself in the mouth. And I mean hard. His lip busts and starts bleeding. I'm so surprised that I sit back down and just stare at him. Next morning, the same thing. Brett stands in front of me and hits himself in the face. Twice. I don't say a thing. I just watch. Sometimes him doing it himself, instead of me, made us laugh. Together. The only time we did that. Laugh. *(Beat.)* I knew Brett ran that train. It wasn't the first time. Maybe it was fate.

DALTON: It wasn't fate. It was a train. Five hundred and sixty tons of it.

CHAS: He was. My son. He was waiting. For me to give him something. I couldn't stand it; I didn't have anything to give him. A key to a cell, maybe. A broom to go with it. Is that what you give your child when he grows up? I didn't have anything to give him. So I hit him. I could give him that.

(Dalton puts his hands in the feathers. He looks up.)

DALTON: How do the birds get in? There's no hole in this roof.

CHAS: What do we do afterwards? I loved him. Years from now?

DALTON: What we wanted. It was to live. Just to live.

(Chas begins sweeping again. As he sweeps up, he drags the broom across Dalton's hands.)

CHAS: I got to finish up here. Word is there's gonna be trouble down at the Plate Glass Factory. Might be some new guests to replace you any day now.

DALTON: About your son. I'm sorry.

CHAS: Ah. It seems so long ago now; it's all I think about. *(Beat.)* Hey, last chance, kid. Guess what I am?

(Chas sweeps the broom a little wider, almost a figure eight motion, but without much effort.)

DALTON: A giraffe. Grazing. The broom's your neck.

CHAS: No. Just an old man. Sweeping the floor of his cell.

(Dalton stops the broom with his hand.)

DALTON: Tell them I'm ready to talk.

CHAS: We're all asleep. It'll have to wait till morning.

(Chas leaves.)

DALTON: Hey. I want to talk now. Open the door. Open up the fucking door! I got something to say.

(At first he shouts to Chas, who is offstage, then he speaks to himself and finally he is telling us, as though we were the jury, what happened.)

DALTON: *(Shouting.)* Pace wanted to make the run that night. I wouldn't do it. I was afraid. No, I was angry.

(Pace appears. Dalton doesn't "see" her but sometimes senses she might be there.)

PACE: You messed all over my dress!

DALTON: *(Turning back to his cell door.)* But I didn't touch her! I was. Upside down. I was. Goddamn it—

PACE: You don't know what you were.

DALTON: I told her to run it alone.

PACE: You dared me.

DALTON: Pace never could say no to a dare. She stood on the tracks. She was covered in sweat. I stood below the trestle. She looked small up there, near a hundred feet above me. But until she started to run, I never thought she'd do it without me.

PACE: I had it made. Bastard. I wanted you to watch—

DALTON: I could hear her footsteps. Fast, fast—

PACE: Because we can't watch ourselves. We can't remember ourselves. Not like we need to.

DALTON: Christ, I didn't know she could run like that! She was halfway. She had it crossed. But then I.

PACE: Turned around. You just. Did it.

(Pace "disappears.")

DALTON: Then I. Just did it. I turned. Around.

(Dalton is propelled into the past moment. Now he can "see" Pace. But where he looks to see her, high up, we see nothing. The Pace that Dalton sees we cannot see, and the Pace we see is not the Pace Dalton sees. Elsewhere, we see Pace climbing up the trestle. Dalton shouts at the Pace we can't see.)

DALTON: No! No way! I won't be your fucking witness! You're warped. That's what you are. Everybody says it. *(Beat.)* Stop. You better stop!

PACE: *(Pace reappears, very high up on a what might be a piece of track. She calls to him.)* Dalton. Watch me. Hey! Watch me.

DALTON: No. Damn you.

(Dalton turns around, so that his back is to both the Pace we can see, and the other Pace we cannot see.)

PACE: Dalton. Turn around. Watch me.

DALTON: *(Dalton is furious and torn as he covers his ears and shouts.)* Goddamn you, Pace Creagan! *(Now he is back in the present, and he speaks to us. Pace remains very still on the track.)* But I wouldn't turn around. Pace must've slowed down. And lost her speed, when she was calling to me. Pace started to run back but she knew she'd never make it. And then she turned. Even from where I was at, I could see she was shaking her head. Back and forth, like she was saying: No. No. No. (Beat.) She didn't want to die. *(Pace puts her arms over her head, like she is going to dive.)* And then she did something funny. Pace couldn't even swim and there was no water in the creek, but she was going to dive.

PACE: Watch me. Dalton.

(This time Dalton turns around, and for the first time looks at the Pace that we can also see. This time we all watch Pace.)

DALTON: And this time. I watched her. *(Pace moves as if to dive, there is the tremendous, deafening roaring of a train that sounds almost like an explosion, different from the other train sounds we have heard. Then Pace is "gone" and we see nothing more of her.)* Pace lay beside the trestle. She wasn't mashed up from the fall. Only the back of her head. I started to shout at her. Called her every name I could think of. Even a few she'd taught me herself. *(Beat.)* And then. And then I did something. Something I can't. I don't know. It was. Maybe. It was. Unforgivable: I knelt beside her. *(Dalton stands looking down at the feathers his father left behind. He kneels beside the feathers. He is still, quiet, as he speaks.)* Pace never let me kiss her, like that. So I did. And she didn't try to stop me. How could she? That's what I can't forget. She once said to me, Dalton, you can't take anything from me I don't want to give you. But then she opened her mouth. She was dead. But she opened her mouth. And I kissed her, the way I'd always wanted to. And she let me. *(Beat.)* She let me. I have to believe that. *(Dalton swipes the feathers aside. End of scene.)*

SCENE EIGHT

Gin appears and watches Dray. She is holding a large piece of glass in her hands, which has a small break on one side. Then we see that the shadow Dray is making is a gun. And it's not a shadow.

GIN: We've swept the place out. Most of the machinery's all right. Glass everywhere. Like hail. We scooped it up. By the bucketful. Three girls from my work are with me. About thirty others. From all over. We threw lots of this out. Thought I'd bring some home. We can use it in the back door. *(Calmly.)* Put that away.

DRAY: I went to see Dalton. He said at night when he slept, his face was full of nails. All these years. And I didn't know. *(Beat.)* Come here.

GIN: I've got to get back to the plant. Are you coming with me?

DRAY: Just come here. *(Gin stands by him.)* Here.

(He gives her the gun. She just stands there with it.)

GIN: Almost a shame to sweep up that glass. It was so bright in there. The sun through the windows, hitting the glass on the floor.

DRAY: *(He turns to Gin and lifts her hand so the gun is at his forehead.)* Ginny.

GIN: Like we were standing on a lake of ice that was turning to fire right under our feet.

DRAY: Change me. *(Gin does not respond.)* Please. Please. Change me.

GIN: No. Not like that.

(She puts the gun down between them and moves away.)

DRAY: Are you coming with me?

(Dray doesn't answer. Dray makes a shadow on the wall. Then another.)

DRAY: What is it? A horse? A dog? I don't know anymore.

GIN: This is the last time I ask you: Are you coming with me?

DRAY: *(Dropping his hands.)* Shadows. Just fucking shadows. *(Gin leaves. Dray stands up, suddenly, knocking over his chair as he does so. He looks in the direction of Gin's exit and speaks softly.)* Yes. I am.

(End of scene.)

SCENE NINE

Dalton is in his cell, with a candle, making shadows on the wall, as in the prologue. Pace appears behind him. They are both in the cell and at the trestle at one and the same time. Pace is dressed in her brother's clothes. She carries her dress. She lays it on the ground and spreads it out carefully.

PACE: That's a bird, stupid. A pigeon. *(Dalton slowly turns around)* Like the kind that live under the trestle. Haven't you heard them? At dawn they make a racket. *(She's finished laying the dress out. She stands back, perhaps on an elevated site.)* Lie down on it.

DALTON: Why?

PACE: Just do it. Or you'll be sorry. Last chance, Chance.

(Dalton lies down on the dress.)

DALTON: What're you gonna do?

PACE: Make something happen.

DALTON: Are you going to kick me? Are you mad at me?

PACE: Open your shirt.

DALTON: What?

PACE: Just shut up and do what I tell you. Open your shirt. *(Dalton opens his shirt. Throughout their dialogue, Pace never touches herself. Nor do they look at one another.)* Now. Touch me. *(Dalton makes a movement as though to reach and touch her, but he reaches towards a Pace we can't see. Meanwhile, Pace is standing elsewhere. She cuts him off.)* No. Stay still. Right there. And do this. *(Pace raises her own hands to her chest, though she doesn't touch herself.)* Go on. *(Dalton copies her.)* Right. Now close your eyes. And touch me. It's simple. *(Dalton hesitates, then he closes his eyes and touches his own bare chest. Pace is very still, her arms at her side.)* Yes. There. You won't hurt me. *(Beat.)* Go on. That's right. You're touching me. I want you to touch me. *(Pace turns around and raises her arms.)* It's going to happen! To both of us. Go on. Open your legs. *(Beat.)* Do it. *(Dalton opens his legs.)* Now touch me. There. Just touch me. *(Dalton touches himself.)* Can you feel me? I'm hard. *(Dalton moans. He turns over onto his stomach.)* I want to be inside you.

DALTON: Pace.

PACE: Let me inside you.

DALTON: Go on.

(Dalton makes a sharp intake of breath.)

PACE: Does it hurt?

DALTON: Yeah.

PACE: Good. I can't stop. *(Dalton moans again, as though in both pain and pleasure.)* Now. Yes. Can you feel me?

DALTON: I'll make your dress wet—

PACE: Can you feel me?

DALTON: Yes.

PACE: Where? Tell me. Where can you feel me?

DALTON: Inside. Everywhere. Pace. *(Beat.)* You're inside me.

(Dalton comes. They are quiet some moments.)

PACE: There. We're something else now. *(Pace turns around and looks at the public, as though it were Dalton.)* You see? We're in another place. *(Dalton opens his eyes. He slowly sits up, and is still. Neither of them "looks" at the other. Pace walks quietly over to the candle and stands over it a moment. Then she blows it out.)*

END OF PLAY

Let the Big Dog Eat
by Elizabeth Wong

BIOGRAPHY

Elizabeth Wong has a Masters from New York University. Her play *Letters to a Student Revolutionary* premiered off-Broadway and has received productions abroad (Singapore Arts Festival and Tokyo's Brecht Festival) and in numerous U.S. cities, including Los Angeles, Seattle and Philadelphia. Her play *Kimchee and Chitlins* had its debut at Victory Gardens Theatre in Chicago and was also produced in Atlanta and Los Angeles. Both plays are published by Dramatic Publishing Company and in other anthologies. Her latest plays, *The Happy Prince* and *The Play Formerly Known as The Happy Prince,* are adaptations of an Oscar Wilde short story, commissioned by the Kennedy Center for the Performing Arts. Ms. Wong also was commissioned by Omaha Magic Theatre to collaborate with Megan Terry and JoAnn Schmidman on *Explor-a-tori-yum,* funded by the Rockefeller Foundation. Ms. Wong was a staff writer for the ABC sitcom *All-American Girl,* an opinion/editorial columnist for the *Los Angeles Times,* a playwright-in-residence at Bowdoin College (funded by the Luce Foundation) and she has received fellowships from Yaddo, Ucross and Walt Disney Studios. Ms. Wong is a Dramatists Guild member and teaches playwriting at University of Southern California and University of California at Santa Barbara. Along with Wole Soyinka, Alfred Uhry and Wendy Wasserstein, she is an advisory board member of Theatre Emory in Atlanta. Her one-woman play *Downsized* was recently commissioned by the Mark Taper Forum; and she'll be adapting a Greek myth for Denver Center Theatre. Ms. Wong is also working on *China Doll,* a play that spans five decades and imagines the glamorous but tragic life of actress Anna May Wong during the halcyon days of studio movie-making. Ms. Wong lives in Los Angeles.

HUMANA FESTIVAL PRODUCTION

Let the Big Dog Eat was commissioned by Actors Theatre of Louisville and premiered at the Humana Festival of New American Plays in March of 1998. It was directed by Frank Deal with the following cast:

Ted .... William McNulty
Bill .... Brian Keeler
Michael .... Fred Major
Warren .... William Cain

and the following production staff:

Scenic Designer .... Paul Owen
Costume Designer .... Kevin R. McLeod

Lighting Designer . . . . Greg Sullivan
Sound Designer . . . . Mark Huang
Properties Designer . . . . Mark Walston
Stage Manager . . . . Heather Fields
Dramaturgs . . . . Meghan Davis & Michael Bigelow Dixon

CHARACTERS

TED

BILL

MICHAEL

WARREN

(Four men, ages 40 to 70)

PLACE

A prestigious golf course. At the first tee.

TIME

The present.

PLAYWRIGHT'S NOTE

The men are avid golfers. They look like pro golfers, impeccably attired in tasteful clothes befitting their status. They take their golf game seriously. Golf is precision.

Hierarchy, competition, alliances, and realignments of power and position are a necessary part of the play's subtextual infrastructure, reflected by actors, spatially. Golf is stillness.

The play is not a cartoon, or a caricature, but must be fun, fraternal—full of ribbing, teasing, verbal roughhousing, occasional school-boy antics and boyish earnestness. But make no mistake—they are powerful, confident, deferring to none, including their peers.

In the Actors Theatre of Louisville production, the play began with a "rain shower" of over-sized money of various denominations, floating onto the playing area, augmented by a subtle green strobe, to a sound mix of cash registers and the song, "For The Love of Money" by the O'Jay. This special effect was fun, highly effective, and worked sublimely as the golf course.

William Cain, Brian Keeler, William McNulty and Fred Major
in *Let The Big Dog Eat* by Elizabeth Wong

22nd Annual Humana Festival of New American Plays
Actors Theatre of Louisville, 1998
photo by Richard Trigg

Let the Big Dog Eat

A golf course. At the first hole. Warren and Michael, Bill and Ted—four captains of industry at play, about to tee off. They are relaxed, convivial, fraternal.

BILL: *(To Ted.)* Gee whiz, that's kinda hard-core, Ted. We cannot be the lousiest golfers in the Fortune 500.

TED: *(To Bill.)* We suck. In God we trust, and in golf we suck. That's why I'm taking up fly-fishin', and you're taking the honor. After you, my friend.

WARREN: *(To Michael.)* The Shark handed me his driver, I swing, I hear a whoosh, I look up. I don't see it. That's because the ball is four inches from my left foot. In front of Greg Norman, I dinked! Twice! It was so humiliating. Dink!

MICHAEL: *(To Warren.)* You wanna talk humiliation. I'm at the shotgun start of my own tournament on my own network, I whiff. From to coast in living color, from Epcot to Anaheim. Whiff. The sound of empty air. That's embarrassment!

TED: *(Interrupting.)* Hell Mikey, that's nothing. I was at Kapalua with Arnie and Jack, couldn't hit it past the goddamned ladies tees, those guys invoked the goddamned rule. Had to play the rest of the hole with my dick hanging o.u.t.

(Bill emits a LOUD RASPBERRY.)

MICHAEL: That's it. I declare a winner. Show us your big swing, Ted. We've all ready seen your big wallet!

BILL: First on the first tee, and first in charit-TEE!!!

WARREN: You win Ted! Let the big dog eat!

BILL:/MICHAEL:/WARREN: Chomp! Chomp!/ Arrrooooo!/ Woof woof!

TED: Now, that's just it. I'm sick of being just a big growling stomach. A gigantic digestive tract, with dollars dripping from my maw. Chomp chomp chomp. Hell, I'm no poorer than I was nine months ago, and the world is maybe a lot better off. *(Beat.)* Okay, all right, what do you say, we play penny per hole, greenies get a nickel, par gets a dime. High score buys a round of milk at the 19th.

BILL: Whew! For a minute there, I thought I'd have to pledge a billion to the Red Cross just to play this round.

TED: Okay! Now you're talkin'.

WARREN: Don't worry Bill, I'll spot you. Better yet, I'll take back a few million shares of Cap Cities, if Mike here doesn't mind. That should make a nice, sizable contribution to the Mickey Mouse Fan Club.

MICHAEL: *(Goodnaturedly.)* Come on Ted, face it, you turned us into measly cheapskates. Bill here gave some $135, $136 million away last year, and now it sounds like chump change. Hell, you're making us all look bad. Right Warren?

TED: Redeem your immortal soul! Now, one of you guys tee up!

WARREN: Well, Mike, I know how you can redeem your *immoral* soul. Sell off your hockey team. Disperse the funds in 10-year increments, $100,000 per annum, to Greenpeace or Save The Rain Forest.

MICHAEL: Not my team! I love my team. Ted got to keep his team. I'll sell off the Magic Kingdom first.

BILL: *(Earnestly.)* Oh nooooo! Not Mickey! Don't liquidate Mickey!

WARREN: Next thing you know, Mickey and Minnie will be living out of a cardboard box, and sellin' shares of Disney in front of Mr. Toad's Wild Ride.

BILL:/MICHAEL:/WARREN: *(Harmonizing beautifully.)* M.O.U.S.Eeeeeee eeeeeee...for sale!

TED: Hell, that sounds all right. Let's pass a law! Lobby! Make *that* the goddamned national anthem.

MICHAEL: Now that's a good idea. I'll have my people get some people to hire some people to work on that.

WARREN: Gentlemen, nothing wrong with a little strategic philanthropy, few things lubricate power faster than a well-placed seven-figure check to the right hospital or university.

TED: That's right, T-bone. Turn over a few shares of Time Warner every year, I feel good about that. Nothing wrong with working for a more humane world.

BILL: *(To Warren.)* But Brother T-bone, Brother Ted has fallen from the pure of faith. He no longer takes joy, as we do, in the pleasure of sheer accumulation. *(To Ted.)* Blasphemer!

TED: Sure it's fun making money, watchin' it grow. Making so much, you never have to write a check or carry cash in your wallet. So many damned zeros and commas to make your mamma proud.

WARREN:/BILL:/MICHAEL: Amen./I heard dat./*Watch it grow!*

TED: Sure, money is a measure of success. I won't deny that, heck, we all have lived by its dipstick.

WARREN:/BILL:/MICHAEL: Whoever has the most!/*Biggest dip wins!* That's right, uh huh!/Winner take all.

TED: But boys, I'm upping the ante. I'm playin' a *new* game, with a *new* scorecard. Who's in with me? It's not how much you make, but how much you can give, give, give!

WARREN: Bill, I think Ted not only wants to top the Forbes' 400 list, but he wants to be tops on the list in *American Benefactor* magazine too. We all know how photogenic you are Ted, and you too Michael.

MICHAEL: Thank you Warren, you are so kind. True, I'm happier donating to my own foundation since most non-profits are lousy at money management, and it gives my wife something to...

BILL: *(Interrupting.)* Move over George Soros! George is running scared, Skipper! The Ted wants to run with the big dogs—Feeney, Getty, Annenberg, Carnegie, Rockefeller. *(Bill runs in place.)* You know, Ted, when T-bone isn't eating steaks, he's a real shark at bridge. King of the trump. In one night, I bet he could win a billion easy.

TED: A *billion* is a nice round number.

WARREN: *(Raising right hand.)* I pledge to donate all my winnings to... Gamblers Anonymous.

BILL: Ohmigosh T-bone, you have to give up cigars! The money you spend on Cohibas you could finance a small war.

WARREN: But I love my Cohibas. I can't give 'em up. Don't make me. They are so delicate.

MICHAEL: Well Warren, you could roll your own. I've been rolling my own since...

BILL: *(Interrupting.)* Mikey, you spoiled my surprise. Tee, I bought you this old wooden cigar thing from Cuba, been in Castro's family years. But sssshhh. Don't tell Ted. Or he'll make me take it back, and donate the money to the *(Pointedly.)* American Lung Association.

TED: If you boys are through. We got 382 yards from the black to the pin. And we're burning daylight.

MICHAEL: I was saying, my buddy Schwartzenegger got me into packin' and rollin' my own stogies. Okay, I admit the first few I rolled were a bit bumpy and lumpy…

TED: *(Interrupting.)* Dopey, Sleepy, Bumpy, Lumpy! Sounds like the goddamned seven dwarfs. Hell, maybe some of those good ol' boys want to play some goddamned golf!

WARREN: Now, gentlemen, the dwarfs are a pivotal variable. Huge valuation disparity relative to the market. Balance sheets haven't looked better in 30 years, they are awash in cash flow. Maybe the dwarfs should turn over their stock outright to a nice little public foundation, and claim 30 percent of their adjusted gross income in deductions. Avoid capital-gains tax on any increases in value. Of course, Ted knows all about those juicy tax deductions, right Skipper?

TED: Tax nothing! It's a third of my net worth! This is going to cost me!

BILL: Nah, I see your game, old boy. You give it to the UN and the UN lets you broadcast TBS, CNN and the Atlanta Brave home games to the nice people of Timbuktu! Rumor has it, he may also buy out Barry, and send 'em The Home Shopping Network, you sly dog! Arrrooo!

MICHAEL: Not at all, gentlemen. I heard through very reliable sources, the poor man had to get his wife off his back! Jane wanted him to open up an acting school in Hanoi, and a health club in Ho Chi Minh City!

(They congratulate Mike, with pats on the back and handshakes. Mike beams.)

BILL:/WARREN: You win that one, Michael! Arrrrooo!/Good one, Michael! Let the big dog eat! Arrrrooooo!

TED: It's about compassion, boys. I gotta believe when you give from your heart, you got yourself a win/win situation.

MICHAEL: Speaking of heart, what about you, Bill? Not everyday we have a tri-zillionaire among us. Ready for that win/win scenario? When are you gonna ante up? Ted's waiting for you to fold, call, or raise.

BILL: Well Michael, I was thinking about that. Gee whiz, well, I could sell my house, it's worth about $40 million, but then my wife would really be mad at me.

MICHAEL: It's a good thing, Bill, you added that trampoline before The Ted here put us all on the hot seat.

WARREN: A man's castle isn't complete without his trampoline room.

BILL: Hey, it's great. I'm serious, you all should try it. It's really a good workout! I like to bounce. *(Bill bounces!)* Helps me think when I'm bouncing. I got the idea to startup MSNBC with a front-twisting somersault and landing on my *butt*. It's fun! Maybe when I'm bouncing, I'll think of a way to trump The Ted. Outdoing a billion-dollar giveaway takes some considerable bouncing.

TED: Well boys, maybe y'all should bounce on it. *(Ted bounces, leads all in a lively bounce fest.)* Belly up to a man's game. Stop playing that tired two-dollar table. Shake loose something more than just measly pocket change.

MICHAEL: *(Coyly.)* By God, I think he's right. Compared to you guys, all I got is pocket change. I'm just a lowly billionaire in waiting.

WARREN: You are catching up fast, that's what counts. But you better hurry it up, because the future makes me feel like an over-sexed guy in a whore-house. The future is ripe for making more money. It's like this beautiful green manicured golf course. The fairway of opportunity, lots of hazards, but we know where they all are, and when we hit the green, we drain that bad boy for a million, ten million! My boy, the future is bright.

MICHAEL: The future is bright.

BILL: And ripe.

TED: It sure is.

(All look dreamily down the fairway, relishing the idea of a lucrative future.)

BILL: *(Gently.)* You know Ted, it's not like we don't give. We give. Right Michael?

MICHAEL: That's right. And Warren is going to be the biggest of the big-time givers. *Beyond* big. Don't be modest, Warren. Some $21 billion, after you know what happens, croak city, then *BAM,* everybody wins. Everybody goes to the bank.

BILL: It's cosmic the amount he'll leave behind. Beyond cosmic!

TED: *After,* Warren? But then you'll be dead. Give a billion right now, T-bone, you can make it back, then give a billion more. Enjoy the smile on some poor kid's face. Hell, put a thousand smiles on a thousand faces. You can't get that kinda pleasure from *worms,* six feet under.

BILL: Warren and I talked long about this. Even my kids won't get a big piece. I want them to understand the value of hard work. Make their own opportunities. I'm giving it all away, after.

WARREN: Right! You could say, we are working and saving for the future. It's a long-term thing, that's how we are doing it. Not before, *AFTER.*

BILL: After.

TED: Boys, what we got here is a dogleg right, with the green trapped left. Best line is straight out from the tee. There is our future, boys. Who's it gonna be? *(All back away from tee mound.)* This is gonna sound crazy. But

Warren, I had this dream. It was like that movie *Road Warrior*. Chaos everywhere. Everybody starving. People resorted to cannibalism. I think about that all the time. People eating each other to survive. Chomp chomp. It was terrible. The worst-case scenario. But I refuse to be a cannibal. I would rather starve.

BILL: A billion dollars to feed the pigeons!

TED: I refuse to eat my fellow human beings. I would rather starve to death than be a cannibal.

BILL: A billion dollars to feed the ducks!

MICHAEL: A billion for the battle of the bulge! A billion for the war on pimples! Come on Warren, it's fun!

(Warren waves him off. He keeps his eyes on Ted.)

BILL: A billion to feed the hungry.

TED: Exactly.

MICHAEL: A billion to heal the sick.

TED: Exactly.

WARREN: Ted, you are so full of shit.

(Ted's next speech** overlaps with the following chant by Bill, Michael and Warren.)

BILL:/MICHAEL:/WARREN: *(One-upping each other.)*

A billion to house the homeless.
A billion to shelter refugees.
A billion.
A billion to educate children.
A billion for a cure for AIDS.
A billion for a cure for cancer.
A billion for humane treatment of animals.
A billion to teach people to read.
A billion for national health care.
One billion.
A billion to end suffering.
A billion to end pain.
A billion for peace.
A billion to spread *luvvvv.*

TED: **Very funny. Who's gonna tee off first? Warren? Bill? Michael? Okay, all right, you had your fun. You guys are doing this because you don't want to go first. Cowards. I'm onto your game. You'll do anything as long as some other sucker tees off first. Cowards! Fuckin' pansies! We came to play some golf. I'm onto your game. Let's play. Let's go! You self-ish bastards! *(Bill, Michael and Warren have ended their chant, and Ted continues.)* Move aside. I'll show ya'll how it's done again! Here it is—for a penny! Goddammit!

(Ted swings his driver. Whoosh. He freezes at the end of his follow-through. Blackout.)

END OF PLAY